American Jewish Organizations & Israel

LEE O'BRIEN

Institute for Palestine Studies
Washington, D.C.

© Copyright, 1986, by the Institute for Palestine Studies.
All rights reserved under International
and Pan-American Copyright Conventions.
Published by the Institute for Palestine Studies, Washington, D.C.

The Institute for Palestine Studies, founded in Beirut in 1963, is
an independent, non-profit Arab research and publication center,
which is not affiliated with any political organization or government.
The opinions expressed in its publications do not necessarily
reflect those of the Institute.

Grateful acknowledgement is made to Steven M. Cohen for permission
to reprint *Attitudes of American Jews Toward Israel and Israelis:
The 1983 National Survey of American Jews and Jewish Communal Leaders*
(Institute on American Jewish-Israel Relations,
the American Jewish Committee).

Library of Congress Cataloging in Publication Data

O'Brien, Lee.
American Jewish organizations and Israel.

Bibliography: p.
Includes index.
1. Jews—United States—Attitudes toward Israel. 2. Jews—United States—
Societies, etc. 3. Zionism—United States—Societies, etc. 4. Christian Zionism—
United States—Societies, etc. 5. Israel—Foreign opinion, American. 6. Public
opinion—United States. I. Title.

E184.J5027 1986	956.94'001'0973	85-29117
ISBN 0-88728-153-2		
ISBN 0-88728-154-0 (pbk.)		

Designed by Pat Taylor, Inc.

Typeset by the Popular Culture Press
of Bowling Green State University, Bowling Green, Ohio

Printed in the United States of America
by Progressive Litho., Inc., Alexandria, Virginia

*To my parents and
to the many people
whose time and knowledge
made this book possible.*

Contents

Preface   1
List of Organizations   3

INTRODUCTION: AMERICAN JEWS AND THE   5
ASCENDANCY OF ISRAEL

CHAPTER I: ZIONIST ORGANIZATIONS   13

World Zionist Organization and the Jewish Agency   19
Jewish Agency for Israel   24
World Zionist Organization-American Section   26
American Zionist Federation   29
Hadassah   34
Zionist Organization of America   38
Association of Reform Zionists of America   42

CHAPTER II: COMMUNITY ORGANIZATIONS   47

Council of Jewish Federations   56
National Jewish Community Relations Advisory Council   63
American Jewish Committee   72
American Jewish Congress   84
Anti-Defamation League of B'nai B'rith   93

CHAPTER III: FUNDING   107

United Jewish Appeal   114
United Israel Appeal   126
American Jewish Joint Distribution Committee   128
Jewish National Fund   130
PEF Israel Endowment Funds   135
State of Israel Bonds Organization   137
AMPAL-American Israel Corporation   142
PEC Israel Economic Corporation   143
New Israel Fund   144
Institutionally-Specific Funding Organizations   146

CHAPTER IV: THE PRO-ISRAEL LOBBY AND THE   151
POLITICAL PROCESS

    American Israel Public Affairs Committee   158
    Political Action Committees (PACs)   183
    National Political Action Committee   188
    Other Pro-Israel PACs   190
    Conference of Presidents of Major American Jewish   191
      Organizations
    Jewish Institute for National Security Affairs   203

CHAPTER V: TARGET AREAS AND SPECIAL   211
FOCUS ORGANIZATIONS

    Campus   213
      American Professors for Peace in the Middle East 223
    Church   227
    Special Focus Organizations   243
      America-Israel Friendship League   243
      Youth Institute for Peace in the Middle East   247
      National Committee for Labor Israel   249
      American Trade Union Council for Histadrut   251
      Americans for a Safe Israel   253
      National Council of Young Israel   256

CONCLUSION: THE PRO-ISRAEL PARADIGM   265

Appendix   273
Bibliography   285
Index   321

Preface

This is a study of the major Jewish establishment organizations in the United States and the content and impact of their Israel support work. It is intended to delineate their organizational structure and political agenda within a historical and contemporary context.

The sheer number and complexity of American Jewish organizations greatly complicated the task. Numerous sociologists and political scientists have published studies of American Jewry's communal structure, but there is as yet no single, definitive analysis, nor do I attempt such here. Of the scores of groups engaged in Israel support work, time and space limitations have forced me to discuss only the most well-known, active, or representative. In addition, while recognizing that the American Jewish community is not monolithic, even in its identification with Israel, I have excluded all "dissent" groups and organizations, such as the New Jewish Agenda, the American Council for Judaism, and American Jewish Alternatives to Zionism, on the grounds that they are not representative of the views of the Jewish establishment.

A word about my methodology: first, my rationale for classification of the various organizations was primarily functional and based on self-definition. In other words, I grouped together organizations that share similar priorities in their pro-Israel agenda and define themselves accordingly. I have tried, as much as possible, to refrain from imposing my own classification on the organizations. I have elected, whenever possible, to rely on sources of information made public by the organizations themselves, or on organizational documents to which the public may have access, or on secondary sources written with the approval of the organizations in question or from a sympathetic perspective. I want the available material to speak for itself.

In the course of my research, I was confronted with a number of important issues that require separate and exhaustive investigation and analysis, such as the socioeconomic makeup of the American Jewish community as it relates to pro-Israel work; the larger American context within which a noticeable shift in the agenda of Jewish organizations has occurred; the evolutionary developments in the relationship between the Jewish community and other groups, including Blacks, organized labor, and the Christian churches; the Jewish community's gradual shift to the

1

right and the implications of this shift for its historical, social, and political agenda, to name only a few. My hope is that I have provided a base for future work on these and other relevant topics.

Finally, I would like to express my thanks to Larry Ekin, who wrote the Church section (Chapter 5), and to Kathryn Silver and Marty Rosenbluth, for their research on the pro-Israel activities of the U.S. labor movement.

Lee O'Brien

Washington, D.C.
March 1986

List of Organizations

Organizations appear in alphabetical order by most commonly used abbreviation or acronym.

ADL	Anti-Defamation League of B'nai B'rith
AFSI	Americans for a Safe Israel
AIFL	American-Israel Friendship League
AIPAC	American Israel Public Affairs Committee
AJC	American Jewish Committee
AJCongress	American Jewish Congress
AMPAL	American Israel Corporation
APPME	American Professors for Peace in the Middle East
ARZA	Association of Reform Zionists of America
ATUCH	American Trade Union Council for Histadrut
AZF	American Zionist Federation
CJF	Council of Jewish Federations
Hadassah	Hadassah, The Women's Zionist Organization of America
IBO	State of Israel Bonds Organization
JA	Jewish Agency
JA-American Section	Jewish Agency-American Section
JDC	American Jewish Joint Distribution Committee
JINSA	Jewish Institute for National Security Affairs
JNF	Jewish National Fund
NatPAC	National Public Affairs Committee
NCLI	National Committee for Labor Israel
NIF	New Israel Fund
NJCRAC	National Jewish Community Relations Advisory Council
PEC	Palestine Economic Corporation (now PEC Israel Economic Corporation)
PEF	Palestine Economic Fund (now PEF Israel Endowment Funds)
Presidents Conference	Conference of Presidents of Major American Jewish Organizations
UIA	United Israel Appeal
UJA	United Jewish Appeal
WZO	World Zionist Organization
WZO-American Section	World Zionist Organization-American Section
YIPME	Youth Institute for Peace in the Middle East
ZOA	Zionist Organization of America

American Jews and the Ascendancy of Israel

American Jews and the Ascendancy of Israel

There are approximately 5.5 million Jews in the United States today, comprising about 2 percent of the total population. In 1825, there were only some 10,000 Jews in the country; German-Jewish immigrants raised the numbers to nearly 250,000 by 1880. The most dramatic influx came in the years from 1881 to 1941, when close to 4 million mainly poor and Yiddish-speaking Jews fled the pogroms, ghettos, poverty, and political crises of central and eastern Europe.[1] Most American Jews are still concentrated in the large northeastern cities* where their grandparents originally settled, but increasing numbers are moving to smaller communities throughout the country. A low birthrate—coupled with increased intermarriage—has resulted in a recent, steady decline in the Jewish population,** which some experts estimate may decrease by as much as a half million by the year 2000.[4]

More than any other twentieth-century immigrant group, Jews have achieved successful integration into American society. Sociologist Steven M. Cohen, associate professor of sociology at Queen's College, CUNY, and Brandeis University's Center for Modern Jewish Studies, notes in his study, *American Modernity & Jewish Identity:*

The extraordinary speed with which most American Jews have attained middle-class if not upper-class status in the last hundred years has been thoroughly documented. Observers reckon that nearly all American Jews of college age attend college; that Jews have been entering the professions in highly disproportionate numbers since the 1920s, if not earlier; and that the average affluence of American Jews equals if not surpasses that of Episcopalians, the wealthiest major religious denomination, and exceeds that of all other major U.S. ethnic groups. Despite

---

* 1.1 million Jews live in New York City; in Manhattan alone, 22.4 percent of all households are Jewish.[2]

** Jewish population in the northeast has declined from 68 percent in 1930 to 54 percent in 1984, and total Jewish population has declined from 5 to 10 percent since 1972 (the absence of a conclusive census leaves the actual figures—but not the declining trend—open to debate.) The birthrate is approximately 1.5 children per lifetime, or two-thirds that of the rest of America; the rate of intermarriage is estimated at one out of every four Jews.[3]

large numbers of poor urban Jews, the overall high position of Jews' mean scores of standard measures of social status is undisputed. In fact, the most recent research reports that in the last ten years they have continued to advance, obtaining some of the most elite positions in society, as US senators, corporate leaders, and heads of Ivy League universities and professional schools.[5]

The upward mobility of American Jews reflects both the process and the result of their successful integration into American society. Integration, however, should not be confused with assimilation. While the traditional religious practices of the first-generation immigrants no longer constitute the basis of Jewish identity, other forms of ethnic and religious identity have arisen. For some, Judaism is a religion; for others, it is a secular manifestation of their ethnic or cultural heritage. The concept of a Jewish people gained adherents with the emergence of political Zionism in the latter part of the nineteenth century, and since the establishment of Israel, Judaism has become a basis for modern-day nationality. For many, Judaism is not inevitably or uniquely expressed through religious practice, since the secular and ethnic components are equally strong.

Since the mid-twentieth century, Israel has increasingly become a source of emotional identification for American Jews, secular and religious, Orthodox and Conservative, rich and poor, Democrat and Republican. The Israeli victory in the 1967 war reinforced these feelings; writing in the August 1967 issue of *Commentary,* Rabbi Arthur Hertzberg noted that the June War created a new "network of claims" not directly related to the religious tradition of Judaism:

The sense of belonging to a worldwide Jewish people, of which Israel is the center, is a religious sentiment, but it seems to persist even among Jews who regard themselves as secularists or atheists. There are no conventional theological terms with which to explain this. . . .[6]

The process by which the American Jewish establishment and an overwhelming number of American Jews reached a pro-Israel consensus spanned a number of decades. In its pre-1948 form, political Zionism was not particularly attractive to an immigrant population attempting to integrate into a new world. The Zionist demand that Jews abandon the diaspora and settle in Palestine met largely with indifference, or even scorn, from those who hoped to find safety and prosperity—at least for their children—in America. Established Jewish leaders were concerned with possible negative repercussions from the arrival of millions of Eastern European immigrants to the United States; they viewed Zionism "as endangering successful integration into the larger society. They believed that if Jews would act as Zionists, that is, if they behaved as a separate national identity, their allegiance to the United States would be threatened."[7] Indeed, the political ideology that most appealed to American

8

Jews in this period was liberalism, a development that Steven Cohen links to "the politics of group integration."*[8]

By the 1940s, integration was no longer a distant goal but a reality for many second- and third-generation American Jews, who, following full revelation of the scope and horror of the Holocaust, were now increasingly concerned with group survivalist issues. Most American Jews eschewed the tenets of classical Zionism in favor of a more emotional identification with the existence of Israel, both as a symbol of the survival and victory of the Jews and as a center of Jewish identity and authority. According to political scientist Charles Liebman, " . . . support for Israel becomes not only support for a state . . . or for its inhabitants—rather, support for Israel is the symbol of one's Jewish identity. . . ."[10]

The phenomenon of American Jewry's emotional identification with and support for Israel is now commonly referred to as pro-Israelism, as distinct from Zionism.

Pro-Israelism and the American Jewish Establishment

The *American Jewish Yearbook* lists over two hundred national Jewish organizations, which make Jews the most institutionally organized minority group in the United States. There are synagogues, youth centers, community relations agencies, federations, fundraising organizations, cultural and educational groups, fraternal lodges, and organizations that address specific issues, such as Israel and Soviet Jewry. Many engage in social, cultural, or philanthropic activities that serve the broader non-Jewish community in meaningful ways. The majority are essentially secular, their membership and activities based on an ethnic and communal definition of Judaism.**

---

* In brief, the progressive concerns of liberalism—intergroup tolerance, civil and religious liberties, social and economic justice—served to protect Jews from anti-Semitism *and* facilitate their integration into American society, albeit into a position to the left of most Americans. Cohen accounts for continued Jewish identification with liberalism by positing that the direction taken by the Democratic Party and American liberalism coincided with the developing interests of American Jewry: "Far from undermining liberal commitments, Jews' changing class character has, in fact, harmonized with liberalism's changing style and content in recent years."[9] See Chapter 2, introduction, and the Conclusion for further discussion of liberalism.

** The 1972 National Jewish Population Survey reported synagogue membership at 46.9 percent and organizational membership at 41.8 percent; the 1983 National Survey of American Jews reported the same two categories at 59 and 44 percent, respectively. While synagogue membership shows an increase, this is not a definitive index of religiosity as opposed to ethnicity. For one thing, a high proportion of Jews attends services only on high holidays. More important, American synagogues have also adapted to the secular trend. When the core of Jewish identity was religious practice, synagogues offered prayer, Hebrew scholarship, and spiritual authority. Today's synagogues provide much more than religious services to members: they have become, in effect, modern community institutions sponsoring a full range of social, cultural, and even political programs from day care and singles clubs to campaigns that mobilize the congregation to lobby for Israel or march for Soviet Jewry.

Clearly, as Jewish immigrants became increasingly Americanized, they did not abandon their Jewish identity, but instead asserted it in a form better suited to American society. The structural result was the proliferation of Jewish institutions and organizations established in the first half of this century, a development summed up by the late sociologist Harold Weisberg's often quoted phrase " . . . to be a Jew is to belong to a [Jewish] organization."[11] In the words of political scientist Daniel Elazar, who is now president of the Jerusalem Center for Public Affairs: "In the process of modernization . . .organic ties disappeared for Jews, as they have for other peoples who have gone through the same process. . . . Organized activity . . . has come to be the most common manifestation of Judaism, replacing prayer, study, and the normal private intercourse of kin as a means of being Jewish."[12]

The phrase "American Jewish establishment" refers throughout this book to both organizations and their leadership. The overall structure of Jewish community-based organizations is often termed confederational: membership and degree of participation is voluntary, based on predilection, commitment, and the luxury of free time. Though formally democratic, this structure early on encouraged the emergence of a relatively small, self-perpetuating, and interlocking leadership, drawn mainly from traditionally wealthy families or otherwise high-status Jewish elites. According to a study done after World War II, "in eight major national Jewish organizations . . . 28 individuals occupied a total of 108 director-ships. . . . "[13] This phenomenon has diminished only somewhat with time; in a 1981 study on American Jewish leadership, Melvin Urofsky found that "two-thirds belong to 5 or more Jewish organizations exclusive of synagogal or local affiliations, while a similar percentage belong to 5 or less non-Jewish agencies. Some 7 out of 10 also hold offices in more than one national [Jewish] group."[14] (A recent exception to this trend is the emergence of the Jewish professional bureaucrat or manager, whose appointed — rather than elected — position results from specific experience and organizational skills.)

The Jewish community has never been monolithic. Its institutions are characterized by the absence of central authority, duplication of functions, and political, ideological, and religious differences. It is against this background that historian Melvin Urofsky describes the most profound impact of pro-Israelism:

. . . the hallmark of American Jewry is its diversity. Being a Jew does not automatically endow one with a set of values and ideas shared by all others who are called Jews. . . . The community can only be united insofar as it has areas of mutual concern to all its members; within American Jewry, there is one primary concern, namely Israel. . . . Every effort to coordinate Jewish activities in other areas has failed miserably. . . . [15]

Jewish establishment organizations now provide the structural framework for expressing ethnic identity and promoting group interest (or survival). By extension, pro-Israelism has become the dominant ideological construct; the result is that various forms of Israel support work are on the agenda of virtually all Jewish establishment organizations, be they communal, welfare, religious, or educational.

Notes*

1. Marshall Sklare, (ed.), *The Jewish Community in America.* New York: Behrman House, 1974: 232.

2. *Jewish Week,* 9 May 1982.

3. *Wall Street Journal,* 13 April 1984.

4. *Washington Post,* 25 March 1984.

5. Steven M. Cohen, *American Modernity & Jewish Identity.* New York and London: Tavistock Publications, 1983: 76.

6. Arthur Hertzberg, "Israel and American Jewry," *Commentary* 44/2 (August 1967).

7. Cohen: 154.

8. *Ibid:* 134.

9. *Ibid:* 137.

10. Charles Liebman, quoted in Gary S. Schiff, "American Jews and Israel: A Study in Political and Organizational Priorities," in M. L. Raphael, ed., *Understanding American Jewish Philanthropy.* New York: KTAV Publishers, 1979: 167.

11. Harold Weisberg, "Ideologies of the American Jews," quoted in Will Maslow, *The Structure and Functioning of the American Jewish Community.* New York: published jointly by the American Jewish Congress and the American Section of the World Jewish Congress, 1974: 5.

12. Daniel Elazar, *Community and Policy: The Organizational Dynamics of American Jewry,* quoted in Cohen: 44.

13. Arthur Liebman, *Jews and the Left.* New York: Wiley, 1979: 396.

14. Melvin I. Urofsky, "American Jewish Leadership," *American Jewish History* 70/4 (June 1981): 405.

15. *Ibid:* 414.

*Editor's Note: Throughout the text a number of footnote source materials came from undated organizational brochures, pamphlets and flyers. Please see the bibliography for full citation.

Zionist Organizations

CHAPTER I

Zionist Organizations

Introduction: An Emerging Ideology

It is estimated today that about one million American Jews, or about one-sixth of the total American Jewish population, are enrolled in a variety of official Zionist organizations.[1] These groups define and promote themselves as Zionist, adhere to the contemporary definition of Zionism as articulated in the 1968 Jerusalem Program of the World Zionist Organization (WZO) and are represented in the WZO through its American branch, the American Zionist Federation (AZF), or by affiliation with the World Confederation of United Zionists (WCUZ). All share a commitment, in varying degrees, to the two concepts that have historically defined Zionism: that Jews everywhere constitute a people with common cultural, national, and political aspirations and that, since the Jewish state is the highest fulfillment of those aspirations, the goal and duty of every Jew should be to immigrate to Israel, to make *aliyah*. Programmatically, American Zionist organizations promote and facilitate *aliyah* and Hebrew education, sponsor political and cultural pro-Israel activities, help sell Israel Bonds, raise money for the United Jewish Appeal (UJA) Federation campaigns, and often provide financial sponsorship for a particular kibbutz or project in Israel. They also participate in Israel support work under the aegis of the American Israel Public Affairs Committee, the domestic pro-Israel lobby, and the Conference of Presidents of Major American Jewish Organizations. Almost all have youth auxiliaries, composed mainly of high school students.

The role, function, and importance of American Zionist groups have always varied according to the definition and development of the world Zionist movement. The official program adopted by the first Zionist Congress, held in Basle, Switzerland in 1897, proclaimed: "Zionism seeks for the Jewish People a publicly recognized, legally secured homeland in Palestine," and proposed achieving this goal:

    1. By fostering the settlement of Palestine with farmers, laborers, and artisans;

    2. By organizing the whole of Jewry in suitable local and general bodies in accordance with the laws of their respective countries;

    3. By strengthening the National Jewish feeling and National consciousness;

4. By taking preparatory steps to attain government consent which may be necessary to reach the aim of Zionism.[2]

Since that time the meaning and focus of Zionism have undergone several permutations. During the initial colonization process, before 1948, the emphasis was on developing a separate Jewish economy and society in Palestine and promoting Jewish immigration: creating "facts" on the ground. American Zionist organizations devoted all their energies to working within the Jewish community and in U.S. policy circles for acceptance of and support for a Jewish state in Palestine. Their main areas of responsibility were political affairs, Jewish and Hebrew education, *aliyah*, and, most important, fundraising. While their membership was never large, these early Zionist groups were notable for the passionate and often divisive ardor with which they advocated their cause. The Zionist Organization of America (ZOA), Hadassah, Mizrachi, and Poale Zion spearheaded the drive to wrest the financial and political allegiance of American Jews from the traditional Jewish establishment. During the 1940s, with the revelation of the scope and horror of the Nazi Holocaust, the lack of alternatives for the remnants of European Jewry, and the growing support of the U.S. government for the idea of a Jewish state, these Zionist groups met with increasing success.

Inevitably, but nonetheless ironically, the official American Zionists suffered their greatest organizational reversal as a direct result of the attainment of their political goal—the establishment of Israel. Almost immediately after 1948, political and programmatic dilemmas arose to haunt American Zionist organizations. Most had been connected to particular ideological groupings within the Zionist movement: after the founding of the state, these groupings were transformed into political parties whose priorities were rooted in the Israeli political structure and only peripherally in the American scene. Simultaneously, the task of fundraising shifted to their former adversaries—specifically, the non-Zionist federations—who had become convinced of the need to support Israel and whose years of experience and strong base in the community made them more successful at generating funds than any Zionist organization could hope to be. The Israeli government did not fail to perceive this situation and at the time, serious consideration was given to dissolving the World Zionist Organization on the grounds that with the establishment of Israel its task was accomplished. American Zionist organizations were described by historian Melvin Urofsky as finding themselves "in the position of a mother who has given her last child in marriage."[3] Only a rare group like Hadassah, which had specific goals, programs, and a mass base, retained its strength.

In 1951, the twenty-third Zionist Congress reformulated the task of Zionism as "the consolidation of the State of Israel; the ingathering of the exiles in Eretz Israel; and the fostering of the unity of the Jewish people."[4]

16

The issue of *aliyah*, however, left many American Zionists in a peculiar position. While they did not want to become "just 'friends' of Israel," like the non-Zionist community groups, they were "unalterably opposed to a definition of Zionism limited to *aliyah*. . . ."[5] In their attempt to resolve this ideological conflict, and to justify the continued existence of and need for self-defined Zionists who did not themselves make *aliyah*, American Zionists stressed the Jewish people concept in the post-state stages: they defined " . . . the continuing mission of Zionism to be the perpetuation of a Jewish people united not only by ethical ideas and religious observance, but by nationalism as well."[6]

A major factor contributing to the decline of American Zionism was the growing lack of any real distinction between Zionist and non-Zionist organizations—Urofsky called it "a distinction without a difference."[7] In the period before 1948, the commitment to the goal of creating a Jewish national home clearly separated the Zionist organizations from their non-Zionist counterparts, who referred to themselves as "defense organizations" and saw their primary task as defending Jewish rights wherever Jews were living. But with the 1967 war, when pro-Israelism swept across Jewish community groups, all organized Jewry took on Israel support work: the non-Zionists became "neo-Zionists," or what Norman Podhoretz dubbed "instant Zionists." One result could be seen in the plight of the Zionist Organization of America, which "foundered, losing members, groping for something to do, watching helplessly while new institutions and agencies, non-Zionist for the most part, assumed the work of public relations, lobbying, and fundraising on behalf of Israel, tasks which the ZOA had always assumed would be its responsibilities after the creation of the state."[8]

For their part, however, Israelis tended to reject any definition of Zionism that did not make the test of *aliyah* its primary component. In 1961, David Ben-Gurion, the first prime minister of Israel, made this clear in his speech before the twenty-fifth Zionist Congress: "Since the day the Jewish State was established and the gates of Israel were flung open to every Jew who wanted to come, every religious Jew has daily violated the precepts of Judaism and the Torah of Israel by remaining in the Diaspora."[9]

It was not until the 1967 war and the emergence of pro-Israelism as a mass phenomenon among American Jews that an expanded and more flexible definition of Zionism was accepted by Israel and the world Zionist movement. This was forthcoming in 1968 at the twenty-seventh Zionist Congress, where the aims of contemporary Zionism were laid out in what is now known as the Jerusalem Program:

1. The unity of the Jewish people and the centrality of Israel in Jewish life;

2. The ingathering of the Jewish people in its historical homeland, Eretz Yisrael, through *aliyah* from all countries;

3. The strengthening of the State of Israel which is based on the prophetic vision of justice and peace;

4. The preservation of the identity of the Jewish people through the fostering of Jewish and Hebrew education and of Jewish spiritual and cultural values;

5. The protection of Jewish rights everywhere.[10]

The Jerusalem Program delineates the ideological framework within which the Zionist establishment is willing to coexist with the pro-Israelism of American Jews. An analysis issued by the American Zionist Federation states:

The Zionism of the Jerusalem Program implicitly rejects a "Diaspora-centered" Zionism which emphasizes a "political solution"—*aliyah*—for oppressed Jews, while requiring only political and financial support for Israel from Jews in the democratic West. It likewise eschews the belief of some Zionists in *Shlilat Hagolah*, the "negation of the Diaspora." Under this doctrine, all Diaspora Jewish identity was seen as more or less compromised and fated to yield to the forces of either anti-Semitism or assimilation. Rather, today's Zionism—influenced by the strong bonds among all Jews forged by Israel over the past 34 years, and by their resistance to the international campaign to delegitimize the Jewish state—views a strong Israel and a vital Diaspora as interdependent and mutually supportive, as the two complementary parts of "one people."[11]

World Zionist Organization and the Jewish Agency

The primary structural framework for the interaction of American Zionist and non-Zionist groups within the Zionist establishment is provided by the World Zionist Organization (WZO) and the Jewish Agency (JA), respectively. Article 4 of the League of Nations Mandate for Palestine recognized the WZO as an independent body of the "Jewish people" and stipulated that, should it be desired at any time to establish an "agency" to consist not only of Zionist membership but also of other Jews who might wish to partake in the building of the country, this "agency" would also be recognized. In 1919, the WZO became that body; in 1929, it was supplemented by the Enlarged Jewish Agency, conceived as the forum for non-Zionist participation in the Zionist structure.* The 1929 agreement specified that JA membership would be determined on the basis of parity, with 50 percent nominated by the WZO and the other 50 percent by Jewish communities and personalities representing the non-Zionists. By the 1930s, however, it was clear that this arrangement was not being implemented as planned. In practice, the WZO was appointing not only its allotted half of the JA membership, but also the non-Zionist representatives from countries where American non-Zionists had no organizational base or constituency. In addition, since the American non-Zionists had no central coordinating body of their own, they were at a disadvantage when confronted by the highly organized representatives of the WZO. As a result, the JA, nominally the "sister organization" of the WZO, gradually evolved into its "operative arm."

In 1944, the JA opened an office in New York City for its agent in the United States. Five years later, the office was changed to a full-fledged corporation, registered in New York under the name of the Jewish Agency, Inc., and registered with the U.S. Department of Justice as a foreign agent working on behalf of the parent organization in Jerusalem.

In 1952, the Israeli Knesset promulgated a law on the status of the WZO-JA, establishing it as a legally registered, tax-exempt organization and regulating the relationship between the WZO-JA and the Israeli government. The 1952 law and the ensuing Covenant of 1954 set up the WZO and its arm, the JA, as an extraterritorial Zionist institution. According to the Covenant, its functions were to be:

The organization of immigration abroad and the transfer of immigrants and their property to Israel; participation in the absorption of immigrants in Israel; Youth Immigration; agricultural settlement in Israel; the acquisition and amelioration of land in Israel by institutions of the Zionist Organization, the Keren Kayemeth Le Israel and the Keren Hayesod; participation in the establishment and the

* See Chapter 2, section on Council of Jewish Federations and Chapter 3, introduction.

expansion of development enterprises in Israel; the encouragement of private capital investments in Israel; assistance to cultural enterprises and institutions of higher learning in Israel; the mobilization of resources for financing these functions; the coordination of the activities in Israel of Jewish institutions and organizations acting within the sphere of these functions with the aid of public funds.[12]

In 1959, the name "Jewish Agency, Inc." was changed to "Jewish Agency for Israel, Inc." A year later, the Jewish Agency for Israel, Inc. was reorganized, according to JA officials, "in order to provide a closer identification on the part of the people who raised funds with the problems of actual operations in the field, and in order to satisfy the requirements of the Internal Revenue Service."[13] As a result of the reorganization, the Jewish Agency for Israel, Inc. cancelled its registration as a foreign agent and was granted tax-exempt status. An additional organization, the Jewish Agency-American Section, was created in New York and registered as the new foreign agent working on behalf of the JA in Jerusalem.

At that point, the activities of the Jewish Agency for Israel, Inc. were to be confined to "the administration of the expenditure of United Jewish Appeal proceeds intended for Israel." In actuality, as the Fulbright hearings showed in 1963, the JA did more than administer the Israel-bound UJA funds. It used the American Zionist Council (AZC), among other organizations, as a conduit for the disbursement of funds in the United States in accordance with directions from the WZO-JA in Jerusalem. In the aftermath of the hearings, the Department of Justice amended the Foreign Agents Registration Act of 1938, and the AZC was abolished. In 1969, the Justice Department forced the JA-American Section to file the 1954 Covenant as a required document in its foreign agent registration.[14]

With the JA increasingly turning into an arm of the Israeli state, and the role of diaspora Jewish communities confined to fundraising, the ambiguous status of the JA was bringing pressure to bear on the tax-exempt status of the United Jewish Appeal (UJA). At the same time that American Jews became more active in pro-Israel work after 1967 and the amount of money raised for Israel dramatically increased, the non-Zionist members demanded greater diaspora participation in the JA's decision-making process. The first step toward resolving both of these problems was the Reconstitution Agreement of 1971, concluded between the WZO (represented by Louis Pincus, chairman of the JA Executive) and the United Israel Appeal (UIA) and Keren Hayesod (Foundation Fund) on behalf of Jewish fundraising bodies throughout the world (represented by Max Fisher, president of UIA and Jewish affairs advisor to President Richard Nixon).

One major result of the reorganization that was formalized in this agreement was the functional separation — on paper at least — of the JA and the WZO, mainly in order to protect the tax-exempt status of UJA funds channeled to the JA through the UIA. According to the agreement, "The functions and tasks and programs administered by the Agency or to which it may contribute funds shall be only such as may be carried out by tax-exempt organizations," and these tasks were to include "immigration and absorption, support for educational and youth activities, particularly Youth Aliyah, absorption in agricultural settlements, and immigrant housing."[15]

As for the WZO, the Reconstitution Agreement stipulates that, "The WZO and its institutions will continue as the organs of the Zionist Movement for the fulfillment of Zionist programs and ideals and, save as hereinafter stated, will continue to perform the functions and tasks enumerated in the said Law of Status and the said Covenant."[16]

More specifically, in 1971 the WZO "... accepted the tasks of *aliyah* from the free nations of the world, education and culture in the Diaspora, information services, organization and membership, youth and *hechalutz* [pioneer] activities, and the functions of the Jewish National Fund."[17]

The other change mandated by the Reconstitution Agreement was a restructuring of the parity system for delegate selection in order to guarantee that the non-Zionist organizations were fairly represented. The 50 percent non-Zionist membership of the JA was now to be appointed by Keren Hayesod (or, in the United States, by the UIA, which is Keren Hayesod's American branch), thus providing the non-Zionists with an organizational structure, as well as increased political clout.

In practice, however, separation between the WZO and JA since 1971 is difficult to discern. WZO and JA world executives share the same chairman—since 1977, Leon Arieh Dulzin in Jerusalem. In the U.S., the WZO and JA have the same offices; many of the same people sit on their respective boards. The agencies have the same director general, have shared the same treasurer, and utilize the same publishing house. Genuine separation between the WZO-American Section and the reconstituted JA is further called into question by the fact that Bernice S. Tannenbaum, president of the WZO-American Section, is chairperson of the JA-American Section. Major departments of immigration and absorption and agricultural settlements have two co-chairs, one each from the JA and the WZO. There is one trade union for employees of both organizations. In spite of the 1971 agreement, Israeli political parties have been unwilling to relinquish their control over an agency with such huge resources.[18]

In February 1981, the JA board of governors convened a conference in Caesarea, Israel "to review ten years of the reconstitution of the Jewish Agency and how the partnership is working out."[19] The three issues posed for discussion were:

1. Assuming the unity of the Jewish People, shall we assume the centrality and primacy of Israel?

2. After ten years of reconstitution, and accepting the import of Israel, is the

21

Jewish Agency doing what it should be doing (or are we doing what we are because we have always done it)?

3. How do you—the members of the Board—see the image of the Jewish Agency? What can we, as Board members, do to strengthen it?[20]

The results of the Caesarea Conference (also known as the Caesarea Process) show that while there are still ideological differences between Zionists and non-Zionists, these have become so secondary that they have lost any real impact. The concern of the non-Zionists was a pragmatic one: they tended to urge more diaspora participation and less association with the WZO in the belief that such a focus would increase the efficacy of the JA. The Zionists pushed for non-Zionist endorsement of the Jerusalem Program—and received it—but in a fashion that participant Rabbi Alexander Schindler, president of the Union of American Hebrew Congregations, says " . . . represented no ideological victory for the Zionist cause. It was more an act of courtesy than an expression of new-found commitment."[21] In his summation, the program director of the conference expressed the consensus reached as:

. . . the well-being and destiny of the Jewish state is the business of all Jews, whether they live in Israel or the Diaspora; the well-being and destiny of the Jewish people is the business of all Jews, whether they live in Israel or the Diaspora; the well-being and destiny of Israel and the Jewish people are one concern.[22]

In June 1983, the Zionist General Council passed a unanimous resolution in support of the Caesarea Process—an apparent act of reciprocity for the acceptance of the Jerusalem Program by the diaspora-based fundraisers of the Jewish Agency. Commenting on these events, the World Confederation of United Zionists (WCUZ) notes:

This implies on the one hand a "Zionization" of the Jewish Agency and, on the other, some depoliticization of the World Zionist Organization. It is no secret, however, that some parties in the WZO have their reservations about this in that they fear a possible watering down of Zionist ideologies by those who call themselves neo-Zionist [i.e. pro-Israeli American Jews] and a curtailment of the influence of the parties in the WZO. It is clear, however, that the fundraisers in the Jewish Agency are now inclined to accept the Zionist Program and to be involved in areas like Jewish education and support for Aliya in addition to their traditional fundraising activities.[23]

At present, more than a third of WZO members are Israelis, who are delegates of political parties or specific Zionist groupings; the remaining 62 percent are representatives of Zionist organizations in the United States or other countries, also aligned with a specific Israeli political party or trend. American Zionists actively participate with their Israeli counterparts in the debates of the Zionist Congress, held every four years. On the whole, delineations are based on political and ideological allegiances as opposed to identity conflicts between diaspora and Israeli Jews, with the occasional exception of the minority non-party Zionists.

JA members are now equally divided between WZO appointees (from Israeli political parties and Zionist groups) and United Israel Appeal (UIA) appointees from the diaspora (such as the leadership of the federations and the UJA) in what is essentially a partnership between the WZO and the neo-Zionist fundraisers. The JA is the recipient of the bulk of the UJA-Federation annual campaign funds raised by American Jews and earmarked for Israel; its function is to supply the funds and supervise the activities in the fields of "immigration, absorption, agricultural settlement, education, health and welfare," while political activities are left to the WZO.

Jewish Agency for Israel

Year established: 1929; reorganized: 1960, 1971
Executive Chairwoman: Bernice Tannenbaum
Address: 515 Park Avenue, New York, NY 10022

The JA-American Section, which had been registered as the agent for the JA in Jerusalem, deregistered as a foreign agent in October 1971, while the WZO-American Section registered in September 1971 as the foreign agent of the WZO Executive in Jerusalem. With no further justification for the JA-American Section, the JA for Israel, Inc., a tax-exempt corporation in New York, became the sole legal recipient of the Israel-bound funds raised by the UJA-Federation annual appeals.

Structure

The reconstituted JA is governed by an assembly, a Board of Governors (BOG), and the Executive. The assembly meets once a year to receive reports from the BOG and the Executive, to review needs and programs, to determine basic policies, to consider and act upon budgets submitted by the BOG, and to elect officers. It is composed of 340 members, 170 for the WZO and 170 for diaspora Jews. The 170 appointed by the WZO include 38 percent from Israeli Zionist political parties, in proportion to their actual Knesset representation, and 62 percent non-Zionists, most of whom are connected to political parties in Israel. The 170 appointed by diaspora communities include 30 percent appointed by the UIA (UJA) and 20 percent by Keren Hayesod.

The BOG, with sixty-two members appointed in the same proportions as the assembly, manages the affairs of the JA and controls its activities. It appoints the members of the standing Budget and Finance Committee and other standing and *ad hoc* committees as it sees fit. The thirty-one WZO delegates to the BOG serve at the same time as members in the management of WZO. As a rule, the chair of the BOG is a non-Israeli Jew.

The Executive is responsible for the day-to-day operations of the JA, subject to the control of the BOG. The Executive has thirteen members, usually seven Israelis and six diaspora Jews, including the chair of the assembly (also the chair of the Executive), the chair of the BOG, the treasurer, the heads of the departments of Immigration and Absorption, Youth Aliyah, and Rural Settlement, the national chair of the UJA, the world chair of Keren Hayesod, and four members from the BOG not designated by the WZO (of whom two or three are designated by the UIA). The Executive, based in Jerusalem, constitutes the "cabinet" of the JA. Indeed, holders of major posts in the Executive are paid on the same scale as the Israeli cabinet members. Competition for the heads of important departments and control over the budget generally takes place at the

Zionist Congress. When vacancies develop — as with the November 1989 removal of Rafael Kotlowitz as chair of the *aliyah* department—political fights occur outside the context of the Congress. In this case, Ariel Sharon was nominated as the Herut candidate to chair both the WZO and JA *aliyah* divisions, since one person traditionally fills both posts.*

The Jewish Agency for Israel, Inc. in New York is a corporation organized under the membership corporation law of the state of New York. In 1963, the members of the corporation were the UIA and the JA-American Section. The corporation is governed by a board of directors of twenty-seven members, two-thirds designated by the UIA and one-third by the JA-American Section.

Funding

The JA's annual budget is covered primarily from funds raised by American Jewry (through the UJA) and by world Jewry (through Keren Hayesod). The UJA income through the UIA constitutes more than 60 percent of the JA's annual operating budget. Since 1971, the UJA/UIA alone has provided about $3 billion to the JA, more than 65 percent of the Agency's operating budget. The JA's share of the American money is much greater if one takes into consideration the more than $240 million provided by the U.S. government between 1972 and 1982 toward the resettlement of Soviet and Eastern European Jews. These funds have constituted nearly 7 percent of the JA's total budget. Since 1948, the JA has expended at least $6.5 billion in Israel; about 70 percent was spent since its reorganization in 1971.

Though UJA's funds go to the JA (and not the WZO), the UJA does finance a part of the WZO's budget indirectly. WZO's income for 1981/1982 consisted of $36.5 million from Keren Hayesod and $15.5 million from the Israeli government. The JA's income that year consisted mainly of UIA funds ($247.2 million) and Keren Hayesod funds ($35.9 million). To cover the JA's $60.8 million debt payments for that year, UIA paid about 75 percent ($45.6 million) and Keren Hayesod, about 25 percent ($15.2 million).[25]

---

*Another nominee, the deputy chair of the Jewish National Fund, told the *Jerusalem Post* that the candidate would be selected "not according to one's qualifications, but according to which political groupings in Herut and elsewhere support the candidate." Sharon was defeated, despite strong support from Prime Minister Shamir, by a vote of 59 to 48.[24]

World Zionist Organization-American Section

Year established: 1971
President: Bernice S. Tannenbaum
Vice-President: Jacques Torczyner
Executive Vice Chairman: Isadore Hamlin
Address: 515 Park Avenue, New York, NY 10022

General Background

In accord with the 1971 Reconstitution Agreement, the WZO-American Section operates in the United States as the agent for the WZO Executive in Jerusalem; it is composed of those members of the Executive who reside in the United States. The WZO is registered with the U.S. Department of Justice under Section 2 of the Foreign Agents Registration Act of 1938, as amended, and it files its six-month registration, as required by law. But it also files Form 990 (Return of Organization Exempt from Income Tax) as a 501 (c) (3) tax-exempt organization under the Internal Revenue Code, and it is exempted from filing annual reports with the New York Office of Charities Registration on the grounds that it is a "religious organization." WZO's territorial branch in the United States, the American Zionist Federation (AZF), is an umbrella organization that includes all U.S. Zionist organizations. In reaction to the affiliation of most American Zionist groups to political parties in Israel, another umbrella organization, the World Confederation of United Zionists (WCUZ), was created to provide coordination among the non-party American Zionists.

Structure and Function

The general objectives of WZO, as stated in the WZO-American Section's registration statements on file with the U.S. Department of Justice, are:

To foster the ideals of Zionism and Judaism, and the unity of the Jewish people; to encourage the immigration of Jews to Israel and their resettlement and rehabilitation therein in industry, agriculture, commerce and the trades; and to assist and further their cultural, educational, religious, social, artistic and scientific endeavors. To encourage, foster and promote the knowledge and study of the Hebrew language and literature, Jewish culture, history, philosophy and traditions, and the achievements of the Zionist ideal; and in connection therewith, to disseminate, publish and otherwise make available cultural, literary, religious, social, artistic, scientific and other publications and works relating to Judaism, Zionism, Israel and kindred subjects."

The purpose of the WZO-American Section "is to gain the increasing and continued support of the American Jewish community for the above-mentioned objectives."[26] Its jurisdiction includes Canada and Mexico.

To a large extent, the range of activities of the WZO-American Section mirrors the activities of the WZO in Jerusalem, with special attention given to the Jewish/Zionist situation in the United States. It operates through a number of fixed departments:

Education and Culture — Programs include the Bible context, the Hebrew Language Division, *Yediat* [knowledge of] Israel, Early Childhood Division, Israel Program Section (conducts recruitment, screening, and registration of students who wish to enroll in the programs in Israel), publications, and educational centers.

Torah (Religious) Education and Culture — Responsible for the preparation of educational materials for religious schools and tutoring workshops intended to introduce modern pedagogical techniques (between April and June 1983, forty such workshops were held in ten cities). Educational materials prepared in 1983 covered topics such as "the unity of Israel," "Turn from evil and do good," and "Love your neighbor." Workshops for school principals and senior teachers included Hebrew studies on curriculum, geography of Israel, and Jewish history.

Theodor Herzl Institute — Conducts lectures and evening programs. In addition to Jewish and Zionist history, topics discussed in 1983 included "Ultimate Israeli concerns," "In search of Jewish role models," "Behind the headlines," "Zionism and the Holocaust," "Moslem fundamentalism and Arab nationalism," and "Controversial issues in current Zionism." Among the special events held at the Institute were a commemoration of the Holocaust, an Israel Independence Day celebration, and a seminar on "Why the world is anti-Israel."

Herzl Press — Publishes books and monographs on Judaism, Zionism, and Israel.

Theodor Herzl Foundation — Publishes *Midstream,* "a monthly literary magazine devoted to Jewish and Zionist problems of general and current interest."

Interreligious and Community Relations Department — Maintains liaison with various Christian organizations. In 1983, this department sent a delegation of twelve presidents of Christian universities to Israel.

Public Information and Press Department — Issues press releases and assists in publishing *Israel Scene* and the annual *Guide to Israel Programs.*

Youth Department, Youth Aliyah Department, and Dor Hemshech/Young Leadership Department — All three departments organize workshops on Zionism and Israel, Israel-based study programs, and frequent delegations to Israel; they also maintain contacts with other Zionist and Jewish youth organizations in the United States.

Zionist Archives and Library — Maintained at the office in New York City.[27]

Funding

As the agent of the WZO in Jerusalem, the WZO-American Section received annual funding from its parent organization. According to its registration statement, the total receipts of the WZO-American Section for the year from 1 October 1982 through 30 September 1983 were slightly over $10 million. The largest expenditure (about $4.5 million) covered the compensation and maintenance of about 150 WZO "envoys" (*shlihim*) engaged in WZO-related activities. About $3.3 million was spent on administrative and functional costs, about $1.3 million on grants, sub-fractions, and service fees, and about $819,000 on WZO employees in Latin America and Canada.

According to the 1982-1983 statement, grants were disbursed in varying amounts, ranging from less than $1,000 to over $100,000. The recipients were a variety of Zionist and Jewish organizations and centers in the United States, Mexico and Canada. Recipients in the United States included the Presidents Conference (membership fee), B'nai B'rith, Hadassah, Jewish Telegraphic Agency (for providing daily news to WZO offices throughout the world), Israel Students Organizations, National Council of Young Israel, Mizrachi-Religious Zionists of America, Union of American Hebrew Congregations, Center for Jewish Studies at Harvard, Center for Jewish Studies at Temple University, Zionist Organization of America, Americans for a Safe Israel, World Confederation of United Zionists and the National Conference on Soviet Jewry. Most of the grants seem to have been earmarked for youth-related activities, visits to Israel, encouragement of settlement, and youth-directed pro-Israel information. Hebrew education and Jewish studies also received support.

American Zionist Federation

Year established: 1970
President: Benjamin Cohen
Executive Director: Karen J. Rubinstein
Address: 515 Park Avenue, New York, NY 10022
Publications: *Spectrum, Issue Analysis*

General Background

The AZF went through a number of permutations prior to 1970, when it became the loosely organized umbrella body for American Zionism. The first impetus for collective Zionist planning in the United States followed the promulgation of the British White Paper of 1939, which called for restricted Jewish immigration to Palestine. Recognizing the need to pressure the U.S. government to take a stand against that development, Chaim Weizmann, then head of the WZO, visited the United States and urged existing Zionist organizations to unite for one plan of action. The result of his call was the formation of the Emergency Committee for Zionist Affairs in 1939. Weizmann's "quiet diplomacy" was not satisfactory to everyone, however, and in protest against it, the militant Rabbi Abba Hillel Silver soon called for "loud diplomacy" from the Jewish masses in the United States. With the failure of the Emergency Committee to generate an agreement on a unified course of action, the ground was prepared for Silver's call to be translated, in 1943, into a new national apparatus, known as the American Zionist Emergency Committee (AZEC). AZEC included the four largest Zionist organizations in the United States at that time: the Zionist Organization of America, Hadassah, Mizrachi, and the Poale Zion. A year later, the AZEC had managed to set up no less than two hundred local emergency committees, and the number soon doubled. The AZEC played an important role in instructing local operatives on "how to make their voices heard more effectively," and continued to function until after the creation of Israel.

The twenty-seventh World Zionist Congress, held in Jerusalem in 1968, resolved to strengthen the Zionist movement worldwide through the establishment of "Zionist territorial organizations," or federations, in countries throughout the world. In the Ratification Assembly held in Philadelphia, the AZF was created "by unanimous decision of all the Zionist organizations in the United States." Recognizing the need to broaden the base of American Zionism, they established the AZF as a central body "to bring the Zionist message to the grass-roots of American Jewry ... and to interpret developments in the Middle East for the American public."[28]

Structure and Role

The AZF is registered in the state of New York as a membership organization which is tax-exempt under the Internal Revenue Code. Its constituent members are the sixteen Zionist organizations in the United States and their youth auxiliaries,* but American Jews who identify. themselves as Zionist may join the umbrella organization directly. (This is the first umbrella organization to permit such individual memberships.) AZF membership is also open to other national Jewish organizations and institutions that are not necessarily Zionist; these come under two additional membership categories: (1) "affiliated organizations," which accept the Jerusalem Program, but whose members are not necessarily declared Zionists, and (2) "related agencies," which are "Zionist-sponsored national institutions which have always had an ongoing relationship to the Zionist movement."[29] AZF's three affiliated organizations are the American Sephardi Federation, the Association of Parents of American Israelis, and the Women's League for Israel; its related agencies are the American Zionist Youth Foundation and the Jewish National Fund. In 1983, the AZF put its aggregate membership at more than one million.

Initially, AZF's regional structure relied on twenty-three local federations to coordinate local Zionist activities, but this system did not prove to be efficient, and it was decided to establish a full-fledged regional structure because of "limited funds and manpower." By 1980, regional offices were located in three "home cities," Boston, Chicago and Los Angeles, serving the East, Midwest and West, respectively. These regional offices, administered by a president and an executive director, supervise Zionist activities in another twenty-two "satellite cities."**

*The sixteen constituent members of AZF are the following (where applicable, ideological or political party affiliations are included in parentheses):
American Zionist Youth Council (umbrella group)
American Jewish League (WCUZ, no party affiliation)
American Mizrachi Women (unofficially, National Religious Party)
Americans for Progressive Israel (Mapam)
Association of Reform Zionists of America (Reform movement in Israel)
B'nai Zion (WCUZ, no party affiliation)
Emunah Women (National Religious Party)
Hadassah (WCUZ, no party affiliation)
Mercaz (Conservative movement in Israel)
Labor Zionist Alliance (Labor Party)
North American Aliyah Movement (umbrella organization)
Pioneer Women /Na'amat (Labor Party)
Religious Zionists of America (National Religious Party)
United Zionists—Revisionists/Herut (Herut)
Zionist Organization of America (Liberal Party)
Zionist Student Movement (*ad hoc* campus group)

**Eastern Region—Albany, Boston, Buffalo, Hartford, Providence, and Rochester; Mid-Western Region—Chicago, Cincinnati, Cleveland, Columbus, Houston, Milwaukee, Minneapolis, and St. Paul; Western Region—Los Angeles, Oakland, Phoenix, Portland, San

According to the *American Jewish Yearbook*, the AZF "consolidates the efforts of the existing constituency in such areas as public and communal affairs, education, youth and *aliyah*, and invites the affiliation and participation of like-minded individuals and organizations in the community-at-large." It also "seeks to conduct a Zionist program designed to create a greater appreciation of Jewish culture within the American Jewish community in furtherance of the continuity of Jewish life and the spiritual centrality of Israel as the Jewish homeland." Interpreting its responsibility as implementing the provisions of the "Jerusalem Program," the AZF strives to reach two audiences: the American Jewish community and the broader American community. Within the American Jewish community, its goal is to strengthen its commitment to Zionist objectives, pivoted on the principles of the centrality of Israel, Jewish peoplehood, and *aliyah.*

In the broader American community, the AZF sees its main goal as "interpreting" Israel—"its problems and accomplishments, its social ideas, its affinity to American democratic values and the identity of American and Israeli interests."[31] However, AZF suffers from the same general decline in importance and effectiveness that has afflicted most official American Zionist groups, as noted by Avraham Schenker, a member of the Executive of the WZO:

The territorial Zionist Federations ... have not developed into a vibrant, active and influential factor within the Jewish community. Their activity, at best, was restricted to coordination and representation ... Locally, UJA and Keren Hayesod view the Zionist Federations as an impediment, a competitor, and even as superfluous in presenting the case of Israel before the public.[32]

Israel Support Work

The AZF responds actively to criticisms of Israel. In September 1982, following the invasion of Lebanon and the Beirut massacre, AZF's outgoing president Rabbi Joseph Sternstein, expressed the prevailing opinion of American Zionist leadership regarding the Beirut massacre: "We are confident the Israelis are not culpable. They don't do it in war, lining up people and shooting . . . . It is not the Jewish way."[33] A year later, in *Spectrum*, AZF's official publication, newly elected President Raymond Patt argued that the Jewish state was being measured by an unfair double

Diego, San Francisco, Seattle, and Tucson. The national office covers thirteen other locations with local Zionist federations: Atlanta, Baltimore, the Bronx, Brooklyn, Denver, Detroit, Miami, Long Island, New Jersey, Philadelphia, Pittsburgh, Queens and Washington, D.C. Each regional office also has a governing board that includes officers and committee heads elected from the "home city" as well as local Zionists and members of Zionist organizations from the "satellite cities." The AZF is governed by a national board of directors of approximately 350 members which meets twice a year. A smaller executive committee, consisting of about 100 members, meets once a month.[30]

standard. "Only if we Zionists maintain our vigilance," Patt wrote, "is there any hope that the big lie and the double standard will ever begin to fade, and some degree of objectivity will be restored where Israel is concerned."[34]

The AZF maintains a general information campaign, directed primarily at its own members. In late 1975, for example, following the United Nations resolution on Zionism and racism, the AZF prepared and circulated to its members *A Manual for a Zionist Information and Education Program in the United States.* The manual, dated November 1975 and stamped "for internal use only," contains a program outline on how to defend Zionism, which includes: reaching the general community with guidance on speaker orientation and briefing; utilization of radio and TV, newspapers, and the "involvement of Christian personalities"; and informing and involving the Jewish community through cassettes from Israel, training conferences, and material from the synagogues, such as bulletins and sermons. The general spirit of the manual is conveyed in this excerpt from the introduction:

The basic approach of the program is that the "enemies of Zion," Sadat, Amin, Qaddafi, Arafat* and the Russians, etc., have shifted their attack from Israel as a state, people and concept, to Zionism as international Jewish conspiracy. This is the first stage of a concentrated, coordinated attack on the Jewish people as a whole, whether they live in Jerusalem, or Gary, Indiana. We must interpret to committed Jews, whether they are card-carrying Zionists or not, that if we do not counteract this anti-Zionist onslaught immediately and interpret to the general community what Zionism is really all about, we soon will have to deal with stage two: the direct challenge of anti-Semitic propaganda in our local communities throughout the United States.[35]

To connect the American Jewish community with Israel, the AZF, in cooperation with the American Zionist Youth Foundation, maintains a "scholars-in-residence" program. Through this program, Israeli scholars, journalists, educators, and government officials are brought to the United States for two-week visits to Jewish communities. During their stays, they participate in meetings, lectures, and discussion groups that are used to transmit information about Israel.

The AZF's travel arm, the Israel Seminar Foundation, also sponsors individual delegations to Israel for professionals, academics, clergy, and business and community groups. In cooperation with the North American Aliyah Movement and the Israel Aliyah Center, for example, the AZF works to encourage Jewish immigration to Israel by seeking out conferences, fairs, and exhibits that introduce the public to opportunities

* Anwar al-Sadat, President of Egypt, 1970-1981; Idi Amin, President of Uganda, 1971-1979; Mu'ammar al-Qaddafi, Chief of State of Libya, 1969-present; Yasir Arafat, PLO Chairman, 1969-present.

in Israel.

Through its regional Zionist federations, the AZF conducts annual public events. For instance, the highly visible celebrations of Israel's Independence Day through parades, dancing, concerts, booths, and so forth aim to get Israel and its actions in the public eye. The focus of the "Jerusalem Day" is to call for international recognition of Jerusalem as Israel's capital. In 1980, there were eighty-six observations of "Jerusalem Day" in Jewish communities throughout the United States. The "Zionist caravan," a traveling resource center cosponsored by the WZO Department of Information and staffed by American Jews who have lived in Israel, visits about twenty cities in the United States each year. For the academic audience, the AZF established the Zionist Academic Council, with the specific goal of mobilizing "faculty members at universities throughout the country on behalf of Israel and the Zionist Ideal."[36] In 1982, the Zionist Academic Council published and widely disseminated a *Guide for the University Teaching of Zionism and Israel.* The thirty-six page *Guide* covers the history of Zionism and Israel, accompanied by basic questions and a selection of resources oriented to the Zionist perspective.

Hadassah
(The Women's Zionist Organization of America)

Year established: 1912
President: Ruth Popkin
Address: 50 West 58th Street, New York, NY 10019
Publications: *Update, Headlines, Hadassah Magazine*

General Background

Hadassah (a Hebrew word for "myrtle," the name of the biblical Queen Esther) was established in 1912 when a twelve-member group of the Daughters of Zion Study Circle decided to expand into a national organization, under the leadership of Henrietta Szold. Their twin goal at the time was to foster Zionist and Jewish education in the United States and to begin public health nursing and nurse training in Palestine. Henrietta Szold's leadership and ideas led to the creation of the Zionist organization with the largest membership in the world, now said to number 370,000 in the United States and Puerto Rico.

Henrietta Szold started her first career as a teacher and educational administrator in Baltimore, where she taught school for sixteen years and organized and ran a night school for Russian Jewish immigrants. Her second career, as the secretary of the editorial board of the Jewish Publications Society, lasted twenty-three years. Then, in 1916, at the age of fifty-six, she began her third career, as "a full-time propagandist for Palestine and a vigorous booster of Hadassah."[37] In 1920, she went to Palestine, and except for a three-year stay in New York, she remained in Palestine until her death in 1945. The vigorous membership organization Szold created has been continuously involved in Zionist activities and fundraising since its founding; unlike the other American Zionist organizations, it did not experience a decline in membership after 1948.

Structure and Funding

Hadassah is incorporated in the state of New York as a non-profit, tax-exempt membership organization. For the purpose of the New York State law, it is registered as a "religious" organization, a status that exempts it from submitting an annual report, which would be publicly available.

Hadassah is perhaps the only genuinely mass-membership Zionist organization; its ranks include Jewish women of all ages and occupations, who belong to more than fourteen hundred local chapters organized around age and interest groups.*

*Indication of its mass outreach are the Hadassah posters in the New York subway and buses. They read: "Some of man's greatest achievers have been women. Join Hadassah."

Its highest policy-making body is the national board, which is composed of about 140 members and meets twice a year to consider major . policy decisions. Minor policy decisions are made by the executive board in New York and transmitted to local chapters and members. A recent study compares the national president of Hadassah to the president of a major corporation: "The Hadassah president must supervise a multimillion dollar yearly budget, a constituency of over 350,000 members, a national board, and thirty regional presidents."[38]

As a Zionist organization, Hadassah is a member of the AZF in the United States and is related to the world Zionist movement through the non-party World Confederation of United Zionists (WCUZ). In its promotional literature, Hadassah stresses that it is independent of any political party in Israel.

Hadassah has a volunteer representative in Washington who attends State Department briefings. The organization also holds non-governmental organization status at the United Nations and is an accredited observer at the U.S. Mission to the UN.

According to its Internal Revenue Service Form 990 for 1981, Hadassah received a total revenue for the year 1 July 1981 to 30 June 1982 of $10 million. Of that, about one-half came from "direct public support," $2.8 million from membership dues, $1.1 million from dividends and interests, and about $900,000 from programs. On the other hand, of the total expenditures of $9.1 million, 45 percent went to program services, 43 percent for fundraising, and 12 percent for management. Hadassah's net worth at the end of the year was put at $22.8 million. In 1982-83, Hadassah raised close to $49 million.

Until 1983, Hadassah was an American Zionist organization with a membership of American citizens. At its sixty-ninth annual convention (August 1983), however, the national board decided that Hadassah would become an international organization and create membership and fund-raising groups outside the United States. To protect its tax-exempt status under U.S. law, Hadassah's non-American membership and fundraising units were to be affiliated with its parallel corporate entity, the Hadassah Medical Relief Association, for purposes of channeling funds for Israeli projects.[39]

Israel Support Work

Like other American Zionist organizations, Hadassah performs two general tasks: it provides information on Israel to the American people, and it raises funds for specific programs in Israel.

By far Hadassah's most important role since its establishment has been supporting and creating health institutions in Israel, particularly the Hadassah University Hospital and the Hebrew University-Hadassah Medical School in Jerusalem. In addition, Hadassah has helped create schools of nursing and dental medicine, outpatient clinics, and community

35

health centers. It is also involved in raising funds for a variety of other programs in Israel, including Youth Aliyah, a vocational training program for disadvantaged Jewish youth in Israel. Hadassah is one of the largest organizational contributors to Youth Aliyah in the world.[40] In cooperation with the Absorption Department of the JA and the Israeli Ministry of Labor, Hadassah has built six day care centers.

Hadassah also identifies itself as "an integral partner of the Jewish National Fund (JNF)," and it is the JNF's "largest single contributor . . . in the world."[41] Since 1926, Hadassah has committed itself to the support of twenty JNF special projects and now supports a new JNF project every three years.

On the American scene, Hadassah provides "factual information on the development and security of Israel to the American public." In practice, this information is often a reiteration of official Israeli pronouncements enhanced through Hadassah's public standing and medical connections. On 18 July 1982, for example, while Israeli planes were bombarding Beirut, Hadassah sponsored a full-page ad in the *New York Times* signed by eleven medical doctors from leading universities and medical centers. Under the heading, "these members of the Medical Advisory Board of Hadassah would like to share the following facts with the American people," the text of the ad indicated that the 1975 civil war in Lebanon had devastated the health care system, especially in the south, and that in 1976 the Israeli government and organizations like Hadassah had stepped in to provide badly needed health care to the people in southern Lebanon. These statements did not mention the massive Israeli devastation of an existing health care infrastructure that had been effectively provided by the Palestine Red Crescent Society and the Lebanese National Movement since 1975.

At the sixty-ninth annual convention in August 1983, Jeane J. Kirkpatrick, U.S. permanent representative to the UN, opened the first plenary session and received the Henrietta Szold Award, Hadassah's highest honor. The convention banquet was addressed by Israel's ambassador to the United States, Meir Rosenne, and Senator Joseph Biden of Delaware. Costa Rica's permanent representative to the UN, Jorge Urbina, was presented with a Hadassah citation "for his country's friendship to Israel and for transferring its embassy from Tel Aviv to Jerusalem."[42]

Like other Zionist organizations, Hadassah pays particular attention to youth. According to "Facts about Hadassah,"

Through its youth movement, *Hashachar* (The Dawn) with its Youth Judean summer camps, year-round clubs, leadership training seminars and Israel programs, Hadassah offers young people a varied program of Jewish identity within a Zionist framework. A national peer-led youth movement, it has 8,000 members on two levels: Young Judea, for boys and girls 9 through high school; *Hamagshimin* (the

Fulfillers) whose college age through 30 members provide Zionist centers on college campuses and *aliyah* support groups. Younger members receive the *Young Judean*, oldest Jewish children's magazine in the United States. Camp Tel Yehudah, the national senior leadership camp and five regional Young Judea camps are summer extensions of *Hashachar*. [43]

Hadassah's Zionist Youth Movement reports that over two thousand students have signed up for its six Young Judea Camps, and that in 1983 eight hundred enrolled at Camp Tel Yehuda. Hadassah also sponsors summer leadership training seminars and "Destination Israel" summer tours for teenagers.

Zionist Organization of America

Year established: 1897
President: Alleck Resnick
National Executive Director: Paul Flacks
Address: 4 East 34th Street, New York, NY 10016
Publications: *The American Zionist* (quarterly), *The Zionist Information News Service* (ZINS, weekly)

General Background

Although its date of establishment is officially the same as that of the first Zionist Congress, ZOA did not really exist as such until 1918. Twenty years earlier, Zionists in America had formed the loosely organized Federation of American Zionists, which acted primarily as "an extension of the European Zionist movement." The Zionist organization in America was described at the beginning of 1914 as "small and weak, in great financial distress, and low in morale."[44] In 1918, American Zionist leader Louis Brandeis proposed to transform this loosely federated structure into a centralized organization, controlled by a national office. The new body that emerged was the ZOA. Its initial framework was that of a mass movement, with dues-paying members; by 1920, "the principle of organization was becoming that of a cadre party. But an elected national executive and annual conventions were retained." ZOA's only goal was "rebuilding Palestine," and its image was that of the American branch of the Zionist movement.[45]

Convinced that the work of the new organization should focus on supporting the economic development of Palestine, Brandeis saw fundraising as the main function of ZOA during this period, but the organization was not particularly successful at this task. Without concerning itself too much with the "Zionist doctrine," its leaders "pinned their hopes on the appeal of Palestine." Even so, ZOA's appeal as an organization remained weak. From 149,000 members in 1918, the year after the Balfour Declaration, its membership dropped to no more than 18,000 in 1929.[46] As a Zionist organization, it failed to capture the Jewish masses in the United States until after the establishment of the state of Israel.

Structure and Funding

ZOA is a non-profit, tax-exempt membership organization, registered in the state of New York. All contributions and dues to ZOA are tax deductible.

During the last few years, ZOA has launched an aggressive campaign to recruit members; current membership is put at approximately forty-five thousand. While its official literature continues to appeal for membership, ZOA's outgoing president, Ivan Novick, claimed in 1983

38

that "notwithstanding the fact that most Jewish organizations are having problems sustaining membership, ZOA has been able to maintain its strength."[47]

In addition to its national headquarters in New York City, ZOA conducts its Zionist activities in the United States through a network of twenty professionally staffed regional offices and three hundred local districts.* About 265 local representatives sit on the national executive committee. The national office, which houses ZOA's Women's Division and the New York metropolitan regions, has a staff of twelve. In Israel, ZOA maintains two permanent offices, one at the ZOA House in Tel Aviv, and the other at the Kfar Silver ZOA Campus in Ashkelon. ZOA's activities are supported by a fundraising arm, the American Zionist Fund. According to *The American Zionist* (April-May 1983), this fund has raised more than $1 million a year for the past several years.

Israel Support Work

ZOA's ideological stand within political Zionism is identified with that of the Likud coalition in Israel. As such, ZOA emphasizes free-enterprise Zionism, reiterates the validity of official Israel policy, and promotes the integral connection between the United States and Israel on the axis of freedom, democracy and opposition to Soviet influence in the Middle East.

From its literature, ZOA appears to be still grappling with the questions of its relevance to the Zionist enterprise and its service to the Jewish state. In its efforts to justify its historical continuity, ZOA dubs itself as "the cutting edge of American Jewry" and maintains that it "led the campaign to achieve the political acceptance of Israel by American and world leaders" and thus "helped to establish Israel." Today, it sees its role as helping "to defend Israel."[48] However, it makes a point of distinguishing itself from other Jewish organizations that defend Israel by highlighting the relevance of its political Zionism: the ZOA stand, it reaffirms, is not merely pro-Israelism. Accordingly, the theme of its eighty-third national convention (spring 1983) was "the Guardians of the Dream." That convention included a number of sessions on anti-Semitism, Soviet Jews, the "oil weapon," U.S.-Israeli relations, Israel and the Zionist movement, the "Jewish Evangelical Coalition," and Israel and American Jews. Among the major speakers were Elliott Abrams, U.S. assistant secretary of state; Gideon Patt, Israeli minister of commerce and industry; Harry Hurwitz from the Israeli Embassy; Senator Arlen Specter, Republican from Pennsylvania; and several State Department representatives. Paul Flacks, ZOA's national executive director, set the tone for the meeting in his address:

---

*The regional offices are distributed in Connecticut, New York, Illinois, Ohio, Michigan, Pennsylvania, Massachusetts, New Jersey, California, Maryland, Florida, and Texas.

We must continue to explain to American Jews that the Zionist Organization of America is the advocate of the free enterprise system, the American system of freedom which we espouse and support as citizens of our beloved nation. As General Zionists we appeal to *all* religious groupings and political affiliations, and as such, represent the focal point of Jewish concerns and the base of real Jewish unity [emphasis in original].[49]

In a June 1983 meeting of the Jewish Community Council of Greater Washington, an umbrella organization of 260 Jewish groups, the delegate assembly of the Council voted 98 to 70 against admitting the New Jewish Agenda (NJA), a social action group that differs from other Jewish organizations in its willingness to concede the principle of Palestinian self-determination. ZOA was one of the two organizations that openly campaigned to exclude the NJA. In defense of its position, Irwin Stein, president of ZOA's local chapter, said that "we feel a group like this is not within the mainstream of thinking of the Jewish community.... They don't fall within the kind of thinking that is current in the Jewish community."[50]

In the United States, ZOA monitors the activities of Congress, the White House, and government offices in Washington. Through its *Zionist Information News Service* (ZINS), ZOA distributes to its sponsor members a weekly news bulletin "filled with vital information not usually found elsewhere." It provides its sustaining, patron, and sponsor members with public affairs memoranda that include copies of all Israel-related memos that ZOA circulates to government officials and to the press, plus action guidelines. ZOA is a member of the National Inter-Religious Task Force on Soviet Jewry. It recently cosponsored a New York City symposium on "Catholics and Jews" with other Jewish organizations and the Archdiocese of New York. It cooperates with the "Christian Embassy" in Jerusalem through the External Affairs Department of the WZO-American Section.

In what it launched as "Project Energy Independence," described as an "educational campaign devoted to disarming OPEC's hold on our nation,"[51] ZOA mounted virulent attacks on Arab oil producers. Following an unattributed bombing in New York's La Guardia airport, ZOA placed an ad in the 12 January 1976 *Washington Star* that read, "Regardless of who placed the bomb at La Guardia Airport, there can be no doubt that the terror climate fostered in the world by the *Arab* states and the PLO caused this outrage. The *Arab* states and the PLO have created a terror climate of epidemic proportions" (emphasis in original). The reader was then urged to join ZOA in order "to fight terror."

Unlike some other Zionist organizations in the United States, ZOA adheres to official Israeli policy. In response to the Israeli invasion of Lebanon in 1982, ZOA president Ivan Novick told the national executive committee, "By its action in Lebanon, Israel has bravely confronted the terrorist PLO which had demonstrated its contempt for human life by its inhuman shelling of Israel's population centers in its continuing violent objectives aimed at destroying the Jewish state."[52] In August 1982, ZOA leaders went on a "solitary mission ... to stand by Israel in these trying times."[53] In addition to touring military installations in Lebanon, they met privately with Prime Minister Begin and Foreign Minister Shamir. After the massacre in Sabra and Shatila camps, Novick commented, "Israel would not knowingly be a participant in such carnage ... the entire thing is contrary to everything Jews hold sacred."[54]

In 1984, ZOA sponsored an ad in the *New York Times* under the title "Hosni Mubarak and the Plot to Murder Peace." The ad urged the United States to act now and denounce "Egypt's plot against peace."[55]

ZOA's youth programs encompass what it describes as Hebrew, Yiddish, and Zionist education. It organizes workshops and forums on college campuses to combat what it terms "anti-Israel Arab propaganda" and maintains a youth auxiliary called Masada (the name of the ancient fortress where Jewish fighters commited mass suicide rather than surrender to the Romans). Operating under the direction of ZOA's Youth Department, Masada has chapters in high schools and colleges throughout the United States and publishes the quarterly *Ayin L'Tzion* (An Eye Toward Zion). Masada youth are involved in New York City's annual "Israel Day Parade," in the Chanukah Torch Relay to hundreds of Jewish communities in the United States, and in pro-Israel political activities. The organization estimates that about one thousand Jewish young people participated in its activities in 1982-1983.

Perhaps the main activity of ZOA's Youth Department is the summer visit to Israel for teenagers and young adults (ages thirteen through twenty-three). The program lasts forty days and culminates in a visit to Masada. During the summer of 1982, ZOA's Youth Department sent 311 young American Jews to Israel. Throughout these programs, Jewish youth are encouraged to reach the "ultimate goal" of the Zionist movement— immigration: "The Masada Movement of the ZOA is anxious for our young people to fall in love with Israel, to return time and time again, and to make Aliyah."[56]

ZOA's major activities in Israel are twofold: cultural, through the ZOA House in Tel Aviv, and educational, through the Kfar Silver Campus complex in Ashkelon. Established in 1953, the ZOA House offers a variety of seminars, symposia, exhibits, and celebrations intended to foster U.S.-Israeli cultural relations and facilitate the adjustment of American immigrants to Israel. Among the English-language programs of the House are the Institute for Israel Studies and the Monthly Dinner Club, which features Israeli political personalities and American Jewish leaders. The Kfar Silver Campus (named after Rabbi Abba Hillel Silver and established in 1955) includes agricultural, technical, aviation, nursing, and academic schools, with an enrollment of about seven hundred Israeli students.

Association of Reform Zionists of America

Year established: 1977
President: Rabbi Charles Kroloff
Executive Director: Rabbi Eric Yoffie
Address: 838 Fifth Avenue, New York, NY 10021
Publication: *ARZA Newsletter*

General Background

ARZA is the first American Zionist organization created since 1948, and the first to be established by a major religious organization. To understand its historical background, it is necessary to examine the history of Reform Judaism in the United States, and specifically the development of its parent organization, the Union of American Hebrew Congregations (UAHC). The UAHC was founded by Rabbi Isaac Wise in Cincinnati in 1873, more than twenty years before the first Zionist Congress met in Basle. Its purpose then, as stated in its bylaws, was "to encourage and aid the organization and development of Jewish congregations; to promote Jewish education and enrich and intensify Jewish life; to maintain the Hebrew Union College [and] to foster other activities for the perpetuation and advancement of Judaism."

Even before the first Zionist Congress, the anti-Zionist direction of American Reform rabbis was very evident. At their 1886 convention in Pittsburgh, they declared in their platform, "we consider ourselves no longer a nation but a religious community, and therefore expect neither a return to Palestine . . . nor a restoration of any of the laws concerning a Jewish state."[57] Following the formulation of the Zionist program, Theodor Herzl's action was branded as "Zionmania," and Zionist sympathizers were purged from the UAHC.

The anti-Zionist direction of the UAHC had been shaped by its founder, Rabbi Isaac Wise. While Wise had no objection to Jewish settlement in Palestine, especially for those who had nowhere else to go, he did not consider such settlement as the only means of Jewish fulfillment. "The idea of the Jews returning to Palestine is no part of our creed," he declared. "The political restoration of Israel cannot be accomplished in Palestine." He further emphasized that "in religion alone are we Jews, in all other respects we are American citizens."[58]

But like the other Jewish organizations in the United States that opposed the Zionist program during the pre-1948 period, UAHC gradually reversed its direction following the establishment of the state of Israel. In 1973, the UAHC amended its constitution to include among the objectives of the Union "the enrichment and strengthening of the State of Israel, as a vibrant exemplar of eternal Jewish values." Following the amendment of the constitution, Rabbi Alexander M. Schindler, president of UAHC, urged Reform Jews to develop a vehicle through which they could express their Zionist commitment. In 1975, the World Union for Progressive Judaism, the international arm of the Reform movement, joined the WZO, but it remained an associate member with limited voting rights, since it was not a Zionist individual membership organization. At this point the UAHC leadership began to consider the formation of a Zionist membership organization to represent the concerns of the Reform movement within the Zionist establishment, and, in 1977, the UAHC biennial convention voted to create ARZA (the acronym is also a Hebrew word that means "to the homeland") as the needed vehicle. As such, ARZA sent nine delegates to the twenty-ninth Zionist Congress, held in 1978.

Structure and Role

ARZA is an affiliate of the UAHC and a member of the AZF; it is represented on the executive committee of the AZF and holds a seat on the WZO Executive. It is the first affiliate of the UAHC created on the basis of ideological commitment rather than gender or professsional association. It has recently been accepted for membership in the Presidents Conference and in the North American Section of the World Jewish Congress. When it was established in 1977, it enlisted 9,500 members; at present, it claims about 70,000.[59] As a Zionist membership organization representing the Reform movement in the United States, its members are drawn primarily from Reform congregations throughout the United States, with the long-established UAHC providing an existing structure for recruitment and ongoing activities. The annual national assembly develops broad policy guidelines, while specific policies are promulgated by a sixty-five-member board of directors. ARZA's regional activities are conducted through 250 regional chapters and the UAHC regional councils and federations across the United States.

In order to create an international network of Reform Zionist organizations, counterparts to ARZA were established in Canada, Great Britain, South Africa, Australia, and the Netherlands. In 1980, the six groups formed the International Association of Reform Zionist Organizations (known as ARZENU, which also means "our land"), which has been officially recognized by the WZO.

ARZA characterizes itself as the means by which "Reform Judaism completed its . . . progression from anti-Zionism to a strongly Zionist position."[60] In addition to its commitment to "achieving Jewish pluralism in Israel and strengthening the Israeli Reform movement," ARZA's activities in the United States focus on "strengthening American public support for Israel."[61]

The overall contours of its agenda are delineated in its "ideological platform," adopted by the first national assembly in 1978. The platform includes eight points:

1. To contribute to Israel's security in all its aspects.
2. To work for authentic Jewish pluralism in Israel ...
3. To encourage *aliya* and to assist those American Jews who, as individuals or in groups, are committed to *aliya*.
4. To create opportunities for volunteer services in Israel...
5. To foster the development of Israel Reform Judaism.
6. To promote tourism by individuals and congregational groups [to Israel] ...
7. To enhance the quality of Israeli life.
8. To inspire creative Israel-oriented activity in American Reform synagogues.[62]

Israel Support Work

ARZA's specific pro-Israel activities are intertwined with those of UAHC. ARZA maintains constant communication with the White House, the State Department, and the Congress, in order to "insure America's unswerving commitment to Israel's security." In 1979, ARZA presented the White House with a petition demanding a U.S. commitment for a united Jerusalem under Israeli sovereignty. ARZA attempts to build support for Israel through a program that brings a variety of Israeli speakers to its local chapters throughout the United States, and ARZA and its parent organization also disseminate information for the Israeli government. In September 1982, for example, the Jewish press reported that UAHC was the U.S. distributor for a videocassette "depicting PLO terrorist tactics." The 15½-minute color tape was prepared by the Israel Defense Forces, in order to put Israel's invasion of Lebanon into "historical perspective."[63]

Since ARZA's founding, a substantial portion of its annual budget has been allotted for Reform projects in Israel. Beginning with fiscal year 1983/1984, ARZA's board voted a fixed portion of the income from membership dues to go directly to specific Reform projects in Israel. Among those projects that aim specifically to encourage immigration are two settlement "nuclei": Kibbutz Yahel in the south and Mitzpeh Har Chalutz, a "free-enterprise community of Reform families" which is part of "a vast pioneering effort ... in the Galilee."[64]

Notes

Introduction

1. Melvin I. Urofsky, "A Cause in Search of Itself: American Zionism after the State," *American Jewish History* (September 1979): 91.
2. David Szonyi, "The Jerusalem Program: Its Meaning and Implications for American Jewry," *AZF Issue Analysis* no. 19 (June 1982): 2.
3. *Ibid.*: 1.
4. Urofsky: 86.
5. *Ibid.: 86.*
6. *Ibid.*: 87.
7. *Ibid.*: 91.
8. *Ibid.*: 84.
9. *Jewish Newsletter,* 9 January 1961.
10. Szonyi: 1.
11. *Ibid.*: 6.

WZO and JA

12. Covenant Between the Government of Israel and the Zionist Executive Also Called the Executive of the Jewish Agency, Jerusalem, 26 July 1954. Copy on file with the U.S. Department of Justice.
13. U.S. Senate, *Activities of Nondiplomatic Representatives of Foreign Principals in the United States,* Hearings before the Committee on Foreign Relations, 88th Congress, First Session, 23 May 1963. (Fulbright Hearings.)
14. Nancy Jo Nelson, "The Zionist Organizational Structure," *Journal of Palestine Studies,* 10/1 (Autumn 1980): 89.
15. Quotation from the 1971 Reconstitution Agreement, cited in "The Jewish Agency for Israel: A Brief Description." UJA (ca. 1981).
16. Founding Assembly of the Reconstituted Jewish Agency, Jerusalem, June 1971.
17. WZO, Organization and Information Department. "The World Zionist Organization." 1972: 24.
18. Eliezer Jaffe, "Philanthropic Politics," *Ha'aretz,* 22 June 1983.
19. *Forum,* special issue on "Caesarea: The Jerusalem Program," 41 (Spring/Summer 1981).
20. *Ibid.*: 25.
21. *Ibid.*: 8.
22. *Ibid.*: 10.
23. WCUZ, "In the Zionist Arena," *Zionist Information Views,* August-September 1983.
24. *Jerusalem Post,* 1 January 1984; *Washington Post,* 12 January 1984.
25. Sources for JA structure and funding: Eliezer Jaffe, "Wanted: A New Agency," *Moment,* April 1983: 62-63; "The Jewish Agency for Israel: A Brief Description;" JA-American Section IRS Form 990 for the year from 1 April 1982 to 31 March 1983.

WZO-American Section

26. WZO-American Section registration statements filed with the U.S. Department of Justice.
27. WZO-American Section, "A Guide to Israel Programs," 1983.

AZF

28. AZF. "The American Zionist Federation," June 1983.
29. AZF "Report to the American Zionist Federation Sixth Biennial Convention," 9-11

November 1980, New York: Grossingers, 1980: 2.

30. *Ibid.*

31. AZF, "The American Zionist Federation."

32. Avraham Schenker, "Zionism in Distress," *Forum* 46/47 (Fall/Winter 1982): 7-23.

33. *New York Times,* 21 September 1982.

34. *Spectrum,* Summer 1983.

35. AZF, "A Manual for a Zionist Information and Education Program in the United States." November 1975: Introduction.

36. AZF, "The American Zionist Federation."

Hadassah

37. June Sochen, *Consecrate Every Day: The Public Lives of Jewish Women.* Albany: SUNY Press, 1981.

38. *Ibid.*: 80-81.

39. WCUZ, "69th Annual Convention Report," *Zionist Information Views,* August-September, 1983.

40. Hadassah, "Facts About Hadassah," May 1983.

41. *Ibid.*

42. WCUZ, "69th Annual Convention Report."

43. Hadassah, "Facts About Hadassah."

ZOA

44. Yonathan Shapiro, *Leadership of the American Zionist Organization 1897-1930.* Urbana: University of Illinois Press, 1971: 25-53.

45. *Ibid:* 160, 119.

46. *Ibid:* 203, 175.

47. Ivan J. Novick, "President's Page," ZOA, *The American Zionist,* April-May 1983:3.

48. ZOA, "ZOA Impact: In the U.S., In Israel, On Jewish American Youth," (ca. 1982).

49. ZOA, *The American Zionist,* April-May 1983: 23.

50. *Washington Post,* 4 June 1983.

51. ZOA, "ZOA Impact. . . . "

52. *Jewish Telegraphic Agency,* "ZOA Leader Urges Reagan to 'Grasp the Moment' in Lebanon," 14 June 1982.

53. ZOA, "ZOA in Review," *The American Zionist,* April-May 1983: 25.

54. *New York Times,* 21 September 1982.

55. *New York Times,* 26 January 1984 (advertisement).

56. ZOA, *The American Zionist,* April-May 1983: 3.

ARZA

57. Howard M. Sachar, *A History of Israel From the Rise of Zionism to Our Time.* New York: Alfred A. Knopf, 1982: 52-53.

58. Peter Grose, *Israel in the Mind of America.* New York: Alfred A. Knopf: 1983: 29.

59. ARZA, "Almost Everything You Wanted to Know About ARZA," September 1980; *ARZA Newsletter* 6/3 (March-April 1983): 1.

60. *Ibid.*

61. *Ibid.*

62. *Ibid.*

63. *Jewish Telegraphic Agency,* 1 September 1982; *Jewish Week,* 3 September 1982.

64. ARZA *Newsletter,* Fall 1983; UAHC, "Mitzpeh Har Chalutz".

Community Organizations

CHAPTER II

Community Organizations

Introduction: The Transformation of an Agenda

Since the beginning of this century, the major community-based forums for the secular activities of American Jewry have been defense organizations and Jewish federations. The three major defense groups, the American Jewish Committee (AJC), the American Jewish Congress (AJCongress) and the Anti-Defamation League of B'nai B'rith (ADL), arose in the early 1900s. Their original role was to defend against prejudice and discrimination caused by anti-Semitism, and to represent their communities' interests in local, national, and international affairs. After World War II, the agenda of these groups was expanded, however; they dropped the label "defense" and redefined themselves as community relations agencies. Their major concerns reflected the Jewish liberal tradition: intergroup relations, civil rights, religious freedom and separation of church and state, the situation of international Jewry, and Israel support work. Today, in addition to the AJC, AJCongress, and ADL, eight other national organizations include some form of community relations on their agenda: Hadassah, Jewish Labor Committee, Jewish War Veterans, National Council of Jewish Women, Union of American Hebrew Congregations, Union of Orthodox Jewish Congregations, National Women's League for Conservative Judaism and Women's American Organization for Rehabilitation through Training. There are also over one hundred local community relations councils, which are usually branches of the AJC, ADL, or AJCongress, or affiliated to one of the hundreds of local federations.

For their part, the federations (now synonymous with welfare funds) are local agencies responsible for funding, planning, and coordinating a wide range of Jewish services, from domestic institutions, such as hospitals and schools, to the bulk of the money sent overseas to Israel. Both the community relations agencies and the federations are coordinated by their own umbrella organizations, the National Jewish Community Relations Advisory Council (NJCRAC) and the Council of Jewish Federations (CJF), respectively. These two bodies, along with their constituents, provide the institutional channels through which the program and political agenda of American Jewry are formulated, funded, and implemented on the community level.

Today, Israel support work stands at the head of virtually all of these agenda. This reality—the acceptance of Israel's centrality and authority by the Jewish community and its representative organizations—is the bulwark of pro-Israelism in the United States, for the network of community groups provides the funds, mass base, and political legitimacy that support Zionist organizations like Hadassah, fundraising institutions like the UJA, and lobbying groups like the American Israel Public Affairs Committee. But unlike many other Jewish organizations, the community nexus was not Zionist from the beginning, since its historic concerns tended to be domestic and focused on the improvement of largely immigrant Jewry's position within American society.

Because of their key control over funding, the federations became actively involved in Israel support work earlier than the community relations organizations. Before 1948, CJF and the federations resisted allocating disproportionately large percentages of their funds to the Zionist enterprise, and what they did give was based on humanitarian and philanthropic rather than political or ideological grounds, a situation that led pro-Zionists to refer to federation leaders as "men who viewed the idea of Palestine as just another Jewish refugee haven.... "[1] As a result, American Zionists undertook a campaign to "Conquer the local Jewish Federations!" and to "Infiltrate the Welfare funds!"[2] Despite the success of these tactics on the local level (from 1941 to 1945, about 50 percent of the federations' campaign funds went to Palestine through the UJA), the CJF continued to resist Zionist priorities until the late 1940s. In the aftermath of the war and the establishment of Israel, however, CJF and its member federations became a major funding source and, eventually, the bulwark of mass support for Israel in Jewish communal life.

The community relations organizations (with the exception of the AJCongress, which had been staunchly Zionist since its inception) maintained a non-Zionist position even after 1948. This is not to imply that they were actively anti-Zionist, but simply that they were not very involved with Israel or Zionism. In the May 1948 issue of *ADL Bulletin,* for example, there was no mention of the establishment of Israel, while in 1952 both the AJC and the ADL withdrew from the United Jewish Fund in opposition to the large amount of aid allocated to Israel. A major cause of this coolness toward Zionism was that the main goal of defense/community organizations had been to integrate Jews into American society. Thus, the basic Zionist notion of the Jewish people—a national identity—conflicted with the beliefs held by most of the American Jewish establishment, who defined Judaism in pluralistic America as a religion with ethnic overtones and sought to protect and integrate Jews by adhering to an agenda focusing on domestic concerns. Commenting on this early tension, Yonathan Shapiro notes: "Acculturated Jews felt that acceptance of the Zionist version of Jewish nationalism would cut them off from the country in which they now belonged. Jews in Eastern Europe did not consider themselves Poles or Russians. The situation of American Jews was different; they considered themselves Americans, though their belonging to America was never free of doubts. . . . "[3]

This outlook changed drastically in the period between 1967 and 1974, with what can be termed the "Israelization" of the community relations field. Analyzing the transformation for the Synagogue Council of America, Leonard Fein writes:

Whatever historic ambivalence American Jews had felt toward the State of Israel from the time of its founding was, for all practical purposes, dissipated in the wake of the Six Day War. The period between 1967-73 was one of dramatic development within the American Jewish community. The community was united as never before in its commitment to Israel. . . . The reasons for this important set of developments have to do very much with secular developments in the United States during the period from November 22, 1963. Among those of primary importance were the powerful, and sometimes volatile, thrust of the Black community toward ethnic assertiveness, the disillusionment with American possibilities occasioned by a full decade of American agonies; the emergence of a set of political issues with particular relevance for Jews (such as affirmative action, the McGovern-Nixon Israel positions, and community control); and, of course, the Six Day War itself, with its early evocation of Holocaust memories and its later support of Jewish self-confidence.[4]

These factors converged with the ongoing need to fill the void in American Jewish life caused by a weakening of traditional religious values, by successful assimilation, and by the lack of any central, unifying consciousness to make Israel the dominant issue for American Jews.[5] During the 1970s, this process was strongly reinforced when Israel was perceived as dangerously threatened by the 1973 war and the emergence of international support for the Palestinians. Particularly disturbing to American Jews was the November 1975 United Nations Resolution 3379 that labeled Zionism a form of racism; the reaction included slogans such as "We are one" and "We are all Zionists."

The full extent of the "Israelization" of community organizations can be seen in a major policy speech by former NJCRAC chairman Bennett Yanowitz, which was reprinted in full in NJCRAC's *1983-84 Joint Program Plan for Jewish Community Relations:*

. . . the very essence of Zionism has always been the recognition that the land of Israel belongs to all of the Jewish people, that we are full partners in Zion—in the building of a Jewish homeland—a Jewish state, the center of Jewish life. Our image of ourselves as American Jews over the past 35 years has been sharply influenced by our image of Israel. Our sense of security within the American society has fluctuated in direct relationship to our perception of the acceptance and security of Israel over these past 35 years. The intensity of our concern over anti-Semitism and Jewish security throughout the world parallels the favorable perception of Israel in countries throughout the world. Our own sense of security is tied to our sense of security for Israel.[6]

51

Agenda Transformed

Community organizations have long been the forum for Jewish liberalism, and their agenda today still reflect classic liberal concerns: social and economic justice, civil rights, Black-Jewish relations, anti-Semitism, separation of church and state. Their positions on most of these issues continue to fall within the liberal/Democratic camp, well to the left of the majority of Americans. Since 1967, however, the acceptance of the centrality and priority of Israel for American Jews has led to major changes in the political, ideological, and programmatic thrust of these community organizations. In his policy speech, Yanowitz described the new task of Jewish community groups:

By reason of these ties that bind us, all Jews have a stake in the security and survival of Israel as a Jewish state. As an American Jewish community, destiny has imposed upon us a special obligation to help maintain that security.... What this nation does or does not do has the most significant effect on the security of Israel; what we as an American Jewish community do or don't do makes a difference in how this nation responds to Israel's economic, diplomatic and military needs....[7]

Dominating but not fully replacing the original liberal concerns, Israel support work has moved to the top of the Jewish communal agenda. As Steven Cohen writes: "The departures from the pattern of disproportionate Jewish liberalism are also instructive. They hint at a selective erosion of liberalism wherever Jewish group interests are at stake. Thus, perhaps owing to anxiety about Israel's security, American Jewish support for defense spending roughly equaled that of other Americans."[8] (NJCRAC guidelines, for example, advocate an increased U.S. military presence in the Middle East.) On the whole, however, community groups have reconciled liberalism and pro-Israelism, asserting that adherence to a liberal agenda actually strengthens Israel support work, as spelled out by Yanowitz:

Our visible and forceful presence in fighting for better schools, better housing, full employment, in short, a strong, democratic, humane America, will convey better than any dissenting views of the Jewish community on Israel the perception and reality of the American Jewish community's concern about the best interests of the United States. Regrettably, we have not played this role as actively as we did in earlier years. Our failure to do so may be more responsible for our being seen as a one-issue community than any other factor. The fact that the Jewish community relations field is concerned with the total American agenda makes it the effective advocate of Israel.[9]

There is no doubt that community relations groups have become one of the most effective and active forums for Israel support work. Among the factors contributing to the success are their long history and experience, respectability, well-developed organizational structure, mass-based constituency and connections to elites, and familiarity with outreach and public relations. But it must also be recognized that the very nature of their traditional agenda lends itself to promoting Israel; the original functions of the community relations organizations could be easily adapted to the preeminence of Israel support work, with amended themes and targets.

Intergroup Relations. Promoting intergroup dialogue is a traditional focus of Jewish community groups, which have longstanding relations with various sectors of American society, including Blacks, Christians, labor, and youth. The basis of these relations and dialogue has now shifted from domestic social concerns to what can only be termed an Israeli context. The litmus test of relations with other groups is no longer their attitudes toward American Jewry *per se*, but toward Israel. The community groups use their established relations and legitimacy to promote support for Israel; if another group is critical of Israel, it may be charged with insensitivity or anti-Semitism. Jewish groups exert pressure by threatening to withdraw from dialogues or coalitions; at the same time, they are eager to provide these forums with programs ranging from ongoing dialogues about Israel and the dissemination of films and literature to delegations to Israel and scholarships for study there.

Monitoring Anti-Semitism. A primary component of the original agenda of community organizations was exposing and denouncing prejudice or civil rights infringements against Jews and others. Traditionally the focus was on the extreme right (the Ku Klux Klan, neo-Nazis) and on government and business sectors (discriminatory housing, quotas, civil rights laws). Since "Israelization," the traditional targets of the Jewish community organizations have been radically expanded to include those individuals, groups and sectors that have, in varying degrees, expressed criticism of Israel. These include segments of the political left; important sectors of the Protestant church establishment, with particular criticism leveled against the National Council of Churches and the American Friends Service Committee for their advocacy of Palestinian rights; all organizations engaged in forms of Palestinian support work, whether political groups, humanitarian organizations, or academic and research institutions; establishment figures and institutions that are considered pro-Arab, such as State Department "Arabists," the Bechtel Corporation, and the major oil companies; dissenting Jewish organizations and individuals, including the American Council for Judaism, American Jewish Alternatives to Zionism, Breira, Rabbi Elmer Berger, Professor Noam Chomsky, and others. The program work that was once turned primarily against the Ku Klux Klan, the John Birch Society, and other reactionary groups— monitoring, exposés, and public accusations of anti-Semitism—is now frequently used against the critics of Israel.

Public Opinion and Public Relations. This is again a traditional role that is now applied to Israel support work. With scores of years of media

53

expertise and connections behind them, and an effective and experienced organizational structure in place, the community relations organizations clearly play the leading role in projecting a positive image of Israel in the hearts and minds of Americans. Through activities that include vast publishing operations, media monitoring, editorial and letter-writing campaigns, and sponsorship of public events and speaking tours, they have firmly supplanted the official Zionist organizations.

The full impact of these activities can only be appreciated in relation to broader operating policies. First, all of these organizations frequently hold press conferences and these are generally well attended. Thus, media exposure can routinely be provided whenever the results of a study or poll are issued, a new book published, a policy statement issued, or an Israeli politician brought to town. Second, the groups have developed large mailing lists over the years, and these are also activated for publicity. Last, and most important, is the unique dimension that these groups provide through their liaison with other organizations, institutions and social sectors. A mailing list, for example, will not be limited to Jewish organizations, but will include churches and unions across the country, minority group organizations, and probably every politician in the House and Senate, together with their aides. Publications can be sent to groups representing other sectors and given to their constituents; speakers can find a forum in a local union hall or church.

Foreign Policy. The original domestic thrust of the community organizations has been greatly expanded to include a major focus on foreign policy, which, with the exception of Soviet Jewry, operates almost solely within the Israel support context. While all the groups assert their independence from Israel, they nonetheless tend to echo its basic political line as a natural and inevitable consequence of "Israelization." This foreign affairs involvement manifests itself in a number of ways: lobbying or political intervention, which can occur directly through a representative in Washington, membership in AIPAC, the Presidents Conference of Major American Jewish Organizations (commonly known as the Presidents Conference), or the coordinated activities of the umbrella groups, NJCRAC and CJF; adopting resolutions that advocate certain policies internationally; cultivating leading U.S. politicians, who receive honoraria to address the groups' constant stream of dinners, banquets and conferences; using their close relations with Israel to provide an established and public forum for visiting Israeli leaders; and mobilizing their constituency to act on issues affecting Israel, through such tactics as letter or telegram campaigns, arranging visits of key local people to their congressional representatives, demonstrations, and boycotts. A basic source of these groups' ability to intervene effectively in foreign policy is their legitimate claim to represent the community (and thus voters and campaign contributors) and, for the national organizations, their unquestionable credentials as establishment organizations of many years' standing.

One particular focus of foreign policy activity is the Arab role in domestic and international affairs. The anti-Arab stance of the various organizations is expressed in a number of common themes: (1) Arab petrodollars threaten the integrity of the United States: the Arabs are "buying up America." The AJC's Washington representative, Hyman Bookbinder, pointed to the ease of exploiting this claim: "It's easy to sloganize by saying oil profits are being put ahead of America's honor in the world. We're not above doing that from time to time."[10] (2) Arab petrodollars are being used to fund a massive propaganda and lobbying campaign aimed at destroying the special relationship between the United States and Israel; Arab money is somehow behind all manifestations of pro-Palestinian activity or criticism of Israel. (3) The Arab boycott of Israel is not only anti-Semitic, but anti-American in intent, as it discriminates against American Jewish citizens and violates the American principle of free trade. (4) The Arabs (considered indistinguishable from OPEC) bear responsibility for the energy crisis and high fuel costs and have a dangerous amount of control over U.S. policy because of their oil resources. (5) The PLO (Palestine Liberation Organization) is a terrorist gang that not only is the ultimate enemy of Israel but, in its role as the center of international terrorism, is a threat to the free world. A related assertion is that Arab and Palestinian organizations in the United States, regardless of their agenda, are somehow agents of the PLO.

Council of Jewish Federations

Year established: 1932
President: Shoshana S. Cardin
Executive Vice-President: Carmi Schwartz
Address: 575 Lexington Avenue, New York, NY 10022
Publication: *What's New in the Federations?* (newsletter)

General Backg·ound

In its original form, a Jewish federation was a joint fundraising effort involving all the various local social welfare agencies in a given community; a welfare fund was a similar effort for national and overseas needs. The first federation was established in Boston in 1895, and the concept spread rapidly across the country. Eventually, CJF was founded as a national coordinating body, an "association of 200 Federations, Welfare Funds and Community Councils serving nearly 800 communities which embrace over 95% of the Jewish population in the United States and Canada."[11]

While CJF began primarily as a fundraising coordinator, it developed into a central planning agency for organized American Jewry in the late 1940s and 1950s, when the amount of funds raised by the federations greatly increased, mainly in response to the needs of displaced Jews in Europe. The federations supported Israel from its inception for humanitarian reasons, since it was seen as the solution to the plight of European Jews. Especially after 1967, Israel became the means for soliciting millions of dollars from American Jews, even though the funds from the annual UJA-Federation campaigns go to both domestic and international needs. Since 1980, these funds have totaled over a half billion dollars a year.

As an umbrella body, CJF does not actually raise or possess the annual millions itself, but it coordinates, represents, and advises the hundreds of local federations that do and thus is granted a significant impact on Jewish communal life.* At the same time, CJF's close involvement with raising and distributing such large sums of money has inevitably led to a deepening of its relations with Israel, so that today CJF is a virtual partner of the Jewish Agency (JA), the official Zionist funding arm since before the establishment of Israel. This is how CJF describes its current relationship with the JA:

To carry out collectively the same trusteeship for funds which go overseas as is exercised by Federations locally and to assure that the most important needs will be dealt with most effectively, CJF, in cooperation with UJA and its partner agencies, UIA and Joint Distribution Committee, has assisted the Jewish Agency

---

* The process by which approximately two-thirds of the local Federations' fundraising totals are transferred to the United Jewish Appeal (UJA), the United Israel Appeal (UIA), and then to the Jewish Agency and Israel is detailed in Chapter 3.

for Israel to review its operations and structure. The Jewish Agency receives through UJA and UIA, nearly two-thirds of all Federation allocations. Together with leaders of UIA and UJA, CJF leadership has made recommendations to the Jewish Agency to strengthen its fiscal planning and budget procedures, initiate new and coordinating arrangements in the activities of the Agency, and undertake changes in the administrative procedures, especially regarding immigration and absorption.[12]

The involvement of American Jewish communal leaders was formalized in the 1971 reconstruction of the JA; Daniel Elazar notes in his 1973 study that since then, the JA has "virtually coopted the federation leadership as its 'non-Zionist' representatives, creating an even tighter bond between the institutionalized representatives of the World Zionist movement and the American Jewish community than ever before."[13] A prime example here is Martin Citrin, who, when president of CJF, also served the JA as a member of the board of governors, co-chair of the Commission of Jewish Education, and member of the Immigration and Absorption Committee and the Comptroller Committee; in addition he is on UJA's board of trustees and UIA's board of directors and executive committee.

Structure and Role

As their fundraising totals have grown, the federations have increasingly taken over the task of Jewish community planning. Local federations are responsible for allotting funds from the annual campaign to community projects such as hospitals, schools, and other institutions, many of which serve people outside of the Jewish community. While the funds allotted for domestic needs are only about 20 percent of the annual campaign total of over one-half billion dollars, they are still substantial.

As coordinator of the local federations and their affiliates, CJF acts as the overall budgetary, planning, allocating, and supervisory body of the organized American Jewish community. Its role is to be a national instrument to strengthen the work of local federations; to provide leadership to locals in developing programs; to be a forum for the exchange of experience; to provide guidelines for fundraising and operations; and to present joint national planning on common purposes dealing with local, national, and international needs. The services CJF offers to its affiliates within this framework include:

Community Services Committee and Consultants — Provides local federation activists with a "national perspective on major Jewish communal issues."

Campaign Planning and Community Building — Long-range fundraising strategy based on demographic and sociological studies, development of leadership cadre, and pilot fundraising projects (coordinated through the CJF-UJA Liaison Committee).

Endowment Development — Intended to increase federation endowment funds, which totaled more than $600 million in 1981.

Washington Action Office—Assists local federations to obtain federal funds for social services and cultural programs.

Community Planning—Assists local federations to improve structures and procedures, to provide liaison with national agencies, and to implement demographic studies.

Emerging Planning Areas—Consultation regarding targeted populations including the aged, Jewish singles, Jewish disabled, and child day care.

Long-Range Planning Committee—Develops a national data base and pilot projects for efficient long-range planning.

Jewish Education Service of North America—Provides recommendations and funding for projects.

CJF Task Force on Federation-Synagogue Relations—Coordinates work with the Synagogue Council of America, the Union of American Hebrew Congregations, and other national congregational bodies.

College Services—Administers the finances of Hillel (B'nai B'rith's campus organization).

Soviet Jewish Resettlement Project—Administered by the CJF, with funds from the Hebrew Immigrant Aid Society (HIAS) and the U.S. Department of Health and Human Services.

Joint CJF/UJA/Jewish Welfare Board (JWB) Task Force on Television—Develops a weekly television program to focus on issues relevant to the Jewish community.

CJF-UJA Regional Public Relations Institutes—Provides day-long workshops on innovative ideas and techniques for public relations.

Leadership Development—Part of CJF's Human Resources Development Department, whose aim is "recruiting outstanding leaders who have attained high positions in business and the professions but who have not become part of the leadership cadre of the Federations." There is also a Young Leadership program and a Women's Division.[14]

An important CJF service is the Large City Budgeting Conference (LCBC). Most Jewish community organizations, from national groups like the AJC and ADL to local agencies, receive funding from the LCBC, which "...includes 29 of the largest Federations working together to analyze the programs and finances of 30 national and overseas agencies and to develop joint recommendations on funding them. It is housed in CJF and serviced by CJF, while its basic expenses are met by dues from the participating Federations."[15] CJF also issues budget digest reports on over fifty agencies, which are used to assess budget allocation. This control over financial resources is the base of CJF's power in the community.

CJF is governed by three bodies: the year-round delegates, the board of directors, and the executive committee. The year-round delegates represent local communities and participate in the annual General Assembly, where they elect officers and board members and help plan the coming year's agenda. They also serve on various committees and task forces and provide the effective link between CJF and the local federations.

There are 720 such delegates, from whose numbers come the board of directors. The executive committee is appointed each year by the president, with agreement of the board. Financially, CJF is supported by dues from its constituents; these are set on a sliding scale.

According to CJF's *1982 Annual Report—Charitable Organization filed with New York State Department of State,* its total revenues were $9,266,520. Of that, $4,075,171 went to member services, $3,896,145 to Soviet Jewish resettlement, $23,641 to student aid, $95,684 to LCBC administration, and $700,876 for general management.

Israel Support Work

According to CJF's 1982 *Annual Report:*

American understanding and support for Israel is a priority concern to CJF. It is approached in conjunction with a number of organizations but primarily through the National Jewish Community Relations Advisory Council (NJCRAC), whose responsibility is to coordinate central planning strategy and programs of the national Jewish community relations and local community relations agencies. In order to bolster U.S. Administration and Congressional support for Israel, as well as America's understanding of Israel's vital role, the Council has organized meetings with Administration and Congressional leaders in Washington, which have been attended by Federation presidents of major cities, to discuss foreign affairs.

Since the 1973 war, CJF has actively pressured Jewish community groups to make Israel support work a priority on their community relations agendas. At that time, CJF formed an Emergency Advisory Committee on Community Relations in the Middle East and sponsored meetings with NJCRAC and the AJC, AJCongress, and ADL. The result of these meetings, announced at the November 1973 CJF General Assembly, was the formation of the special NJCRAC Israel Task Force to channel funds to the community relations agencies for Israel support projects; its initial budget was over one million dollars, with the funds allotted from the annual UJA-Federation campaign revenues.[16]

CJF's grassroots network of local affiliates provides a direct link to the general Jewish community that is unmatched by any other single organization. The nature of their activities can be gauged from the CJF newsletter, *What's New in the Federations?* Among the activities noted in the February and July 1983 issues, for example are:

Cleveland, Ohio—A comprehensive information program on Israel aimed at non-Jewish community leaders. Organized by the Cleveland Federation Israel Task Force and financed by CJF's Federation Endowment Fund, the program included special missions to Israel, such as a March 1983 trip for business leaders; a June 1983 meeting that brought former U.S. Undersecretary of State Joseph Sisco together with more than one hundred community leaders; and a local newsletter, *FYI: Israel Update.*

Rochester, New York — A month-long celebration of Israel's thirty-fifth anniversary sponsored by the Rochester community federation. Events included a special philharmonic orchestra performance, a screening of *Exodus,* and a thirty-second public-service TV announcement showing footage of David Ben-Gurion and the first Jewish settlers.

Denver, Colorado — The Leadership Roundtable, a program sponsored by the Allied Jewish Federation of Denver for outreach to leaders in business, industry, and the professions. Their first briefing session on the Middle East was addressed by former Israeli Prime Minister Yitzhak Rabin.

Maine — "Israel and the U.S. — Promise and Fulfillment," a four-seminar series organized by the Southern Maine Federation. Aimed at church and service groups, the seminars covered Zionism up to 1948; Arab claims to Palestine and the Arab national movement, with emphasis on Israeli options for the refugee situation; oil, political power, and the development of U.S. policy; and public relations and the emergence of pro-Arab lobby groups.

On the national level, CJF's General Assembly, which is billed as the "largest annual gathering of Jewish organizational life in America,"[17] has become the major annual event of the organized Jewish community. According to Melvin I. Urofsky, " . . . the real power in Jewish life is found at the community level. If one wants to see the nearest thing to a truly representative Jewish parliament, the place to go is the General Assembly of the CJFWF. There the gut issues of the day are dealt with, as problems of quotas, allocations, community relations and programming are hammered out and the communal agenda set."[18]

The General Assembly also provides the thousands of local activist federation members who attend with specific programs, training and political direction for Israel support work. The participation of other national organizations, such as AIPAC, WZO, NJCRAC, ADL, and AJC, further increases the effectiveness and scope of this process.

Among the presentations at the 1979, 1980, and 1981 General Assemblies were:

• "Making Israel a Living Experience: Community Involvement with Israel Programs, Information Desks and Aliyah Activity," with speakers from the Jewish Welfare Board (JWB) and the World Zionist Organization (WZO).
• "Inside the Arab World," a forum arranged by the American Professors for Peace in the Middle East (APPME).
• "Community Relations Priorities in the 1980s: Three Issues — Israel and the Middle East, Urban Affairs, Interreligious Activities," with speakers from NJCRAC, AIPAC, ADL, AJC, and AJCongress.
• "College Youth and Faculty: Arab propaganda on the college campus, an informal discussion," presented by Hillel.
• "Strengthening Links Between the North American Jewish Community and

Israel—a panel discussion with Americans who have gone on Aliyah," sponsored by JWB, the Israel Aliyah Center, and the North American Aliyah Movement.
• "Revolutionary Changes in the Islamic World," arranged by APPME.
• "Israel as an Educational Resource: Principles and Programs—An Exploration of Formal and Informal Approaches," prepared by the Jewish Agency and WZO.
• "Israel and the Arab World: Changes and Challenges, Post-Sadat Implications," prepared by APPME.
• "Peace in the Middle-East—The Role of North American Jewry," with participants from NJCRAC, AIPAC, and AJCongress, as well as Dan Patir, advisor to former Israeli prime ministers Yitzhak Rabin and Menachem Begin.
• "Israel-Diaspora Relations: Strengthening Links with Israel through North American Olim," presented by the Israel Aliyah Center.

At the 1982 General Assembly, a number of workshops addressed the conflict in the community caused by the Lebanon war:

• "North American Jewry and Israel in the Post-Lebanon Climate: Assessing Consequences of Recent Events and Their Implications For Communities."
• "New Challenges of the Media: Improving Governmental Relations. Making the national-local network more effective and improving the *hasbara* [information] effect," presented by AIPAC, NJCRAC, AJC, AJCongress.
• "Community Relations Issues of the Middle East: Opportunities for Expressing and Dealing With Differences of Opinion Within the Jewish Community."
• "Arab Propaganda on the College Campus: Impact and Response. Arab propaganda is in high gear on the campus and is undermining Jewish student self-acceptance and the academic commitment to Israel."
• "The Jewish Community Newspaper," stressing the importance of developing a newspaper in each community since recent events have shown that the general media is unreliable on Israel.
• "Successful Student Programs," including a report from the Campus Friends of Israel Task Force.

CJF's role as the foremost national forum for pro-Israel politicking in the United States also emerges most clearly in the General Assembly. With more than two thousand participants from virtually every major Jewish community and Zionist group in the United States, it is the most desirable platform for both Israeli and American leaders who desire to touch base with Jewish grassroots and leadership. Former Israeli Prime Minister Menachem Begin was scheduled as the keynote speaker in 1980 and 1982 (although he was forced to cancel his appearance in 1982 because of his wife's death). In 1981, Moshe Arens, then a member of the Knesset and chairman of the Foreign Affairs and Security Committee (and later Israeli defense minister), presented an analysis of the Saudi peace plan. In 1983, Israeli President Chaim Herzog timed his visit to the States to coincide with the General Assembly and spoke there, as did U.S. Secretary of State George Shultz, who presented a major policy statement on the Middle East.

Among the political resolutions passed at the 1983 General Assembly was one on the situation in Lebanon, said to "demonstrate anew that Israel is America's sole stable and dependable ally in the region and hence, the necessity for strengthening United States-Israeli cooperation."[19] Other resolutions urged continuing and increased U.S. aid to Israel, including "the technical and financial means to independently build the Lavi fighter aircraft" — a request granted by the Reagan administration shortly thereafter. Significantly, certain issues under debate within the Jewish community were not put to a vote at the General Assembly: a resolution proposing a freeze on Israeli settlements in the West Bank, for example, was tabled despite reported support from a number of delegates.[20]

National Jewish Community Relations Advisory Council

Year established: 1944
Chair: Jacqueline K. Levine
Executive Vice Chairman: Albert D. Chernin
Address: 443 Park Avenue South, New York, NY 10016
Publication: *Joint Program Plan for Jewish Community Relations*

General Background, Structure, and Role

NJCRAC was formed in the 1940s as a voluntary coordinating council for the proliferating Jewish community relations agencies. Today NJCRAC's affiliates include 11 national and 111 local organizations. The national community relations agencies represented are: AJC, AJCongress, ADL, Hadassah, Jewish Labor Committee, Jewish War Veterans, National Council of Jewish Women, Union of American Hebrew Congregations, Union of Orthodox Jewish Congregations, United Synagogue of America, National Women's League for Conservative Judaism, and Women's American ORT. Membership is not as random as it may appear at first glance; in addition to the three defense organizations that redefined themselves as community relations agencies after World War II (AJC, AJCongress, and ADL), the national congregational bodies are represented because they have all formed internal commissions on social action.

The local organizations are divided into three categories: Community Relations Committees (CRCs), Jewish Community Councils (JCCs), and Jewish Community Relations Councils (JCRCs). Some are autonomous organizations; some are affiliates of local federations or welfare funds, and others are chapters of national agencies. These groups serve as functional agencies for community activities and often as coordinating agencies for local Jewish institutions.

According to Gary S. Schiff, "It was the CJFW, representing the local communities, with its desire to avoid wasteful duplication in community relations programming and unnecessary expenditures of Jewish communal funds, that was the motivating force behind the initial establishment of NJCRAC." However, NJCRAC has never been able to play the enforcement role needed to prevent the duplication of tasks rampant among both national and local CRCs; as Schiff notes, NJCRAC is careful "to keep its activities within the sphere of the 'information, consultative, coordinating and advisory' roles it is limited to, and out of the realm of programmatic activity reserved to the functional agencies."[21]

The major challenge to this now-accepted *status quo* came in 1951, when CJF initiated an investigation of the national organizations affiliated with NJCRAC. Robert MacIver, an eminent Columbia University sociologist, conducted a study that found the charges of duplication fully justified and recommended that particular functions be assigned to particular agencies; for example, he urged that all legal and legislative work be allotted to the AJCongress and no longer be done by the AJC and ADL. His recommendations were accepted by the majority of NJCRAC members but were never implemented because the AJC and ADL withdrew their membership in protest; they faced no sanctions and simply rejoined NJCRAC fifteen years later when attempts at enforcement had become a moot issue.[22]

The major reason for NJCRAC's inability to enforce decisions is that all its national members are powerful organizations in their own right that are unwilling to relinquish their freedom of individual action to anyone. An additional cause of NJCRAC's relative weakness is its lack of control over funding. All CRCs, both local and national, are funded through the federations' annual local campaigns. The CRCs' allocations are decided through the Large City Budgeting Conference of the CJF. While this allocation may provide a major part of a local CRC's budget, the larger, mainly national organizations conduct their own fundraising campaigns to raise additional revenues, indeed, usually the bulk of their budget. All of the CRCs enjoy tax-exempt status.

While NJCRAC does not impose any structure or division of labor on its members, it still plays a very important role as consultant and policy formulator. NJCRAC uses its umbrella status to present the annual consensus of its constituents regarding the programmatic work of the organized American Jewish community.

Israel Support Work: The Joint Program Plan

Nowhere are the political concerns and actual program agenda of the Jewish community groups delineated so clearly as in NJCRAC's major annual document, the *Joint Program Plan for Jewish Community Relations,* which addresses all topics on the agenda of Jewish community relations agencies, including economic and social matters, intergroup relations, and anti-Semitism. The *Plan* is formulated with input from each national affiliate and representatives from local CRCs (who meet at the annual plenary session) and then is written, published, and distributed by NJCRAC staff. NJCRAC describes the *Plan* as

. . . products of the continual national planning process of the Jewish community relations field. Offered as a general guide for Jewish community relations programming, each Plan is meant to be used by member agencies as a basis for their own program planning, with each accepting or rejecting, modifying or expanding—according to its individual judgments, resources and needs—any of the recommendations made. . . . Joint Program Plans seek primarily to identify and appraise changing conditions and trends that have occurred during the preceding year and their potential impact on Jewish community relations goals and concerns. This assessment provides a basis for projecting responsive positions, priorities and programs.[23]

The emergence of Israel as the central concern and unifying factor for CRCs since 1967 is strikingly demonstrated by the increasing priority given to Israel-related topics and programs in these *Joint Program Plan*[s]. Since the political positions and action goals advocated by the NJCRAC reflect the views of those guiding mainstream, organized American Jewry, it is useful to look with some detail at the Israel-related sections of the *1982-83* and *1983-84 Joint Program Plan.*

The overview section of the *1982-83 Plan* notes with concern tensions between the United States and Israel, owing to what is called the U.S. policy of "appeasement" toward Arab states such as Saudi Arabia. The overall assessment, however, is that these problems are not insurmountable:

The American Jewish community, an integral part of American life in every city of the United States, has a network of national and local agencies with the resources, will and sophistication that make them a significant factor in the shaping of public policy.

We are not alone and so we need not march in splendid isolation. As we indicated, strong support for Israel as a valued friend and ally exists, particularly in the Congress of the United States, both major parties, the trade union movement, even within the world of business (witness the *Wall Street Journal*), and among Christian religious movements. The American people as a whole see Israel as a true friend and Saudi Arabia as a nation who threatens the interests of the United States. ...

Finally, Saudi pressures on U.S. policy require that we renew the lagging interest of the Jewish community relations field in U.S. energy policy. ... The most difficult part of the problem may not be the question of expanding energy conservation but in finding ways to limit the leverage of petrodollars upon American decision-making.[24]

The Israel section of the *Plan* contains a strong statement of support for and legitimation of the Israeli invasion of Lebanon. (The *1982-83 Plan* was adopted on 14 June 1982.) It also reiterates support for the Camp David process and rejects the Prince Fahd peace plan. Concern is expressed over the Reagan administration's concept of strategic consensus insofar as it involves strengthening the alliance with anti-communist Arab states. The *Plan* notes: "The term 'strategic consensus' masks that foreign policy tilt. That tilt has objectively downgraded Israel's importance for the United States and downplayed any program of strategic cooperation with Israel itself. It gambles with Israel's security and in the end, inhibits the establishment of any effective pro-Western security system in the Middle East. It also has increased Israel's vulnerability, which may require greater reliance on a strategic doctrine emphasizing the preemptive option."[25]

There are also subsections on "Saudi Arabia and Appeasement" and on "Israel and American Public Opinion." The latter deplores what it terms the "distortions" of the mass media's coverage of Israel but notes

65

that public opinion is still firmly pro-Israel, despite a pro-Arab "well financed campaign to sway popular opinion. . . ."[26]

The Israel section of the *1982-83 Joint Program Plan* concludes with the following "Action Goals" or recommendations for the Israel support work of community relations agencies:

• We recommend interpretive programs which stress that new U.S. initiatives in the wake of Lebanon to protect the interests of America and the free world would contain a fatal internal contradiction if those arrangements do not include as a basic premise recognition of a strong and secure Israel as vital to U.S. interests. Such recognition would require that:

the U.S. continue to provide such economic and military aid as is necessary for Israel's defense, while taking tangible steps to implement U.S./Israel strategic cooperation;

the U.S. provide such aid in a grant/loan balance which is sensitive to the new demands on Israel's strained economy engendered by the Sinai withdrawal and the explosive growth of Arab armories;

the U.S. insist that, as a condition of alliance, potential Arab partners credibly renounce any intent of destroying Israel;

the U.S. not inadvertently shift the balance of arms in the Middle East and erode Israeli security by the sale of arms to Arab regimes, who refuse to negotiate peace with Israel.

The interpretive program should further stress that an effective security system in the Middle East requires an increased U.S. military presence in the region.

• We recommend a new stress on the theme that appeasement feeds rather than moderates extremism; and that concessions to Saudi, Jordanian, and other Arab-state demands be made only within the framework of their making essential concessions to American needs, including the acceptance of the Camp David peace process. We therefore further recommend the rejection of arms sales to Saudi Arabia, Jordan, and other Arab states unless and until these conditions are met.

• We recommend an intensified program to expose the PLO as not only a terrorist organization dedicated to the destruction of the State of Israel, but also a basic anti-American force in the Middle East. There is a critical need for the United States to resist resuscitation of the PLO after its crushing defeat in Lebanon. The folly of an appeasement policy on this score should be stressed, along with an indication of alternatives, within the Camp David process, which are compatible with American national interest.

• We recommend that major emphasis be given to efforts to moderate negative treatment of Israel, particularly at the national level as demonstrated by the mass media treatment of the war in Lebanon.

• We recommend strongly urging the United States to play a vigorous role in supporting the Camp David process, to reject Western European and Saudi proposals given new impetus by the Lebanese crisis, and to deepen public understanding of the Camp David Accords. The American role should also ensure that Egypt continue to honor its Camp David agreements after the Sinai withdrawal, and actively pursue the normalization of Egyptian/Israeli relations at all levels.

• We recommend an intensified interpretive program on the specific issue in the framework of stressing the positive Western aspects of Israel's politics, culture and society. This program should include an emphasis on Israel's aspirations and efforts for peace, despite its continued vulnerability. These values should be contrasted with those of the Arab nations outside the Camp David process.[27]

The subject of American attitudes toward Israel also arises in the "Jewish Security and Individual Freedom" section, under the heading of "Anti-Semitism." Here it is noted that traditional anti-Semitism has declined, but concern is expressed about new anti-Semitism as might be provoked by the AWACS debate:

Some surveys show a rise in the proportion of Americans who believe that American Jews are more loyal to Israel than to America. That is a matter of concern, since there is no incompatibility in supporting American and Israeli interests in the Middle East. And indeed, according to the evidence, most Americans do not feel hostile towards American Jewish activity on behalf of Israel, presumably because most Americans also see the compatibility between American and Israeli interests.

However, if the public were to lose its sense of that compatibility, it could presumably become hostile towards American Jewish activity on Israel's behalf. Thus, if the American Jewish community were to reduce its efforts to interpret Israel positively, that might paradoxically serve to increase rather than reduce levels of anti-Jewish hostility.[28]

The overview section of the *1983-84 Plan* reiterates support for the Israeli invasion of Lebanon and criticizes the United States for not strongly pursuing a treaty between Israel and Lebanon and for "retreating from the Camp David process." The last section of the overview, however, presents a new theme as it calls upon the Jewish community to reach out and form coalitions around broad issues, especially the domestic economic crisis, despite the strained relations and the isolation of the past decades. The *Plan* notes:

The security of the Jewish community and the needs of this nation require us to reach out to narrow the distance between ourselves and those who had once been our allies, even in the face of their enmity. They, as well as we, must recognize the critical need for coalitions to confront the great problems that we are facing. If we cannot act together, at minimum we have to learn once again to talk to each other.[29]

The Israel section of the *1983-84 Plan* is divided into subsections on Lebanon, Camp David, U.S. arms sales to Arab countries, and U.S. public opinion:

Lebanon. NJCRAC applauds the Lebanon-Israel treaty as an important step toward peace but expresses much dismay over Soviet, Syrian, and PLO positions and actions: "The developments underscored the central reality of the Arab-Israeli conflict: that Israel negotiates in good faith, making substantial accommodations in the search for peace, while the rejectionist Arabs maintain their refusal to make any accommodations with Israel, and reject measures that could bring peace to Lebanon."[30]

67

Moving the Camp David Peace Process Forward. This subsection is mainly a rejection of the Reagan plan of September 1982 on the grounds that it is "contrary to the spirit" of the Camp David Accords. A memorandum dealing with the consensus of the NJCRAC Israel Task Force on the Reagan and Fez plans is reprinted in full. While "sympathetic understanding" is expressed toward Reagan's proposals, they are rejected for being premature, too inclusive, and outside the Camp David framework. The Fez plan is described as a "sharp rejection" of the U.S. initiative. The memorandum, from Bennett Yanowitz, NJCRAC chair, to NJCRAC and CJF member agencies, concludes with the following guidelines on the Reagan plan for the Jewish community:

The Task Force felt that the Jewish community's posture should stress that agreement on autonomy and the ultimate comprehensive settlement must be the product of the hard, difficult, direct negotiating process urged by President Reagan, sought by the government of Israel and envisioned by the Camp David Accords. Thus, as in the past, there is no need now for the Jewish community to force a consensus judgment on the final status of Judea and Samaria (West Bank) and Gaza. Such a debate of what are now essentially academic questions deflects attention from the current reality that these issues are not under negotiation because of the refusal of the Arab states to come to the negotiating table. The President's speech and the subsequent reactions deal with issues of long-run nature. Thus urgent debate and confrontation within the Jewish community on specific details only serves to polarize the Jewish community and the U.S. and Israel.[31]

U.S. Arms Sales to Jordan and Saudi Arabia. This subsection simply reiterates NJCRAC's opposition to any U.S. arms sales to Arab countries. Both Jordan and Saudi Arabia are cited as "rejectionists"; concern is also expressed over the ability of Congress to veto such arms sales, given the June 1983 Supreme Court decision that invalidated the legislative veto (on an unrelated issue). Also reprinted here is a *Wall Street Journal* article by Amos Perlmutter, editor of the *Journal for Strategic Studies*, on "The Saudis — Ultimate Rejectionists."

The Middle East and American Public Opinion. This subsection notes a slight increase in pro-Palestinian perceptions but expresses confidence that pro-Israel feelings are dominant in public opinion and in Congress. There is concern over "controversial media coverage of the war," the tendency of some foreign policy elites toward "appeasement," and "evidence of greater activity on the part of pro-Arab advocates, including increasingly active Arab-American associations which began to employ sophisticated political and public affairs techniques and constitute a potential force that bears monitoring in the future.... College campuses have long been vulnerable in anti-Israeli activities, a problem addressed by NJCRAC through the creation, in 1982, of the Campus Advisory Committee of the Israel Task Force; to function as a clearing house and coordinator of campus activities. The level of pro-PLO and anti-Israel activity rose significantly after the Lebanon war."[32]

Issues related to Israel carry over to other sections of *1983-84 Plan* as well. Thus, the use of a pro-Israel yardstick to measure community relations is found throughout. For example, a section urging Jewish groups to seek dialogue and coalitions with the Hispanic community concludes: "It is important to convey the views of the Jewish community on Mideast issues to the Hispanic community, which has not focused particular attention on the Middle East. This should be one of the items on the agenda for Hispanic-Jewish relations."[33]

Likewise, the issue of anti-Semitism is measured and addressed mainly in terms of American attitudes toward Israel: " . . . the pervasive mood of foreboding among American Jews seems most directly linked to the growing sense of Israel's international isolation, and the close identification of American Jews with Israel. Concern has been expressed as to whether this is leading to anti-Jewish hostility among some in the women's movement. The media's treatment of the Lebanon war, and the increase in Arab propaganda efforts in the U.S., contributed to the sense of apprehension." According to NJCRAC, "The fundamental remedy, in this case, lies not so much in an abstract campaign against anti-Semitism, but in a continuing campaign to underline the convergence of Israeli and American national interests and political cultures."[34]

The *Plan* addresses the issue of dissent versus unity in the reprint of a speech by former NJCRAC chair Bennett Yanowitz, entitled "Democracy and Discipline in the American Jewish Community: The Utility and Morality of Unity." Here Yanowitz states that, while individual Jews have the right to dissent, unity is required within the community relations field, as it is a "critical factor in our ability to effectively influence public policy." He asserts that suppression of dissent is not the issue—there is no suppression, simply a belief that dissent should take place only "within the tent" of NJCRAC and should not be published. Dissenters who use public forums, he says, are trying to pressure, not persuade; they bring charges of suppression only because their views are not accepted by the majority. He goes on to say that public dissent is dangerous because it is exploited by the media and used to undermine support for Israel, making it difficult for pro-Israel forces, such as Congress, to act. Acknowledging that one may feel "uncertainty or unhappiness with a specific Israeli action," Yanowitz puts forward these alternatives to dissent: "choosing to remain silent as a statement of our doubt," or "postponing confrontation on an issue until it is ripe for resolution." However, Yanowitz warns that even these alternatives need to be exercised with "enormous restraint and caution."[35]

Other Forms of Israel Support Work

In November 1973, CJF, AJC, AJCongress, and ADL set up the special

69

NJCRAC Israel Task Force with an initial budget of $1,090,000, most of which came from the UJA-Federation campaign and NJCRAC's constituents. NJCRAC also added an Israel specialist to its staff. The aim of the Task Force is to strengthen Israel programming; its activities include funding AJC opinion surveys on public attitudes toward Israel; underwriting a Jewish Labor Committee project for strengthening U.S. labor's ties to Israel in areas where strong pro-Israel attitudes do not exist; and funding NJCRAC's program to set up local Israel Task Forces in small communities. A number of media-related projects were funded as well. They include the following:

One, a national speakers bureau to coordinate the appearance of pro-Israel speakers across the country, was set up (at a cost of $150,000) as an independent agency, with no ostensible Jewish identification, so as not to impugn its credibility in the general community.

Similarly, the services of a private, non-profit research organization, Near East Research Inc., were engaged to prepare interpretative material on Israel for Washington-based columnists, commentators and reporters ($30,000). A television feature film on Israel was produced by Dore Schary, the well-known producer prominently identified with ADL ($30,000). Another joint media project ($35,000) between the two leading community relations agencies was the development of ties with specialized trade technical publications, journals, etc., in order to introduce news of Israel, even of a purely technical nature, into this area of the media and thereby into this new constituency. The ADL undertook the production of two to three minute bi-weekly news analyses on Israel and the Middle East for some 100 radio stations ($12,000). The last media project was a program working with black media people, cultivating their confidence, and supplying them with factual and analytical material.[36]

NJCRAC also makes specific recommendations to its member agencies. In 1977 for example, the American Friends Service Committee (AFSC) sponsored a conference on the Middle East with Israeli general (ret.) Matityahu Peled and Palestinian activist Issam Sartawi (who did not attend, but sent a written statement); NJCRAC took the lead in imposing a boycott against Peled by sending all member agencies a letter that "strongly urged that Jewish organizations not be drawn into this propaganda trap by participating in and/or attending the conference."[37] More recently, NJCRAC sent a letter to member groups on the subject of the March on Washington for Jobs, Peace and Freedom, held on 27 August 1983 to commemorate Dr. Martin Luther King's march twenty years earlier. The letter urged Jewish organizations "to use caution in any involvement in the march."[38] The participation of former Senator James Abourezk, known for his advocacy of U.S. recognition of the PLO, was singled out for criticism; also, objections were posed to a section of the "Call to the Nation" statement that read: "We oppose the militarization of internal conflicts, often abetted and even encouraged by massive U.S. arms exports, in areas of the world such as the Middle East and Central America, while their basic human problems are neglected."

In March 1982, a letter signed by the leaders of the 120 member groups of NJCRAC was sent to President Reagan to protest continuing U.S. arms sales to Arab states, especially the proposals to sell weapons to Jordan.[39] In June 1982, after NJCRAC member agencies were briefed by visiting Israeli general Natan Sharon, NJCRAC chair Yanowitz sent Reagan a telegram on U.S. policy in Lebanon, in which he called for "arrangements that will avoid Israel's need to act again in its self-defense," for not pushing for Israeli withdrawal from Lebanon, and for standing against "punitive action directed at Israel by the U.N. or even by officials of our own government."[40]

NJCRAC holds annual conferences that are used to prepare for the *Joint Program Plan* but also serve as a forum for American and Israeli politicians.

American Jewish Committee

Date established: 1906
President: Howard I. Friedman
Executive Vice President: David M. Gordis
Chair, Executive Committee: Rita E. Hauser
Address: 165 East 56th Street, New York, NY 10022
Publications: *American Jewish Yearbook, Commentary, In the Communities, News and Views, Present Tense*

General Background

The AJC was established in 1906 in reaction to the 1903 and 1905 Kishinev pogroms in Russia. Its stated goal was to defend the civil and religious rights of Jews in the United States and abroad. The AJC's founders were a select group of "uptown" New York German Jews who, in contrast to the waves of poor immigrants from eastern Europe filling the city's "downtown" tenements, were the successful elite of American Jewry. This elitism was a conscious policy; when it was suggested that the AJC should be formed with a broader base, B'nai B'rith President Adolf Kraus responded: "If the Committee represents the representative and high class Jews of America, that is enough."[41]

In its first decades, the AJC was mainly involved with providing immigrant aid and education, combatting eastern European anti-Semitism, and supporting civil rights legislation against religious discrimination. Its approach was to avoid overt controversy: wealthy, powerful, and intellectual members would approach their counterparts in government, business, or the media and quietly negotiate. This tactic reflected the class position and perspective of an acculturated sector whose aspiration was to fit securely into mainstream American life. Thus, the established German Jews of the AJC were unreceptive to both the Zionism and the radical socialism that the newer eastern European immigrants brought to America. Describing this early period, one recent AJC pamphlet notes: " . . . while the members of the Committee spoke of their 'religious brethren,' the 'downtowners' spoke of 'peoplehood' . . . ."[42]

The first direct challenge to AJC leadership came in 1915 from prominent Zionists such as Rabbi Stephen Wise and Louis Brandeis. The following year they convened an American Jewish Congress as an immediate response to the crisis in Europe, but with the idea of forming a democratically elected umbrella organization for all Jewish groups. However, the broader aims of the Congress failed (it led only to the creation of the AJCongress as a separate organization). Not until the 1940s, when AJC was unable to respond adequately to Nazi genocide in Europe or to present a viable alternative to Zionism, did its dominance diminish. The AJC's approach of quiet negotiation, no fuss, no demonstrations was

72

so unsuited to the scope of the Holocaust that other organizations and groups were able to move into leadership roles in Jewish life.

Like the AJCongress and ADL, the AJC turned to community relations after World War II. In a retrospective pamphlet called *Milestones,* the AJC cites the following post-war activities (apart from Israel-related programs): sponsoring major studies on topics such as the authoritarian personality, executive suite discrimination, and intermarriage; participating in interreligious dialogues, often on a high level; filing an amicus brief in the Bakke case against affirmative action quotas; creating the Institute of Human Relations; sponsoring *Commentary,* an important magazine of opinion.

While the AJC has expanded its base and membership, it is still known as an essentially "select" organization. Daniel Elazar notes that the AJC's major criterion for membership seems to be actual or potential influence, and that its membership is especially powerful because it is strategically placed in leadership positions of other organizations, such as the federations and synagogues. When former AJC President Morris Abram was asked by Israeli Prime Minister Ben-Gurion how many members the AJC had, Abram answered: "We don't count AJC members, Mr. Prime Minister, we weigh them."[43] While this is not quite so true today, the AJC continues to be the Jewish organization with the most direct access to the "corridors of power" by virtue of its leadership connections and class position rather than the size and activity of its membership.

The AJC and Zionism

In its current pamphlets, the AJC highlights its historic support for Zionism, including endorsement of the Balfour Declaration in 1917, opposition to the British White Paper of 1939, cooperation with the Jewish Agency, and support for the UN Partition Plan of 1947. However, in the pre-1948 days, the AJC was known as the leading non-Zionist American Jewish organization. Its formulation of Judaism as a religious or, at most, a cultural identity existing within a pluralistic America precluded an acceptance of Jewish peoplehood. Also, since the AJC's leadership had emigrated freely to the United States and successfully become part of American society, they found the Zionist vision of immigration to Palestine unattractive. Thus, when the American Jewish Congress reconvened in 1943 to deal with the crisis in Europe, the only four votes against a Jewish state in Palestine were cast by the AJC. In fact, the AJC withdrew from the Congress in opposition to the demand for a state, and Zionist sympathizers in turn left the AJC. In 1944, a resolution put before the U.S. Congress included a call for the encouragement of colonization in Palestine leading to a Jewish commonwealth. Greatly to the dismay of the Zionist movement, opposition from and debate within the Jewish community caused the resolution to be shelved. Now-declassified documents on the subject from the Office of Strategic Services note: "American Jewish Committee, which is non- but not anti-Zionist, presented a statement suggesting an amendment to the Resolution which would defer final determination of the question of a Jewish Commonwealth."[44]

Even as the AJC's rejection of a Jewish state changed after World War II, in direct response to the needs of the thousands of survivors and displaced people flooding Europe, and although they supported and lobbied for the creation of Israel, it is clear that an ambivalent attitude persisted. The nationality or "peoplehood" issue was still a sticking point, as witnessed by the joint statement of Ben-Gurion and AJC President Blaustein at the time, which emphasized that "Israel represents and speaks only in behalf of its own citizens." It was only after 1967 that the AJC actively and wholeheartedly took up pro-Israel work, to the extent of opening an office in Israel. By 1981, AJC President Maynard Wishner could say in a speech: "Let no one misunderstand the rock of commitment and love of Israel that shapes the work we do. . . . We will demonstrate that devotion day in and day out. . . . We shall do it with mind and heart and resources and energy. We have no higher priority."[45]

Structure and Funding

The AJC is still a relatively small organization, with less than fifty thousand members nationally. Its literature lists twenty-three regional offices that serve eighty chapters and units in over six hundred communities. In addition, there is a Washington, D.C. office and an overseas service with offices in Paris, Rio de Janeiro, Mexico City, and Jerusalem. The headquarters in New York houses the AJC's Institute of Human Relations, with a staff of over 250 professionals, including specialists in community relations, education, law, social science research, social work, religion, foreign affairs, communications, and the mass media. The AJC's organizational structure includes a board of trustees and all attendant officers, with vice presidents representing various regions. The honorary chair of the national executive council is Max M. Fisher, a leader of the Republican National Jewish Coalition and member of the board of governors of the Jewish Agency, while the list of honorary presidents includes Morris B. Abram, former president of Brandeis University and co-chair of the White House Conference on Civil Rights in 1965 (1964-1968); Arthur J. Goldberg, former associate justice of the U.S. Supreme Court (1968-1969); Philip E. Hoffman, a former member of the UN Human Rights Commission, as well as state and national civil rights commissions (1967-1973); Richard Maass, former mayor of White Plains, N.Y. and former chair of the National Conference on Soviet Jewry (1977-1980); Elmer L. Winter (1973-1977); and Maynard Wishner, a Chicago executive active in the local federation and Hillel (1980-1983). The current president is Howard I. Friedman, a Los Angeles attorney and federation leader.

The AJC's organizational structure appears to be closely linked to fundraising: there are numerous committees, task forces, institutes, and

74

special studies that arise primarily through endowments or special fundraising campaigns. According to a 1983 pamphlet, "AJC's funds are provided through its nationwide Appeal for Human Relations. In New York City and Chicago the Committee conducts its own direct fundraising campaign. Outside these cities its support comes from Jewish Welfare Funds, direct individual gifts and support for special projects, endowments, bequests and legacies."[46] What this means in practice is that as a community relations agency, the AJC participates in CJF's Large City Budget Conference (LCBC) and receives an annual allocation from the welfare fund. However, because this allocation is relatively small, the AJC also conducts its private fundraising campaign, which is structured not to overlap with the UJA-Federation appeal. This system was instituted after 1962, when the AJC ended its joint fundraising program with the ADL. The AJC is a non-profit, tax-exempt organization under the Internal Revenue Code.

Some of the major ongoing programs that the AJC has established, primarily through endowments, are the Jacob Blaustein Institute for the Advancement of Human Rights, the Jacob and Hilda Blaustein Center for Human Relations Research, the Academy for Jewish Studies Without Walls, the William Petschek National Jewish Family Center, the National Committee on the Role of Women, the Leonard and Rose A. Sperry International Center for the Resolution of Group Conflict, the Morris and Adele Bergreen Institute for Foreign Policy Studies, the William E. Wiener Oral History Library, and the new Institute on American Jewish-Israeli Relations. There are also divisions within the national Institute of Human Relations, such as domestic affairs, energy, foreign affairs, and interreligious affairs.

In its IRS Form 990 return for calendar year 1982, the AJC reports a total revenue of nearly $14 million, 79 percent of which was generated from direct and indirect public support (namely contributions and allotments), and 7 percent from membership dues. Of the total expenditures for that year, nearly 81 percent went to program services and 12 percent to fundraising.

Israel Support Work

The shift to Israel support work that characterizes Jewish community relations agencies is most strikingly seen with the AJC: once the leading non-Zionist organization, it has adopted a stance whereby, according to a leading staff member, "Community relations around Israel and the Middle East is the number one subject in the AJ Committee. There is no question about that."[47]

Describing its current program, the AJC stresses

...the development of early warning systems to alert us when dangers threaten, effective counteraction, and an ongoing tracking of American public attitudes toward Jews, Israel and other issues which require our attention. Personal representations to government officials as well as widely read AJC background memoranda, pamphlets and briefing papers help interpret Israel's position to U.S. policy makers, business, church and labor leaders, newspaper columnists and radio and TV broadcasters. Meetings of AJC leaders with officials of the State Department, the Commerce Department, the World Bank, and the Federal Reserve Board have sought to combat the Arab boycott and alert Americans to the dangers of Arab economic warfare. Soviet anti-Semitism . . . the subversion of the United Nations . . . the new challenges to Jewish security and well-being in America . . . all have shaped AJC's worldwide efforts to defend Jewish security.[48]

Much of the AJC's Israel-related work takes place on two main levels: (1) writing, publishing, and disseminating information and position papers, and (2) continuing its traditional approach of quiet but influential pressure meetings with prominent individuals and groups representing other sectors (such as politicians, labor, and ethnic leaders), with special emphasis on the Christian religious establishment. The effectiveness of these tactics rests on the prominence and influence of the AJC's leadership, their intellectual and establishment credentials, and their personal and organizational connections with the various sectors of American society.

Since 1967, the AJC's Washington representative has been Hyman Bookbinder, a former special assistant to Hubert Humphrey. Bookbinder maintains especially good relations with the White House and the State Department—an informal division of labor that leaves Congress mainly within AIPAC's scope. In a 1978 interview, Bookbinder described how that special relationship works:

[E]very Administration has been friendly, access to this one has been, if anything, better than average. . . . There are many people I deal with in the White House quite regularly. Not just the Jews—Lipschutz and Eizenstat—but also [Hamilton] Jordan and even [Vice President] Mondale. He calls me regularly to ask how I react to things, and I can get through to him when I call. So we have a good relationship.[49]

Indeed, one reason that the AJC has not joined the Conference of Presidents of Major American Jewish Organizations but remains only an observer, is its reluctance to relinquish the freedom of action granted by its own special relationship with the executive branch. (The reason publicly cited by the AJC is that the monolithic image of the Presidents Conference is an inappropriate one for American Jewry.)

The AJC is not a registered lobby; however, Bookbinder has been very clear as to what his role entails: "I consider it my job, as an involved, acknowledged, unembarrassed friend of Israel, to get whatever information I can from the Israelis, from our State Department, from any sources, and to put the best possible light on the Israeli case."[50]

An example of his quiet diplomacy was seen in 1974, when then Chief of Naval Operations Admiral Elmo Zumwalt had some pro-Nixon Jewish businessmen invite Jewish leaders to his home, where he argued for an increased military budget, citing concern over adequate arms for Israel. It was Bookbinder who, following the talk with Zumwalt, called a meeting of American Jewish groups "to take another look at the arms budget."[51]

Though the AJC does deal with other issues in Washington, its priority is clearly Israel-related. In 1981, both budget cuts and the Voting Rights Act were on the AJC's agenda, but the only mass membership mailing to Congress was one opposing arms sales to Saudi Arabia. In 1983, the AJC took credit for lobbying Interior Secretary James Watt to rule that Santa Fe International, an American oil company owned by Kuwait, could not hold oil and gas leased on federal land, on the grounds that Kuwait discriminated against U.S. oil companies.

The AJC's political clout and positions can also be seen in the proceedings of its annual meetings. At the 1976 meeting, the agenda included off-the-record briefings with the Israeli Embassy, the White House, the State Department, the Department of Health, Education, and Welfare and the Department of Housing and Urban Development. Areas covered included the Middle East situation and the Arab boycott of Israel (a major issue for the AJC), as well as domestic concerns. The general meeting was addressed by President Gerald Ford, Senator Hubert Humphrey, State Department official Joseph Sisco, Israeli ambassador Simcha Dinitz, and Chaim Herzog, then Israeli representative at the UN. In the 1983 meeting the major speaker was Secretary of Defense Caspar Weinberger.

The AJC's annual meetings also provide a forum for passing political resolutions, which are then issued and distributed as statements to the media, other organizations, and politicians. A resolution adopted at the seventy-fourth annual meeting in 1980, for example, reaffirms the importance of the Camp David Accords, while attacking Western European initiatives as "engaging in patent appeasement of the Arabs at Israel's expense for reasons of oil and hoped-for economic gain." It also criticizes the Carter administration for its stand on Israeli settlement policy:

[W]e believe that they are not contrary to international law where required for security purposes. We further believe that Jews have a right to live on the West Bank. While recognizing this right, however, we note that there has been much criticism in Israel and abroad in recent months as to the political wisdom of the establishment of additional Israeli settlements on the West Bank. Only Israel can decide through its democratic process what its settlement policy should be. Nonetheless, to prevent erosion of support, we urge Israel, its right notwithstanding, to show restraint in the creation of new settlements at this time. In the meantime, continued emphasis by the U.S. on the alleged illegality of Israeli settlements in administered territories serves no useful purpose.[52]

According to the resolution, the real obstacle to peace is not settlements, but the intransigence of the Arab countries.

In addition to overt political intervention, the AJC serves as a think tank for pro-Israel activity. Important to this role are the many public opinion polls and special studies that the AJC either researches directly or commissions from others; many of the polls have been underwritten by funds allotted from NJCRAC's Israel Task Force, indicating that the other community relations agencies in fact accept the AJC's claim to this role.

One recent study, prepared in 1981 by Gary S. Schiff, addresses "Middle East Centers at Selected American Universities." As the conclusions indicate, the primary concern of the report, which examines the Middle East Centers at Columbia, the University of Michigan, Princeton, New York University, the University of Pennsylvania, and the University of California at Los Angeles, is not with academic excellence but with the orientation of the centers in relation to Israel. The report accuses all the centers of a "growing tendency to regard Israel as an entity separate from the rest of the Middle East," citing as evidence a lack of federal funding for the study or teaching of Hebrew; the acceptance of funding from Arab governments or corporations that deal with Arab countries, which, "guidelines notwithstanding, exercises at least a subliminal influence. . . . "; and the tendency for Jewish graduate students to enroll in Jewish studies rather than Middle East studies programs. The report concludes with the following recommendation:

Since no realistic view of the Middle East can deny the existence of Israel, this enumeration of trends suggests that, at a minimum, the federal government should reevaluate its priorities for its support of language and area studies. Moreover, the extreme importance and sensitivity of the issues aroused by any consideration of the Middle East suggest that universities offering Middle East studies should exercise close oversight of appointments, course content, source of funding, and outreach programs in the interest of preserving the scholarly objectivity which they have traditionally valued so highly. In the case of outreach programs, closer university oversight might perhaps be reinforced by federal oversight . . . in the meanwhile, however, the tendency to deny Israel and the Hebrew language their fair share of attention and resources in the universities should be recognized and resisted, not only by the federal government and the universities themselves, but also by anyone concerned to preserve peace in the Middle East, and perhaps, the world.[53]

Another AJC study reports findings of a 1981 national survey sponsored by the AJC to measure anti-Semitism in the United States. Prepared by Yankelovich, Skelly and White, Inc., a national research organization, the study attempts to measure whether anti-Semitism has increased or decreased by comparing the 1981 survey results with past surveys. According to this scale, which is based on a measurement of traditional anti-Semitism, the AJC concludes that anti-Semitism has decreased in the United States. However, the 1981 survey also measures anti-Semitism in terms of

78

attitudes toward Israel and perceptions of American Jewry's relation with Israel. The results here indicate some erosion of America's support for Israel and a large increase in the view that American Jews are more loyal to Israel than to the United States. The study concludes: "Since support for Israel is so pervasive at the current time, the impact of attitudes toward Israel on negative attitudes toward American Jews has been quite small. However, the relationship which does exist between attitudes toward Israel and attitudes toward American Jews raises the issue of the possible future deterioration in American attitudes toward Israel on the position of American Jews."[54]

In 1982, the AJC established the Institute on American Jewish-Israeli Relations "to increase understanding and dialogue between the two largest, most vibrant Jewish communities in the world." The Institute's activities are intended to survey opinion, to facilitate an exchange of views on controversial issues, and to develop programs to overcome stereotyping and misunderstandings. One of its first major projects was the study, *Attitudes of American Jews Toward Israel and Israelis: The 1983 National Survey of American Jews and Jewish Communal Leaders,* mentioned in the Introduction (see Appendix).

Publications

The AJC's think tank role has generated a large publications network; in fact, among all the organizations dealt with in this study, the AJC publishes the greatest number of magazines, pamphlets and memos, while relying least on the electronic media or mass mobilization. At the same time, the AJC is clearly aware that the production of these written materials calls for an equal effort in terms of distribution. To this end, pamphlets or articles excerpted from its magazines are regularly sent off to the appropriate politicians, church and labor leaders, AJC members, or other Israel support groups, depending on the nature of the materials. With the mailing is a personalized cover letter, signed by the AJC president or other officers. For publications a press conference is called, as was the case with George Gruen's 1982 book, *The Palestinians in Perspective.*

Periodicals

Commentary, established in the 1940s, is the best known of AJC's periodicals and the one aimed at the broadest audience, especially in political and intellectual circles. Recognized today as a leading advocate of neoconservatism, the magazine was originally rather liberal, with a focus on cultural rather than political affairs. Though editorially independent of the AJC, it receives an endowment of approximately $150,000 a year.

Norman Podhoretz is the name most associated with *Commentary.* Podhoretz became editor in 1960, and his leadership soon made *Commentary* greatly respected as a forum for new Jewish fiction, criticism, and ideas. Its pages were filled with the work of writers such as Saul Bellow, Isaac Bashevis Singer, Bernard Malamud, Philip Roth, and Norman Mailer. Liberal social critics Paul Goodman, Irving Howe, Alfred Kazin, and Jane Jacobs used *Commentary* as a forum for their ideas. As early as 1964 and 1965, strong positions were taken against the Vietnam war and the invasion of the Dominican Republic.[55]

During this period, *Commentary's* attitude toward Zionism was similar to that of the AJC: supportive but critical. (Indeed, *Midstream* was founded by the Theodor Herzl Institute to be a more pro-Zionist alternative.) Among the articles published in the 1960s was a strong criticism of the Israeli Supreme Court decision in the "Brother Daniel" case (where a Jew who had converted to Catholicism during the war and later became a monk, yet still claimed he was ethnically Jewish, was denied admission to Israel under the Law of Return, although he was allowed to settle there.) In the August 1967 issue, after the June War, the absence of jubilation or gloating is striking; rather, that issue contained an article by Israeli writer Amos Elon warning against the future dangers of occupation and a thoughtful piece by rabbi and historian Arthur Hertzberg on the Zionization of secular Jews in the wake of the war.[56]

1967 soon proved to be a turning point for *Commentary*, however, with the adoption of increasingly conservative positions on both domestic and international issues. *Commentary* since 1967 has been described as approaching every issue by asking "Is it good or bad for the Jews?" It perceives American Jewry as a corporate entity or special interest group, whose very survival—much less success—necessitates abandoning traditional liberal positions. On the domestic level, authors such as sociologist Nathan Glazer proclaimed that social planning and affirmative action were bad for Jews, while Milton Himmelfarb (of *Commentary's* editorial board) posited that even the Democratic Party was bad, and that Jews had to break with their liberal alliances to move ahead in American society. In a critique of Himmelfarb's article later published in the more liberal Jewish magazine *Dissent*, Bernard Avishai pointed out how this attitude is related to the perception of Israel:

Israel might now be a cause for celebration—the same issue boasted a piece by Gil Carl Alroy suggesting that tough, technological Israel could trounce any combination of Arab armies for a generation—but it was Israel's image, not its culture or problems, that the new *Commentary* wanted. What would 'Israel' do if it lived in Brooklyn and not among the Arabs? It would, Himmelfarb suggested, vote Republican, or at least threaten the Democrats with abandonment.[57]

A basic tenet of Himmelfarb's argument, and of *Commentary* as a whole, is that Jews must shift to the right because "only a strong America can guarantee the existence of Israel." A "strong America" also involves advocating extreme anti-communism and forceful U.S. intervention internationally. The expansion of U.S. power was linked to support for

Israel by such figures as UN representative Jeane Kirkpatrick, Robert W. Tucker, professor of international relations at Johns Hopkins University, and Edward Luttwak, senior fellow at Georgetown's Center for Strategic and International Studies—all popular *Commentary* writers.

Commentary has taken the lead in advocating hawkish positions on Middle East issues. A January 1975 article by Robert W. Tucker urged U.S. military intervention in the Gulf as the solution to the energy crisis; in November of the same year he proposed that Israeli military strategy should be based on nuclear weapons. In 1977, *Commentary* printed a scathing denouncement of Breira, a Jewish organization formed in the early 1970s by moderate supporters of Israel who were critical of Israeli government policies and advocated the need to search for peace through negotiations with the Palestinians (*Breira* means "alternative" in Hebrew). Other critics of Israeli policy, such as the American Friends of Peace Now, have also come under attack in its pages. In September 1982 Norman Podhoretz issued his own version of Emile Zola's "J'Accuse," now a passionate vindication of Israel's invasion of Lebanon and denunciation of the media and those liberals who criticized the war.[58]

In recent years, *Commentary*'s subscribers have actually decreased in number, from 60,000 in 1971 to 38,500 in 1981, but the magazine's impact should not be measured by this criterion alone. Especially with the advent of the Reagan administration, the magazine has gained credibility. UN Representative Jeane Kirkpatrick and Carl Gershman, her official counselor, both used *Commentary* as a forum for their views before their 1981 appointments. Richard Pipes' Cold War view of the Soviets and advocacy of a hard-line nuclear policy—as printed in *Commentary*—are said to have led to his 1981 appointment to the National Security Council. Likewise, it was after Menachem Milson's views on Israeli policy in the occupied territories were published in *Commentary* that he was appointed by Defense Minister Ariel Sharon as civil administrator of the West Bank in November 1981.[59]

The AJC's other major periodical is *Present Tense,* a glossy quarterly that was established in the 1970s with a grant from the AJC's Bergreen Institute of Foreign Policy Studies. Its stated aim is "to broaden American Jewry's understanding of the condition of world Jewry." Unlike *Commentary*, its audience is limited to AJC members and the general Jewish organizational community; it is also much less political and dogmatic, and thus provides a counterpoint to *Commentary's* increasingly neoconservative and hawkish positions. The advisory board includes such writers as Betty Friedan, Alvin Toffler, and Elie Wiesel. There is at least one article on Israel and/or the Middle East in each issue; if a topic is controversial, usually both extremist and moderate positions will be printed.

Two periodicals that are geared solely for the membership and other Jewish community groups are *News and Views* and *In the Communities.* The first reports on activities within the Committee itself, mainly on the national level; the second, issued by the AJC's Community Service Department three or four times a year, reports on various local chapter activities.

The AJC has also co-published and prepared *The American Jewish Yearbook* for over seventy years. The *Yearbook*, currently edited by Milton Himmelfarb, includes a directory of Jewish organizations along with several articles on major demographic, social and political issues; it is widely considered the definitive reference work on Jewish communal life in North America.

Occasional Publications

The AJC also issues materials through its various departments and sections to respond to current events, provide information, or make a political statement. During the 1981 AWACS debate, for example, it issued "15 Questions and Answers on U.S. Arms for Saudi Arabia," (and similarly, "10 Questions and Answers on Lebanon," published during the 1982 invasion), both of which present the official Israeli position on the issues involved. This kind of Israel support work is not limited to AJC's Foreign Affairs Department; Israel-related material is also published by such divisions as the Public Relations Department, the Energy Information Service, and the Discrimination Division of the Domestic Affairs Department.

AJC's Energy Information Service reprints and distributes articles stressing the danger of Arab dominance over Middle East oil. In 1982, reprints published by the Energy Information Service included "Oil, Petrodollars and the U.S. Economy," by Dr. Peter B. Kenen, Walker Professor of Economics and International Finance at Princeton; "The Diminishing Importance of Middle East Oil: Its Future Implications," by Eliyahu Kanovsky, professor of economics at Bar Ilan University; and "Hastening OPEC's Demise," by Dr. Lawrence Goldmuntz, chair of the AJC's National Energy Committee and the president of Economics and Science Planning, a Washington, D.C. consulting firm.

Foreign Affairs Department Background Memoranda are brief memos on topical issues sent out under personal cover letters to the media, politicians, minority organizations, women's groups, AJC members and supporters, labor unions, and churches. Often enclosed in the mailings are copies of newspaper or magazine articles or transcripts of speeches that support the view presented in the memorandum. Memoranda dealing with Israel have included "Israeli, U.S. and Egyptian Positions on Jerusalem," by George E. Gruen, director of AJC's Middle East Affairs Division (21 January 1980); "Jerusalem: Renewed Focus of Controversy," by George E. Gruen (29 September 1980; this memo was published one month after the Israeli Embassy issued an information background sheet on Jerusalem that was virtually identical not only in information but also in language):

"The Golan Heights Controversy: Symptom of a Deeper Crisis in U.S.-Israeli Relations," by George E. Gruen (23 December 1981); "The Golan Heights Controversy as Seen in Israel," by Gershon Avner, director of political affairs, AJC Jerusalem office (20 January 1982); "President Reagan's Middle East Initiative," by George E. Gruen (15 September 1982); "United States-Saudi Relations: Time for a Reevaluation," by Lois Gottesman, research analyst, Middle East Affairs Division (March 1983); and "Moscow's Moves in the Mideast," by Allen L. Kagedon, research analyst, Foreign Affairs Department (16 May 1983).

News from the Committee are press releases issued by the AJC's Public Relations Department. These often contain a summary of the AJC's recent research and are linked to current events. In February 1983, for example, one of these press releases reported the results of an AJC-commissioned Gallup poll on U.S. citizens' support for Israel; issued during a time when the situation in Lebanon had resulted in extreme friction between the United States and Israel, it thus served to remind the U.S. government of the weight of pro-Israel public opinion.

The AJC's Trends Analysis Department identifies and studies general issues or specific events of concern to the Jewish community, and its findings are printed in periodic reports. After the 1981 AWACS vote, a *Trends Analysis Report* entitled "The AWACS Debate: Is There an Anti-Semitic Fallout?" was published by the Domestic Affairs Department of AJC's Discrimination Division. Based on monitoring of the media and interviews with various public figures, the report concludes that there was little or no rise in traditional anti-Semitism. However, certain "dangerous trends," considered actually or potentially anti-Semitic, are stressed: criticism of Israel's special relationship with the United States; criticism of the Israeli government's strong public position against the AWACS sale; criticism of or even any reference to the pro-Israel or Jewish lobby in the United States, and especially any statement implying its disproportionate strength; any implication that American Jews may face a conflict between Israeli and U.S. interests; and all activities supporting the AWACS sale. Another *Trends Analysis Report* is titled "Ad Hoc Groups: New Pleaders for the Arab Cause" (11 October 1982). Prepared by AJC staff member Sheba Mittleman, it discusses the emergence of what are characterized as new "anti-Israel" groups after the Lebanon war, but is actually a very brief synopsis of studies done by the ADL and AIPAC.

American Jewish Congress

Year established: 1918
President: Theodore Mann
Executive Director: Henry Siegman
Chair, Governing Council: Paul Berger
Address: 15 East 84th Street, New York, NY 10028
Publications: *Congress Monthly, Judaism, Boycott Report*

General Background

The AJCongress emerged in the early 1900s from a trend known as the "congress movement," whose original impetus was to provide an alternative to the AJC. The movement was sponsored by such prominent American Zionists as Louis D. Brandeis, Stephen S. Wise, Julian W. Mack, Horace Meyer Kallen, and Felix Frankfurter, all of whom had been deeply involved in progressive or liberal politics and reformist crusades. Their opposition to the AJC was based not simply on its rejection of Zionism, but also on what they perceived as its elitist and anti-democratic structure and policies.

In 1915, Brandeis and Wise led the call for the formation of an American Jewish Congress to be a democratic, national umbrella body composed of existing Jewish organizations. Despite opposition from the AJC, a preliminary meeting of the Congress was held in Philadelphia in March 1916, with thirty-three national groups represented. The Congress floundered, however, and its members did not convene again till 1918, when they were galvanized by the crisis in Europe. This 1918 meeting decided to send a delegation to the Versailles Peace Conference with two demands: (1) to ensure that provisions protecting the rights of Jews and other minority peoples went into the peace treaties with defeated nations and (2) to press for recognition of "the aspiration and historic claims of the Jewish people with regard to Palestine" in accordance with the Balfour Declaration, and "to assure the development of Palestine into a Jewish commonwealth."[60]

The original conception of the AJCongress as a broad-based umbrella alternative to the AJC never materialized; instead, the AJCongress became yet another organization, though one with a substantially more populist, activist, and pro-Zionist program than the AJC. These differences were most marked in the 1930s, when the AJCongress took the lead in anti-Nazi work in the United States. At a time when the AJC was advocating "quiet diplomacy," the AJCongress sponsored a massive demonstration in Madison Square Garden, launched a world boycott of Nazi goods and services, founded international appeals, and established a National Women's Division to increase mobilization. It was also in this period that the AJCongress made its final switch from organizational to individual membership.

84

Historically, the AJCongress was the most Zionist of all the community organizations, an orientation due in large part to its founder and first president, Rabbi Stephen Wise, a passionate and committed activist in Zionist organizations and campaigns. The AJCongress' adherence to Zionism was intense and unswerving, but was noteworthy for functioning on an emotional rather than a doctrinaire level. Its allegiance was to Jewish peoplehood and right to a state, not to a particular Zionist organization or trend. After the establishment of Israel in 1948, the AJCongress issued a statement that read in part: "There is no room in AJCongress for those who are not certain of the right of the Jewish people at last to establish the Jewish National Home in Palestine...."[61] The AJCongress criticized the AJC and ADL for being elitist, appeasing, and—by AJCongress standards—anti-Zionist. At the same time, they charged official Zionist organizations with being bureaucratic and incapable of leading American Jews and with failing adequately to reformulate Zionism after the creation of Israel.

When the AJCongress broadened its scope to include community relations following World War II, it placed particular stress on defending civil rights and liberties. It established the Commission on Law and Social Action and became known for focusing on the use of legislation and litigation to press for social change. Maintaining its populist tendencies, the AJCongress was more liberal than the AJC or ADL on such issues as McCarthyism and civil rights and was much more active with the concerns of the poor and inner city Jews. It also took a progressive stand on certain foreign policy issues and adopted a resolution against the Vietnam War in 1966.

Structure and Funding

The AJCongress is a tax-exempt religious organization with a national membership of approximately forty to fifty thousand. It is not as decentralized as the ADL or AJC; most of its activities and members are based in New York. It also receives much less funding than the other two national community relations agencies; in 1972, its budget was $2.5 million, compared to the AJC's $7.3 million and the ADL's $5 million, and this disparity is said to continue.[62] Like the ADL and AJC, it receives a financial allotment from the federations in addition to its private funding from gifts, bequests, membership dues, special campaigns, and a variety of other activities, such as sponsorship of tours to Israel.

According to the AJCongress' IRS Form 990, its total income for the year ending 1982 was $4,232,661, of which $2,119,730 came from direct and indirect public support. Disbursements for salaries and wages accounted for $2.2 million; expenses for program services were listed as follows: Israel and the Middle East—$857,967; Jewish Identity—$381,193; Church, State and Religious Freedom—$366,647; Other International Affairs —$189,469. Also listed is an expenditure of approximately one-half million dollars for grassroots and legislative lobbying between 1979 and 1982.

The AJCongress' regular publications are *Judaism,* a quarterly journal focusing on Jewish scholarship, and *Congress Monthly,* a magazine featuring general articles of interest to Jews, with a strong stress on Israel-related subjects and Jewish community activities. *Congress Monthly* is distributed free to members.

Israel Support Work

The 1983 program of the AJCongress lists the following issues (in this order):

- Fostering U.S. support for Israel's defense and security needs.
- Exposing the well-financed Arab propaganda campaign depicting Israel as an aggressor and the PLO as victim.
- Informing the American public that the Arabs' refusal to negotiate, not Israel's policies, has been and remains the real obstacle to Middle East peace.
- Uncovering efforts to compel illegal participation in the Arab sponsored anti-Israel boycott.
- Combatting anti-Semitism, whether crude hate-mongering or subtle discrimination.
- Unlocking emigration doors that have swung shut for Soviet Jews and beleaguered Jewish communities anywhere.
- Advancing the struggle for human rights, women's rights, and civil liberties.
- Challenging efforts to breach the Constitutional wall between church and state.
- Fighting legislative attempts to strip federal courts of jurisdiction in issues like abortion and public school prayer.
- Opposing the moral vigilantism of those who seek to impose their own breed of religious fundamentalism on the rest of American society.
- Preserving the vitality of our democratic institutions on which the security and well-being of American Jews and all minorities depend.
- Mobilizing support for compassionate social and economic policies during the current era of deep recession and high unemployment.
- Building coalitions with other minorities in pursuit of commonly shared goals.
- Strengthening Jewish life and culture through activities of the Martin Sternberg Center for Jewish artists, the University Summer Seminar programs and the publications *Judaism* and *Congress Monthly.*[63]

While the AJCongress clearly stresses Israel support work, it has rejected neoconservatism and still maintains much of its traditional liberal agenda. It seems less inclined than other Jewish establishment organizations to adapt its political positions to Israeli interests, as illustrated by its position on the following issues:

The Evangelical Right. A resolution passed at its National Governing Council on 4 October 1981 strongly denounces the program and ideology of the New Right. In its current literature, the AJCongress rejects an alliance with such groups, noting, " . . . we are mindful that many of their leaders and spokesmen defend and support the state of Israel. We acknowledge that support, but we regard it as irrelevant to our assessment of their domestic programs. The damage done by their efforts to curtail domestic freedom is not made less by the sympathy they voice for Israel. Their support for the Jewish State has in no way caused us to mitigate or modify our opposition to the many policies and practices of the Evangelical Right with which we disagree."[64]

Domestic Policy. In a 1982 *New York Times* ad entitled "America Must Not Quit on Social Justice," the AJCongress criticized President Reagan's cutbacks in social welfare because "it is the poorest in our midst who are being asked to suffer the most."[65] In other literature, the AJCongress strongly defends the Equal Rights Amendment, the right to abortion, and other civil liberties under attack by the current administration.

Foreign Policy. After an aide to UN Representative Jeane Kirkpatrick addressed an AJCongress meeting in 1981, an official response to the speech was issued by the AJCongress' executive director, Henry Siegman, criticizing the outline of President Reagan's human rights policy and calling the distinction between "authoritarian" and "totalitarian" regimes "pernicious and untenable." The *New York Times* ad mentioned above deplored U.S. reliance on military strength alone and noted, "Over-population, depletion of resources, starvation and nuclear prolifera-tion . . . remain America's enemies and the enemies of all who hope to build a more stable, freer world. These problems will not yield to a foreign policy based solely on resisting Soviet expansion."

Nonetheless, it is important not to confuse the AJCongress' liberal tendency with serious dissent. The AJCongress has consistently adhered to a pro-Israel position; it diverges from the pro-Israel mainstream only on issues where it is impossible to reconcile its traditional agenda with a particular policy, such as alliances with the Evangelical Right or the hawkish "strategic cooperation" concept as the basis for U.S.-Israeli relations. The AJCongress does not waver on supporting Israel—rather, it occasionally questions what the ideological basis of that support should be. The heirs of Brandeis, Wise, and the "downtowners" cannot embrace all the policies of the Reagan and Likud governments without abandoning the assumption that the very establishment of the AJCongress was predicated on, namely that there is no conflict between Zionism and liberalism. Former AJCongress President Arthur Hertzberg addressed this issue in a 1980 interview, saying: "The problem with all this strategic nonsense is that it makes support for Israel conditional on its importance as a strategic asset." Disagreeing also with the domestic policies that such "strategic" thinking leads to, he argued that American Jews should strengthen their alliance with Blacks and speak out against the Reagan program; pointing to a link between anti-Semitism and economic instability, he warned that " . . . in difficult days, midwestern WASPs will not be our shield and buckler, our refuge and fortress."[66]

Despite this tension within the AJCongress, its pro-Israel activities are indistinguishable from those of other American Jewish organizations. In its literature, the Congress writes that it

... continues to work closely with the makers of public opinion and public policy to demonstrate how the cause of Middle East peace and America's vital strategic interests are served by an economically and militarily strong Israel with defensible and recognized borders. We play a leadership role in fighting the sale of AWACS and other sophisticated equipment to Saudi Arabia and we continue to campaign against any tendency in the White House to bypass or abandon the Camp David process.[67]

During the 1973 war, the AJCongress led a major mobilization, calling on its members to give to the UJA and Israel Bonds and to agitate for rearming Israel. Following the 1976 UN resolution on Zionism and racism, it published a full-page ad in the *New York Times,* headed "Proud to be Jews, Proud to be Zionists." (Rabbi Arthur Hertzberg was the president of the AJCongress at the time.) The AJCongress strongly supported the 1982 Israeli invasion of Lebanon, which it characterized as necessary for peace;[68] during the war, AJCongress sponsored a *New York Times* ad (4 August 1982) listing "politicians and columnists ... who supported the action in Lebanon."[69] *Congress Monthly* published articles claiming that there was a disinformation campaign against Israel, denying the existence of any division among American Jews, and describing the invasion as liberating Lebanon from the "grip" of the PLO.[70]

The AJCongress' focus on Israel support work is also reflected in its biennial conferences, which feature as keynote speakers either prominent Israelis or U.S. politicians. In the past decade, speakers at the biennials have included former Secretary of State Henry Kissinger, Senator Edward Kennedy, Israeli ambassadors Simcha Dinitz, Abba Eban, and Avraham Harom, Senator Daniel Moynihan, AFL-CIO President Lane Kirkland, and the late Senator Frank Church.

AJCongress programs involving Israel have included the following:

The Overseas Travel Program, set up in 1958 to promote tourism in Israel. The first trip involved only twenty-three people; today it is the largest such tour in the Jewish community, with approximately seven thousand people participating each year.

The Louise Waterman Wise Youth Hostel in Jerusalem. The largest such facility in Israel, it is not simply a youth hostel, but also offers special citizenship training programs for new immigrant children.

Arrangements for mayors of major U.S. cities to go to Jerusalem for the annual International Conference of Mayors, where, according to an organizational brochure, participants "learn at first hand the importance to Israel's security of a unified Jerusalem under Israeli sovereignty. Particularly gratifying have been the activities of the Mayors on their return home supporting Israel's enlightened administration of the city—a major goal in our effort to build public understanding of Israel's security requirements as essential to our own country's strategic interests."[71]

The American-Israel Dialogue, instituted in 1962. This is a symposium held in Jerusalem for American Jews and Israelis. Among the Israeli participants have been former prime ministers David Ben-Gurion, Golda Meir, and Menachem Begin, Moshe Sharett, Abba Eban, and writers Amos Elon and Amos Oz; Americans have included leaders of the AJCongress along with writers and other intellectuals such as Arthur Hertzberg, Philip Roth, Cynthia Ozick, Irving Kristol, Leonard Fein, and Chaim Potok. The symposium transcript is published by the AJCongress each year. According to the Congress, "The 'Dialogue' is AJCongress's response to the need we feel to forge a closer understanding and a profounder unity between Israel and American Jewry."[72]

A statement on the mass media adopted by the National Governing Council on 6 March 1983 notes, "The need to counter inaccurate or tendentious coverage in the media is a formidable challenge, but a critical requirement in the ongoing battle to defend the security and welfare of Israel and of Jews everywhere." The statement concludes with a list of specific recommendations for the Congress and the Jewish community to adopt, reproduced here in full:

1. Cultivate publishers, editors and other media executives during periods of non-crisis. This gives an opportunity to provide them with long range perspectives and establishes accessibility during moments of crisis.
2. Inform editors in your local area where an organizational news source can be reached at any time of day or night so they can obtain information or verification on breaking news stories. A mini-media directory should be compiled for ready reference as to where and to whom to send letters of complaint or congratulations.
3. When errors of commission or ommission occur, call the attention of the reporters and editors to the inaccuracy as soon as possible. Don't wait until the issue is a dead letter. Charges of inaccuracy should be carefully documented.
4. Whenever possible, statements to the press should be issued in written form. This reduces inaccuracies and assures that the information given is in the proper context.
5. Organize special programs to encourage select media personnel to visit Israel. A first-hand view of the Jewish state is an excellent way to sensitize newspeople to Israel's problems and achievements.
6. Use letters to the editor as a primary means of correcting newspaper inaccuracies. The letters column is the most widely read department in any newspaper. Similarly, reply editorials should be used to answer commentary on local radio and T.V. stations. Under government regulation, electronic media are required to provide opportunities for listeners to present opposing points of view. Wherever possible letter and op-ed banks should be established in anticipation of events.
7. Establish national and local monitoring systems. Call the attention of Jewish community members to the importance of such activity by establishing formal task forces for this purpose.
8. Since effective monitoring requires knowledgeable scanners, national organizations should use newsletter bulletins, hot lines and press releases to supplement

material available to the Jewish community in local Anglo-Jewish newspapers.

9. Identify effective spokesmen among the local membership who can be encouraged to prepare op-ed columns on particular issues and who can effectively appear on the electronic media.

10. In flagrant instances of misreporting, imbalance or bias, seek a meeting with news executives to ask for redress and to prevent recurrence. In such encounters remain calm and civil, be prepared with the facts, make certain the news official is someone in real authority rather than a surrogate assigned to run interference.

11. Paid advertisements should be used sparingly and only when efforts to get letters, op-ed articles or other replies prove unavailable. Ads, however, should not be precluded altogether. They should be used when the message is important and other means of obtaining access fail.

12. No matter how exercised a community may be about an inaccurate news item, care should be taken to avoid any inference that efforts will be made to apply pressure on the editorial side through recourse to advertisers. Except in unusually rare instances such efforts are likely to prove counterproductive and ought not to be employed.[73]

The AJCongress' Israel work is more limited than that of other organizations by its lack of comparable funding; however, this constraint is compensated for in various ways. For one, the AJCongress draws on its liberal credentials in devising "programs targetted on specific groups in the community with which we have particular contact ... [the] Negro community ... [the] 'peace community' [anti-Vietnam War groups]...."[74] Thus, when the issue of Israel's connection to South Africa was raised in the 1970s, the AJCongress published two studies detailing the trade relations of nineteen Black African states with South Africa and revealing arms traffic among Europe, the Arab states, and South Africa. Another report was published on Israel's aid programs to Black Africa. Regarding the peace movement, the AJCongress published and distributed, with the ADL, an attack on the American Friends Service Committee and has published criticism of such individuals and groups as Noam Chomsky, Jacobo Timerman, Vanessa Redgrave, and the National Council of Churches in the *Congress Monthly*.* The AJCongress also supplements its own Israel support programs by working closely with the Conference of Presidents of Major American Jewish Organizations, of which it is a member, preparing many of its *Middle East Memos* and public statements; AJCongress president Howard Squadron was head of the Presidents Conference from 1980 to 1982.

The AJCongress and the "Arab Threat"

In the late 1960s and early 1970s, AJCongress began focusing on the Arab boycott of Israel and Arab oil. The ADL, AJC, AJCongress and the

---

* For example, in a review of Jacobo Timerman's book on the invasion of Lebanon, *The Longest War*, Louis Rapoport charged: "He is simply out to capitalize on his new Israeli identity. Like so many bleeding hearts who make their careers on the freedom circuit, he has an authoritarian problem of his own."[75]

Business Roundtable all cooperated on pushing through anti-boycott legislation. The AJCongress continues to monitor the Department of Commerce for enforcement of this legislation and issues its findings in a regular publication called *Boycott Report*. In one of its brochures, the AJCongress characterizes this work as "Fighting the Arab boycott" and explains that it is deeply involved in efforts to protect the rights of American Jews from Arab attack and to defend the American principle of free trade as it affects commerce with Israel.[76]

Following the 1973 war and the Arab oil embargo, the AJCongress put out a number of publications about the oil crisis, including "Fact and Fiction about the Oil Crisis" and "Towards a National Energy Program." In recent years, there has been more emphasis on the specter of Arab wealth controlling America. A recent leaflet, "Why Join the American Jewish Congress?" proclaims that "Arabs are buying influence over American policy."

As the community relations agency most known for recourse to lawsuits and other forms of legal activities, the AJCongress has also turned to the courts to confront the "Arab threat." Major legal actions in the 1980s have included:

(1) A "sweeping Freedom of Information request to more than 100 agencies" calling for the release of all "unclassified documents on the Palestine Liberation Organization and its personnel and supporters in this country." The FOIA request was a step in a suit filed on behalf of twenty-nine Israelis killed and sixty-five injured during a Palestinian operation in 1978; the suit seeks damages against the Libyan government, the PLO, and three U.S. groups: the Palestine Information Office, the National Association of Arab Americans, and the Palestine Congress of North America.[77]

(2) Another suit, based on the Freedom of Information Act, to compel the Treasury Department to disclose the financial holdings of Saudi Arabia, Kuwait, and the United Arab Emirates in U.S. mainland banks. In 1982, the Federal District Court upheld the Treasury Department's refusal to divulge such information, but the AJCongress is currently appealing the decision.[78]

(3) The "Shareholders Project." Following the battle over the sale of AWACS to Saudi Arabia, the AJCongress initiated a campaign to force disclosure of pro-AWACS lobbying by corporations; through the use of shareholder proxy resolutions, stock owners sympathetic to AJCongress goals can bring the lobbying issue to a vote at the annual meetings of corporations. The strategic goal of the campaign is to prevent such arms sales in the future; as Will Maslow, general counsel of the AJCongress, noted, "The AWACS issue may be old, but the Jordanian arms issue is just coming up. About half the companies we've talked to said they will not be involved in a Jordanian arms deal. As far as we are concerned this was a success." A major article on the campaign published in *The Christian*

Science Monitor was reprinted by the AJCongress under the heading, "This is one of the ways the American Jewish Congress challenges the pro-Arab lobby...." Ironically, the campaign is based on the very tactics it claims to criticize: money and pressure. One targeted company filed a complaint with the Securities and Exchange Commission, on the grounds that the campaign was intended "to harass the corporation so as to create a chilling effect deterring them from taking positions opposed to those taken by the American Jewish Congress."[79]

Anti-Defamation League of B'nai B'rith

Year established: 1913
National Chairman: Kenneth J. Bialkin
National Executive Committee Chairman: Burton Levinson
National Director: Nathan Perlmutter
Address: 823 United Nations Plaza, New York, NY 10017
Publications: *ADL Bulletin; Face to Face: An Interreligious Bulletin; Fact Finding Report; Israel Backgrounder; Law Notes, Rights, Law; Research and Evaluation Report; Discriminations Report*

General Background

The development of the ADL has to be placed in the context of the B'nai B'rith International, ADL's parent organization. B'nai B'rith (Sons of the Covenant) was established in 1843 as a fraternal Jewish order; at present, it has affiliates in forty-two countries, and it places a major emphasis on "preserving Judaism through projects in and for Israel and for Soviet Jewry." Its American membership has increased from 23,000 Jewish males in 1910 to over 200,000 in 1965. A female counterpart, B'nai B'rith Women, was established in 1897; it "supports a variety of services to Israel."[80] In 1913, Sigmund Livingston, an attorney from Bloomington, Illinois, persuaded B'nai B'rith to establish the ADL to target overt anti-Semitism. The new organization was headquartered in Chicago, with Livingston as its first national chair, a position he held until his death in 1945. To form its first executive committee, 150 leaders "representing a cross-section of Jewish communal life and interests" were invited to join; among them was Adolph Ochs, publisher of the *New York Times*.[81] In 1947, ADL headquarters were moved to New York City, and the regional office structure was expanded.

According to ADL's 1913 charter, "The immediate object of the League is to stop, by appeals to reason and conscience, and if necessary, by appeals to law, the defamation of the Jewish People. Its ultimate purpose is to secure justice and fair treatment to all citizens alike, and to put an end forever to unjust and unfair discrimination against, and ridicule of any sect or body of citizens."[82]

In its first few decades, the ADL's major arena of work was clearly the United States, where it struggled to protect Jews and other minority groups from discrimination and civil rights abuse. It helped focus attention on the various racist and fascist movements in the country, such as the Ku Klux Klan; Henry Ford's newspaper, *The Dearborn Independent;* the American Nazi Party; and the John Birch Society. In the 1950s, important action issues included quotas in education, restricted housing and resorts, Jim Crow laws, and employment discrimination. The ADL was continuously concerned with Christian-Jewish relations and, in the

1960s, Black-Jewish relations; the Civil Rights Act of 1964 was a major focus of activity. The ADL also responded strongly to individual events, such as outbreaks of anti-Semitic vandalism, or specific instances of discrimination in hiring, housing, and so forth. On the international level, from the 1930s on, the major issue was the Holocaust and then the rebuilding of Germany, where the ADL was concerned over the failure to punish Nazi war criminals and the persistence of former Nazis in government positions. The ADL also produced reports on the situation of Jews throughout the world.

It is on the basis of this domestic-based, prejudice-targeting agenda that the ADL has acquired its moral legitimacy and prestige. Harry Truman described ADL efforts as "a rose in the hearts and minds of the American people." "By educating our citizens to overcome the evils of prejudice," Dwight Eisenhower told the ADL, "you have helped to make our land a better place to live in." John F. Kennedy characterized the ADL's "tireless pursuit of equality of treatment for all Americans," as having made "a lasting and substantial contribution to our democracy." Lyndon Johnson expressed his support with more poetic enthusiasm: "Wherever your torches burn, tolerance, decency and charity have been illuminated. Bigots and bias hide wherever you come into view."[83] President Reagan signed a joint Congressional resolution proclaiming 12 November 1983 as ADL Day.[84]

Structure

The ADL's highest decision-making body is the 110-member national commission, which is equivalent to a board of directors and meets annually. Fifty-two members are drawn from the American Jewish community at large, and fifty-eight from B'nai B'rith channels. There is also an executive committee. The most active individual leaders are the national chair, national director, chair of the executive committee, national staff, and other officers. Each of the ADL's twenty-seven regional offices is guided by its own advisory board drawn from community figures.*

The ADL's work is divided into four major categories, each constituting an independent division: civil rights, communications, community service, and program. All deal with both national and international issues.

---

*The regional offices include Central Pacific (San Francisco), Connecticut (New Haven), D.C.-Maryland (Washington, D.C.), Florida (Miami), Long Island (East Meadow, N.Y.), Michigan (Detroit), Midwest (Chicago), Minnesota and the Dakotas (Minneapolis), Missouri-Southern Illinois (Clayton, Mo.), Mountain States (Denver), New England (Boston), New Jersey (Livingston), New York (N.Y.), New York State (N.Y.), North Carolina-Virginia (Richmond), Northwest Texas-Oklahoma (Dallas), Ohio-Kentucky-Indiana (Columbus), Pacific Northwest (Seattle), Pacific Southwest (Los Angeles), Palm Beach County (West Palm Beach), Pennsylvania-West Virginia-Delaware (Philadelphia), Plains States (Omaha), San Diego-Arizona (San Diego), South Central (New Orleans), Southeastern (Atlanta), Southwest (Houston), and Wisconsin-Upper Midwest (Milwaukee). There are ADL offices in Jerusalem, Paris, and Rome.

Although an issue may fall into the domain of one division, it often passes through other divisions for coordinated attention. The ADL also sets up numerous departments, committees, and task forces to deal with specific issues. Perhaps the most distinctive of these are the "domestic fact-finding" and "research and evaluation" departments, both of which are basically involved in data gathering (including surveillance) and data retrieval, activities that other Jewish organizations do not pursue to anywhere near the same degree.

The ADL is registered as a tax-exempt religious organization. Like the AJC, it withdrew from the United Jewish Fund in 1952 out of opposition to the large allotment of aid going overseas, and the two organizations formed the Joint Defense Appeal. This effort collapsed in 1963, when the AJC reorganized to concentrate more on international work, and each organization then initiated a separate fundraising campaign, an arrangement that proved more successful. In addition to its own fundraising, the ADL receives a yearly allocation from the federations' Welfare Fund and is a member of CJF's Large City Budgeting Conference.

In 1913, the ADL started with a budget of $200 and two desks; by 1974, the annual budget was more than $5 million.[85] Total revenue for fiscal year 1981-82 was nearly $15 million; about 95 percent was generated from direct and indirect public support, and slightly over a half million dollars came from government grants. Total expenditures were $14.7 million — 69 percent for program services, 21 percent for fundraising, and the rest for management and general expenditures.[86]

Since finances generally reflect priorities, it is informative to examine the breakdown of Program Services expenditures, which constitute over two-thirds of total expenditures in the 1981-82 IRS report. The largest disbursement in this category (46 percent) was for the operations of the twenty-eight professionally staffed offices. The second highest expenditure (20 percent) was for publications and communications. About 12 percent was spent on "national affairs" for maintenance of "all research, library files, and investigation data relating to anti-Semitism, anti-Semitic trends, bigotry, and hate movements." Only 6 percent is listed for "Mid-East," but this figure is misleading, because Israel support work is in fact on the agenda of virtually all departments. The remaining 12 percent of the budget was for interreligious, legal, and foreign affairs, and for leadership recruitment.

Israel Support Work

With its priority on domestic issues and the very real problem of anti-Semitism in America, the ADL historically distanced itself from the issues of Israel and Zionism. In 1949, the ADL published this policy statement:

After several months of study, the Executive Committee of ADL's National

Commission formalized organizational policy to meet issues raised by the creation of Israel and the impact of these problems on the fight against anti-Semitism. The policy is:

1. Augmenting the currently favorable attitude of Americans to Israel. ADL will dramatize the historical and cultural background of Israel's development and struggle for independence as a force for developing better group relations in America.

2. Supporting B'nai B'rith's position—urging *de jure* recognition and Israel's admission to full U.N. membership. It will be the province of ADL's program division to point up how the accomplishments and philosophy of Israel parallel the growth and development of American freedom, stressing these themes:

-contributions of the Israeli [*sic*] in World War II and their subsequent heroic struggle for independence, not unlike the birth of the U.S. in 1776, and the pioneering efforts of the Israeli in reclaiming Palestine's desert much as American pioneers of the 19th century pushed back the frontiers to the Pacific.

-ADL will cooperate with the American Jewish Committee and other members of the NJCRAC, as well as the Zionist Emergency Council in developing its Israel program.

-The League emphasizes that it will not become involved in Israel's political problems, holding these to be strictly the concern of the new state.[87]

Although this policy statement embodies Zionist assumptions about Palestine and the indigenous population, it does not assert the centrality of Israel or an organic linkage between American Jews and Israel. Indeed, the recurrent use of the word "Israel" illustrates the ADL's outlook in 1949: support for Israel, but with a clear differentiation between Israelis and American Jewry. The fact that the ADL had not yet embraced the Jewish people concept that lies at the core of Zionism is further illustrated by themes covered in the *ADL Bulletin* up to 1966. In general, there are remarkably few articles dealing with Israel, Zionism, or the Middle East, and most of these consist of attacks on the activities of Arab or pro-Arab groups in the United States, on the grounds that they are anti-Semitic. (It should be noted, however, that these articles already exhibit the anti-Arab slant that became more virulent in the 1970s and 1980s.) There is an upsurge in articles in 1956 because of the Suez crisis, but from 1957 to 1959 there are no Israel-related articles at all.

The "Israelization" of ADL

The shift that occurs in the ADL, which can be described as an almost complete "Israelization" of its programs, priorities, and actions, coincides with the 1967 Arab-Israeli war. The *ADL Bulletin* hailed the 1967 war as "The Miracle Victory," and, indeed, for mainstream American Jews Israel's military success in 1967 led to a sense of identification with and support for Israel that the creation of the state had not. By the mid-1970s, this sentiment had pervaded the Jewish community, and the ADL leadership had adopted an active, aggressive pro-Israel position.

Particularly relevant to the present focus of the ADL—indeed, its cornerstone—is the assumption that anti-Zionism equals anti-Semitism, and the corollary that criticism of Israel reflects insensitivity to American Jews and constitutes a form of anti-Semitism. Thus, the ADL's original role of combatting anti-Semitism in the United States has come to be dominated by Israel defense work. In *The New Anti-Semitism*, a book written in 1974 by ADL's general counsel Arnold Forster and national director Benjamin Epstein, "insensitivity," undistinguished from anti-Semitism, is the most evident word in the entire volume.* In equating anti-Zionism with anti-Semitism, the ADL officials write that "today the left and the far right are again patent fellow travelers in their hatred of Israel and its position as ally of the United States."[89] This assertion represents a substantial departure from the ADL's traditional emphasis on the "hate groups" of the far right. But by including the left, the ADL attempts to legitimize its attacks on any expression of solidarity with the Palestinian cause—or what ADL calls "politically powered anti-Semitism."

For Nathan Perlmutter, ADL national director, the fight against selling the AWACS to Saudi Arabia reveals the "real anti-Semitism in America." These "real" anti-Semites are the "Semitically-neutral arms salesmen who talked of jobs, of black ink for the aerospace industry and of recycling petrodollars. These are today a thousandfold more telling adversaries [of the Jews] than juveniles painting swastikas on Jewish-owned buildings."[90] (He develops this theme further in *The Real Anti-Semitism in America*, co-authored with Ruth Perlmutter in 1982.)

The ADL now maintains a staunch anti-Soviet position. In a 1984 letter to the editor in the *New York Times*, Abraham Foxman, ADL associate national director, wrote: "The Soviets feed on endemic Middle East radicalism, which exists independent of Israeli policies or of alleged American assertiveness. Basic hostility to the West, social and economic dissatisfaction, opposition to Arab moderates and rejection of Israel's right to exist are all sources of this regional radicalism and nicely dovetail with Soviet radicalism."[91]

The extent to which the ADL has become "Israelized" can be demonstrated clearly by juxtaposing its positions in 1966 with those from the beginning of the 1980s:

*The book contains such inconsistencies that critic Walter Goodman, in his review of it in *The New Leader*, concluded that "a good deal of what is presented here as the new anti-Semitism is not anti-Semitism at all. Every criticism is not a defamation, and unless the ADL is careful, it's going to give anti-Semitism a good name."[88]

ADL: Purpose & Program (1966)	*ADL: Campaign '80 (1980)*
1. Uncover anti-Semitism	1. Combat anti-Semitism
2. Strengthen interreligious understanding	2. Tell Israel's story
3. Expose the radical right	3. Rescue Soviet Jewry
4. Secure equal rights for all	4. Protect world Jewry
5. End discrimination	5. Expose extremism
6. Insure the safety of Jews abroad	6. Strengthen interfaith understanding
7. Inform opinion molders	7. End discrimination
8. Improve school curricula	
9. Instruct teachers	
10. Strengthen the local community	

In the goals put forward in 1966, the only mention of Israel is confined to one sentence on the Arab boycott and the Arab League, under the category of "Insure the safety of Jews abroad."[92]

The ADL's "Israelized" position is also reflected in the set of resolutions adopted by the national commission during its sixty-ninth meeting, on 3 June 1982, just before the Israeli invasion of Lebanon. Six of the nine resolutions adopted dealt directly with Israel and the Middle East:

Criticizing the National Council of Churches' statement on the Middle East as "biased, misinformed and insensitive," the ADL urged "all religiously motivated persons to assert their religious traditions of social justice and reconciliation by speaking out and rejecting those who support terrorists and their methods."

The ADL called on the American government to launch a diplomatic offensive against the PLO and pledged to "devote maximum efforts to educate the public, the media, and American officials as to the need for such an active and new policy by the U.S."

The ADL expressed opposition to the sale of jet fighters and missiles to Jordan.

The ADL called on the United States to withdraw its support from the United Nations if that organization acts to expel Israel.

The ADL commended the governments of Zaire and Costa Rica for taking diplomatic steps favorable to Israel: Zaire for re-establishing its diplomatic relations with Israel, and Costa Rica for moving its embassy to Jerusalem.

In the last resolution, the ADL "called on Congress to enact legislation to remove the secrecy surrounding Arab petrodollar investments in the United States that threaten American 'independence' in the formulation of domestic and foreign policy."[93]

The ADL's actions have become so predicated on the primacy of Israel that some liberal-minded American Jewish leaders have offered public criticism. Rabbi Alexander Schindler, the president of the United

American Hebrew Congregations (UAHC) and former president of the Presidents Conference, for example, deplored this trend in a 1980 sermon delivered before trustees of the UAHC: "When the Jabotinsky foundation presents its award to Jerry Falwell ... for his support of Israel and the Anti-Defamation League offers its platform to Pat Robertson of the Christian Broadcasting Network to speak about Jerusalem, it is madness—and suicide."[94]

Operations

In its early decades, the ADL would approach persons or institutions considered to be anti-Semitic and privately attempt to persuade or reason them into retracting abusive statements and correcting offensive behavior. In later years, ADL has turned to more public and aggressive measures, which it classifies as "Educational," "Vigilance Work," and "Legislation." In fact, "Vigilance Work" has become outright surveillance of individuals and groups, the results of which are fed into both the Israeli intelligence-gathering apparatus, via their consulates and embassy, and American domestic intelligence, via the FBI. Top ADL officials have admitted the use of clandestine surveillance techniques. *Not the Work of A Day*, the official account of the rise of the ADL, reports that in 1936, the "ADL managed to expose many Americans who supported Kuhn [leader of the Bund, the anti-Zionist Jewish socialists.]" Although the Bund's membership lists were kept secret, "the League had its own undercover investigators, one of them being Kuhn's personal chauffeur."[95] Today, the ADL is much more active than other community relations organizations in the use of its regional offices and constituency for information gathering, and dissemination. The central headquarters in New York City provides regional offices with analysis sheets, sample letters to the editor to be placed in local media, biographies of Israeli leaders and anti-Zionist speakers, and directives on how to deal with topical issues. The regional offices in turn monitor all Israel-related or Middle East-related activities in their areas, such as the media, campus speakers, and films. By bringing the local events to the attention of the central headquarters, they play a pivotal role in ADL's overall supervision of the national scene.

Stifling Dissent

In an internal memorandum of 18 September 1970, from Abraham Foxman to the ADL regional offices, Jewish organizations are advised "not to sponsor or co-sponsor" the appearances of Israeli journalist and Knesset member Uri Avnery and "not engage in public debate with him." Avnery's nationwide tour was sponsored by the Fellowship of Reconciliation and the American Friends Service Committee. Labeling Avnery "an opponent of the traditional concepts of Zionism and Judaism," Foxman warned that he "may say things which will trouble and even embarrass the Jewish community." Various Jewish student groups on campus and the

Israeli Student Association had been notified of Avnery's itinerary, the memo went on, and "will challenge him whenever necessary." Attached to the memo was a "fact sheet" outlining Avnery's views that was prepared by ADL's Research and Evaluation Department. Copies of the memo were sent also to the Community Relations Councils.

One Jewish activist critical of Israeli policies discovered in 1983 that the ADL maintained a file on him going back to 1970; it included information on the subject gathered from local newspapers, talks on campuses, interoffice memos (from the institution where the subject teaches), business meetings, talks on radio and TV, and press and other miscellaneous materials. As the file revealed, specific individuals had been assigned to monitor this person's lectures, either by tape recordings and verbatim transcriptions, or by detailed summaries of what the subject spoke about, the context of the lecture, other participants, size of audience, questions from the floor, mood of the audience, and so forth. In some cases, these observers successfully penetrated closed meetings in which the subject participated. Subsequently, the ADL prepared and disseminated a short primer on this person, following the "myth" and "fact" format, and distributed it to their agents for use at future speaking engagements.

The file reveals a fixed pattern regarding the flow of information between ADL headquarters and the regional offices. Most of the information was forwarded from the regional offices to the subject's file in New York. A local Jewish federation also cooperated by forwarding summaries of lectures by the subject to New York. At one point, ADL headquarters sent a memo to the responsible regional office with a copy of a letter, bearing the subject's signature, which invited friends to join in a new group that would look critically at the Middle East. Upon receiving this letter, the regional office sent a copy of it, with a memorandum labeled "confidential," to the Israeli consul in that city, commenting that the consul might be interested in the document.

In 1982, the ADL produced a very extensive "Curriculum Guide" to help teachers expose "extremist groups in the United States." In the section of the guide that deals with "the common elements of extremism of the left and right," two "instructional objectives" are presented: to teach the students that (1) both left and right share the same beliefs in "hostility to democratic ideas," "faith in conspiracy theories," "anti-Semitism," and "enmity to Israel"; and (2) that both share the same behavior in "violence and terrorism," "slavish adherence to a party line," and "actions aimed at the destabilization and destruction of our democratic system." After the students are taken through a series of highly selective readings about western and eastern Europe, they are presented with reasons for the "anti-Israel emphasis of the Radical Left":

a. Both the Soviet Union and China support the Arabs.
   (1) Russia has a heavy stake in the Arab world, having invested vast sums in military and economic aid.

(2) China, in an attempt to wean the Arab world away from the Soviet Union, outdoes the Russians in its anti-Israel rhetoric.

(3) Thus, all shades of the radical spectrum, whether pro-Soviet or pro-Chinese can agree on an anti-Israel position.

b. The United States supports Israel.

(1) The Radical Left's most important objective is the destruction of the United States, the prime example of a democratic, capitalist society.

(2) The destruction of a democratic state with close ties to the United States, and through whom America can exercise influence in the Middle East is an excellent way of diminishing America's power and position in the world.

c. To strike against Israel is also a way of striking against Jews in general.

(1) Jews viewed as part of the affluent, smug, white, capitalist class that "oppresses" the racial minorities.

(2) Jews with their liberal attitudes and voting patterns viewed as obstacles to the growth of revolutionary consciousness by their perpetuation of the "myth" that progress can be achieved peacefully through normal democratic processes.[96]

The ADL's New England Regional Office circulated a confidential letter to "Campus Jewish Leaders," dated November 1983, informing Jewish campus leaders that the ADL was willing to help them to combat "anti-Semitism and anti-Israel propaganda and create positive images of Jews and Israel," to which end that office had established a part-time campus coordinator for their campus "Hasbara [information] Network."

In December 1983, about twenty New Jewish Agenda members in the Boston area received hate mail after cars belonging to three of them were vandalized. New Jewish Agenda, which is largely composed of dovish Zionists, asked ADL's regional office in Boston to look into these incidents of harassment, but the ADL refused.

Around the same time, following the release of Costa Gavras' film *Hanna K.,* which deals with the Palestinian issue through the experiences of an American Jewish woman who migrates to Israel and becomes a lawyer there, ADL headquarters circulated a memo to its regional offices "to provide ... a means to respond to problems that might arise with regard to the film." The memo, dated 10 October 1983, included one review by Shimon Samuels, director of ADL's European office, and another by Abba Cohen, assistant director of its Middle Eastern Department, both of which accused the film of being inaccurate and distorting Israel's positions and actions.

The ADL responded even more aggressively in the case of another film, *Women Under Siege,* which is a twenty-minute documentary about Palestinian women in Rashidiyeh camp in southern Lebanon. *Women Under Seige* is part of a three-film series on women in changing Middle Eastern societies produced by Elizabeth Fernea, a lecturer at the University of Texas at Austin, and the entire project received some of its funding from the National Endowment for the Humanities. Charging that the film is "unabashed propaganda for the Palestine Liberation Organization," the

ADL complained to the National Endowment and argued that "obviously, American taxpayers never intended their money to be used for such a purpose."[97] The National Endowment, perhaps reflecting an alteration in its political orientation under the Reagan administration, concurred with ADL's charges and stated that the film should not have received NEH funding.

The Lebanon War

The ADL circulated a number of in-house memoranda during and after the 1982 war in Lebanon.* The subject of a 16 June memo to regional offices was "Israel's military action against the PLO." Included with the memo was a question and answer piece on Israel's military action prepared by Harry Wall, ADL's Israel director, and press reports favorable to Israel and anti-PLO. The memo's suggestion to the regional office was to "emphasize the gains to U.S. interests as a result of Israel's defeat of two Soviet allies."

On 28 June, the same packet was sent to rabbis, under the signature of the co-chair of ADL's Interfaith Affairs Committee. The message this time was to engage your "colleagues in the Christian community" in conversations on the situation. On 10 December 1982, a memo on "Israel and the Middle East after Lebanon" was sent to the regional office under the signature of ADL's associate director, Abraham Foxman. The thrust of the five-page essay is that, like other wars, the war in Lebanon has generated its own myths, which Foxman summarizes as follows: (1) "Israel is no longer the moral society it once was"; (2) "The PLO has gained a political victory out of military defeat in Lebanon"; (3) "U.S. interests have been harmed by its support of Israel in the war"; and (4) "Israel's operation in Lebanon has made peace even more remote." The memo urges the regional offices to use the article "extensively with influentials in your region, particularly in trying to place as many as possible in your area newspapers."

With the debate on American policy in Lebanon heating up, another memo was sent to the regional offices on 1 September 1983. It included what was termed a "disturbing" *New York Times* editorial that blamed Israel "for dragging Americans into this venture," and the ADL response. Two weeks later, following Prime Minister Menachem Begin's declared intention to resign, a memo was sent to all regional directors, praising Begin as "a man of history." The text of the statement lauding Begin was intentionally sent on plain paper, and the regional directors were urged to "place it as an Op-Ed piece in the general press of your area."

After another two weeks, the ambiguity generated by the situation in Lebanon, in terms of both U.S. and Israeli positions, prompted ADL central headquarters to offer further clarifications to its regional offices.

---

*A list of the memoranda can be found in the Bibliography.

Thus, a 5 October 1983 "not for publication" memo from Foxman to the regional directors provided a brief analysis of American policy in Lebanon, prepared by Ken Jacobson, ADL director of Middle Eastern affairs. Implied in the analysis is a lamentation of indecisive American policy in Lebanon, which would inevitably force the Americans into "political negotiations with the Syrians, undoubtedly resulting in major concessions to Syria" and potentially adverse effects on Israel. The analysis sees the Saudis and Syrians gaining with the United States at Israel's expense. It concludes that "everything should be done to support an equitable settlement that helps stabilize Lebanon, that helps reduce Syrian influence and that allows Israel to maintain peace and security in its northern towns."

Finally, on 8 March 1984, ADL placed a paid advertisement in the *New York Times*, where it mourned the loss of "peace between Israel and Lebanon," as a result of "Syrian poison and international neglect." Peace died, according to the ad, after having been "subjected to that 36 year-old Middle Eastern disease, Arab rejectionism. Syria and Saudi Arabia, joined by the Soviet Union and Iranian terrorists, worked overtime to snuff out its life." Its passing should be mourned not only by ADL but by "those who care about the triumph of civilization over barbarism. . . ."[98]

Publications

In addition to *ADL Bulletin*, the ADL has an extensive publishing program that includes both printed and audio-visual materials. Its audio-visual program consists of a number of short films, filmstrips, and slides designed specifically for use on TV and in classrooms and discussion groups.

The ADL publishes dozens of books, covering the entire range of its concerns. The two books that most reflect the changing agenda of the ADL are *Target USA: The Arab Propaganda Offensive* (November 1975) and *Pro-Arab Propaganda in America: Vehicles and Voices* (January 1983), both of which purport to expose and discredit Arab propaganda in the United States.

Notes

Introduction

1. Samuel Halperin, *The Political World of American Zionism.* Detroit: Wayne State University Press, 1961: 193.

2. *Ibid:* 200.

3. Yonathan Shapiro, *Leadership of the American Zionist Organization, 1879-1930* (1971), quoted in Steven M. Cohen, *American Modernity and Jewish Identity.* New York and London: Tavistock Publications, 1983: 47.

4. Leonard Fein, "The Domestic Element: American Jewry and U.S. Israel Relations," *Analysis,* no. 49 (1 December 1974).

5. See Jonathan S. Woocher, "The American Jewish Polity in Transition," *Forum,* Fall/Winter 1982; and Cohen: 154-170. The transformation of the Jewish communal agenda is examined by Gary S. Schiff, "American Jews and Israel: A Study in Political and Organizational Priorities," in *Understanding American Jewish Philanthropy,* edited by M. L. Raphael. New York: KTAV Publishers, 1979.

6. Bennett Yanowitz, "Democracy and Discipline in the American Jewish Community: The Utility and Morality of Unity," in NJCRAC, *1983-84 Joint Program Plan for Jewish Community Relations:* 20-21.

7. *Ibid:* 21.

8. Cohen: 143.

9. Yanowitz: 21.

10. *Congressional Quarterly Weekly Report,* "Middle East Lobbying," 39/34 (22 August 1981).

CJF

11. *CJF 51st General Assembly Program and 1982 Annual Report.*

12. *Ibid.*

13. Daniel J. Elazar, "Decision Making in the American Jewish Community," in *American Jews/A Reader,* edited by Marshall Sklare. New York: Behrman House Inc., 1983.

14. *CJF 51st General Assembly Program and 1982 Annual Report.*

15. *Ibid.*

16. Schiff: 187.

17. *CJF 51st General Assembly Program and 1982 Annual Report.*

18. Melvin I. Urofsky, "American Jewish Leadership," *American Jewish History* 70/4 (June 1981): 415-416.

19. *Jewish Telegraphic Agency,* 23 November 1983.

20. *Ibid.*

NJCRAC

21. Schiff, p. 173.

22. Will Maslow, *The Structure and Functioning of the American Jewish Community.* New York: Published jointly by the American Jewish Congress and the American Section of the World Jewish Congress, 1974: 23.

23. NJCRAC, *1983-84 Joint Program Plan for Jewish Community Relations,* Introduction.

24. NJCRAC, *1982-83 Joint Program Plan for Jewish Community Relations:* 7.

25. *Ibid:* 15.

26. *Ibid:* 17-18.

27. *Ibid:* 20.

28. *Ibid:* 46.

29. *1983-84 Joint Program Plan:* 10.

30. *Ibid:* 11.

31. *Ibid:* 14.

32. *Ibid:* 17.
33. *Ibid:* 45.
34. *Ibid:* 53-54.
35. *Ibid:* 20-24.
36. Schiff: 187-189.
37. *Jewish Exponent,* 18 February 1977.
38. *Washington Post,* 23 July 1983.
39. *Jewish Press,* 5 March 1982.
40. *Jewish Telegraphic Agency,* 9 June 1982.

AJC

41. Melvin I. Urofsky, "Do American Jews Want Democracy in Jewish Life?" *interChange,* March 1976.
42. Henry L. Feingold, "A Jewish Survival Enigma. The Strange Case of the American Jewish Committee," AJC, May 1981: 2.
43. Feingold: 11.
44. OSS Document No. B-165, "American Zionists and the Palestine Resolution," 9 March 1944.
45. Feingold: 15.
46. AJC, "Decades of Decision: A Brief History of the American Jewish Committee," May 1983.
47. Quoted in Schiff: 177.
48. AJC, "Decades of Decision ... "
49. William J. Lanouette, "The Many Faces of the Jewish Lobby in America," *National Journal,* 13 May 1978.
50. *Ibid.*
51. *Detroit Free Press,* 18 April 1974.
52. AJC, "Statement on Arab-Israel Peace and the Middle East," adopted 18 May 1980.
53. Gary S. Schiff, "Middle East Centers at Selected American Universities," a report presented to the American Jewish Committee. AJC, 1981: 39.
54. Yankelovich, Skelly, and White, *Anti-Semitism in the United States,* vol. 1, *The Summary Report.* AJC Study, 1981: 45-46.
55. See Oscar Gass, "Vietnam—Resistance or Withdrawal?" *Commentary* 37/5 (May 1964); David Halberstam, "Getting the Story in Vietnam," *Commentary* 39/1 (January 1965); Maurice J. Goldbloom, "Foreign Policy," *Commentary* 39/6 (June 1965); Theodore Draper, "The Dominican Crisis," *Commentary* 40/6 (December 1965).
56. See Marc Galanter, "A Dissent on Brother Daniel," *Commentary* 36/1 (July 1963); Amos Elon, "Letter from the Sinai Front;" and Arthur Hertzberg, "Israel and American Jewry," *Commentary* 44/2 (August 1967).
57. See Nathan Glazer, "The Limits of Social Policy," *Commentary* 52/3 (September 1971), and "The Exposed American Jew," *Commentary* 59/6 (June 1979); Milton Himmelfarb, "Is American Jewry in Crisis?" *Commentary* 47/3 (March 1969); Bernard Avishai, "Breaking Faith: Commentary and the American Jews," *Dissent,* Spring 1981.
58. Joseph Shanan, "Why Breira?" *Commentary* 63/4 (April 1977); also Ruth Wisse, " 'Peace Now' & American Jews," *Commentary* 70/2 (August 1980).
59. See Jeane Kirkpatrick, "Dictatorship and Double Standards," *Commentary* 68/5 (November 1979); Richard Pipes, "Soviet Global Strategy," *Commentary* 69/4 (April 1980); Menachem Milson, "How to Make Peace with the Palestinians," *Commentary* 71/5 (May 1981).

AJCongress

60. AJCongress, "Not Charity But Justice: The Story of the American Jewish Congress:" 6.
61. AJCongress, *Congress Monthly,* May 1948.
62. Maslow: 22.

63. AJCongress, "A Program for the American Jewish Congress in 1983."

64. AJCongress, "Not Charity But Justice . . .": 19.

65. Reprinted as an undated AJCongress flyer.

66. *Jerusalem Post International Edition*, 7-13 December 1980.

67. AJCongress, "Not Charity But Justice . . .": 15.

68. *Jewish Telegraphic Agency*, 8 June 1982.

69. AJCongress, "AJCongress Update," *Congress Monthly*, September/October 1982.

70. Henry Siegman, "Israel in Lebanon: Are American Jews Divided?"; Henry Feingold, "How Israel Lost the War of Information"; Nancy Miller, "Years of Upheaval: The PLO in Lebanon," AJCongress, *Congress Monthly*, September/October 1982.

71. AJCongress, "Not Charity But Justice . . .": 15.

72. *Ibid:* 17.

73. AJCongress, "Where We Stand: The Mass Media," adopted by the AJCongress National Governing Council, 6 March 1983.

74. Schiff: 185.

75. Louis Rapoport, "A Man Whose 'Reflections' Cannot be Trusted," AJCongress, *Congress Monthly*, November 1982.

76. AJCongress, "Not Charity But Justice . . .": 15.

77. *Washington Post*, 12 March 1981.

78. *Jewish Telegraphic Agency*, 7 October 1983.

79. *Christian Science Monitor*, 17 March 1983.

ADL

80. Edward E. Grusd, *B'nai B'rith: The Story of a Covenant.* New York: Appleton-Century, 1966.

81. ADL, "Not the Work of a Day: The Story of the Anti-Defamation League of B'nai Brith," 1965.

82. *Ibid.*

83. Quotes from ADL, "ADL: Purpose and Program," 1966.

84. *Jewish Telegraphic Agency*, 18 November, 1983.

85. Maslow: 23-24.

86. ADL, IRS Form 990 for fiscal year 1 July 1981 to 30 June 1982.

87. ADL, *ADL Bulletin*, January 1949.

88. *The New Leader*, 27 May 1974.

89. Arnold Forster and Benjamin Epstein, *The New Anti-Semitism.* New York: McGraw Hill, 1974.

90. ADL, *ADL Bulletin*, September 1982.

91. *New York Times*, 1 January 1984.

92. ADL, "ADL: Purpose and Program": 8-9.

93. ADL, *ADL Bulletin*, September 1982.

94. *Jewish Telegraphic Agency*, 24 November 1980.

95. ADL, "Not the Work of a Day . . . ": 32.

96. ADL, "Extremist Groups in the United States: A Curriculum Guide," 1982.

97. *New York Times*, 25 June 1983.

98. *New York Times*, 8 March 1984.

Funding

CHAPTER III

Funding

Introduction: Channeling Resources

Within a year after the beginning of the June 1982 war in Lebanon, Israeli Prime Minister Menachem Begin was touring the United States and appealing for funds: three months later, the Israeli treasury had received $100 million in donations from American Jews.[1] On an annual basis, in addition to about $2.5 billion in direct U.S. government aid, Israel now receives nearly one billion dollars from organized fundraising in the American Jewish communities.[2] Money raised through this process falls into two categories: donations generated primarily by the UJA-Federation campaigns, and investment funds repayable at low interest within fifteen years, raised mainly by the Israel Bonds Organization. Israeli officials depend heavily on such fundraising as a source of quick cash injections into the economy, especially during periods of crisis, such as the Lebanon War or the tension-filled period prior to and during the June 1967 war. Some of the funds raised, especially those from the sale of Israel Bonds, are pumped directly into Israel's development budget and in fact constitute a substantial portion of it.[3] This mechanism frees funds for major items in Israel's regular budget, including military expenditure, while preserving the technically correct claim that American Jewish contributions to Israel are solely for humanitarian and developmental purposes.

Money raised for Israel by Jewish diaspora communities possesses a high symbolic value: it is a solid and obvious indication of diaspora Jewish identity with Jews in Israel and with what happens there. Irrespective of the amount collected every year, the process by which money is raised for Israel affects the American Jewish community in a number of ways: (1) it maintains the centrality of Israel in the campaign and keeps Israel-related issues on top of the agenda; (2) it steers the issues of discourse on Israel away from criticism of certain Israeli policies and toward a preoccupation with Israel's humanitarian, cultural, and educational needs; (3) it generates a positive and morally valid image of Israel for Jews and non-Jews alike.

American Jews are rightly known for their generous charitable support—support that has never been limited to Jewish causes alone. Their philanthropy is rooted in both religious tradition and social consciousness. Organized communal fundraising, specifically by Jews for Jews, can be

109

traced to the last decade of the nineteenth century, when the plight of Jewish immigrants to the United States and that of Jewish communities abroad inspired diverse charitable efforts.[4] The high degree of community involvement and concern was epitomized by the ubiquitous blue collection-box (*pushke*), carried door to door by thousands of Jewish children and always present in Jewish homes, shops, and centers, where coins were deposited in it as a matter of daily routine. Until the beginning of World War I, the organization of fundraising reflected existing division within American Jewry: between Zionists and non-Zionists, Russian and German Jews, Reform and Orthodox, and so forth. In 1914, when it became apparent that European Jewish communities needed enormous amounts of money, the AJC convened a conference to unify the fundraising of all national Jewish organizations for this purpose. The conference appointed a five-member committee representing the various trends in the Jewish community and charged them to select one hundred "leading American Jews" to constitute the American Jewish Relief Committee. Louis Marshall was the president and Felix M. Warburg, the treasurer. On 27 November 1914, an umbrella organization, the Joint Distribution Committee of American Funds for the Relief of Jewish War Sufferers (JDC), was set up and entrusted with the distribution of funds collected for the relief of Jewish communities, primarily in Europe.

By the end of the war, however, the Zionist/non-Zionist dichotomy within the American Jewish community had become the most divisive factor in fundraising and the distribution of funds, pitting committed Zionists against those they called "social service barons"—the wealthy, philanthropic elite of the Jewish establishment.[5] American Zionists complained that not enough funds were being channeled to Palestine Jewry (the *Yishuv*). The low percentage of funds that went to Palestine between the two world wars reflects the fact that the non-Zionists then had the upper hand, but the allocation of funds remained a major focus of discussion within American Jewish philanthropy.

In 1925, angered by the minimal allotment of funds to Jews in Palestine, the Zionists withdrew from the united Jewish campaign and organized a separate United Palestine Appeal. Four years later, Chaim Weizmann, in his capacity as president of the WZO, established the Enlarged Jewish Agency (commonly known as the Jewish Agency), primarily in order to attract non-Zionist Jewish personalities, such as Albert Einstein, Felix Warburg, Louis Marshall, and the Rothschild family, to support the Zionist program.

As a response to the 1929 anti-Zionist riots in Palestine, the JDC and the American members of the JA agreed to join in an Allied Jewish Campaign, with a goal of raising $6 million. This united effort at fundraising was short-lived, however. The Allied Jewish Campaign was soon dissolved, ostensibly to permit "as much freedom of choice and support as possible." In fact, the Allied campaign was not succeeding: only

$1.5 million of the $6 million campaign goal had been collected.[6]

With Hitler's rise to power in 1933, another attempt at joint fundraising among American Jewry took the form of the United Jewish Appeal, but this effort also broke apart, and did not unite again on a permanent basis until the magnitude and aims of Nazi anti-Semitism became devastatingly clear in 1939. On the local level, however, there was increasing pressure to unify community fundraising drives. In 1937, the Council of Jewish Federations and Welfare Funds (CJF) took a leading role in initiating consultations with the JDC and JA "with a view of promoting the fullest cooperation between them and of securing from local Jewish welfare funds the maximum response to their appeals."[7] CJF's approach succeeded in involving local federations in the fundraising process by allowing the two organizations to cooperate while remaining separate. In this period the CJF began to acquire considerable influence, which was reflected in the emergence of the role of the local community organizations—the federations—in coordinating and conducting fundraising campaigns.

By 1939, and in response to the crisis in Europe, the JDC, the United Palestine Appeal (UPA), and the National Coordinating Committee Fund joined together to form the United Jewish Appeal for Refugee and Overseas Needs (UJA); they then announced a campaign for $20 million, of which over $15 million was actually raised. At the beginning of the 1941 fundraising campaign, the UJA was reconstituted in a way that would guarantee its continuity and avoid the need to renegotiate the basis of a united campaign each year. A new formula for dividing the funds was also devised, and during this period less than half the funds raised was allotted to UJA. The weight was gradually shifting from the national agencies to the local communities; the effective communal apparatus for raising the funds had become the local federation.

The 1948 campaign raised nearly $200 million, but the sums raised in the following year dropped by 30 percent.[8] This decline brought the tension to the surface: again the UJA complained that while it raised the issues that inspired contributions (in this case, Israel), the local welfare funds were keeping more and more of the money for community use. From 1945 to 1947, UJA's share of all community funds raised was about 72 percent. Following 1948, however, and until the 1967 war, that percentage dropped to 55 percent.[9]

After the passage of the 1947 UN resolution for the partition of Palestine, Golda Meir was dispatched to the United States to raise money for weapons. "The Jewish community in Palestine," she told her American Jewish audiences, "is going to fight to the very end. If we have arms to fight with, we will fight with them. If not, we will fight with stones in our hands. The Egyptian government can vote a budget to aid our antagonists. The Syrian government can do the same. We have no government. But we have millions of Jews in the Diaspora . . . I believe that they will realize the peril of our situation and do what they have to do." Golda Meir's

111

American Jewish audiences "listened . . . wept and . . . pledged money. By the time I came back to Palestine in March," she wrote in her autobiography, "I had raised $50 million, which was turned over at once for the Haganah's secret purchases of arms in Europe."[10]

Since that American fundraising tour by Meir, Israeli objectives have defined the specific issues for the annual campaigns; at various times, the acquisition of arms, the establishment of settlements for Jewish immigrants, and the extraordinary economic burdens of continuous hostilities with the Arabs have provided the broad issues. Only in 1978, and under domestic Israeli pressure, did the specific issue of rehabilitation of impoverished Jewish slums become a fundraising campaign focus, which took the form of UJA's Project Renewal.

American Jewish fundraising has become a well organized, highly professional, and deeply entrenched activity, focused to a great degree on Israeli needs. The fundraising network comprises two categories of organizations. The first grouping, whose funds are raised through tax-exempt contributions, includes UJA, UIA, JDC, Jewish National Fund of America, PEF Israel Endowment Funds, and the recently established New Israel Fund (NIF). In addition to these major organizations, scores of groups raise funds directly for specific Israeli institutions, such as universities, hospitals, and museums.

The second category attracts investment funds to Israel and puts money at the disposal of the Israeli government for borrowing on favorable terms. Major organizations in this category are: the State of Israel Bonds Organization (IBO), PEC Israel Economic Corporation, and AMPAL-American Israel Corporation. The funds these organizations invest are taxable under American law.

The flow of funds through these various organizations is represented schematically on the following chart:

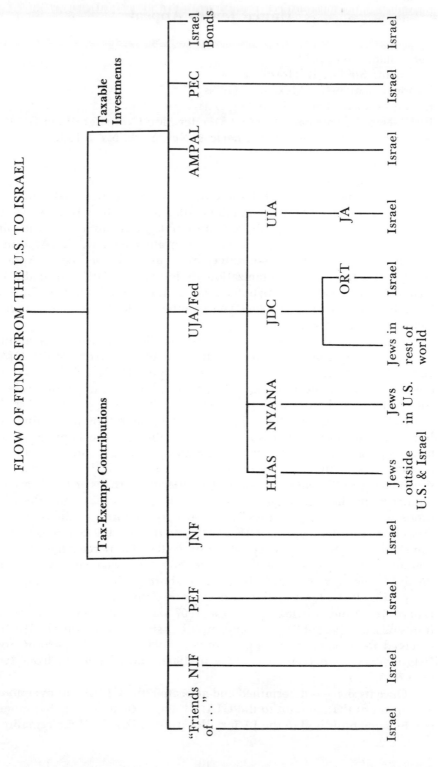

FLOW OF FUNDS FROM THE U.S. TO ISRAEL

United Jewish Appeal

Year established: 1939
President: Stanley B. Horowitz
National Chairman: Alexander Grass
Executive Vice-Chairman: Irving Bernstein
1985 General Chairman of the UJA-Federation Campaign: Ivan Boesky
Address: 1290 Avenue of the Americas, New York, NY 10104

General Background

Since its inception in 1939, the UJA has been the principal American Jewish fundraising organization in the United States. The UJA is registered with the IRS as "a not-for-profit corporation organized to serve as the joint fundraising organization for its two corporate members, the American Jewish Joint Distribution Committee, Inc. and the United Israel Appeal, Inc." It is a tax-exempt organization under Section 501(c)(3) of the Internal Revenue Code; contributors can deduct their UJA contributions from their taxable income. The UJA's counterpart for fundraising in other countries is Keren Hayesod.

The source of the UJA's funds is its allotment from the annual UJA-Federation central campaign; since about 80 percent of the UJA's annual revenue is channeled to Israel, support for Jewish life there is obviously paramount on its agenda. The fundraising campaign has been community-based from the outset, with the local federations doing the actual fundraising and the UJA national organization presenting the Israel-related issues. Concessions between the two are hammered out before the campaign starts ("pre-campaign budgeting") and again after it is over ("post-campaign allocating"). M.L. Raphael, in his *Understanding American Jewish Philanthropy*, asserts that "there is perhaps no single area as important in the campaign as that of ranking priorities and allocating funds among these priorities."[11] Usually communities adhere to the guidelines supplied by the CJF and UJA; in fact, the major direction comes from the Jewish Agency, which indicates what percentage or dollar amount it anticipates from the United States for that year. Generally, the guidelines give the UJA the greatest share of the regular campaign, along with all the funds collected from special appeals, such as the Israel Emergency Fund instituted after the 1967 war. Of the total community funds raised as part of the regular campaigns since World War II, UJA has received about 60 percent: 47 percent from 1939 to 1944; 72 percent from 1945 to 1948; 55 percent from 1948 to 1966; and 67 percent from 1967 to 1978.[12]

Once its share is determined and allocated, the UJA hands over about 80 percent of that amount to the UIA, which, in turn, moves that money (in the same building) to the JA for allocation to Israel. Of the remaining part of UJA's share, 10 to 12 percent is allocated to the JDC, and about 3 percent to the New York Association for New Americans (NYANA) and the Hebrew Immigrant Aid Society (HIAS). Of the allocations that it receives from the UJA, the JDC spends about 32 percent in Israel. On the average, therefore, about half of the total funds raised by the UJA-Federation central campaign goes to Israel. The other half of the money raised is distributed primarily for the support of Jewish community needs in the United States through community-based projects and major community organizations, which receive a certain annual budget. Some of the money is allocated to support Jewish communities in other parts of the world through the JDC. (See the chart below.)

UJA/FEDERATION COMMUNITY CAMPAIGN FUNDS

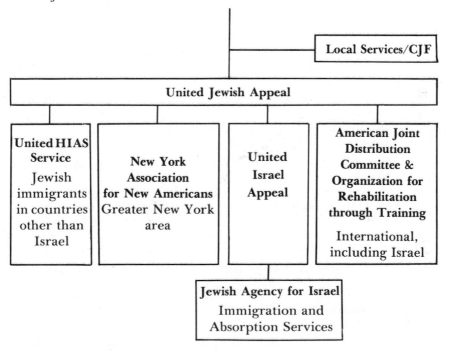

Who Gives to UJA?

As the UJA's 1981 annual report states: "From its inception through December 31, 1980, UJA received $5.1 billion as its share of community campaigns, expended $218 million for its national operations, and distributed $4.9 billion to its beneficiary organizations." These are impressive sums; Jews comprise only 3 percent of the total U.S. population, yet the UJA's budget is one-third that of United Way.[13] In 1980, the UJA-Federation central campaign, raised $508 million; the UJA's allotment came to $307 million, or 60 percent, from which $261 million went to the

UIA and on to Israel. Since then, the central campaign has continued to raise over one half billion dollars annually, with steady increases each year. The goal for 1983 was a 40 percent increase over the 1982 total of $567 million. Because a large proportion of the money raised is in the form of large gifts, the UJA operates on an overhead of about 4.5 percent.[14]

About 44 percent of total campaign funds comes from contributions of between $10,000 and $500,000. In the 1973 UJA-Federation campaign, four families in New York each contributed $5 million. Eighteen percent of UJA donors contribute 80 percent of the total funds. In 1979, there were 649 donors in the $50,000 to $100,000 category, and in 1980, over 700; the 1981 UJA annual report announced the decision to "upgrade" these donations by a minimum of 25 percent. In the same time period, more than 800 people made contributions of $100,000 and over. Observers estimate that about 50 percent of American Jews donate to the UJA, although the range differs from one Jewish community to the next. Wolf Blitzer, the Washington correspondent of the *Jerusalem Post*, recently wrote that "only around 10 percent of 500,000 Jews in the Los Angeles area give to the local federation.... In the smaller communities, the percentages increase.... In the approximately 12,000 member Jewish community of Columbus, Ohio, ... some 60 or 70 percent give to the local federation.... In the tiny Jewish communities scattered around southern Illinois, the local federation reaches out to around 90 percent of the Jews...."[15]

In 1983, UJA received more than $1,000 through one New York taxi driver, Leo Edelstein, who has driven a cab for twenty-five of his sixty-eight years. He told this story:

> The other day, a man asked how much for an hour's ride. "Twenty dollars," I said. After two and a half hours, the man prepared to pay. "It's $50," I said, "but how would you like to write a check to UJA for a little more?"
>
> The man wrote a $100 check and he wasn't even Jewish, he was Irish. The passenger said he was in a high tax bracket. How do I know? Who cares? UJA got $100. That I know.[16]

Role: The Politics of Fundraising

The UJA's primary and explicit function is fundraising; *The American Jewish Yearbook* describes the UJA as an organization that "channels funds for overseas humanitarian aid, supporting immigration and settlement in Israel, rehabilitation and relief in 30 nations, and refugee assistance in [the] U.S. through [the] Joint Distribution Committee, United Israel Appeal, United HIAS Service, and New York Association for New Americans."[17] According to the *Wall Street Journal*, UJA's Israel-bound funds are "providing a major portion of that country's special-welfare budget."[18] However, the methods, results, and impact of UJA's fundraising have always been closely intertwined with political developments in Israel and among American Jews.

The peak of UJA's fundraising activities was reached during the 1974

Yom Kippur War Campaign, which raised $660 million. More than half the donations in that year came from contributions of $10,000 and over. By 1979, the UJA-Federation campaign had experienced a decline of 27 percent in the amount raised; UJA officials explain this trend in terms of the changing demography of the Jewish population in the United States, rather than as a result of popular misgivings toward the UJA. In any case, it is evident that Israel's involvement in wars, regardless of the outcome of the conflict, affects to a large degree the level of money raised.

In 1948, for example, when the newly-established Israel was at war with Arab countries, an unprecedented $200 million was raised; however, the 1951-1955 central campaigns averaged only $115 million a year, and the percentage allocated to domestic community needs increased. This decline may be attributed to two main factors: first, once Israel was actually established and the 1948 war threat had passed, American Jews turned more to their own communal needs; and second, most European Jews had already been resettled in Israel, and the priority of the Israeli government was funding *aliyah* from Arab countries. As Abraham J. Karp noted in his history of the UJA: "The needs of the Jews in Moslem lands were not as dramatic as those of the postwar refugees in Europe. Their need to emigrate did not seem quite so urgent. American Jewry, almost wholly of European origin, could identify more with the plight of European Jews."[19] The galvanizing effects of the 1967 and 1977 wars were also clearly reflected by the fundraising figures. The 1967-1978 central campaigns raised more than $4.7 billion, of which the UJA's allocation was about $3.2 billion, approximately 67 percent of the total.[20]

In addition to raising funds, UJA's promotional campaigns perform an important public relations function that touches hundreds of Jewish communities throughout the United States. These events are well publicized in strictly humanitarian terms of meeting social needs within Israel. "The yearly UJA-Federation Appeal," as one observer put it, "is perceived by its American Jewish donors as a way to contribute money to Israel. In fact, UJA promotes itself as an Israel-related organization."[21] Through the annual fundraising process, the UJA fosters a positive climate for specific Israeli needs, and also strengthens the emotional bonds between Israel and American Jews. The UJA's most well known slogan—"We Are One"—expresses the ideological basis of pro-Israelism and urges Jews to reaffirm their solidarity by the act of giving. In an instruction booklet for solicitors, the UJA put it this way:

When you ask for a gift you're talking about the most important needs affecting our Jewish people in Israel, at home and in other lands. At the same time you are giving your prospect the opportunity to express his Jewish identification in a way that counts...*Do* make your listener feel that giving is not charity but self-taxation—paying his or her fair share to assure Jewish survival and continuity and to preserve the quality of Jewish life everywhere.[22]

117

In the UJA's 1983 promotional literature, potential donors were urged to "share the vision, give to life," by supporting programs for children from single parent families, for senior citizens in American Jewish communities, for "purchase of specialized farm equipment for one family on a new border *moshav*" in Israel, for a Jewish day school in North Africa or a Jewish home for the aged in Eastern Europe.[23] Beyond the image of comprehensive concern for the Jews of the world, contributing to the UJA specifically serves to reinforce psychological support for the state of Israel as a haven for the homeless in a hostile world.

In the view of Irving Bernstein, the UJA's executive vice-chairman, "in many American communities the UJA has become a surrogate synagogue. For the secular and assimilated Jews of America, the UJA Campaign provides the sole link between the Jews and the spirituality and centrality of Israel."[24] How this link is interpreted, however, is determined by events in Israel, the region, and internationally. In the fall of 1976, responding to the 1975 UN resolution on Zionism and racism, the UJA organized an event called "This Year in Jerusalem," during which a flotilla of jets "carrying three thousand Jewish men and women from hundreds of communities of all sizes in all fifty states" flew to Israel. More than any other activity, observed one sympathetic writer, this event "underlined the power of Israel in the life of American Jewish communities, exposed the emotional heart of their essentially Israel-oriented campaigns and highlighted the UJA's role as a catalyst in providing the means for effective community expression of oneness with Israel's people."[25]

In 1978, the UJA launched Project Renewal—a sweeping rehabilitation program for Israel's impoverished Jewish immigrant neighborhoods. The program has achieved a departmental status in the JA, and the UJA has established a National Project Renewal Committee for it. Through the UJA, U.S. donors have pledged more than $100 million to Project Renewal since it was inaugurated. When Robert Loup visited Israel upon his election as UJA's national chairman following the Camp David Accords, he denied that peace with Egypt constituted a potential problem for UJA's fundraising efforts. Citing Project Renewal in particular, he emphasized that "United States Jewry has got to understand that our partnership, through the UJA, is not based on war or peace—but on a desire to enhance the quality of Jewish life, both in Israel and the U.S." Thus, Project Renewal is "becoming increasingly focal in UJA campaigning." It represents, he said, "the opportunity for our generation, for those who were not able to contribute towards Israel's birth, to be part of Israel's rebirth."[26]

The UJA, Loup maintained, is interested in "raising Jews through education as much as in raising money."[27] Or, as longtime UJA leader Irving Bernstein once put it, "At one time we used the campaign to raise money. Now we use the campaign to raise Jews."[28]

Based on its bylaws (as amended in 1980), the UJA corporation is composed of the two members on whose behalf it raises funds, and the UIA. The UJA is governed by a forty-three member board of trustees, twelve of whom are selected by the JDC, twelve by the UIA, seven by the CJF, seven by the national campaign officers, the president of the board, the national chair, and the last three living past presidents of the UJA. In addition to a standing executive committee, management policy and operations committee, and transactions committee, the board is empowered to create any number of additional committees it deems necessary; in the past these have included committees for budget and finance, audit, assets realization, legacies, and CJF/UJA liaison.[29]

The entire UJA bureaucracy, with its numerous divisions and committees, is structured around the fundraising process. The most power rests with the officers of the national campaign, headed by the national chair, the executive vice-chair (who is "the principal professional manager of the Annual Campaign"), and a number of associate and assistant executive vice-chairs, as deemed necessary.

The UJA's fundraising effectiveness is derived from its ability to mobilize hundreds of local Jewish communities in coordination with the local federations. Regional operations come under the direction of one vice-chair. On the local level, 200 front-line professional staff members administer eight regions, including 210 federated and 455 non-federated communities throughout the United States.*

To enhance its ability to raise funds from specialized sectors of the Jewish population, the UJA has created six organizational components: the Women's Division, the Young Leadership Cabinet, the Young Women's Leadership Cabinet, the Rabbinic Cabinet, the Faculty Cabinet, and the University Programs Department. For each major division, headed by a chairperson and a director, there is a nationally distributed newsletter that serves to connect the members and keep them abreast of relevant developments in the United States and Israel.

UJA's National Women's Division, established in 1946, is the oldest of the major organizational components, and at present, about 200,000 women in 335 communities are said to participate actively. The Women's Division issues a *News Update* for campaign chairs, speakers, and national board members, and also provides fundraising suggestions and instructions for their implementation. A divisional speakers' bureau sends women to some two hundred major annual events throughout the United States. Funds collected are allocated for such Israel-based projects as the absorption

---

*The regional divisions, with their headquarters, are: Northeast (New York City); Mid-Atlantic (Philadelphia); Southeast (Atlanta); Florida (Miami); East Central (Cleveland); West Central (Chicago); Southwest (Dallas); and Western (Los Angeles). Each division has a regional chairperson.

of Jewish immigrants, the building of nursery schools and libraries, the expansion of vocational training programs, and the improvement of housing.

The Young Leadership Cabinet, established in 1977, is "committed to the creative survival of Jews, Judaism and Israel through dialogues with leading scholars and writers, and through peer exchanges at retreats, conferences, missions to Israel and special programs." Annual leadership conferences in March of each year bring Jewish teenagers together for what is described as Jewish consciousness-building and a "return to the days of the old." A recent profile of the 1980 UJA Young Leadership Cabinet described "a cadre of well-educated, upwardly mobile, communally active young Jewish men who . . . share an intense commitment to Jewish survival, security and well-being and who identify strongly with the Jewish people and its religious and cultural traditions."[30]

The Rabbinic Cabinet was established in 1972 "to promote rabbinic leadership support for local and national UJA campaigns through education and personal commitment; to make use of rabbinic resources on behalf of UJA and Israel." The Faculty Cabinet, established in 1975, serves a parallel function for the campus, while UJA's other campus division, the University Programs Department, established in 1970, is intended "to crystallize Jewish commitment on the campus through an educational fundraising campaign involving various programs, leadership training, and opportunities for participation in community functions."

In addition to these basic structural components, the UJA maintains a separate public information section that includes a speakers' bureau, a public relations department, a creative and educational programs department, and a research department.

Fundraising Programs

The UJA apparatus includes numerous programs and committees that sponsor national fundraising events and overseas missions, devise programs to target particular donation categories, provide solicitor training, and organize special or emergency appeals. While these programs are generally ongoing, they are not all employed in each annual campaign.

Since the 1981 campaign, increased executive attention has been given to the Major Gifts Program (donations of $10,000 and over). Three national committees have been set up, targeting contributions of $100,000 and over, $50,000 to $100,000, and $10,000 to $50,000. The $10,000 to $50,000 committee sponsors "missions" to Washington, where its contributors meet with high government officials. In 1980, 165 participants in this one-day "mission" met with Vice President George Bush and attended a reception with thirty-five senators. For its part, the $100,000-minimum committee (called the *hineni* committee, from the Hebrew "here I am") attracts new donations through even more elaborate events, such as the 1981 "Prime Minister's Mission"—a guided tour to Israel that featured a meeting with the prime minister—and the International Leadership Meeting, reserved for contributors of $250,000 or more. The Major Gifts Program gets further support from Operation Breakthrough, a program that includes solicitor training in individual communities and leadership training sessions, long-range community consultation projects, training missions conducted in cooperation with the Overseas Programs Department, and direct solicitation.

Contributions of $10,000 and under fall into UJA's Intermediate and Small Gifts Program, which is subdivided into three categories—$1,000 to $10,000, under $1,000, and a New Gifts Program. Operation Upgrade solicits donors of $1,000 to $10,000 through close community work. Intensive training seminars, involving the top leadership, are aimed at new solicitors as well as experienced ones. Individuals contributing $1,000 and less are targeted through the Department of Special Appeals, which uses mass campaign programs such as the National Super Sunday, the National Walk-A-Thon, and direct mail solicitation. The Department of Special Appeals also offers training in appointment making and telephone techniques.

The New Gifts Program was established in 1980 as a "pragmatic response to critical issues affecting campaigns in the '80s, including the potential for growth in campaigns among non-givers, shifts in the distribution of the American Jewish population towards Sunbelt communities, and significant changes in the social, marital, professional and religious characteristics of American Jews in the 25-40 age group.[31] Among the tools this program has developed to identify and solicit new contributors are the Standard Jewish Demographic Kit, designed to help communities in campaign planning, and the "Jewish Families on the Move" demonstration project, intended to provide a national system to track down the 500,000 Jewish households that change residence each year.

In 1981, some 5,500 people from 340 Jewish communities in all 50 states participated in UJA-sponsored missions to Israel. The emotional impact of such missions greatly increases contributions and activism. After a previously uninvolved New York businessman, Don Gould, attended a six-day Men's Mini-Mission to Israel in 1968, his contributions to UJA went up 1,000 percent, and by 1973 he was chairman of UJA's National Young Leadership Conference.[32] Similarly, a Washington, D.C. investment banker who went on a one-week "discovery mission" to Israel in 1980 increased his annual donation from one thousand to twenty-one thousand dollars a year. He has also been instrumental in soliciting twenty-five additional donations a year, ranging from five hundred to twenty-five thousand dollars.[33]

The first UJA Winter President's Mission raised almost $3.3 million for the 1982 campaign. One hundred thirty-three participants from thirty-six communities throughout the United States spent five days in Israel and increased their total contributions at the end of the event by 33 percent over 1981. Their program included an opening dinner where they met with "46 new immigrants from threatened Jewish communities throughout the world and heard moving stories of their lives and experiences." They visited "settlements in the Negev, where Sinai farming families are being relocated by the Jewish Agency," and received "a special background briefing in Ariel, a settlement on the West Bank," by defense minister Ariel Sharon. They also toured Project Renewal neighborhoods and visited homes of "prominent Israelis," such as Jerusalem mayor Teddy Kollek and members of the Knesset. The mission culminated in a visit with the president of Israel.[34]

Process: The Annual Campaign

The UJA-Federation fundraising process has become fairly established, with tested techniques and a fixed annual schedule. The main components are: missions of selected contributors to Israel and Washington, Super Sunday telethons, regional major gifts meetings, kick-off "pace-setter" luncheons and banquets, and specific divisional activities.

The private phase of the campaign starts with closed-door consultations between representatives of the Jewish community in the United States and JA officials. During these meetings, the JA presents its needs for the following calendar year, and concessions and compromises are worked out between the local needs of the Jewish community and the Israel-based needs of the JA. Once an acceptable formula is reached, a tentative plan for raising the necessary funds is developed by the national chair and the executive vice-chair. These officers are in charge of the important Long Range Planning Committee, the main function of which is to develop an annual profile of existing and potential contributors; in this task they are assisted by the advisory National Leadership Campaign Policy Board and the marketing research firm of Yankelovich, Skelly, and White. Once the profile is prepared, usually by July, executive-level briefings are conducted in the company of key community leaders, in order to explore the ways in which the UJA can be most effective in the overall operation of the annual campaign. The plan is then presented to the National Leadership Conference.

In the first half of the year, fundraising drives open in all eight national regions. Many Israeli officials and top personalities crisscross the country on behalf of the UJA while lining up meetings with key U.S. congressional, executive, and foreign policy decision-makers. The full year of luncheons, banquets, telephoning, direct mail, missions, and face-to-face solicitation culminates in a closed-door pledge banquet in December.

The UJA accelerates its fundraising during the religious holidays. These periods mark a renewal of communal contacts, which become opportunities for the reaffirmation of Jewish identity via participation in the efforts of the UJA. The holidays also create a time for positive news, which indirectly aids the work of the UJA as well. During the 1981 Passover season, for example, President Reagan issued a message and later proclaimed the week of May 10 as Jewish Heritage Week. The public, mass-appeal phase of the national campaign opens later, in January or February, with the Super Sunday volunteer telethon.[35] In different Jewish communities across the United States, thousands of volunteers staff the phones at UJA-Federation offices and solicit pledges from prospective donors. In greater New York and Manhattan, 2230 volunteers calling on one Sunday in February 1982 secured pledges of over $2 million. In eastern Long Island, during the same period, 250 volunteers obtained pledges totaling $271,000. In the Washington, D.C. area, in late January 1983, 1500 volunteers called 50,000 of the city's 180,000 Jews; by 9:00 p.m. they had reached their goal of $1.7 million. Super Sunday '82 raised a total of $25,260,091 through volunteer telethons involving 26,114 volunteers in 102 communities. The 1981 Super Sunday had raised $19.1 million.

Gearing up for and carrying out the annual campaign involve the active participation of the entire UJA-CJF network. Volunteers in local federations are encouraged to study Dun and Bradstreet, deed transfers, and corporate proxies in order to identify and estimate the net worth of wealthy Jews in their communities. These contacts are then encouraged to "discuss what they know about the finances of neighbors, friends and colleagues. A physician who gives might be expected to help assess the finances of other physicians."[36]

Personal solicitation is one of the major techniques used in UJA fundraising. The communal fundraising network is further reinforced through a publication called the *Book of Life*, containing the names and addresses of individual contributors and the amounts donated. The book is circulated among members of the Jewish community. A fundraising technique known as "card calling" involves a roll call of guests at major meetings and banquets. Starting with the names of the biggest givers, the amount of each pledge is read aloud and the donor stands for recognition. Future pledges are secured by another method known as a "declaration of intent," whereby prospective donors promise certain gifts during their lifetimes or in their wills.

UJA contributors are urged to contact non-contributors. As one UJA official put it, "It's not enough to give your money; we like to see people helping others to give."[37] There is a big reliance on psychic rewards and community pressure. Large donors receive awards at UJA dinners, are named to chair committees, and are lionized in Jewish newspapers. Those who decline to contribute can face pressure and ostracism. In Pittsburgh's heavily Jewish Westmoreland Country Club, according to the *Wall Street Journal*, "If a non-giver wants to join, someone will mention, in a nice way of course, that behaving responsibly means remembering Jewish philanthropies. . . . An influential lawyer active in several charities favors tougher methods, including ostracism if friendly persuasion doesn't work."[38]

Most training of volunteer solicitors is done on the job. In addition, they see films about Israel and about successful UJA programs in other Jewish communities, and they are taught how to educate prospective donors about the financial needs of the Jewish community and Israel. They are encouraged to use emotion-packed topics in their appeal, such as the Holocaust, terrorist attacks, and anti-Semitism. "I call this educational process," said Aryeh Nesher, UJA's head of training, "Jewish spiritual circumcision."[39] Telethon callers work from a prepared script. Those in the New York UJA-Federation headquarters can watch a teleprompter with the message, "You reunited families... Every gift is a gift of love... More because more people need us... Every gift is a gift of life... You re-settle Israeli families... You help the deaf to hear."

The 1983 Campaign

The UJA's response to the Israeli invasion of Lebanon was to redouble its campaign efforts. Events were geared to demonstrating American Jewry's moral support to Israel in the face of international criticism and to providing financial aid. The 1983 campaign was inaugurated in September 1982 with what National Chairman Loup called "Liftoff '83"—a three-day meeting in New York for 150 major contributors who had each pledged a minimum of $100,000. The roster of speakers at the meeting included Secretary of State George Shultz, former Israeli foreign minister Abba Eban, and Moshe Arens, then Israeli ambassador to the United States. Accompanied by actress Molly Picon and former New York mayor Abe Beame, the group visited Ellis Island—the first landing point for millions of Jewish immigrants to the United States. Evening entertainment included a dinner performance by Oscar-winning composer Marvin M. Hamlisch and visits to the homes of prominent New Yorkers.

The three-day kick-off led into a "National Fly-In"; between Rosh Hashana and Yom Kippur, three teams of leading Israeli personalities and politicians, together with UJA leaders, canvassed cities all over the United States in an intensive fundraising effort, with the Israelis speaking about Israeli achievements and needs and the Americans soliciting. This stage of the campaign was not directed at the grassroots, but at wealthy Jews who, in the estimation of the UJA, could contribute more than they had in the past. Contributors in outlying areas might be flown to the larger cities to meet with important personalities.[40]

The main event of the campaign was the October 1982 Campaign Leadership Mission to Israel, organized during the National Fly-In for contributors of $10,000 or more. Approximately one thousand UJA supporters from all over the country participated; in a public demonstration of solidarity, the group marched through Jerusalem to the Western

Wall, singing and dancing and carrying banners with the UJA slogan, "We Are One." At the West Bank settlement of Elkanna, defense minister Ariel Sharon, in a widely covered speech, called on U.S. Jews for support. At the final gathering, which was attended by Menachem Begin, it was announced that the mission had generated a total of $24 million in pledges.[41]

Targeting big givers for the 1983 campaign continued with specialized events; contributors of $250,000 and over were flown to Geneva to meet with delegations from various countries; contributors of $50,000 or more were treated to exclusive meetings in Washington with representatives of the White House, the Pentagon, the Congress, and high-ranking Israeli diplomats.

The "pace-setter" banquets also started during this time and continued into the early part of 1983. In November 1982, the banquet launching the South Shore, Long Island 1983 drive brought over four hundred guests to hear former secretary of state Alexander Haig. Haig spoke of the "non-confrontational stance" between the United States and Israel in Lebanon, against the PLO, and in favor of the "vital importance of maintaining the spirit of Camp David." The South Shore Jewish leaders pledged nearly $4 million to the UJA-Federation 1983 Campaign—a 20 percent increase over the year before.[42]

United Israel Appeal

Year established: 1925
Chairman: Irwin S. Field
Executive Vice-Chairman: Irving Kessler
Address: 515 Park Avenue, New York, NY 10022
Publications: *Briefings*

General Background

In 1921, Chaim Weizmann, then president of the WZO, established Keren Hayesod (the [Palestine] Foundation Fund) in the United States in order to tap money from American Jewry in support of the Zionist program in Palestine. Though Zionist leaders such as Louis Brandeis discouraged him at first from setting high expectations for American Jewish support, Weizmann went ahead, and the initial response proved him right. Simultaneously, however, the JNF also claimed to be the sole fundraising arm for the WZO. The two began competing over the same source of money for the same cause, although Keren Hayesod had a more generalized appeal than the JNF, which focused on land reclamation. In 1925, the two organizations were combined for fundraising purposes, and, in 1927, they became the United Palestine Appeal (UPA).

This situation lasted until 1939 when, because of the need for much larger amounts of money, the UJA was created as the principal fundraising organization for both the UPA (which became the UIA after 1948) and the JDC. At that point UPA/UIA stopped its fundraising activity altogether and became the major beneficiary of UJA funds or, as one official described it, a "standby organization."[43] Thus, while Keren Hayesod became the principal fundraising organization among Jews in over sixty countries throughout the world, the UJA assumed that role in the United States.

Structure and Role

The UIA describes itself as the "link between [the] American Jewish community and [the] Jewish Agency for Israel, its operating agent," and indicates that it "assists in resettlement and absorption of refugees in Israel, and supervises [the] flow of funds and expenditures for this purpose." In other words, as the major recipient of funds raised by the UJA, the UIA serves as a conduit, retaining about four percent of its allocation for administrative and managerial costs and forwarding the rest to the JA.

In addition to the funds it receives annually from the UJA, the UIA has, since 1971, received support from the U.S. government. Between 1972 and 1976, Washington provided the UIA with about $121 million for the "resettlement of Soviet refugees in Israel." In 1980, U.S. government aid to the UIA was $20.2 million, and, in 1981, about $28 million, or about 10 percent of UIA's total income for the year.[44]

The UIA is a tax-exempt corporation registered in the state of New York. According to its bylaws (as amended on 25 January 1953), the UIA consists of 120 persons, 72 representing Keren Hayesod and 48 representing American Jewish communities in consultation with the CJF.[45] This means that the UIA is structurally controlled by Keren Hayesod, which is in turn controlled by the Zionist Organization of America (with majority votes), the Poale Zion Party of America, the Mizrachi Organization of America, and Hadassah (the Women's Zionist Organization of America). Under the specific control of the Zionist establishment in the United States, then, the UIA is the link in the transfer of funds from the American Jewish community to the Jewish Agency for Israel.

American Jewish Joint Distribution Committee

Year established: 1914
President: Heinz Eppler
Executive Vice-President: Saul B. Cohen
Address: 60 East 42nd Street, New York, NY 10165
Publications: *JDC Annual Report, JDC World*

General Background

The JDC was established in November 1914, following the outbreak of World War I. From its original name, the Joint Distribution Committee of American Funds for the Relief of Jewish War Sufferers, it was known for a long time, especially among Jews from Europe, as the "Joint." During its first year, it was entrusted with the funds raised by the Orthodox Central Committee for the Relief of Jews, the American Jewish Relief Committee, and the People's Relief Committee.

The JDC was the charitable arm of the "non-ideological and non-political" Jewish establishment; it was known as "an organization committed to the principle that Jews should be helped to remain in the countries of their birth rather than to emigrate to Palestine."[46] As a result, Zionists considered the JDC a tool of non-Zionist groups such as the AJC, and the pre-1948 period was filled with the virulent clashes between the JDC and the UPA. In 1941, UPA chairman Rabbi Abba Hillel Silver attacked American Jewish philanthropists for giving "all aid to the Jewries of Eastern and Central Europe, but only a pittance to that visionary project of impractical idealists in Palestine." He charged that such JDC projects as refugee resettlement in Soviet Biro-Bidjan or Santo Domingo were actually attempts to "strangle" the Zionist movement by the "single device of starving it to death."[47]

Despite these conflicts, the UPA and the JDC both joined the central UJA campaign from 1941 outward, though for different reasons: events in Europe and community pressure forced the philanthropic leadership out of their anti-Zionist positions, while for their part, the Zionists knew full well that without the support of the Jewish establishment, sufficient funds for Palestine could not be raised. In 1941, the JDC received 63 percent of the UJA allotment, and the UPA, 37 percent. However, the establishment of Israel dramatically reversed this situation: by 1949, the UPA was receiving approximately half of UJA funds, and its total receipts from all funding sources were $8 million, more than JDC's international budget. In addition, the JDC itself altered its stance toward Israel, as evidenced by its allotments to its Palestine/Israel program, which increased from $2 million in 1946 to $24 million in 1949.[48]

Role

The JDC operates under the motto that "Jews in need should be helped and should be helped to live as Jews." According to its statement of purpose, the JDC "organizes, and finances rescue, relief, and rehabilitation programs for imperiled and needy Jews overseas; conducts [a] wide range of health, welfare, rehabilitation, education programs and aid to cultural and religious institutions; programs benefitting 300,000 Jews in 30 countries overseas. Major areas of operation are Israel, North Africa and Europe."

In its 1982 budget, Israel-based programs received the largest share, about 32 percent. The rest of the budget was divided geographically, with 21 percent for "relief-in-transit" (for emigrants from the Soviet Union and Eastern Europe), 19 percent for Eastern Europe, 14 percent for "Moslem countries," 19 percent for Western Europe, 1.8 percent for "Africa and Asia," and 2.9 percent for Latin America.

About a third of JDC's 1982 operating budget was distributed to relief and welfare, and over one-fifth to Jewish education; these are the two largest categories. The rest of the budget was distributed, in decreasing order of magnitude, to services for the aged, health services, program management, social development, advanced education and manpower development, and others.

In 1982, the JDC allocated $11.3 million to Israel for over one hundred programs for the aged, the chronically ill, and the mentally and physically handicapped. The JDC supported over 130 community centers, 170 *yeshivot* (religious schools), and programs for technical and vocational training through the Organization for Rehabilitation through Training (ORT). (American ORT Federation, another New York-based tax-exempt organization, provides vocational training for Jews in fourteen countries, principally in Israel. In 1982 it spent over $7.5 million on its programs.) From 1914 until the end of 1982, the JDC spent a total of $1.4 billion, of which about $278 million (20 percent) went to Israel.

Flow of Funding

Since the JDC is not an active fundraising organization, it relies on allotments from the UJA, which provides between 70 and 90 percent of JDC's annual budget. These funds represent 10 to 12 percent of UJA's total allotments, which means that the JDC is the second largest UJA beneficiary, after the UIA. In addition to the UJA, JDC's other source of funds is the U.S. government, which provides financial support for JDC's programs for the resettlement of Jewish emigrants from the Soviet Union, plus donations-in-kind of foodstuffs and clothing from the U.S. Department of Agriculture. In 1981, JDC's total revenue was close to $52 million, of which approximately $13 million, or one-fourth, was U.S. government aid; the UJA provided $36 million, and private revenues accounted for the remainder. Of the $40-odd million disbursed by the JDC in 1982, $37.8 million came from the UJA, $1.1 million from the U.S. government, and $1.8 million from donations-in-kind. The JDC also receives relatively small contributions from Jewish communities in Canada, Latin America, South Africa, and elsewhere.[49]

129

Jewish National Fund
(Keren Kayemeth LeIsrael)

Year established: 1901
President: Charlotte Jacobson
Executive Vice-President: Samuel I. Cohen
Address: 42 East 69th Street, New York, NY 10021
Publications: *JNF Almanac, Land and Life*

General Background

Hermann Shapira, a Lithuanian rabbi and professor of mathematics, first proposed the creation of a Jewish fund for the acquisition of land in Palestine at the first Zionist Congress, held in Basle, Switzerland in 1897. The proposal did not get enough backing, however, until the fifth Zionist Congress in 1901, when the JNF was created as "a trust for the Jewish people, which can be used exclusively for the purchase of land in Palestine and Syria." With that legal status, the JNF soon became the sole fundraising arm of the WZO for the acquisition of land in Palestine.[50]

Following the creation of Israel, the Knesset adopted the *Keren Kayemeth LeIsrael Law, 5714/1953*, which authorized the minister of justice to incorporate the JNF in Israel "with a view to continuing the activities of the Existing Company that had been founded and incorporated in the Diaspora." In 1954, the new Israeli corporation acquired all the assets and liabilities of the JNF that was incorporated in England in 1907. The "primary object of the Association" was now "to purchase, acquire on lease or in exchange, or receive on lease or otherwise, lands, forests, rights of possession, easements and any similar rights as well as immovable properties of any class, in the prescribed region (which expression shall in this Memorandum mean the State of Israel in any area within the jurisdiction of the Government of Israel) or in any part thereof, for the purpose of settling Jews on such lands and properties" (Clause 3, Subclause a).

In an attempt to clarify the relationship between the JNF and the state of Israel, an agreement was signed in 1960 between the JNF and the Israeli government, stipulating that the JNF "shall continue to operate, as an independent agency of the World Zionist Organization, among the Jewish public in Israel and the Diaspora, raising funds for the redemption of land...and conducting informational and Zionist-Israel educational activities...."[51]

Until it was absorbed into the United Palestine Appeal in 1925, the JNF in the United States claimed to be the sole fundraising arm of the

WZO. Rather than remain a recipient organization of UJA funds, in 1951 the JNF reclaimed its independent status as a Zionist organization whose purpose was to raise funds from American Jewry for the reclamation and afforestation of lands in Israel. Today, the JNF in the United States—the territorial fundraising for the JNF in Israel—is registered in New York as a tax-exempt corporation.

Role

The JNF describes itself as the "exclusive fundraising agency of the world Zionist movement for the afforestation, reclamation, and development of the land of Israel, including the construction of roads and preparation of sites for new settlements," adding that it "helps emphasize the importance of Israel in schools and synagogues throughout the world." Until the creation of Israel, the JNF focused on land purchases. Subsequently, there has been a gradual shift in emphasis from land acquisition to land reclamation, road building, and various forms of assistance to new settlements, including well drilling, construction of dams and irrigation systems, and large-scale afforestation. Thousands of kilometers of Israeli roads connecting numerous and proliferating Jewish settlements all carry the symbol of the JNF; many public parks and forests also carry the JNF insignia. JNF operations since the 1967 war fall into three categories by location: (1) inside Israel's 1948 borders; (2) areas that had been "inaccessible to development" before the 1967 war, such as along the Syrian border and the Yarmuk River, as well as "East Jerusalem whose inclusion in Israel has become an established fact," and (3) "other lands now under Israel's jurisdiction...," referring to the West Bank, Gaza Strip, Golan Heights, and, most recently, the south of Lebanon.[52]

The projects of the JNF have an impact beyond their obvious agricultural and economic significance; in his speech at the eightieth National Assembly, JNF president Rabbi William Berkowitz proclaimed that "the JNF is also creating historic conditions, establishing strategic realities and forming geopolitical security certainties...." Since the 1960s, the JNF has closely cooperated with the Israeli army to build Nahal (Army Pioneer Settler Corps) outpost villages on border sites because of their strategic importance. The JNF has sponsored more than one hundred *mitzpim* (observation and lookout posts) that "put Israeli security into place." Road building also has a strategic importance; as Berkowitz noted: "... if today there is a vital conduit between Israel and her Christian allies in Lebanon, it is because of paved roads on the desolate Lebanese border. And who made it possible? The JNF."[53]

The information disseminated by the JNF in the United States is characterized by a romantic vision of Zionist settlement that either ignores the existence of an indigenous Palestinian population residing within Israeli borders in their own villages and towns or else portrays their very presence as a threat to Israel's security which must be overcome.* The political content of JNF's work is evident in its campaign to develop the Galilee, the area with the greatest Palestinian population concentration (nearly 300,000 people) within the 1967 borders of Israel. While in the Galilee as a whole (including Nahariya and Tiberias, 40 percent of the population is Jewish, as of 1980, in the hill areas Jews numbered only 77,000 out of a total population of 235,000.[55]

The Israeli government has been working to "Judaize the Galilee," in the phrasing of Israeli officials, precisely in order to change the present character of its demography and landholding, an issue that Labor Party Knesset member Gad Ya'acobi described, in comparison to the West Bank and Gaza Strip, as "more sensitive, more critical, and maybe even more problematic to the State of Israel in the years to come."[56] JNF land reclamation efforts conducted within the the Green Line (separating the area ruled by Israel since 1948 from those occupied in 1967) have thus been focused on the Galilee region. Through the efforts of the JNF and other agencies, one hundred settlements were built in the Galilee between 1977 and 1981; most of these are the small *mitzpim* (small outposts) aimed at "establishing a Jewish presence . . . ."[57] The Israel Land Administration and the JA offer special economic incentives to encourage Jewish settlement there.[58] Not surprisingly, the degree of hostility to Arabs is greater among Jews in the Galilee—where settlement efforts are centered—than it is elsewhere in Israel. A survey conducted by the Jewish-Arab Centre, the results of which were presented to a conference at Haifa University in 1984, disclosed that while 49 percent of Jews in Israel as a whole want the state to encourage Arab emigration, 57 percent of Jews in the Galilee share that sentiment, and 72 percent of them want restrictions imposed to prevent the Arabs from becoming a majority.[59]

*This is how Rabbi Berkowitz characterized the Galilee in his 1982 Presidential Address:
    "Let us turn now, and in the Biblical phrase, look to the North.
    "A recent issue of our JNF publication *Land and Life* carried on its cover the headline, 'Galilee: The Empty North' That phrase sums up the challenge Israel faces in the North, for there too, just as in the South, geopolitical and strategic significance attaches itself to the facts we are creating.
    "Are you aware that the population of the area between Acre and Safed is about 220,000 and that of this 65 percent are Arabs? Do you know that in some areas of the Galilee the Arab population has a numerical majority of as much as eight to one? We are speaking of a region that is critically important to the State of Israel, whose size amounts to 275,000 acres, yet whose Jewish population is a mere 32 percent!
    "Need I tell you how delicate the situation is? Need I tell you the implications of these statistics? Need I tell you of the campaign by radical Arabs to seize Jewish-owned land on which there is no visible Jewish presence?
    "Here too the Jewish National Fund is meeting the challenge, creating an infrastructure for the establishment of strategically vital new settlements as well as the expansion of existing settlements."[54]

Historically, the JNF relied on such fundraising techniques as selling trees in Israel, stamps, inscribing the names of large contributors in what was called the Golden Book, and of course, the famous Blue Box, which was used to collect donations. A circular from JNF's Department of Education lamenting the disappearance of the Blue Box from Jewish homes emphasizes its symbolic as well as financial value and urges Jews to reintroduce it to their homes. "Before lighting candles on Shabbat and Holidays," the circular suggests, "make a contribution in the presence of your children and encourage them to do so, giving from their own funds... take time to discuss some aspect of Israel within the family circle.... You can include Zionist personalities and development of Zionism, geography of Eretz Yisrael and modern Israel, plants and animals mentioned in the Bible, and those we find today in the country, and so much more.... Parents and children together will then establish a living link to the Land of our Fathers, Israel."[60]

The era of the small-scale, community-based Blue Box has passed. In the words of Menachem Begin, "The JNF was conceived by people of vision as the instrument of the whole Jewish people to share in the redemption and reclamation of the soil of Eretz Israel. What began as individuals making small weekly contributions to their 'Blue Boxes' developed in time into what is now a vast enterprise...."[61]

In April 1980, the JNF in Jerusalem evaluated its total assets at more than $148 million. The primary sources of income were leases on JNF-owned property, work contracted by the JA and the Israeli government, contributions from world Jewry, and the sale of timber thinned from JNF forests. JNF officials estimate that about one-third of the JNF's independent income comes from inheritances (wills and life insurance policies).

For the JNF in the United States, its annual report for the year ending in September 1982 showed total support and revenue of $7.1 million, with about $7 million from contributions. About $5.8 million was spent on programs, of which about $5.4 million was sent to Israel, and about $400,000 was spent on "public education and cultural activities," presumably within the United States for the most part. About $1.1 million was spent on fundraising and administration.

In the United States, the JNF now uses a variety of fundraising techniques, drawing on a network of "regions and councils" to sponsor seminars, meetings, and dinners for specific JNF projects. All of its informational and fundraising activities stress one theme: support Israel by helping the JNF maintain Jewish control over the land.

During the Eightieth Anniversary Assembly, held in upstate New York in March 1981, JNF's executive vice-president presented a five-point program for the American JNF in the 1980s that included: (1) setting a ten-year income goal of $100 million; (2) structuring a national fundraising cabinet; (3) broadening JNF's organizational base to increase the activities of other Jewish organizations; (4) holding conferences and consultations with public relations firms to bring JNF's message to the Jewish community; and (5) forming a national committee to develop policy guidelines and planning to raise funds in non-Jewish communities in the United States.[62]

Since the JNF claims exclusive responsibility to raise funds for land-related projects, contributions from other American Zionist organizations to the JNF usually take the form of a commitment to fund a specific project, or an aspect of a project, initially proposed by JNF. The United Synagogue of America, the congregational arm of Conservative Judaism, announced during the 1981 JNF Anniversary Assembly that it had just funded its first United Synagogue forest, and that it had started raising funds from its members for another forest. The president of the United Synagogue of America announced at the beginning of 1982 that his organization had decided to launch a major project to establish a national park in Safad in the Galilee, which would be a JNF project. In 1976, the JNF of America launched the American Independence Park outside of Jerusalem in commemoration of the U.S. bicentennial. Pioneer Women (the Labor Zionist Organization of America) made a commitment to the JNF to underwrite the cost of a road in the park, estimated at $600,000 over three years. In 1981, the JNF gave its first "Tree of Life" award to Evangeline Gouletas-Carey, wife of New York's former governor Hugh Carey, and her brother, real estate tycoon Nicholas Gouletas, for establishing a children's recreation park at Givat Homoreh, near Nazareth.

Like other pro-Israel fundraising organizations, the JNF also uses missions or delegations to Israel, as well as to post-Camp David Egypt. During one such delegation, the "JNF Collegiate Winter Seminar in Israel," thirty participants planted trees, visited settlements, and attended workshops with officials of the JNF and the Israeli government.

PEF Israel Endowment Fund

Year established: 1922
President: Sidney Luria
Chairman: Sidney Musher
Address: 342 Madison Avenue, New York, NY 10173

General Background and Structure

In 1922, Justice Louis Brandeis and a small group of American Zionists formed the Palestine Endowment Fund (PEF) as a charitable organization to channel funds to the *Yishuv* in Palestine. After the creation of Israel, the PEF changed its name to PEF Israel Endowment Fund.

The PEF is a tax-exempt "public charity" corporation registered in the state of New York; it also has tax-exempt status in Israel. The organization is governed by a national board of trustees, with 34 members who reside in Israel and the United States. None of its nine officers and trustees receives compensation. The PEF employs only one full-time and two part-time staff members. In Israel, a group of five volunteers supervises its activities. As a result, it has minimal overhead expenses; in 1981, these were only 1.5 percent of total receipts.

Flow of Funding

PEF's goal is to service Israeli institutions by helping American contributors obtain tax exemptions. Prospective donors may contribute to the PEF with a recommendation that their contributions go to a specific institution or purpose. Before consenting to forward the grant, the PEF investigates each institution through consultations with its volunteers in Israel. It accepts small (a minimum of twenty-five dollars) or large gifts and bequests. It maintains extensive files on a wide variety of nonprofit organizations in Israel. Potential recipient institutions in Israel may approach the PEF for advice on funding, and they may recommend that a contribution go through the PEF.

Since its inception, the PEF has forwarded over $45 million to Israel. In 1982, PEF's total receipts were over $6 million, of which over $5 million was distributed to 300 educational, research, religious, health, and other institutions in Israel. There is generally no deduction from the contributions for administration; the small administrative cost is absorbed by the PEF. According to its 1982 annual report, about 77 percent of the total receipts of over $6 million came from "contributions and bequests"; the rest came from "interest and dividends" and "gain from investments." PEF's net worth by November 1982 was over $13 million.

Some of the institutions the PEF supported in 1982 were: the Hebrew University in Jerusalem ($345,664), the secondary school scholarship program ($252,684), the Association for the Welfare of Soldiers ($283,357), and the Association of Americans and Canadians in Israel ($47,450); $89,428 was distributed to 146 other institutions, each of which received less than $2,000.

The PEF has established special funds of $100,000 and over, from which the interest and/or the principal is disbursed to specific institutions. In 1982, PEF had 25 such funds, nine of which paid out interest and/or principal to the Hebrew University in Jerusalem.[63]

State of Israel Bonds Organization

Year established: 1951
President: Brig. Gen. Yehudah Halevy
General Chairman: Sam Rothberg
Executive Vice-President: Morris Sipser
U.S. National Campaign Chairman: David Hermelin
Address: 730 Broadway, New York, NY 10003

General Background

Following the establishment of the Jewish state, and against the background of the ongoing debate over Israel's share of UJA campaign funds, a group of 59 American Jewish leaders visited Israel in September 1950 and met with Prime Minister Ben-Gurion "to consider the economic situation of Israel."[64] Two-thirds of the participants were from the New York-New Jersey area, and the moving force behind the visit was Henry Montor of New York City, who was already very active in UJA fund-raising activities and who was arguing for a bigger Israeli share of the annual receipts.

Realizing that Israel's financial needs at the time were staggering, the group attempted to find another funding channel controlled exclusively by pro-Israel elements. To this end they called for private investment in Israel and for the continuation of the UJA, as well as "a new approach to the scope of the cooperation between the Jews of the United States and the people of Israel," in the belief that "the State of Israel has reached a crucial point of development in which contributions are not adequate to meet long-range economic needs." At the conclusion of their meeting, they pledged themselves "that should the Government of Israel decide to float a public loan in the United States as a means of obtaining funds for the financing of constructive programs, American Jewry will extend its fullest support."[65]

What grew out of that resolution was the American Financial and Development Corporation for Israel, better known as the Israel Bonds Organization (IBO). Besides Montor, the other moving force behind the idea was Henry Morgenthau, Jr., then chairman of the UJA, and formerly secretary of the treasury under Franklin D. Roosevelt. After Morgenthau secured U.S. governmental approval of the idea, Ben-Gurion visited the United States to launch the IBO in May 1951, and Henry Montor left the UJA to nurture the new organization during its first few years.[66]

Structure and Role

The IBO is not a tax-exempt corporation, but an investment corporation. It "seeks to provide large-scale investment funds for the economic development of the State of Israel through the sale of State of

Israel Bonds in the United States, Canada, Western Europe, and other parts of the free world." The sale of Israel Bonds makes development capital available to Israel at a rate below that of any other available money market. The Israeli securities carry from four to seven percent interest and mature in fifteen years. The funds raised from the sale of these securities go directly to the Israeli Ministry of Finance, where they become part of Israel's development budget.[67] The IBO works closely with the Israeli government, especially during what they define as emergency situations, when Israeli needs for cash are transmitted directly and swiftly to IBO officials in the United States.

The impact of bond money is felt in almost every economic project in Israel. Together with German reparations and loans, bond money financed "the growth of Israel's southern industrial towns and factories, the Jordan Valley Water Carrier, the ports of Eilat and Ashdod, the oil pipelines from the Gulf of Aqaba to the Mediterranean, as well as a host of other development projects, including the enlarged Dead Sea Works and the Arad petrochemical complex."[68]

Run simultaneously as a highly structured business and a community organization, the IBO targets the entire American market and not only American Jews. With headquarters in New York City, the IBO has a system of city offices, each responsible for a given area. In addition to the geographical organization, there are sectoral units, such as the Women's Division, the Rabbinate Division, and so forth. All of these regional and sectoral units are controlled by directors and chairpersons responsible to the national executive staff in New York. In Florida, a new position of condominium coordinator was recently introduced.

Flow of Funding

For potential Jewish investors, the purchase of State of Israel Bonds is presented as the "strongest and most direct link with Israel, its people and their future." For non-Jewish American entrepreneurs, the purchase of Israel Bonds is cast as helping "to expand Israel purchases of U.S.-produced machinery, equipment, raw materials and other products, thus providing jobs and business opportunities for Americans," while assisting the economic growth of Israel, "the only democracy in the Middle East."

Many of the techniques the IBO uses to sell its securities are similar to those used by other major fundraising organizations: gala social events, missions to Israel, regional meetings, specialized seminars, and fashion shows. To create a network of bond purchasers, "Prime Minister Clubs" restricted to big investors were created in a number of large U.S. cities. Major purchasers of Israel Bonds are honored with awards such as the Israel Bonds Cultural Award, the Golda Meir Leadership Award, and the Eleanor Roosevelt Humanities Award.

In order to promote its new series of Variable Rate Issue Bonds (VRI) in Detroit, the IBO held small cocktail meetings in doctors' medical suites.

"In each case, the invitation, printed on the doctor's stationery, was mailed to colleagues in the doctor's building. The meeting was conveniently held immediately following office hours and a guest speaker, knowledgeable about VRI and pension and profit-sharing plans, was featured."[69] The success of the plan in 1982 led to its continuation the following year.

Immediately after launching the invasion of Lebanon in 1982, the Israeli government initiated intensive contacts with IBO officials in the United States and urgently requested cash. In conjunction with other major fundraising organizations, the IBO put in motion "Operation Welcome," a U.S. fundraising tour for Prime Minister Begin. At an IBO luncheon held at the Waldorf Astoria in New York on 18 June 1982 American and Canadian Jewish Bonds leaders presented Begin with a check for $35 million, a first installment on the $100 million that they committed themselves to raise by September 1982.[70] At that time, a high-level IBO delegation was in Israel to hand over the balance of their commitment.

In late June 1982, a delegation of thirty Bonds leaders was invited by the Israeli government for consultations. During a 42-hour visit, the delegation met with the prime minister and minister of finance and visited the Beaufort Castle and Israeli troops in Lebanon. A week later Israeli officials invited a second Bonds delegation of 32 members to visit for consultations and progress reports on the emergency drive.

A four-day International Leadership Conference of the IBO was held in Washington, D.C. in late August 1982. The conference was addressed by Israeli defense minister Ariel Sharon and Walter Mondale. Chairman Sam Rothberg set the 1982 goal at $550 million in Bond receipts (the 1981 sales were $432 million) and proceeded to list what he considered the four "major challenges" facing the Bonds program:

(1) to begin a new era of agricultural and industrial development of the Galilee...
(2) to help restore and replenish the economy...
(3) to continue the expansion of the economic structure of the Negev in order to complete the resettlement of the families from Sinai...
(4) to provide seed money for the Mediterranean-Dead Sea Canal.[71]

IBO's interaction with the Israeli government has always followed a fixed pattern: Israeli officials express the volume of their need to IBO officials, and the latter commit themselves to raising it. What happened in the wake of the invasion of Lebanon duplicated the response to earlier "emergencies." These emergencies, however, are not restricted to wars, as the following example illustrates. During the first week of April 1982, as Israel was preparing to pull out from the Sinai, Begin sent an urgent cable to IBO's Rothberg in which he expressed his hope that "the Bond Organization will demonstrate its solidarity by making a special effort in

139

the coming weeks to enable us to back up our endeavor for peace with a strong economy." In response, the IBO declared 25 April 1982 to be "Unity with Israel Day," which would be the culmination of a special campaign of major sales and cash collection.[72]

To target the corporate world, the IBO set up the Israel Bonds Corporate Program in the early 1970s. In 1982, some $160 million in securities offered by the IBO were purchased by corporations, banks, and insurance companies in the United States. Bond securities have also been purchased by 9,500 pension funds, 3,500 banks, 1,500 labor unions, and 500 insurance companies. Among the major purchasers of Bond securities are: the Coca-Cola Company, Melville Corporation, the Borden Corporation, Allied Stores Corporation, U.S. Shoe Corporation, Walter Kidde and Company, the Catalog/Showroom Industry, MGIC Investment Corporation, ARA Services, Inc., the Great Atlantic and Pacific Tea Company, Warner Communications, Inc., Bally Manufacturing Corporation, Supermarkets General Corporation of New Jersey, Associated Wholesale Grocers, Inc., Colonial Stores, the Manufacturers National Bank of Detroit, and the National City Bank of Cleveland.[73] In April 1982, at a gala dinner-dance at the New York Hilton, under the auspices of the IBO, Lord & Taylor was designated to receive the "State of Israel Peace Medal" for its valued service to the state.[74] The purchase of substantial sums in Israel Bonds is probably the most important form of financial assistance that U.S. labor has rendered to Israel. Union pension funds and health and welfare funds buy these securities despite the low rate of interest. About forty unions hold approximately a quarter billion dollars in Israel Bonds in their portfolios.†[75]

---

†The unions holding the bonds include the following (unions with few Jewish members, as indicated by the Israel Bonds Organization, are denoted by an asterisk):

Amalgamated Clothing Workers of America (AFL-CIO)

Amalgamated Lithographers of America (Independent)

*Amalgamated Meat Cutters and Butcher Workmen of North America (AFL-CIO)

American Federation of Musicians (AFL-CIO)

Baker and Confectionery Workers International Union of America (AFL-CIO)

*Bricklayers, Masons and Plasterers International Union of America (AFL-CIO)

Distillery, Rectifying, Wine and Allied Workers International Union of America (AFL-CIO)

Graphic Arts International Union (AFL-CIO)

Hotel and Restaurant Employees' and Bartenders' International Union (AFL-CIO)

*International Association of Bridge and Structural Iron Workers (AFL-CIO)

*International Association of Machinists and Aerospace Workers (AFL-CIO)

*International Brotherhood of Electrical Workers (AFL-CIO)

*International Brotherhood of Painters and Allied Trades of the United States and Canada (AFL-CIO)

*International Brotherhood of Teamsters, Chauffeurs, Warehousemen and Helpers of America (Independent)

International Jewelry Workers Union (AFL-CIO)

International Ladies Garment Workers Union (AFL-CIO)

Since IBO's inception in 1951, more than $6.1 billion in bonds and other Israel securities have been sold, and over $3 billion worth have been redeemed. Although individual German companies and institutions purchased large quantities of State of Israel Bonds in the early 1960s, the majority of sales continue to take place in the United States.

International Leather Goods, Plastics and Novelty Workers Union (AFL-CIO)
*International Longshoresmen's Association (AFL-CIO)
International Typographical Union (AFL-CIO)
International Union of Dolls, Toys, Playthings, Novelties and Allied Products of the United States and Canada (AFL-CIO)
*International Union of Operating Engineers (AFL-CIO)
*International Union of Wood, Wire and Metal Lathers (AFL-CIO)
*Laborers International Union of North America (AFL-CIO)
Laundry, Cleaning and Dye Houseworkers International Union (Independent)
*Longshoremen's and Warehousemen's International (Independent)
Retail Clerks International Association (AFL-CIO)
Retail, Wholesale and Department Store Union (AFL-CIO)
*Seafarers International Union of North America (AFL-CIO)
*Service Employees International Union (AFL-CIO)
*Sheet Metal Workers International Association (AFL-CIO)
Textile Workers Union of America (AFL-CIO)
*United Association of Journeymen and Apprentices of the Plumbing and Pipe Fitting Industry of the United States and Canada (AFL-CIO)
*United Automobile, Aerospace and Agricultural Implement Workers of America (Independent)
*United Brotherhood of Carpenters and Joiners of America (AFL-CIO)
United Furniture Workers of America (AFL-CIO)
United Hatters, Cap and Millinery Workers International Union (AFL-CIO)
*United Paperworkers International Union (AFL-CIO)
*United Steelworkers of America (AFL-CIO)

AMPAL-American Israel Corporation

Year established: 1942
President: Michael Jaffe
Chairman of the Board: Ephraim Reiner
Address: 10 Rockefeller Plaza, New York, NY 10020

AMPAL was established originally as the American Palestine Corporation. By the early 1970s, the corporation had become gradually but completely controlled by the Israeli Bank Hapoalim, a Histadrut company. At the end of 1977, Bank Hapoalim sold one-third of AMPAL's shares to a West German bank but still retained controlling voting rights.

AMPAL is a New York-registered investment corporation. It describes itself as being "primarily engaged in the business of financing . . . industrial, financial, commercial and agricultural enterprises in Israel." In other words, whereas the UJA mobilizes contributions, and the IBO recruits loans for the Israeli government, AMPAL solicits direct investment in business enterprises in Israel.

Until 1977, AMPAL remained a relatively small company, owning three minor banks that provided industrial loans. However, toward the end of the year, AMPAL showed sudden growth and by 1982 its profits had increased threefold, with a net income of $15.2 million. With assets in excess of $900 million, AMPAL represents a big potential for foreign investment in Israel.[76] *Ha'aretz* writer Eliezer Lavin concluded in January 1984, however, that the actual volume of investment funds AMPAL was supposed to have mobilized in the United States was small, and that most of the company's profits were passed on to its American investors instead of being redirected to enterprises in Israel.*[77]

---

*An investigation into AMPAL and other Labor Party-affiliated financial institutions erupted into scandal in February 1984, when AMPAL board chairman Yaacov Levinson killed himself.[78]

PEC Israel Economic Corporation

Year established: 1926
President: Joseph Ciechanover
Chairman of the Board: Raphael Recanati
Address: 511 Fifth Avenue, New York, NY 10017

PEC was established as the Palestine Economic Corporation by American Jewish leaders "to foster economic development and advancement in Israel." It is a profit-generating investment company. Over the five-year period from 1978 to 1982, the company's net income increased from $3.8 million to $14.4 million. PEC's holdings are in finance and banking, manufacturing, high technology, construction and development, and shipping and marketing enterprises.[79]

New Israel Fund

Year established: 1979
President: Jonathan J. Cohen
Executive Director: Jonathan Jacoby
Chairman of Israeli Committee: Richard Laster
Address: 111 West 40th St., New York, New York 10018

General Background, Structure and Role

The NIF is the youngest of all pro-Israel fundraising organizations in the United States and represents a significant departure from its predecessors. Established in the San Francisco area as a protest against traditional fundraising organizations among American Jewry, and especially against perceived links with Israeli government policy, the NIF is more closely allied with the Israeli peace camp.

The NIF is governed by a board of trustees, working in conjunction with one committee in Israel and another in the United States. The U.S. committee is responsible for development of policy, fundraising, and educational outreach; the Israeli committee shares responsibility for development of policy and constitutes NIF's review and allocation committee. The Israeli committee also receives and reviews all requests for grants and assumes a supervising and evaluating role for projects once they are funded.

The NIF is registered as a tax-exempt public charity organization in the state of California and as a foreign, nonprofit institution in Israel. In 1982, NIF's U.S. advisory committee was composed of 61 members; the eleven-member Israeli committee included a number of veteran social activists. The 1981/1982 chairperson, for example, was professor Eliezer D. Jaffe of the social work faculty at the Hebrew University in Jerusalem, who recently wrote an article in *Ha'aretz* criticizing the continued "Zionization" of the JA and the overall politicization of Jewish philanthropies.[80] The NIF is staffed by one part-time worker and twelve volunteers.

According to its own literature, the NIF "complements other philanthropic efforts by involving many individuals who otherwise show little or no inclination to give either to Jewish or to Israeli causes through traditional channels." It pays particular attention to those projects that "fall through the cracks" of traditional Jewish philanthropy. The NIF "offers a unique and innovative partnership between American Jewish resources for the people of Israel....It establishes a structure for exchange of information and involvement among Israelis and Americans committed to a healthy, secure State of Israel." The NIF emphasizes that it does not fund "any activity that originates outside the 'Green Line'."[81]

144

There is a noticeable emphasis on grassroots projects and those with social policy orientation, such as the Association for Civil Rights in Israel.

The NIF awards grants of up to $10,000 each to nonprofit and nongovernmental groups only.

Flow of Funding

NIF's grants consist of general funds or "donor-directed allocations" in which the NIF simply acts as a conduit for channeling funds to pre-designated organizations and institutions in Israel. NIF's grants are distributed in five general categories: civil rights, women's issues, Arab-Jewish relations, innovative services, and community action. In the first funding cycle (April 1980), 22 grants ranging from $1,000 to $5,000 were awarded. In 1982, the NIF doubled its donor base and the funds raised. According to its 1982 Annual Report, the cumulative funds raised totaled $332,500, of which $240,000 (72 percent) were allocated in grants. About one-third of the allocations were in the category of "donor-directed" grants. Close to 28 percent of the funds raised during 1982 was spent on fundraising and development, educational programming, and technical assistance, outreach, and administrative costs in Israel.

Institutionally-Specific Funding Organizations

In addition to the organizations discussed so far in this section, there are scores of "American Friends of . . . " groups that have been established for the sole purpose of promoting and raising funds for particular institutions and organizations in Israel. The earliest of these organizations, American Friends of the Jerusalem Mental Health Center, was set up in 1895. The Israeli beneficiaries include educational, cultural, health, and welfare institutions. All of these organizations are tax-exempt under the U.S. Internal Revenue Code, and many are registered as such in both the United States and Israel.

Below is a partial list of these organizations, with the year in which they were established in parentheses:

(1895) American Friends of the Jerusalem Mental Health Center
(1903) United Charity Institutions of Jerusalem
(1924) American ORT Federation
(1925) American Friends of the Hebrew University
(1928) American-Israeli Lighthouse
(1928) Women's League for Israel
(1937) Women's Social Service for Israel
(1939) American-Israel Cultural Foundation
(1940) American Technion Society
(1940) Federated Council of Israel Institutions
(1941) American Red Magen David for Israel
(1944) American Committee for the Weizman Institute for Science
(1948) Israel Music Foundation
(1948) United States Committee Sports for Israel
(1949) American Committee for Shaare Tzedek Hospital in Jerusalem
(1950) American Physicians Fellowship for Medicine in Israel
(1954) Hebrew University-Technion Joint Maintenance Appeal
(1955) Bar Ilan University in Israel
(1955) American Friends of the Tel Aviv University
(1956) Keren-Or
(1960) Friends of the Rothschild University Hospital
(1963) American Friends of the Rambam Society
(1968) American Friends of the Israel Museum
(1969) American Friends of Haifa University
(1970) Fund for Higher Education
(1973) American Associates of Ben-Gurion University
(1974) American Friends of the Tel Aviv Museum
(1977) American Friends of the Jerusalem Academy
(n.d.) American Friends of the Midrashia

Notes

Introduction

1. Details of the American Jewish funding organizations' response to the 1982 Lebanon war can be found in reports from *Jewish Telegraphic Agency,* July to October 1982; *Jerusalem Post,* 20 June 1982; *Jewish Week,* 11 July 1982; and *New York Times,* 19 June 1982.

2. Ben Bradlee, Jr., "Israel's Lobby," *Boston Globe Magazine,* 29 April 1984.

3. *Washington Post,* 20 February 1972 and 29 August 1982.

4. The primary source for historical background is Abraham J. Karp, *To Give Life: The UJA in the Shaping of the American Jewish Community.* New York: Schocken Books, 1981.

5. A thorough discussion of the historical tension between Zionist and non-Zionist fundraising goals can be found in Samuel Halperin, *The Political World of American Zionism.* Detroit: Wayne State University Press, 1961.

6. *Ibid:* 195.

7. Karp: 65.

8. *Ibid:* 89-90.

9. *Ibid:* 118.

10. Golda Meir, *My Life.* New York: G.P. Putnam and Sons, 1975: 212-214.

UJA

11. "Distributing the Jewish Communal Dollars," in M.L. Raphael, (ed.), *Understanding American Jewish Philanthropy.* New York: KTAV Publishing, 1979: 133.

12. Karp: 169.

13. *Wall Street Journal,* 1 April 1983.

14. *Jewish Digest,* November 1981.

15. Wolf Blitzer, "Who Gives, Who Doesn't—and Why?" *Present Tense,* Summer 1983.

16. *New York Times,* 29 December 1983.

17. All self-definitions in this chapter are quoted from AJC: *The American Jewish Yearbook.* New York, 1983; and Jewish Chronicle Publications, *The Jewish Yearbook.* London, 1982.

18. *Wall Street Journal,* 1 April 1983.

19. Karp: 111.

20. *Ibid:* 170.

21. Michael Rosen, "The UJA as a Detriment to Jewish Survival," *Israel Horizons,* 28/5-6 (May/June 1980).

22. UJA, "Do's & Don'ts of Personal Solicitation."

23. UJA, "We Give To Life," 1983.

24. Wendy Elliman, "Your Dollars and Your Sons," *Forum* 44 (Spring 1982).

25. Karp: 156.

26. *Jewish Telegraphic Agency,* 4 May 1982; *Jerusalem Post,* 6 May 1982.

27. *Jerusalem Post,* 6 May 1982.

28. Melvin I. Urofsky, "American Jewish Leadership," *American Jewish History* 70/4 (June 1981): 415.

29. U.S. Senate, *Activities of Nondiplomatic Representatives of Foreign Principals in the United States,* Hearing Before the Committee on Foreign Relations, 88th Congress, First Session, 23 May 1963 (Fulbright hearings); UJA, "UJA Annual Report," May 1981.

30. Jonathan Woocher, "The 1980 United Jewish Appeal Young Leadership Cabinet: A Profile," *Forum* 42/43 (Winter 1981).

31. UJA, "UJA Annual Report," May 1981.

32. Elliman: 78.

33. *Wall Street Journal,* 1 April 1983.

34. *Jewish Telegraphic Agency,* 23 February 1982.

35. For details of "Super Sunday" and other telethons, see *Jewish Telegraphic Agency,* 24 February 1982; and *Jewish Week,* 21 February 1982.

36. *Wall Street Journal,* 1 April 1983.

37. *Ibid.*

38. *Ibid.*

39. *Ibid.*

40. Information on "Liftoff '83" and the "National Fly-In" was obtained from *Jerusalem Post,* 6 May 1982; *Jewish Week,* 2 May 1982, 16 May 1982, 3 September 1982, 10 September 1982, 15 October 1982.

41. *New York Times,* 13 October 1982; *Jewish Telegraphic Agency,* 15 October 1982.

42. *Jewish Week,* 12 November 1982.

UIA

43. Fulbright hearings.

44. U.S. International Development Cooperation Agency, *Voluntary Foreign Aid Programs, 1980 and 1981.* A.I.D., Bureau for Food, for Peace and Voluntary Cooperation: Washington, D.C.

45. Fulbright hearings.

JDC

46. Halperin: 199.

47. *Ibid:* 205.

48. *Ibid:* 208, 213.

49. See "U.S. Assistance Provided For Resettling Soviet Refugees," Departments of State and Justice. *Report to the Congress by the Comptroller General of the U.S.,* June 20, 1977; *Voluntary Foreign Aid Programs, 1980 and 1981;* and JDC, *1982 Annual Report of the American Jewish Joint Distribution Committee, Inc.*

JNF

50. Walter Lehn, "The Jewish National Fund," *Journal of Palestine Studies* 3/4 (Summer 1974).

51. Government of Israel, *Laws of the State of Israel,* vol. 14 (5720/1960), Jerusalem: 48-52.

52. H. Freeden, *Jewish National Fund — 70 Years of Growth.* JNF: New York.

53. All quotes in this paragraph come from Berkowitz's presidential address, reprinted in JNF, *Land and Life,* Summer 1981.

54. *Jerusalem Post,* 9 May and 21 November 1982.

55. *Land and Life,* Summer 1981.

56. *Jerusalem Post,* 21 November 1982.

57. *Jerusalem Post,* 21 November 1982 and 8 April 1983.

58. *Jerusalem Post,* 24 November 1982.

59. *Ha'aretz,* 1 April 1984.

60. Esther Adler, "The Little Blue Box," JNF.

61. *Land and Life,* Summer 1981.

62. *Ibid.*

PEF

63. Information in this section from PEF, "60th Annual Report, 1982."

IBO

64. Karp: 96-97.

65. *Ibid.*

66. *Ibid.*

67. *Washington Post,* 29 August 1982.

68. Howard M. Sachar, *A History of Israel From the Rise of Zionism to Our Time.* New York: Alfred A. Knopf, 1982: 725.

69. IBO, *Israel Bond Forum,* March 1983.

70. *Jewish Week,* 27 June 1982.

71. *Jewish Week,* 3 September 1982.

72. *Jewish Week,* 11 April 1982.

73. IBO, "The Corporate Share in Building Israel."

74. *Jewish Week,* 21 February 1982.

75. Edward Bernard Glick, *The Triangular Connection: America, Israel and American Jews.* London: George Allen and Unwin, 1982: 113-115.

AMPAL

76. *Jerusalem Post,* 18 October 1982.

77. *Ha'aretz,* 13 January 1981.

78. *Boston Globe,* 26 February 1984.

PEC

79. PEC Israel Economic Corporation, "1982 Annual Report."

NIF

80. *Ha'aretz,* 1 April 1984.

81. NIF, "Annual Report 1982."

The Pro–Israel Lobby and the Political Process

The Pro-Israel Lobby and the Political Process

Introduction: Channeling Opinion

What is usually referred to as the Jewish, Israel, or pro-Israel lobby includes the American Israel Public Affairs Committee (AIPAC), which is the only official, registered lobby "charged with the responsibility for lobbying on behalf of the American Jewish community in support of Israel,"[1] the pro-Israel political action committees (PACs), through which financial contributions are channeled to political candidates; the Conference of Presidents of Major American Jewish Organizations, which functions as the official voice of American Jewry on Israel in both the national and international political arenas; and the Jewish Institute for National Security Affairs (JINSA), which targets the Pentagon and military establishment.

A lobby is a special-interest group working within the political system to affect policies in a way favorable to its cause. Lobbying work can involve numerous forms of political intervention: discussions with congressional and other leaders; the preparation of briefs, memoranda, speeches, legislative analysis, and even the drafting of legislation for committees and congressional representatives; building relations with key legislative aides and other power figures; disseminating information and positions; stimulating mail and telephone calls on issues from constituents; organizing lecture engagements for friendly politicians; and many other types of advocacy. Virtually all of the Israel support organizations discussed in this chapter and elsewhere—community relations, Zionist, funding, fraternal, or religious groups—engage in one or all of these forms of political activity. Membership in AIPAC and the Presidents Conference is the organizational basis of the Israel support lobby.

The question of the power of the Israel lobby in the United States is complex. An abiding myth exaggerates the influence of Jews over government. In the myth's most virulently racist form, as found, for example, in the fictitious and pernicious *Protocols of the Elders of Zion* from czarist Russia (reprinted by Henry Ford in the United States), Jews are accused of conspiratorial control over political and economic life. A variation of this theme is attributable not to classical anti-Semitism, but rather to a political view that does not recognize the compatibility between U.S. and Israeli interests. According to this more sophisticated form of scapegoating, pro-Israel forces are held responsible for forcing the U.S. government to maintain a pro-Israel policy against its own interests and/or ethics.

Recently, another factor has begun to affect the question of influence. Traditionally, most establishment American Jewish organizations and individuals have viewed any implication of political clout or reference to the "Jewish vote" or lobby as potentially threatening and possibly tinged with anti-Semitism; as a result, they downplayed or simply denied their own power and influence. Now, however, the key forces in the lobby — AIPAC and the PACs — actively assert and even exaggerate the scope of their political power. To this end, AIPAC has adopted a posture previously rejected by the American Jewish establishment: in literature, speeches, and interviews, AIPAC claims responsibility for the $12.9 billion in military and economic aid to Israel since 1979, boasts of defeating Illinois Republican congressman Paul Findley and California Republican congressman Paul McCloskey, and claims to have such control over Congress that it can override the administration's wishes, as with the December 1982 conversion of $500 million in aid to Israel from loans to grants. Thomas Dine, AIPAC's executive director, states openly: "We not only express political power, we exercise it."[2] He directly confronts the issues of Jewish power and anti-Semitism. In 1983, Stephen S. Rosenfeld, deputy editorial page editor of the *Washington Post,* wrote:

It (AIPAC) is not shy in claiming credit for the results of its efforts in Congress. Indeed, Dine is forthcoming in defense of lobbying as a proper political activity for the Jewish community. He rejects the idea that Jews should go on tiptoe in order to avoid stirring up anti-Semitism or overloading their fellow citizens' goodwill toward Israel. To him, the post-AWACS warning of a "backlash against too much Jewish advocacy" was "an empty and nefarious threat." He pointed out: "We must also appreciate that overcaution and reticence seem to validate the canard that there is something evil in Jewish political power."[3]

In other words, allegations about an all-powerful "Jewish lobby" no longer come only from disgruntled Arab regimes, State Department Arabists, or anti-Semites, but also from the lobby itself; paradoxically both the pro- and anti-lobby sides now mythologize it. This paradox does not, however, transform the exaggerated assessment of the lobby's power into an accurate evaluation. Neither AIPAC nor any other group is all-powerful. The AWACS vote showed the lobby's limits against a determined administration's efforts.

The main source of the Israel lobby's strength lies in the fact that support for Israel is an inherent component of U.S. strategy, that it has been so through a number of administrations, and that such policies face no significant challenge from forces within the U.S. political mainstream at this time. The lobby is thus not in the position of trying to extract aid to Israel from Congress in conflict with an unwilling administration; it

154

essentially supports aid programs to which the administration has deep strategic commitments. It may, on a tactical level, be requesting somewhat more than the administration has offered, under more favorable terms, and including even more sophisticated weapons. But its ability to achieve success on this tactical level is in great measure a product of the momentum it gathers as a force driving for support of programs to which there is no significant political opposition in the U.S. government.

It is in this context that the factors contributing to the strength and effectiveness of the lobby must be considered. Top among these is its unabashedly single-issue criterion: how pro-Israel a politician, candidate or policy is. This single-issue focus is by and large shared by the lobby's major source of strength, its mass-based support among American Jews. And not only is American Jewry overwhelmingly pro-Israel in its orientation, but it is also activist and already organized into functioning groups, the majority of which are members of AIPAC and the Presidents Conference. The longstanding history of political involvement and organizational experience of American Jews is popularly perceived as and objectively translated into the "Jewish vote," fundraising and contributions, connections to elites, and general impact on the political process.

While the impact of the "Jewish vote" is often exaggerated, the figures do show a degree of participation that must attract the attention of politicians and lend credence to lobbyists. While Jews constitute about 2.5 percent of the population, the rate of Jewish participation in national elections is approximately 90 percent, compared to a national average for the general population varying from 40 to 55 percent. This extra percentage is especially important in major electoral vote states, where Jews are concentrated. In New York State, for example, Jews constitute an estimated 14 percent of the population but cast 16 to 20 percent of the vote; in New York City, the figure rises to one-half the votes in the Democratic primaries. This high level of voter participation goes hand in hand with financial donations to candidates. As a relatively wealthy community with a long tradition of philanthropy, American Jews are estimated to donate more than half the large gifts to national Democratic campaigns, and an increasing amount to Republicans as well.[4] With the formation of PACs, the impact of this money is greater than ever.

Jewish involvement in U.S. politics has traditionally tended toward "behind the scenes" roles as political aides and campaign advisors rather than as candidates for elected offices. This tendency also seems to be changing, however. In 1972, there were two Jewish senators and twelve representatives, all mainly from the northeast; by 1982 there were eight Jewish senators and thirty-one representatives from all over the country, including such states as Alabama, Kansas, Colorado, Nebraska, and Oregon.

The pro-Israel lobby is in the enviable position of benefitting from two interlocking factors: many American Jews vote, give money, and

155

intervene on the basis of a politician's position on Israel, and thus politicians solicit the Jewish vote, money, and support by asserting a pro-Israel stance.*

The *Jerusalem Post* described the 1984 presidential campaign in the following way:

It looks and sounds almost like a United Jewish Appeal parlour meeting. Responding to peer pressure, each man stands, says how much Israel means to him and makes his pledge. The pledges, however, are political in nature, the parlour is the U.S. media, and the man standing up is a candidate for the highest elected office in America. It is presidential election time in the U.S.[5]

Senator Rudy Boschwitz (R-Minn.), chairman of the Senate Foreign Relations Subcommittee on Near Eastern and South Asian Affairs, sent out a fundraising mailing with endorsements that included a letter from Senator Lowell Weicker (R-Conn.). Weicker's letter read, in part, "When it comes to raising money for political campaigns, every politician claims to be a friend of Israel. But Rudy Boschwitz is not like every politician." Boschwitz also sent a similar letter from Senator Robert Packwood (R-Ore.) and a reprint of a *Jerusalem Post* article entitled "The Boschwitz View of Israel as a Strategic Asset."

Another sign of the lobby's clout is its access to those in power, access that is granted to the entire range of pro-Israel organizations. According to a former Jewish liaison officer in the White House, Jewish groups and leaders were granted at least 350 briefings with various level White House, State Department, and Defense Department officials from March 1981 to April 1983—or almost a meeting every other day.[6] The emphasis placed on initiating and maintaining access highlights another characteristic of the lobby: despite the overwhelming pro-Israel stance of U.S. politicians and public, nothing is ever taken for granted, and vigilance is the order of the day. This situation reflects the lobby's ubiquitous fear that a crisis between the United States and Israel may erupt and that American Jews must always be prepared for the worst, namely, some change in the pro-Israel stance of the United States. This single-issue focus also explains why the lobby does not maintain any longstanding ideological coalitions, as demonstrated by the switch to a Republican, neoconservative position under the Reagan administration, and the alliance with fundamentalist Christian groups at the expense of the traditional agenda of American Jewry.

---

* It is in the interest of pro-Israel lobby groups to exaggerate the single-issue voting pattern of American Jews; however, the assertion is not unfounded. In the 1981-1982 National Survey of American Jews, 78 percent of the respondents agreed that "Jews should not vote for candidates unfriendly to Israel"; in the 1983 survey, the figure was 73 percent.

The final source of the pro-Israel lobby's power is that it consists of extremely efficient and committed individuals and organizations who, in the time-honored lobbyist tradition, systematically use their supportive network of elites and mass-based constituents. These organizing skills bring dramatic results because of the predominant moral, ideological and political pro-Israel sentiment in the United States, which thus creates the lobby's unique role of enforcer rather than pleader for a cause.

American Israel Public Affairs Committee

Date established: 1959
Executive Director: Thomas A. Dine
Deputy Director: Arthur Chotin
President: Robert Asher
Senior Vice-President: Michael Stein
Address: 500 North Capitol Street, N.W., Washington, DC 20001
Publication: *Near East Report*

General Background

Though the name AIPAC did not come into use until 1959, the lobby has been in existence since 1951. In that year Isaiah (Si) Kenen, after much discussion and planning with Israeli leaders Abba Eban, Moshe Sharrett, and Teddy Kollek, joined the American Zionist Council (AZC) with the expressed aim of spearheading a pro-Israel lobbying campaign.

The immediate goal of the lobby was to increase U.S. economic aid to Israel. In his book, *Israel's Defense Line: Her Friends and Foes in Washington*, Kenen recalled that in 1951 "Israel needed American economic assistance to enable her to absorb the huge influx of refugees . . . " and to stimulate economic development:

Unfortunately, the Department of State was then opposed to any U.S. grant to Israel because it feared the resentment of the Arabs, who were not requesting U.S. aid. American policy was inhibited by the fear that the Arabs would align with Moscow in the Cold War. The negative attitude of the State Department forced us to appeal to Congress. . . . [7]

The early days of the lobby are very much the story of Si Kenen. An ardent American Zionist, he worked with the now-defunct American Jewish Conference in the 1940s. In 1947, he became a press officer for the Jewish Agency in New York. When the state of Israel was established in 1948, Kenen worked with Ambassador Abba Eban as a spokesperson for the new Israeli delegation to the UN General Assembly. In 1951, when he shifted to the AZC, he notified the Department of Justice that he was withdrawing as an agent of a foreign power and then filed with the Clerk of the House and the Secretary of State as a domestic lobbyist.

Kenen was the Washington representative of the AZC from 1951 to 1953. As a tax-exempt organization, the AZC could not engage in full-time lobbying. In 1954, after rumors of an impending investigation began circulating, Kenen renamed his lobbying committee the American Zionist Committee for Public Affairs, retaining the identical leadership and membership, but no longer accepting tax-exempt financing from the AZC.

The name of the lobby was changed to AIPAC in 1959, mainly

because of pressure from "non-Zionist" defense organizations. These groups, which were unable to lobby full-time themselves owing to their tax-exempt status, played a major role in AIPAC's development. Describing one of his first steps in building the lobby, Kenen recalls, "We enlisted the cooperation of all major Jewish organizations, both 'Zionist' and 'non-Zionist,' such as the defense organizations. They were unwilling to lobby, but they agreed to find prominent constituents to open Congressional doors for us."[8]

The organizations that Kenen listed as most supportive in 1954 include B'nai B'rith, AJC, AJCongress, Jewish War Veterans, the National Council of Jewish Women, and Hadassah. Thus, the lobby arose from one of the earliest genuinely shared ventures between the American Jewish establishment and representatives of the Israeli government.

Structure

When the name AIPAC was adopted in 1959, a national council was formed from representatives of local and national leaders of organizations who were willing to engage in Israel support work and who, as Kenen wrote, "could raise funds for AIPAC or who were on friendly terms with their congressmen. . . ."[9] The executive committee was expanded with the same goal of further incorporating American Jewish groups; today it includes presidents of thirty-eight major American Jewish organizations that claim a total membership of 4.5 million people.

AIPAC regional centers coordinate for local members, in close cooperation with the Washington staff. Members pay minimum dues of $35 a year. Membership reportedly increased from 22,000 to 44,000 in 1982/1983, and there are plans to raise it further by more use of direct mail campaigns.

The Annual Policy Conference brings together active members, community leaders, representatives from target groups or close associates, scores of politicians, and prominent individuals from both Israel and the United States. It is the forum in which AIPAC presents its political positions and current lobby priorities, adopts political resolutions, trains and motivates the membership, and encourages politicians to make public pledges of their support to Israel.

The key position within AIPAC is that of executive director, the post occupied by Kenen from 1954 to 1974. His successor was Morris Amitay, a lawyer and former foreign service officer who, at the time of his AIPAC appointment, was a legislative aide to Senator Abraham Ribicoff (D-Conn.). Kenen describes Amitay as " . . . a tower of strength on the Hill, beginning in 1970 and continuing until I stepped down, as one of a group of legislative aides who helped our cause."[10]

In 1981, Thomas A. Dine replaced Amitay. Dine, a former Peace Corps volunteer, had worked for the State Department, directed national security issues for the Senate Budget Committee, and served as a legislative aide to Senators Edward Kennedy (D-Mass.), Frank Church (D-Id.), and Edward Muskie (D-Me.)—"One of the small group who had been helpful on the Hill," in Kenen's words.[11]

The position of AIPAC president is usually filled by someone wealthy, influential, respected by and belonging to the American Jewish establishment. The first chairman, Rabbi Philip Bernstein of Rochester, New York, who was active in the AJCongress and World Jewish Congress, served until 1968. Irving Kane, president from 1968 to early 1974, had previously headed both CJF and NJCRAC. In 1974, Kenen took the post for a year, in order to be eligible for membership in the Presidents Conference. The next president was Edward Sanders, a lawyer and community leader from Los Angeles who, however, soon resigned to work on the Carter campaign and served as White House Jewish advisor from March 1978 to the next spring. He was replaced by Lawrence Weinberg, a businessman and active pro-Israel community leader from Los Angeles, who served until 1983.

When AIPAC began, Kenen was the only registered lobbyist, working with a staff of four. One of these was Fred Gronich, a former U.S. Army officer who had been Ben-Gurion's advisor on military affairs, and who toured southern states looking for cooperative local leaders. From the late 1960s on, AIPAC began recruiting and hiring young, active staff, most of whom were connected to Congress, to local organizations, or to Jewish institutions. Among the first to be added were Aaron Rosenbaum, the son of a Detroit rabbi, Leonard Davis, a Yeshiva University graduate, and Ken Wollack, who had worked on the McGovern campaign and became AIPAC's legislative director. Later AIPAC lobbyists or staff included Richard Straus, Douglas Bloomfield, F. Stephan McArthur, Michael Gale, who previously worked for the Republican National Committee, Richard Altman, who was AIPAC's political director under Amitay, and Steven Rosen, who joined AIPAC in 1982 as director of research and information, and who had previously been associate director of the National Security Strategies Program at the Rand Corporation and a political science professor at Brandeis.

AIPAC actively looks for staff and supporters among congressional aides and political campaigners. It is now seeking out younger Jewish political activists in local city councils, state legislatures, and the better law firms with the "generous support of local Jewish federations and community relations councils."[12] Along with a good salary, AIPAC offers valuable political experience. It acts as an effective training ground and placement center for those committed to continuing careers around pro-Israel work. Some former AIPAC staff have formed pro-Israel PACs to make direct campaign contributions, which AIPAC cannot do by law, or have moved on to different forms of Israel-support work. For example:

Morris Amitay—Founded pro-Israel Washington PAC and writes a column in *The Jewish Press* called "Report from Washington." Lobbyist for Nathan Lewin (for 47th Street Photo), Northrop Corp., and Pan American Airways.

Ken Wollack — Co-editor of *Middle East Policy Survey (MEPS)*, described as a "bi-weekly Washington DC insiders newsletter."

Richard Straus — Also with *MEPS*.

F. Stephan McArthur — Works with the National Christian Conference for Israel in Washington, D.C.

Richard Altman — Washington, D.C. representative of the largest pro-Israel PAC, NatPAC.

Leonard Davis — Director of American Associates, a political consulting firm in Jerusalem that appears to be the unofficial Israeli connection for AIPAC.

Michael Gale — Deputy special assistant to the President in the White House Office of Public Liaison.

When only thirty-one years old, Michael Gale described his AIPAC-White House journey as follows:

I joined the Republican National Committee in July 1978 and was recruited by AIPAC in late fall 1979 to work with them as a lobbyist particularly. AIPAC sent me to the platform. I spent a lot of time lobbying the RNC to have a pro-Israel plank and we got a fairly good one. After the convention was over I was approached by Bill Casey and asked if I'd be interested in working on the Jewish vote for Reagan. I was interested, so I left AIPAC and worked for Reagan doing the Jewish vote. I went back to AIPAC the Monday after election day, and I was approached in January 1982 about this job . . . I wasn't very interested . . . I thought I could do more for the President and US-Israel relations at AIPAC.[13]

When Gale left his White House position at the end of 1983, he was replaced by Dr. Marshall Breger, an associate at New York Law School and a visiting fellow at the Heritage Foundation.

In AIPAC's 1983 mandatory report filed with the U.S. government, six persons were registered as salaried staff directly engaged in legislative activity, down from the nine listed in 1981 and 1982. Not listed were directors and staff for non-legislative programs, such as leadership development, research and information, political education, and Christian outreach.

Funding

AIPAC's original budget was around $50,000 a year, with Kenen receiving a salary of $13,000. He claims that it was difficult to raise even this much, because of the lack of the tax-exempt status, the concern of constituent organizations with their own needs, and the assumption that the Israeli government would underwrite the lobby. But all this changed with the upsurge of pro-Israel feeling that swept the United States during the 1967 war.

AIPAC is funded by dues and non-tax-deductible contributions from individuals and organizations. Its yearly income has consistently and dramatically increased: in 1973, the budget was reported as $250,000; in 1974, $400,000; and in 1977/1978, it was up to $750,000. Six years later it had more than tripled.

As a registered domestic lobby, AIPAC is obliged to file quarterly financial reports with the Secretary of State and the Clerk of the House of Representatives. For calendar year 1980, AIPAC listed receipts of $1,074,420; for 1982, the figure was slightly over $1.8 million. However, these reports must only show receipts and disbursements that relate to legislative interests, that is, lobbying. A more accurate picture of AIPAC's income emerges from its IRS files. AIPAC's Form 990 for the fiscal year from 1 March 1980 to 28 February 1981 lists total revenue as $1,458,714; total revenue for 1 March 1981 to 28 February 1982 is $2,444,533, and lobbying expenses total $1,551,423. The IRS forms for 1983 were not available; however, the 1983 Annual Report on lobby-related receipts shows contributions just a little short of $2.5 million, so it can be safely assumed that the actual total was substantially higher.

AIPAC targets large, individual givers; there are several hundred members in the Capitol Club, who give $2,000 or more, and plans are underway for a Washington Club for $1,000-plus donors. Of the $2.5 million total for 1983 contributions, over $2 million came from some 1,500 individuals who contributed more than $500 each, and this individual response is even more striking in view of the fact that the money is not tax-deductible.

Who gives to AIPAC? The name, address, and amount donated for every contributor who gives more than $500 are filed with the quarterly financial report. A quick glance shows that the large donations generally come from New York, California, Texas, Florida, and a few pockets in the Midwest.

A closer look at the big donors shows other patterns as well. Consistent contributors are individuals closely connected to AIPAC in particular or to political Israel-support work in general. Thus, AIPAC president Morton Silberman gave $5,000 in 1980, $6,000 in 1981, and $8,500 in 1983; former AIPAC president Lawrence Weinberg gave $25,000 in 1980, $30,000 in 1981 and 1982, and $35,000 in 1983; Leonard Davis gave $5,000 in 1980 and $10,000 each year thereafter; Marvin Josephson gave $5,000 in 1982 and 1983; the Swig family of San Francisco, owners of the Fairmont Hotel, gave $500 in 1980, $2,000 in 1981, $1,000 in 1982, and $10,000 in 1983; Max Fisher of Detroit gave $1,000 in 1980, $5,000 in 1981, $15,000 in 1982 and $5,000 in 1983; and Robert Asher of Chicago, who is AIPAC's current president, gave $15,000 in 1980, $14,000 in 1982, and $12,000 in 1983. These people have in common not only wealth, but also active political involvement. Max Fisher has been a leader of the Jewish Republican Coalition for Reagan-Bush; Weinberg, Josephson, Asher, and the Swigs either formed or support pro-Israel PACs; their names and the others will appear again in this chapter.

Another pattern found among the big-money contributors is a steady and sometimes dramatic increase in successive donations. In part, this tendency reflects AIPAC's ability to prove that it is an organization with political clout, savvy, and connections—that it promises and delivers results—but it also results from solicitations based on specific issues that only AIPAC can fight, since it is the only official lobby (the 1983 AWACS sale to Saudi Arabia is a good example of this). In turn, AIPAC's reputation as an organization with backers who are willing and able to give money further increases its political clout.*

AIPAC reports filed in the House of Representatives Clerk's Office for the 1983-84 election cycle list hundreds of people who gave more than $500 to AIPAC, including the novelist Herman Wouk. In 1984, at least nine individuals gave contributions of $20,000 or more to AIPAC. The highest single contribution was $51,000.[14]

Role and Israel Support Work

More than any other American Jewish organization, AIPAC maintains positions and conducts campaigns that mirror those of the Israeli government in power at any given time. The most publicized exception was Thomas Dine's vague support for the Reagan peace plan of 1 September 1982. After the Israeli government strongly rejected the plan, AIPAC proceeded to lobby against it.

In AIPAC's first decades, its lobbying priority was simply to increase U.S. aid to Israel, but its role later expanded to include lobbying against any arms sales to Arab regimes, beginning with Egypt, then Iraq, Saudi Arabia, and Jordan. In the 1980s, another priority was the conversion of U.S. loans into grants—a request substantially met in 1983. Ideologically, AIPAC has stayed with a few broad themes: it is in America's interest to support Israel; Israel is, like the United States, a democracy and thus reliable; and, more and more in the Reagan years, Israel is the only viable strategic ally in the region able to deter the Soviet Union.

AIPAC has agitated and lobbied on various topical issues as they have arisen. AIPAC took the lead in defending the Israeli invasion of Lebanon

*Some contributors who stand out, either for the sheer size of the sums involved or for the annual increments, include: Jacob Feldman of Commercial Metals Co. of Dallas, who gave $18,000 in 1980, $20,000 in 1981 and 1982, and $25,000 in 1983; B. Gottstein of Alaska, $10,000 in 1980, $15,000 in 1981 and 1982, and $20,000 in 1983; Peter Haas, of San Francisco's Levi Strauss Co., $3,250 in 1980 and $10,500 in 1983; Edward Levy of Detroit, $15,000 in 1980, $20,000 in 1982, and $23,000 in 1983; Albert Nerken of New York, $10,000 in 1980, $13,000 in 1981, $15,000 in 1982, and $20,000 in 1983; Samuel Soreff of Ft. Lauderdale, $17,500 in 1982 and $20,000 in 1983. The Greenbergs of Coleco Industries gave $3,000 in 1982 and $10,000 in 1983; Mote Friedkin of Ohio, $1,000 in 1980 and $12,000 in 1983; Charles Schusterman of Tulsa, $3,000 in 1980, $10,000 in 1981, and $12,000 in 1982 and 1983; Judd Malkin of Chicago, $1,000 in 1980 and $10,000 in 1983; and the Brachman family of Texas increased their 1980 gift of $4,000 to $14,000 in 1983.

(Dine testified before the House Foreign Affairs Subcommittee on Europe and the Middle East on 13 July 1982) and lobbied behind the scenes in support of keeping the U.S. Marines in Lebanon. Other such issues adopted over the years are the same as those taken up by most pro-Israel organizations: the Arab boycott, the United Nations, the PLO, organizations critical of Israel, the myth of the refugees, and so forth.

At the 1982 AIPAC Annual Policy Conference, Dine presented the following demands for U.S. policy toward Israel and the Middle East: (1) conversion of U.S. loans to grants; (2) no arms to Jordan; (3) U.S. support when Israel is forced to respond to the threat in Lebanon; (4) U.S. action regarding the negative role of the United Nations; (5) reversal of the U.S. decision to remove Iraq from the international terrorism list, along with no sale of cargo planes to Iraq; and (6) regarding the peace process, U.S. adherence to Camp David, reaffirmation of its alliance with Israel through strategic cooperation, pressure on Jordan and Saudi Arabia, including punishment of them for unfriendly acts and reprisals for buying arms from the Soviet Union, support for a strong and independent Lebanon, with Syria ousted, and development of a U.S. policy of energy independence.

The 1983 policy conference, held that June, laid out the coming year's lobbying goals in order of priority: (1) higher foreign aid to Israel; (2) greater U.S.-Israel strategic cooperation; (3) U.S. recognition of united Jerusalem as Israel's capital; and (4) more beneficial trade and economic policies for Israel. Each of these four priority issues received serious and systematic attention that went far beyond mere identification. The political arguments in support of each were outlined, as were the specific lobbying targets and actions.

Arguments to support higher U.S. aid included diplomacy (Israel's alignment with and promotion of U.S. interests, its reliability and shared democratic traditions as opposed to the instability of the Arab world, Iran, and Afghanistan); defense (opposition to the U.S.S.R., the sharing of intelligence information, combat testing of U.S. weapons, the future potential for military coordination); economics (the end results of higher aid "are more American jobs and exports and a stronger American economy"); Israel's paying for the Camp David Accords; and that the only reason the money is needed is "the huge Arab military build-up." Over $2.5 billion was requested (and received) for Israel in FY-1984; members of Congress were asked to support both the authorization and appropriation bills, to vote against any attempts to cut aid across-the-board or for Israel specifically, and to vote for final passage.[15]

Strategic cooperation is another AIPAC priority. The major political argument is Israel's unparalleled ability to protect U.S. interests and deter Soviet expansionism, as witnessed by its role in Egypt, Jordan, and Lebanon and generally against "international terrorism." According to a 1983 AIPAC memo: "As a result of these Israeli actions, the eastern

Mediterranean region, which once looked like fertile ground for Soviet adventurism, is now evolving toward stable relations with the Western world. Thanks largely to the actions of Israel, the Mediterranean basin is now virtually an American lake, with the exceptions of Syria and Libya." The memo concluded by listing how the U.S. would benefit from adopting the strategic cooperation agreement suspended in 1982: protection of lines of communication in a crisis, so that U.S. aircraft could be used elsewhere; valuable naval assistance; available airfields and ports; storage site for ammunition, fuel, and equipment; and hospitals for "the large number of American wounded likely to result from a Persian Gulf war. . . . " AIPAC's thrust is to pressure the Department of Defense to use Israel as the staging and supply area for the Rapid Deployment Force and to set up a separate section in that department to oversee the particular military aspects of strategic cooperation.[16]

AIPAC is calling for Congress to support a joint resolution to recognize Jerusalem as Israel's capital and to move the U.S. embassy there from Tel Aviv; this would also involve closing down the U.S. consulate general office in "East" (*sic*) Jerusalem, which is considered to be pro-Palestinian. The trade and economic policies recommended include allowing some "shekel conversion" of U.S. aid; increasing both export opportunities in the United States and U.S. government procurement, especially military, from Israel; securing U.S. assistance for increased NATO procurement of Israeli military production; and enforcing U.S. anti-boycott laws.

AIPAC's complete political resolutions, adopted in 1983 and published in *Near East Report*, covered the following points: legislation ensuring that Israel's annual debt service does not exceed domestic aid received in a given fiscal year; no U.S. arms sales to Jordan; no U.S. recognition of the PLO and no PLO participation in negotiations (with an oblique reference to the Jordanian option that reads, "It should be recognized that Jordan comprises 80% of what was the British Palestinian Mandate and that the majority of Jordan's people are Palestinian Arabs."). Further, the U.S. and its allies should wage war against the international network that includes the PLO, the Soviet Union, and Libya; the Arab lobby campaign to discredit Israel and undermine the U.S.-Israel alliance must be recognized and countered; Israel's friends must establish close relations with the media and provide collective criticism; Jerusalem is the capital of Israel, and the United States should move its embassy there; since Jews have the right to settle anywhere, the occupation of the West Bank and Gaza is not illegal, and settlements are not an obstacle to peace; the United States should encourage production of non-OPEC oil, support price competition, and intensify energy conservation and alternative sources; the United States should continue to threaten withdrawal from the UN if Israel is threatened with expulsion, and the United States should reduce its contributions by the amount that goes to support anti-Israel propaganda.

There were also resolutions on Jews in the Soviet Union and endangered Jewish communities. The last included a request for the U.S. administration "to support compensation from Arab countries for the lost property of thousands of Jews forced to flee since 1948."

A pervasive theme at the conference was the concern that a crisis between Washington and Tel Aviv was inevitably approaching. Members and supporters were urged to be prepared; emphasizing the backwardness and corruption of Arab society was suggested as the most productive counter-argument.

Tactics: AIPAC on the Hill

AIPAC's effectiveness is based on the systematic and assiduous application of tested lobbying techniques. Its special skill is the cultivation and simultaneous interaction of two sets of support networks, the first consisting of powerful elites and the second of an active mass-based constituency.

AIPAC's network of elites has been built up since its inception, with the major focus on Congress. The lobby's first major campaign in the 1950s was the promotion of a $100 million grant to Israel. Si Kenen's first step was to meet with the leadership of established American Jewish organizations and get access to their congressional contacts; he also met with leading Jewish businessmen and personalities. One of these was Barney Balaban, the head of Paramount pictures, whose aide arranged meetings with Senators Wayne Morse (R-Ore.) and Paul H. Douglas (D-Ill.), who became the sponsors of the grant bill. Senator John Sparkman (D-Ala.), also a sponsor, was introduced to Kenen by a local businessman and campaign contributor. The process of building up the network in these early days is described by Kenen:

> I visited many old friends on the Hill and in New York, including John Oakes of the *New York Times* and Harry Baehr of the *New York Herald Tribune,* and both publications carried excellent editorials....
>
> We consulted the two Jewish congressmen on the House Foreign Affairs Committee, Representatives Jacob J. Javits (R-N.Y.) and Abraham Ribicoff (D-Conn.)....
>
> Oveta Culp Hobby, who had led the American WACs and was a Houston publisher, came to Washington to host a dinner party for Eban and the Texas Democratic senators, Tom Connally, chairman of the Senate Committee on Foreign Relations, and his youthful colleague, Lyndon B. Johnson....
>
> Democratic leader Wiley Moore of Atlanta arrived with his friend Abe Goldstein to dine with Eban and Georgia's two Democratic senators, Walter F. George, who later succeeded Connally, and Richard B. Russell, then chairman of the Armed Services Committee.
>
> One widely respected congressman, Brook Hays (D-Ark.), told me that he had been in doubt about the legislation but favored it because a Little Rock rabbi, Ira Sanders, was sympathetic to Israel.
>
> Abraham J. Feinberg of New York, who had helped to start Truman's 1948 campaign train, telephoned many senators and their aides.[17]

Virtually all of these techniques are still used by AIPAC today with great success: cultivation of key people in the media; close consultation and coordination with supporters; hosting dinners and meetings with prestigious visiting Israelis, such as Abba Eban; using politicians' local constituents, such as the Little Rock rabbi, to exert pressure; and benefitting from the Jewish tradition of large campaign contributions, as in the case of Abraham Feinberg. Other techniques were also introduced in the 1950s. In 1951, for example, Kenen escorted a group of congressmen to Israel. Representatives Abraham Ribicoff (D-Conn.), Emanuel Celler (D-N.Y.), Jacob Javits (R-N.Y.), Tom Fugate (D-Va.), Kenneth Keating (R-N.Y.), Donald O'Toole (R-N.Y.), William Barrett (D-Pa.), and Sidney Fine (D-N.Y.) visited the country for twenty-three days. Whether or not a politician has visited Israel, and his or her behavior and comments there, are considered absolutely crucial; at the 1983 policy conference, members were told to avoid supporting even avowedly pro-Israel candidates if they hadn't actually been there.

Another early technique that has proved valuable is the cultivation of legislative aides. Amitay and Dine, among other AIPAC staff, had themselves been aides, and AIPAC has never lacked the support of strongly pro-Israel aides to key members of Congress. These aides have included Max Kampelman (Hubert Humphrey), Roy Millenson and Bess Dick (Jacob Javits and Emanuel Celler), Michael Kraft (Clifford Case), Albert Lakeland (Javits), Richard Perle (Henry Jackson), and Stephen Bryen (Case).*

Legislative aides and congressional staff play an important behind-the-scenes role in advocating policies, presenting particular positions and making contacts for their representatives. Among their duties are correspondence with constituents, researching and writing speeches, serving on various committees or subcommittees, preparing issue papers, and attending meetings with constituents, interest groups, or foreign visitors and summarizing the results.

One example of the use of aides was seen in early 1983, when AIPAC campaigned against the administration's policy toward Israel and Lebanon at that time. On 4 February AIPAC sponsored a briefing for senior aides of about fifty prominent Senate and House members; it was given by an Israeli government specialist on Lebanon, who focused on why Israel had to remain in Lebanon and why the Reagan peace plan would not work.[18]

---

*Bryen, who had worked on the staff of Senator Clifford Case (R-N.J.), left his job with the Senate Foreign Relations Subcommittee on Near Eastern and South Asian Affairs following allegations that he offered classified information to Israeli officials; he went on to work with the Jewish Institute for National Security Affairs, among other activities. Perle was considered instrumental in organizing a pro-Israel caucus within the House and in encouraging the late Senator Henry Jackson's (D-Wash.) pro-Israel position. Today Perle is an assistant secretary of defense and Bryen, one of his assistants, is deputy undersecretary for trade and security policy.

The briefing was followed by memos sent directly to members of Congress on the same subject, and by a 13 February Dine article in the *Washington Post*, "Pressuring Israel is Dumb."[19]

During the 1983 policy conference, when someone questioned Senator John Glenn's (D-Ohio) stand on Israel, Dine's only response was to say that Glenn's aide Carl Ford was "okay by me." Congressional staff present at the conference included James D. Bond, staff director of the Senate Appropriations Subcommittee on Foreign Operations; Richard McCall, deputy staff director of the Senate Democratic Policy Committee; Michelle Van Cleave, Representative Jack Kemp's (R-N.Y.) legislative assistant for defense and foreign policy; Stephen Ockenden, legislative assistant on foreign relations and defense to Senator Dave Durenberger (R-Minn.), and Bernard Friedman, administrative assistant to Representative Larry Smith (D-Fla.). Bond helped conduct a workshop on how to lobby his own committee.

AIPAC's friends embrace all spheres of political life. Morris Amitay created his own informal advisory group, which included John Lehman (secretary of the navy), Elliott Abrams (assistant secretary for international organization affairs), Myer Rashish (undersecretary of state for economic affairs), Ben Wattenberg (American Enterprise Institute), and former Senate aides Jay Berman and Ken Davis.[20] Among political party officials who attended the 1983 conference were the heads of the Democratic National Committee, the Democratic Senatorial Campaign Committee, and the National Republican Senatorial Committee.

A link to the White House has existed through various liaison officers and appears to have been strengthened by the increasing cooperation between the United States and Israel and consequent overlap in lobbying interests, as well as by AIPAC's close relationship to wealthy Republican Jewish supporters of Reagan. However, AIPAC still maintains its traditional policy of concentrating almost solely on Congress rather than the executive branch.

AIPAC's most valuable elite supporters continue to be a large number of pro-Israel representatives and senators from both parties. (Bipartisanship has been a guiding rule of AIPAC since the very first aid request, which was cosponsored by both parties.) Among the staunchest of AIPAC's Senate friends have been Henry Jackson, Howard Metzenbaum (D-Ohio), Robert Packwood, Rudy Boschwitz, Edward Kennedy, Daniel Moynihan (D-N.Y.), Robert Kasten (R-Wis.), Christopher Dodd (D-Conn.), and Joseph Biden (D-Del.). Senator Chic Hecht (R-Nev.) is a former state senate minority leader and active AIPAC member, while the recently elected New Jersey senator, Frank Lautenberg, is a former head of UJA and an AIPAC contributor. In late 1982, the *Jerusalem Post* described a "pro-Israel caucus" in the House under the informal leadership of Sidney Yates (D-Ill.), with members including Stephen Solarz (D-N.Y.), Benjamin Gilman (R-N.Y.), the late Benjamin Rosenthal (D-N.Y.), Henry

Waxman (D-Ca.), Barney Frank (D-Mass.), Jonathan Bingham (D-N.Y.), and Charles Wilson (D-Tex.). The *Post* wrote that they "meet informally to discuss legislative strategy in support of Israel" and noted that Menachem Begin met with them as a group in 1982.[21] Other members of Congress crucial to the caucus were Representatives Howard Berman (D-Ca.), Mel Levine (D-Ca.), Tom Lantos (D-Ca.), and Larry Smith (D-Fla.).

According to AIPAC's *Legislative Update for the Year End Report 1982:*

There was much good news for friends of Israel on November 2 as Campaign '82 concluded.

All 14 prime supporters of Israel whose Senate seats were challenged this year were reelected. Both Jewish Senators up for reelection won handily — Howard Metzenbaum (D-OH) and Edward Zorinsky (D-NE). Two new Jewish Senators were also elected — Chic Hecht (R-NV) and Frank Lautenberg (D-NJ). They will be joining incumbents Rudy Boschwitz (R-MN), Carl Levin (D-MI), Warren Rudman (R-NH) and Arlen Specter (R-PA), for a total of eight.

In the House, every senior supporter of Israel has been returned. Only one of the 24 incumbent Jewish representatives was defeated, freshman Democrat Bob Shamansky of Columbus, OH, a member of the House Foreign Affairs Committee. Seven new Jewish members will be serving in the 98th Congress, raising the total to 30. The new members are: Howard Berman (D-CA-26) (Los Angeles); Barbara Boxer (D-CA-6) (San Francisco); Ben Erdreich (D-AL-6) (Birmingham); Sander Levin (D-MI-17) (Southfield); Mel Levine (D-CA-27) (Los Angeles); Norman Sisisky (D-VA-4) (Petersburg); Larry Smith (D-FL-16) (Hollywood) . . .

In a number of House and Senate races this year, friends of Israel were in the enviable position of having strong supporters of Israel on both sides (e.g., New Jersey, Minnesota, Missouri and Delaware Senate races) and in several House races both candidates were Jewish.

What is most striking about this AIPAC report is the unquestioned assumption that any Jewish representative is automatically pro-Israel and of special value to AIPAC.

One change in AIPAC over the years is that it is now more active in the Senate than in the House, a policy based on the assumption that senators are more valuable allies because of their greater influence and longer time in office. The major focus is on incumbents who belong to key foreign aid or policy committees, other incumbents with influence, and representatives who are heading toward the Senate. In addition, support for Jewish candidates and incumbents is almost always assured. These priorities are generally the same as those followed by pro-Israel PACs, with which AIPAC works very closely.

While both the House and the Senate consistently vote in support of Israel, not all congressmen are ardently pro-Israel, and not all proposed legislation is favorable. For this reason, AIPAC staffers, together with supportive aides and representatives, constantly monitor events in Congress and all actions of congressmen. Particular attention is given to events relating to foreign relations or foreign aid; a congressional aide who works with the House Foreign Relations Committee describes AIPAC as being "like a wet blanket over the Committee." An AIPAC representative attends every open committee meeting and aggressively approaches all staffers, whatever their rank. Closed meetings are always attended by someone from the pro-Israel caucus. Careful record is kept of every representative's speeches, informal remarks, and even letters to constituents. The *Congressional Record* is read regularly, and any remarks which raise concern trigger visits from AIPAC.

AIPAC benefits greatly from its friends in Congress. The most obvious gain is in legislation and the ever-increasing aid to Israel. Other benefits include pro-Israel mailings and speeches that affect constituents. "Friends of Israel in Congress frequently put AIPAC-prepared speeches or AIPAC-prepared research into the *Congressional Record*, and once in this form it is circulated to newspaper editors, editorial writers, broadcast commentators and other opinion makers and community leaders who might be influential in spreading the views expressed." [22] In addition, AIPAC's own influence and power—and thus effectiveness—as an organization increase with each prestigious name or affiliation.*

AIPAC promotional literature, aimed at fundraising and soliciting membership, carries the following salutory quotes:

"Without AIPAC's persistent efforts over the past twenty years, Israel's security, and that of the western alliance in the Middle East might have been severely affected."

Hon. Clifford Case

"When I needed information on the Middle East, it was reassuring to know that I could depend on AIPAC for professional and reliable assistance."

Hon. Frank Church [23]

---

*Speakers at the 1983 policy conference included Senators Christopher Dodd (D-Conn.) and Paul Laxalt (R-Nev.), and Representatives Howard Berman (D-Ca.), Jack Kemp (R-N.Y.), Mel Levine (D-Ca.), Mark Siljander (R-Mich.), Larry Smith (D-Ca.), Robert Torricelli (D-N.J.), and Jim Wright (D-Tex.), all of whom addressed a session called "The Legislative Process." Even more impressive was the list of senators and representatives who attended the evening banquet: Senators Max Baucus (D-Mont.), Jeff Bingaman (D-N.M.), Rudy Boschwitz (R-Minn.), Bill Bradley (D-N.J.), Dennis DeConcini (D-Ariz.), Christopher Dodd, Charles Grassley (R-Iowa), Howell Heflin (D-Ala.), Paul Laxalt, Carl Levin (D-Mich.), Howard Metzenbaum (D-Ohio), Don Nickles (R-Okla.), Claiborne Pell (D-R.I.), Larry Pressler (R-S.D.), Arlen Specter (R-Pa.), and Representatives Joseph Addabbo (D-N.Y.), Don Albosta (D-Mich.), Anthony Beilenson (D-Ca.), Howard Berman (D-Ca.), Michael Bilirakis (R-Fla.), Jim Cooper (D-Tenn.), Richard Durbin (D-Ill.), Jack Edwards (R-Ala.), Ben Erdreich (D-Ala.), Dante Fascell (D-Fla.), Bobbi Fiedler (R-Ca.), Martin Frost (D-Tex.), Benjamin Gilman (R-N.Y.), Tom Harkin (D-Iowa), Steny Hoyer (D-Md.), John Kasich (R-Ohio), Ray Kogovsek (D-Col.), Tom Lantos (D-Ca.), Mel Levine (D-Ca.), Tom Lewis (R-Fla.), Clarence Long (D-Md.), Jim McNulty (D-Ariz.), Connie Mack (R-Fla.), Kenneth MacKay (D-Fla.), Jim Moody (D-Wis.), Solomon Oritz (D-Tex.), Stan Parris (R-Va.), Jerry Patterson (D-Ca.), Claude Pepper (D-Fla.), Larry Smith (D-Fla.), Mike Synar (D-Okla.), Henry Waxman (D-Ca.), Ted Weiss (D-N.Y.), Timothy Wirth (D-Col.), Howard Wolpe (D-Mich.), George Wortley (R-N.Y.), and Sidney Yates (D-Ill.).

AIPAC's mass-based constituency has been drawn primarily from the organized Jewish community through two methods: coordination with the leadership of the established Jewish community and religious and Zionist organizations, most of whom are on AIPAC's board; and the development of AIPAC's own membership. These overlapping sectors are constituents of both AIPAC and of whomever represents them in Washington as senator or representative.

Since its inception, AIPAC has used Jewish community groups to establish contacts and raise funds. Lobbying work is coordinated with the AJC and the ADL, the two community relations groups that devote the most time to the Hill, and with the Conference of Presidents of Major American Jewish Organizations. AIPAC benefits from this existing network; the participation of other, non-lobby groups ensures that AIPAC's "reports on congressional action and its calls for grassroots pressure go far beyond its own contributors or members."[24] During the campaign against the AWACS sale to Saudi Arabia, writer Roberta Feuerlicht described AIPAC's activities:

It must have used every Jewish mailing list in the country. I received several copies of a form letter asking for a contribution because "we intend to stop the sale in its tracks".... With the letter was a memorandum protesting the sale of the AWACS. I was to sign the memo, and a check, and send both back to Washington in the enclosed envelope, with the assurance that my protest would be personally delivered by an AIPAC lobbyist to my senator and representative.[25]

The focus on a wide base reflects AIPAC's vision of itself as much more than a simple lobby. In Thomas Dine's words, "We are not a PAC, we're a movement, a political factor, neither liberal nor conservative, neither Democratic nor Republican. We're the top of the iceberg of the pro-Israel community. We figure to expand support for Israel through the rest of the century."[26]

To achieve this goal, AIPAC has long stressed the need to claim representation of—and to be able to activate—a large mass base, and even more important, a mass base that is politically aware and active. Kenen recalls that "It's always necessary to appeal to the constituency. I urged the other Washington 'reps' to discuss the problems of legislation and to stimulate their constituents to act."[27] Sharing Kenen's concerns with the need for a politically aware community, Thomas Dine notes in an interview: "Every Jew should be a member of a congregation and involved in a local Federation.... Every Jew must be deeply involved in the political process."[28]

AIPAC goes about creating such a constituency by soliciting and educating membership and providing concrete courses of action. The AWACS mailing typically combined both a solicitation for membership

($35) and a specific form of activity (a memo against the AWACS, for example). The use of multiple mailing lists is also common.

A February 1982 mailing aimed at recruiting new members began with the salutation "Dear Fellow American." It continued with a denouncement of the AWACS sale, a mention of how "we almost won!", laudatory comments from the press and politicians about AIPAC, and then a strong pitch for membership that included the following argument:

AIPAC is a lobby and only the direct lobbying of Congress helps make American foreign policy. *What is more, thanks in great part to AIPAC, that foreign policy has, in the past three years, resulted in over six billion dollars of U.S. aid to Israel!*

To look at this figure in terms of what *your own* membership in AIPAC means in aid to Israel, consider this: On a budget of just $1.8 million, AIPAC successfully lobbied Congress in 1981 for $2.2 *BILLION* in foreign aid. *This means that every membership gift of $35 to AIPAC resulted indirectly in $42,777 of U.S. AID TO ISRAEL!* (emphasis in original).

Another membership recruitment mailing, sent out after the Israeli invasion of Lebanon, was headed "Is America for Sale?", with figures on Arab investment in the United States. An enclosed letter from Dine began, "Dear Friend, Israel's enemies have come out in the open." This was followed by examples of criticisms of Israel, and then an ominous call to join AIPAC because:

The need is urgent. The time is now. And it is better to act on principle today than to regret tomorrow the steps that were never taken.

Training, educating, and mobilizing the membership is considered the key component of successful mass-based lobbying. By approaching this task in its usual systematic and exhaustive fashion, AIPAC ensures that its constituency is not simply another large mailing list, but a powerful force in its own right. Frequent mailings go out with information on Congress and current events, and members receive the annual legislative update and the *Near East Report* newsletter.

The Annual Policy Conference is also the major forum for training and involving members in the actual lobby process. Approximately twelve hundred members attended the 1983 conference. They were divided into six groups according to geographic region and each group underwent training sessions focusing on the following skills: how to monitor and influence their local media, how to lobby Washington from their home states throughout the year, and how to lobby Washington when visiting there. A workshop on "The Nuts and Bolts of Political Action" dealt with campaign-related topics such as volunteer aides, fundraising, and media relations; it was led by Ann Frank Lewis, political director of the Democratic National Committee, Mitchell Daniels, executive director of the National Republican Senatorial Committee, and Billy Keyserling, planner of Senator Ernest F. Hollings' presidential campaign. Another workshop, "How to Lobby," was led by AIPAC staff. At a third, called "The Legislative Process," AIPAC members were addressed by Representatives Howard Berman, Mel Levine, Mark Siljander (R-Mich.), Larry Smith, and Robert Torricelli (D-N.J.).*

The general focus at the conference was on Congress, with little or no mention of the executive branch or even the presidential candidates. Much stress was put on urging members to be pleasant and non-antagonistic; for example, they were told never to accuse congressmen of anti-Semitism if statements critical of Israel were made. When some members proposed more confrontational tactics, AIPAC staff responded that the Israel lobby was secure enough to avoid tactics with possible negative side effects.

The conference was used to mobilize the membership and to lobby every senator and almost all representatives. AIPAC staff had previously made appointments on the Hill, and intense strategy sessions were held before sending members out in small groups. The lobbying goals were the same laid out by the conference as a whole for 1983-1984: members were provided with briefing memos outlining the political arguments for each point and the specific courses of action each representative was being asked to follow. In preparation, congressional staff and professional lobbyists briefed each group on the most effective approach.

In addition to the Annual Policy Conference, AIPAC also holds training sessions around the country at regional centers. At one such meeting, held in May 1978, a confidential guide entitled *Effective Community Action* was distributed. Among AIPAC's instructions to members and community activists were the following:

Identify key individuals in each Congressional District who can be called upon to contact your legislators on issues of concern. Such individuals, Jewish and non-Jewish, should know the Congressman well as personal friends, professional acquaintances, campaign workers, or contributors. The list of political contributors to a Congressman, available in the Secretary of State's office in every State House, provides one good source of potential key contacts for that Congressman. As long as they have a basic commitment to Israel's well-being, they can be briefed on specific issues. In districts with existing Federations or CRC's, such key individuals are more easily identifiable. Work within existing organizational frameworks whenever possible—but make sure people charged with the responsibility are really staying in touch with their legislators on our issues—not just casually.

Ideally there should be a few key contacts and they should not be labeled in the Congressman's or Senator's mind as the constituent who calls him only on Israel related matters. In some cases a legislator welcomes someone he can turn to

*Information on the Annual Policy Conference comes from AIPAC printed materials distributed there and from the notes of a conference participant.

exclusively for guidance on "Jewish" issues. A contact should be measured by the results he produced as well as his access.

Be aware of the difference in impact between telegrams (fastest), the personal phone call or letter (most effective) and form letters (easily discounted).

Identify priority issues and distinguish those areas in which Congress can and cannot do much more than criticize one-sided U.S. resolutions or a biased comment in a State Department press conference, but they *can* appropriate more aid for Israel, block arms shipments to Arab countries and strengthen anti-boycott laws. . . .

Particularly in 1978, a Congressional election year, encourage involvement in election campaigns at all levels: fundraising, personal contributions, canvassing, volunteer work and hosting coffees. Be sure that candidates running for Congressional office are well briefed on issues of concern to us and encouraged to take a public stand on them during the campaign. . . .

Encourage your Congressman and Senators and key aides to visit Israel, as nothing "sells" Israel as much as the country and the people themselves. Constituents should consider the possibility of accompanying a Congressman on such a visit.

When a Congressman makes a speech locally about relevant issues or says something important to a constituent, orally or in writing, please let us know about it. Or, if you have identified a friendly aide in the Congressman's office, let AIPAC know about it. When new key contacts are found, make certain that the new contact receives action and information memoranda and other materials.

In the 1980s, AIPAC began a series of political action workshops because:

American Jewish voters need to hone their political skills and sophistication in order to ensure that candidates for national office are supportive of Israel.

These AIPAC Political Action Workshops will provide leadership training for participants who can then transfer their skills to other Jewish voters in their home States.[29]

One such workshop scheduled for Chicago on 16 October 1983 was advertised as a "nuts and bolts workshop on how the political process works and how to become involved in it." The morning session was entitled "U.S.-Israel Relations: A Congressional Perspective," with presentations by Senator Bob Kasten, chairman of the Senate Appropriations Subcommittee on Foreign Operations, and Representative Larry Smith of the House Foreign Affairs Committee. The afternoon sessions included how-to workshops, presented by AIPAC staff, on "Elements of Political Action," "Israel and American Jewry," and the "Campaign to Discredit Israel: How to Respond."

The Intersection of the Elite and Constituent Networks

The key to AIPAC's success is not simply the cooperation of pro-Israel politicians or the mobilization of American Jewry, but AIPAC's ability to use the intersection of the two networks to its advantage. While this intersection exists on a number of levels, it most commonly takes the form of putting pressure on Congress. As one Senate aide has said: "Other lobbies do the same sort of thing, or try to, but AIPAC has its system of playing Congress down to a fine art."[30]

In a 1981 *Foreign Affairs* article, Senator Charles Mathias (R-Md.) had this to say about the lobby:

More important, in the long run, has been the success of the Jewish organizations in maintaining solid congressional support for a high level of military and economic aid to Israel. This is not to suggest that Congress supports Israel for no better reason than fear of the Israel lobby; on the contrary, I know of few members of either house of Congress who do not believe deeply and strongly that support of Israel is both a moral duty and a national interest of the U.S. It is rather to suggest that, as a result of the activities of the lobby, congressional conviction has been measurably reinforced by the knowledge that political sanctions will be applied to any who fail to deliver. When an issue of importance to Israel comes before Congress, AIPAC promptly and unfailingly provides all members with data and documentation, supplemented, as circumstances dictate, with telephone calls and personal visits. Beyond that, signs of hesitation or opposition on the part of a Senator or Representative can usually be relied on to call forth large numbers of letters and telegrams, or visits and phone calls from influential constituents."[31]

A former Senate aide put it even more clearly:

It's a remarkable system they have. If you vote with them, or make a public statement that they like, they get the word out fast through their own publications and through editors around the country who are sympathetic to their cause. It's an instantaneous reward with immediate positive feedback, where the Senator's name, attached to a proposal or idea, becomes the subject of laudatory editorial or news show comment. Of course, it works in reverse as well. If you say or do something they don't like, you can be denounced or censured through the same network. That kind of pressure is bound to affect Senators' thinking, especially if they are wavering or need support.[32]

The issue of AIPAC's role in funding or endorsing politicians is complex, as the organization is officially not supposed to engage in either activity. However, there is no doubt that AIPAC does so, while carefully staying within the letter of the law. The major technique consists of using the political clout of its membership and supporters—clout that is based on their known wealth and size of political contributions, their political activity, and their willingness to follow AIPAC's lead in judging politicians by the single-issue standard of a pro-Israel position. Members are asked to contribute to congressional races in their districts and states and to report their contributions to AIPAC, whose staff can then use them for access, saying to a politician that "We were responsible for your receiving x amount of dollars." Special emphasis is put on contributing early; a refrain at the 1983 policy conference was, "If money talks, early money shouts." AIPAC's ability to control funding and endorsement has been greatly increased by the establishment of the PACs, which are the legal vehicle for campaign contributions; almost all of them were founded or are run by former AIPAC staff and members. Endorsement follows the same lines; AIPAC's publications and statements make clear who is looked on favorably and who is not. Members are urged to act as volunteers on campaigns of known pro-Israel candidates and of "neutral" candidates, where the hope is expressed that the presence of AIPAC-connected Jewish activists will encourage the candidate to become more pro-Israel. At the 1983 conference, it was reported that over three hundred candidates solicited AIPAC support in 1982.

The conference also revealed how funding affects political party organizations as well as individual candidates. One participant in a political action workshop was Lynn Cutler, vice-chair of the Democratic National Committee, who noted the "hunger" of the party for money and the "ease" with which the Jewish community could acquire "quickly and early considerable power" by contributing. AIPAC members were urged to contribute and to request delegate status to the national convention— Cutler even distributed delegate application forms. Mitchell Daniels, executive director of the National Republican Senatorial Committee, spoke along similar lines.

Pressure from the constituency takes other forms as well. One aide said that "it takes just one wishy-washy statement or letter" to be picked up by AIPAC monitors and circulated to synagogues or community groups. Some aides believe that AIPAC has sent letters criticizing Israel to congressmen, simply to test their reactions. While this cannot be documented, the mere fact of such a rumor demonstrates the wariness that AIPAC evokes on the Hill. When it became known that one congressman was considering issuing a critical statement regarding the Lebanon war, a group of rabbis from his home state was flown in to dissuade him. As early as the 1960s, AIPAC began the regular policy of bringing constituents to Washington to appeal to wavering representatives. Kenen notes: "Our technique was always to rouse the constituents to mobilize the Members of Congress to press the Administration that this or that policy was what the American people wanted."[33]

Congressman Mervyn Dymally (D-Ca.), a member of the House Foreign Affairs Committee, has been known to "grumble" over aid to Israel. According to the *Wall Street Journal,*

Whenever Rep. Dymally grumbles, he says, he receives a prompt visitation from AIPAC or one of the Jewish PACs, usually accompanied by someone from his district.

During one recent session, he explained that while he sometimes complains, in the end he always votes for more aid to Israel. "Not once," I told them, "have I ever strayed from the cause."

And they said, "Well, you abstained once." That's how good they are.[34]

AIPAC also uses emotional pressure; during the AWACS debate, for example, every member of Congress received a complimentary copy of the novel *Holocaust*.

Another major technique is the letter campaign. Sometimes this entails postcards, which are distributed and signed in synagogues, B'nai B'rith lodges, and other community centers and sent out in the thousands. Less obvious are campaigns that focus on three or four related themes and use differently worded letters. Congressional aides say that such letter campaigns occur whenever there is a current issue relating to Israel or arms sales to the Middle East. Again, such campaigns often target waverers. In the summer of 1977, Representative Thomas J. Downey (R-N.Y.), an Israel supporter, expressed doubts about a foreign aid bill providing $1.7 billion to Israel.

Downey, whose mail was running high against any foreign aid, said he could vote for the bill only if it got a show of support from his district, which has a Jewish population of only 5 percent. Two days later, Downey got 3,000 telegrams from constituents saying they wanted a "yes" vote. He obliged.[35]

Similar incidents in the same time period involved Senators Adlai Stevenson (D-Ill.) and Abraham Ribicoff. When Stevenson was involved in a mark-up session on anti-boycott legislation, he received one hundred identically worded telegrams from Illinois residents, repeating AIPAC's call to "stand firm" against "weakening amendments." In AIPAC's view, the upshot of the incident came in 1982 when, according to Dine, "The memory of Adlai Stevenson's hostility toward Israel during his Senate tenure lost him the Jewish vote in Illinois—and that cost him the gubernatorial election."[36] When Ribicoff criticized Prime Minister Begin's policies and AIPAC itself as doing "a great disservice to the United States, to Israel and to the Jewish community," telegrams and letters from Connecticut residents poured in. AIPAC sent a memorandum to its Connecticut members charging that Ribicoff had attended a lunch with Yasir Arafat, and the Jewish press then picked up the story.[37]

AIPAC also maintains a computer list of key contacts for every member of Congress, drawn from its own resources and those of other pro-Israel groups around the country, particularly local federations and synagogues. If there is a need to pressure or simply approach a certain politician, the computer generates a list of potential contacts from the at-home constituency and others on the Hill; these might include former campaign workers, known large contributors to campaign funds, local community or religious leaders, or simply a close friend in the Senate or House.

Two 1975 incidents illustrate the peak of AIPAC's reliance on intersecting elite and constituent support. In both instances, the two networks were used to put pressure on the administration. The first occurred in response to the administration's proposal to sell Hawk anti-aircraft batteries to Jordan. Benefitting from the elite network, AIPAC was "leaked" the proposal by aides of former Senator Clifford Case and Congressman Jonathan Bingham. AIPAC head Morris Amitay then checked with the Israeli embassy and proceeded to send out a two-page memorandum against the sale to the entire Congress and to 397 city and regional Jewish organizations.

The second incident is considered AIPAC's "coup": the May 1975 "76 Senators" letter to President Gerald Ford requesting that the White House "be responsive to Israel's urgent military and economic needs." Again, AIPAC worked closely with the elite network: the letter was co-sponsored and signatures solicited by Senators Henry Jackson, Jacob Javits, Abraham Ribicoff, Richard Stone (D-Fla.), Lloyd Bentsen (D-Tex.), Birch Bayh (D-Ind.), Walter Mondale (D-Minn.), Herman Talmadge (D-Ga.), and others. The key contact people were once again friendly legislative aides: Winslow Wheeler in Javits' office and Jay Berman in Bayh's. The letter was drafted by Amitay and reprinted in the *New York Times* and thus became available to pro-Israel groups around the country for use in their own work. The impact of the letter and its public dissemination went ever further; on 27 May 1975, the *New York Times* reported:

Buoyed by recent demonstrations of congressional support, Israel has decided to ignore repeated United States requests that it produce new negotiating proposals before the American-Egyptian meeting in Salzburg next Sunday, according to senior Israeli officials.[38]

This close coordination can also be seen more recently, as in 1983, when AIPAC and its friends in Congress moved to block any arms sales to Jordan. The Kennedy-Heinz Senate resolution and the Addabbo-Corcoran House letter, both opposing the sale, were prepared and circulated with AIPAC support and active coordination. The extent of this cooperation was revealed at the 1983 conference, where a memo on the Jordan arms sales was distributed to members being sent out to lobby. The memo stated in part:

Both the letter and resolution are being held until after the AIPAC Policy Conference in order to get the maximum number of signatures. The House letter will be sent to the President at the end of this week. The Senate resolution will be dropped in the hopper at the same time" (emphasis in original).[39]

Politicians who consistently take a pro-Israel position and work closely with AIPAC are lauded in the lobby's publications and memos and feted at conferences and dinners. Their voting records are prominently distributed, and among the widening AIPAC network they receive the highest accolade: "a true friend of Israel." While the most obvious reward is a positive report to at-home constituents and the assurance of receiving Jewish votes and funding, there are others. These include meetings with high Israeli officials (witness Begin's meeting with the pro-Israel congressional caucus in 1982) and, as reported by some legislative aides, offers from AIPAC to provide their friends with support on other issues that concern a particular politician, even if not related to the Middle East.

Broadening the Agenda: Non-Legislative Target Areas

An increasing proportion of AIPAC's energies is being turned to targets outside its traditional legislative lobby agenda. These reflect concerns shared by most other Israel support organizations. For example, AIPAC is soliciting support from fundamentalist Christian churches because of the more liberal Protestant church establishment's concern for Palestinian human rights. To this end, AIPAC has established a Christian Outreach Program, and the 1983 policy conference was attended by fifty Christians from thirty-five states. Meanwhile, former AIPAC staffer F. Stephan McArthur went on to work for the National Christian Conference for Israel.

In accord with the NJCRAC mandate for Jewish groups to attempt to improve relations and find "common ground" with Black organzations, AIPAC has been holding meetings with Black politicians and organizations. In November 1983, AIPAC convened a weekend conference on "A Sharing of Agendas" with the youth group of the NAACP. The conference was addressed by Thomas Dine and Rev. Edward Hailes, national vice-president of the NAACP. The chair of the Congressional Black Caucus, Representative Julian Dixon (D-Ca.), also spoke and called on Jewish groups, particularly ADL, to ease up on their criticisms of presidential candidate Jesse Jackson. The Jackson campaign was a major source of both tension and dialogue between Jewish and Black groups. As of April 1984, AIPAC had held two meetings with Jackson to discuss these tensions.

A recurring theme at the 1983 policy conference was AIPAC's fear that American Blacks and other minorities were becoming anti-Israel as a result of their Third World orientation. To counteract this, it was suggested that emphasis should be put on the ill-treatment of minorities in the Arab world and on the argument that American Blacks, with their already overcrowded agenda, cannot benefit from supporting the Palestinians. Of the ten Blacks attending the conference, three wore AIPAC staff ribbons.

The major non-legislative activities of AIPAC now focus on the Arab lobby, as well as on the campus (to be discussed in Chapter 5). The resources and energy allotted by AIPAC to these areas show that they are considered political priorities and "targets" particularly suited to AIPAC's skills.

179

The Arab Lobby

The increased focus on what AIPAC terms the "Arab lobby" arises out of concern with some general trends in the U.S. These include a growing sympathy for the Palestinians among such sectors as students, liberal churches, and minorities; increased awareness of Israeli militarism and internal problems; and the formation of new groups that are critical of Israel, as well as the activities of more established groups.

AIPAC has decided that the most appropriate and effective political and ideological response is to portray Israel's Arab neighbors as backward and totalitarian, with emphasis on the oppression of women, the denial of equal rights to Christians (implying that Jerusalem is better off in Israeli hands), and Arab racism, allegedly proven by the historic involvement with the slave trade. All of these arguments are meant not only to defend and legitimize Israel, but also to forestall grassroots support for pro-Palestinian groups and thus prevent any serious challenge to Israel defense work.

Liberal and leftist critics of Israel are simply dismissed as pro-Soviet, anti-American, and extremist (they are only taken seriously in relation to campus work). AIPAC's attitude toward the more establishment groups— the National Association of Arab Americans (NAAA), the Arab Women's Council, the Arab American Anti-Discrimination Committee, the American Educational Trust, the American-Arab Affairs Council—is more ambivalent. These are generally assessed as ineffective because of their lack of a mass base, votes, and often counterproductive campaigns; simultaneously, however, AIPAC lumps them all together as a monolithic, wealthy, and powerful Arab lobby.

In August 1982, AIPAC hired Amy Goott to engage in full-time monitoring and analysis of the Arab lobby. In her prime time speech at the 1983 policy conference, Goott stressed the need for constant monitoring and called on members to send all information and materials to her in the Washington office. (The scope of AIPAC's monitoring became apparent during Goott's speech, when she quoted freely from Gray and Co. memos dealing with their public relations work for the NAAA.) As a major tactic for dealing with the lobby, she recommended stressing that the corporate funding many pro-Arab groups receive is simply a clever substitute for direct funding from Arab states, and thus a form of "Arab blackmail," where the corporations are allegedly repaid by business contracts in the Arab world.

Publications

AIPAC puts out a steady stream of reports, memos, speeches, analyses, and letters. It obtains maximum impact from these materials because of their distribution to elites (senators, representatives and their aides) and to membership. A congressional aide noted that AIPAC materials are used routinely for speeches commemorating Jewish or Israeli holidays and for issues where more specific information is needed, such as arms sale debate.

Near East Report (NER): According to Si Kenen, the *NER* was conceived in 1957, when he spoke at a UJA meeting and was sent payment afterwards. Because a charitable organization cannot contribute to a lobby, he was unable to accept the check for AIPAC, and this incident sparked the idea of a subscription newsletter, legally separate from AIPAC, that could accept such funds.

The *NER* began as an occasional four-page newsletter and became a weekly in 1970. With a circulation of approximately fifty thousand, the *NER* is distributed free to members of Congress, media, embassies and senior administration officials. In addition to individual subscriptions, it is also distributed by other organizations; B'nai B'rith, for example, distributes the *NER* to Hillel and the campuses.

The *NER* has been able to involve the same sort of high-powered staff as AIPAC itself. In addition to the founders, Kenen and Allen Lesser, an AIPAC assistant, the staff has included Wolf Blitzer, Kenen's successor as editor, who went on to become the Washington correspondent for the *Jerusalem Post*; Aaron Rosenbaum; Tina Silber, who later joined the staff of Senator Henry Jackson; Charles Fenyvesi, now editor of the *Washington Jewish Week* and advisor to the *Washington Times*; Susan Dworkin; Leonard Davis; Alan Tigay, who resigned to become executive editor of *Hadassah Magazine;* Moshe Decter; and the current editor, M.J. Rosenberg, a former aide to Congressman Jonathan Bingham.

The content of the *NER* strictly reflects the line of AIPAC and the Israeli government. Coverage includes broad topical issues and Middle East-related current events and detailed information about legislation and voting patterns of all politicians. The *NER* is also used to promote AIPAC events and campaigns and it reprints AIPAC speeches and testimony.

In 1964, the *NER* began issuing special supplements, known as *Myths and Facts.* Topics presented in these supplements include the Middle East arms race, U.S. aid and commitment to the area, Iran, the "myth" of the refugees, candidates' statements, convention platforms, the Arab boycott, and the Arab-Israeli conflict. This publication is widely distributed, especially for campus and community pro-Israel work.

Some other AIPAC publications, briefly noted, include the following:

Saudi (AWACS) Watch: Begun the day after the Senate voted to pass the sale of AWACS to Saudi Arabia in 1981, this is billed as "an ongoing report on Saudi compliance with the assurances they gave at the time of the AWACS sale—a report directed at Capitol Hill." The report focuses on "exposing" Saudi support for "PLO terrorism" and branding Saudi oil policy as anti-American.

The PLO Papers: Described as "updates on current PLO programs and actions, PLO plans, and the background of PLO terrorism."

Legislative Update: An annual report and assessment, in great detail, of all congressional, executive, and United Nations activities relating to the Middle East throughout the year.

The AIPAC Papers on U.S.-Israel Relations: A series of monographs, started in September 1982, that was part of AIPAC's "major new campaign to project Israel as America's best strategic asset in the region."[40]

In June 1983, AIPAC issued *The Campaign to Discredit Israel*, a handbook prepared largely by Amy Goott, the Arab lobby analyst. According to Thomas Dine's introduction, the handbook was prepared because:

In recent years, there has been a considerable growth in activity by other organizations that do not share our basic beliefs. An energetic campaign is being conducted by enemies of the U.S.-Israel relationship to undermine the moral and strategic ties between the two countries. Their method is to focus attention exclusively and relentlessly on any aspect of Israel which puts the Jewish State in a negative light, and thus to erode the relationship.

The handbook includes chapters on "The Artificial Constituency," "The Ideology—and its Weaknesses," "Lebanon and Beyond," and "A Directory of the Actors." This last chapter provides a list, with descriptions, of all organizations and individuals that are part of the "campaign." AIPAC acknowledges that there is great variety among the groups and individuals on the list, and possible doubt as to whether they all aim to "discredit Israel," but their inclusion is justified in the following way:

Many of the organizations describe their goals as fighting discrimination, advancing human rights, defending Lebanon, opposing war, improving U.S. relations with Arab countries, and other positive aims. In themselves, these objectives are not anti-Israel. Yet when an organization criticizes Israel's actions in Lebanon, but is not actively critical of PLO, Syrian and Iranian actions that have caused great suffering in that country, it is clear that the intention is to discredit Israel. Similarly, a committee that describes its purpose as defending human rights, yet concentrates its fire exclusively on alleged Israeli violations while ignoring extensive evidence of repression by Arab governments, manifestly has singled out Israel as a target. Promotion of Arab interests becomes an anti-Israel activity when the main policies being advanced would reduce the security of Israel or weaken the bonds between the United States and Israel.

AIPAC has announced plans to publish expanded and updated versions of the handbook on an annual basis.

Political Action Committees (PACs)

PACs emerged as an important political force after the 1974 and 1976 federal election law reforms, which restricted individual contributions to political candidates to $1,000. Groups of individuals who together form a PAC can now contribute up to $5,000 per candidate, per election.

As of 1982, there were 3,300 PACs in the United States; approximately half represented business interests, but the rest included such disparate groups as the National Rifle Association, the nuclear freeze, labor unions, and Christian evangelicals. Total PAC contributions to congressional candidates were $87.3 million, up from $55.3 million in 1980. Running for federal office is a very expensive undertaking, and PACs are becoming a crucial source of funding. In 1982, a successful candidate for the House of Representatives spent an average of $165,000 — 34 percent of which came from PACs. The average winning senator spent $2 million (up 71 percent from 1980), of which PACs accounted for 22 percent.[41]

The pro-Israel network quickly realized the importance and potential of PACs. Direct financial contributions to candidates had previously been a relatively weak link in the network, given the wealth of the community and its tradition of donating money and organizing fundraising campaigns. But since it is illegal for either lobbies or tax-deductible charitable organizations to give money directly to candidates, AIPAC (which, despite its name, is not a PAC) and virtually all the pro-Israel community organizations were effectively prevented from making direct financial contributions. With the emergence of pro-Israel PACs, almost all of which have been formed since 1980, this situation was transformed.

AIPAC staff and affiliates took the lead in establishing some of the larger pro-Israel PACs, thus providing AIPAC with valuable input into how the money is targeted. When former AIPAC director Morris Amitay left the lobby, he formed Washington PAC. Richard Altman, once AIPAC's political director, left to become the Washington, D.C. representative of the National Political Action Committee (NatPAC). Mark Siegel, a former Carter White House aide who worked closely with AIPAC and provided liaison with the Jewish community, is now director of the National Bipartisan PAC, which "was formed in 1978 by 30 Jewish backers of Senator Henry Jackson's presidential campaign."[42] Prominent AIPAC members and contributors closely connected to pro-Israel PACs include AIPAC senior vice-president Robert Asher of Chicago, former president Lawrence Weinberg of Los Angeles, the Swig family of San Francisco, and Marvin Josephson of New York.

Involvement in the formation of pro-Israel PACs is not limited to the lobby. According to Morris Amitay, PACs include "a wide spectrum of people who are members of establishment Jewish organizations. . . . "[43]

183

Following a visit to the United States, Israeli journalist Yoel Marcus wrote:

There is a massive Jewish organizing effort being made towards November 1984, and there is talk of about 70 to 80 Jewish PACs. However, I will not be surprised if I have been intentionally misled and there will be in the end hundreds of Jewish PACs. Moreover, in some places Jews are setting up PACs jointly with trade unions and evangelist Christians, two groups which are very pro-Israel.[44]

Not one of the thirty-three PACs identified as pro-Israel has a name that refers even obliquely to Israel, the Middle East, or foreign policy. Most likely this reflects a compromise between the more assertive AIPAC members who took the lead in advocating and forming pro-Israel PACs, and the established (and more traditional) Jewish community leaders and constituents, who are understandably wary of evoking references to "Jewish money" or charges of "buying" politicians.

The Wall Street Journal and the book PACs Americana have identified thirty-three pro-Israel PACs that participated in the 1981-1982 election cycle.* They donated $1.87 million to 268 candidates for federal office. This may not seem like a huge sum next to the $87.3 million PAC total, but there are several reasons that pro-Israel PACs have an impact higher than either numbers or finances would suggest. One is that there is simply no opposition. In an article appropriately entitled "A Field Day for Jewish PACS," Morris Amitay noted:

So far there are no pro-Arab PACs operating. When the oil interests and other corporate interests lobby, 99 percent of the time they are acting in what they perceive to be their own self-interest — they lobby on tax bills, but we rarely see them lobbying on foreign policy issues. In a sense we have the field to ourselves. I think we should take advantage of this.[45]

Another reason for the effectiveness of pro-Israel PACs is their careful and systematic use of money. Most follow a policy of making donations to races where contributions can really make a difference. For example, the largest pro-Israel PAC of all, NatPAC, did not contribute to staunchly pro-Israel senators Daniel Moynihan (D-N.Y.) or John Danforth (R-Mo.), who were considered guaranteed winners. Instead they gave to pro-Israel politicians who were facing closer challenges, such as Senators Jim Sasser (D-Tenn.), Lowell Weicker (R-Conn.) and Chic Hecht (R-Nev.), or to Representatives Tom Lantos (D-Ca.), Sam Gejdenson (D-Conn.), Dante Fascell (D-Fla.), Sidney Yates (D-Ill.) and Jack Kemp (R-N.Y.). Senator George Mitchell (D-Maine), who had been challenged by

* According to the New York Times of 16 August 1984, "At least 54 political action committees, with names that do not reveal their political purposes, have mustered more than $4.25 million to influence the 1984 American elections in favor of policies, appropriations and Congressional candidates that support Israel."

Representative David Emery, received $78,807 in contributions from twenty-eight of the pro-Israel PACs, all of which are based outside of his state. In addition, PACs benefit from the fact that pro-Israel candidates are often the incumbents who are likely to win reelection: 74 percent of pro-Israel PAC contributions in the 1982 Senate contests went to the incumbent candidates.

Like the pro-Israel lobby in general, the basic reason for the strength of these PACs is that they focus on a single foreign policy issue, and this strategy allows them to use money in the most effective way. They target politicians who are involved with U.S. aid to the Middle East, both economic and military, or with determining U.S. foreign policy. In the Senate, these include members of the Foreign Relations Committee and its Subcommittee on Near Eastern and South Asian Affairs or the Senate Appropriations Committee, particularly the Subcommittee on Foreign Operations. In the House, they also look to members of the Foreign Affairs and Appropriations Committees and the relevant subcommittees.

According to the *Wall Street Journal*, in 1981-1982 pro-Israel PACs spent $355,550 to elect or defeat members of the House Foreign Affairs Committee and House Appropriations-Foreign Operations Subcommittee. Of the eleven representatives elected in 1982 who received more than $10,000 in pro-Israel PAC money, four were on the Appropriations Committee; these were Representatives Clarence Long (D-Md.), Sidney Yates, Les AuCoin (D-Ore.), and Matthew McHugh (D-N.Y.). Three were on the Foreign Relations Committee: Reps. Dante Fascell, Sam Gejdenson and Tom Lantos. The others were Dick Durbin, who was Rep. Paul Findley's opponent in Illinois, Ike Skelton (D-Mo.), Martin Frost (D-Tex.), and Phillip Burton (D-Ca.). Rep. Clarence Long (D-Md.), chairman of the Foreign Operations Subcommittee and a staunch supporter of Israel, received approximately $30,000 from pro-Israel PACs. He told the *Wall Street Journal*, "I would call this defensive money. They want to try to keep me in Congress."[46] Four other members of his subcommittee received more than seven percent of their contributions from pro-Israel PACs— three times the average from these PACs. In the House Foreign Affairs Committee, Dante Fascell received approximately $40,000 from twenty-two pro-Israel PACs. Clement Zablocki (D-Wis.), who was not very popular with the lobby, was challenged in the last elections by State Senator Lynn Adelman, who is both Jewish and pro-Israel. Adelman received around $10,000 from thirteen pro-Israel PACs. He probably was not given more because Zablocki was a fairly certain winner, because Findley was the main target, and because the "reliable" pro-Israel members of the Foreign Affairs Committee outnumbered other members twenty-one to sixteen. (This margin increased in late 1983 when Zablocki died and was replaced by Fascell, who became acting chairman of the committee.)

It is more difficult to assess the impact of the pro-Israel PACs on the Senate, where there are three separate campaign cycles. (Also, as in the

House, some senators are both pro-Israel and guaranteed winners, so they do not need PAC money). Five incumbent, pro-Israel members of the Appropriations Committee received $232,600: James Sasser, (D-Tenn.), $58,250; Robert Byrd (D-W. Va.), $55,500; Quentin Burdick (D-N.D.), $44,775; Lowell Weicker (R-Conn.), $42,075; and Dennis DeConcini (D-Ariz.), $32,000. In the Senate Foreign Relations Committee, $48,500 went to Paul Sarbanes (D-Md.)

Approximately 60 percent of the total expenditures of pro-Israel PACs in 1981-1982 went to Senate races. In addition to the senators cited above, the following received contributions of more than $10,000: George Mitchell (D-Maine), $77,400; David Durenberger (R-Minn.), $56,000; Chic Hecht (R-Nev.), $46,500; Jeff Bingaman (D-N.M.), $36,575; Howard Metzenbaum (D-Ohio), $35,175; John Heinz (R-Pa.), $15,500; Henry Jackson (D-Wash.), $11,750; William Roth (R-Del.), $11,500; Daniel Moynihan (D-N.Y.), $11,000; Spark Matsunaga (D-Hawaii), $10,000; Frank Lautenberg (D-N.J.), $10,500; and Edward Kennedy (D-Mass.), $10,420.[47]

Pro-Israel support is still overwhelmingly Democratic. The eleven major House recipients of pro-Israel PAC money listed previously were all Democrats; of the twenty-six senators listed, only six were Republicans.

No discussion of the impact of pro-Israel PACs would be complete without mentioning the successful campaign in 1982 to defeat Republican incumbent Paul Findley in Illinois. While the drawing of new district lines in the area, which resulted in a situation where one-third of the voters were new to Findley, certainly contributed to his defeat, the candidates and observers alike agree that PACs played a critical role.

Findley, an incumbent for over twenty years, was the ranking Republican on the House Foreign Affairs Subcommittee that authorized aid to Israel. He was also the leading congressional critic of Israel and had met twice with PLO chairman Yasir Arafat. His opponent in the 1982 race was Dick Durbin, a Catholic lawyer and Democrat. The Middle East and Israel were not big issues in the district, where there are less than two thousand Jewish voters. However, Durbin received more pro-Israel PAC money than any other candidate in the country: approximately $104,000, donated by virtually every pro-Israel PAC in the United States. Defeating Findley was the agreed priority of the pro-Israel network. (AIPAC bussed two hundred student volunteers for Durbin into the district two weeks before the election; as Durbin's winning margin was only 1,400 votes, each student only needed to have persuaded seven voters to defeat Findley.)

One Illinois-based pro-Israel PAC, the Citizens Concerned for the National Interest, contributed their $5,000 maximum to Durbin. Its treasurer "also headed the National Committee to Elect Dick Durbin, which solicited individual donations from Jewish leaders across the country with a letter saying: 'This year we have the best chance we will ever have to remove this dangerous enemy of Israel from Congress. . . . ' "[48]

Lawrence and Barbara Weinberg were organizers of a Los Angelesbanned pro Israel PAC called the Citizens Organized PAC, which donated $5,000 to Durbin. The Weinbergs gave $20,000 to the PAC and an additional $2,000 to Durbin. Another California PAC that contributed to Durbin is the San Franciscans for Good Government, whose founder is Melvin M. Swig, co-owner of San Francisco's Fairmont Hotel. Swig said his PAC is "intended to support candidates whose views are favorable to the State of Israel." His comment on Findley: "We would not like to see him returned to Congress."[49]

The Findley case is an impressive example of the power of PACs when put to intelligent use. In 1980, Findley had been challenged by a former state representative, David Robinson. Though Robinson drew thousands of dollars in donations from individual Jews around the country, this was before the majority of pro-Israel PACs had been formed, so the totals and the organization were much less effective. In addition, it is clear that in 1982 the lobby assessed the situation objectively and realized that the new redistricting—adding many Democratic voters— created an ideal opportunity to unseat Findley. Hence the decision to concentrate on this race.

With each election cycle, it is clear that pro-Israel PACs are steadily increasing in influence and size. According to a February 1985 *Wall Street Journal* article:

Jewish PACs'... overall giving to federal candidates and party organizations in the 1984 campaign almost doubled from 1982, to nearly $3.6 million. Their numbers also doubled, to more than 70 PACs. While the Jewish PACs represented only about 4% of total PAC giving, their power comes from their intense focus on candidates and congressional committees that deal with foreign aid, a subject of little interest to most lobbies....

Of $1.82 million given to Senate candidates, 44% went to opponents of five Republican senators who voted for the controversial 1981 sale of AWACS aircraft to Saudi Arabia, which the Senate approved. Senators Percy of Illinois and Roger Jepsen of Iowa lost re-election, Senators Jesse Helms of North Carolina, Thad Cochran of Mississippi and Gordon Humphrey of New Hampshire won....

Combined giving to defeat Sen. Percy alone totaled $321, 825. Some 21 Jewish PACs gave $51,150 to former Illinois Representative Tom Corcoran, a conservative Republican, in his unsuccessful primary race against Sen. Percy. Then 19 of these groups crossed party lines to join 40 other Jewish PACs in giving $270,675 to Rep. Paul Simon, a liberal Democrat, who beat Sen. Percy in the general election. In addition, Michael R. Goland, a California real estate investor with ties to one of the Jewish PACs, spent $1.1 million in an "independent" TV, direct-mail and billboard campaign against Sen. Percy.[50]

There can be little doubt that PACs are here to stay as a major and important addition to the activities of the Jewish community and the pro-Israel lobby. (ADL head Kenneth Bialkin responded to John Fialka's 1983 *Wall Street Journal* article with a letter defending pro-Israel PACs.)[51]

Their proliferation, of course, strengthens the power and effectiveness of the single-issue PACs, especially if AIPAC provides coordination. The $5,000 or $10,000 ceiling on individual contributions quickly becomes meaningless when there are fifty or more PACs contributing to the same candidate.

National Political Action Committee

Date established: 1982
Chairman of the Board: Marvin Josephson
Executive Director: Richard Altman
Address: 308 East Capitol St., S.E. Washington, DC 20003
Slogan: "Faith in Israel Strengthens America."

NatPAC is the largest, wealthiest, and best-known of the pro-Israel PACs. It was founded by Marvin Josephson, head of International Creative Management, one of the largest theatrical and literary talent agencies in the United States. He states that he was motivated to start the PAC after the AWACS vote, because of the upsurge in anti-Semitism and the disclosure of the role of big business in supporting the arms sale.[52]

NatPAC has a six-member board consisting of Josephson; Barry Dillar, chairman of Paramount Pictures; George Klein, a New York City developer and leading Jewish Republican; Martin Peretz, editor of the *New Republic;* James Wolfensohn, a New York investment banker; and Rita Hauser, a New York lawyer and former chair of the Foreign Affairs Commission of the American Jewish Committee. The Washington, D.C. representative is Richard Altman, who left his position as an AIPAC lobbyist to take the job.[53]

Josephson has built up NatPAC quickly and effectively. He began by soliciting donations of $5,000 or more, which was then used as seed money for advertisements in Jewish and non-Jewish newspapers and for fund-raising appeals. Of all the PACs, NatPAC has taken the most public approach. One of its first steps was a large direct mailing with a cover letter by Woody Allen, which began:

> Mobil Oil has a PAC.
> Bechtel has a PAC.
> Fluor has a PAC.
> Boeing and Amoco and Grumman all have PACs.
> But those of us who believe deeply in this country's long-term stake in Israel's survival have not had a nationwide PAC.

Enclosed with the letter was NatPAC's statement of policy and purpose, which was divided into four sections: (1) "The Problem"—U.S.

commitment to Israel is weakening; (2) "U.S. Long Range Interests Are At Stake"—great damage would be done to America if ties with Israel were eroded; (3) "The Evidence is Unmistakable"—petrodollar ads, an international double standard against Israel, accusations of double loyalty against American Jews, and a "growing sentiment that sticking with Israel is not worth all the headaches. . . . ;" (4) "We Can Act Together"—there must be elected officials from every party who share these concerns, and NatPAC is the vehicle to achieve this.

Among the 166 names on the "partial list of supporters" are Morris Abram, Woody Allen, Bob Hope, Michael Korda, Ralph Lauren, Zubin Mehta, Sue Mengers, Martin Peretz, Itzhak Perlman, Roberta Peters, Rabbi Alexander Schindler, Richard Sennett, Fred Silverman, Laurence Tisch, and Pinchas Zukerman.

By October 1982, when NatPAC had over ten thousand subscribers, it began placing full-page ads in leading newspapers. One of the first of these ads was aimed at recruiting non-Jews as supporters. In large type the ad proclaimed; "Supporting candidates who believe in Israel isn't just good for Jews. It's good for Americans." The smaller text underneath began:

Some people in America today think you have to be Jewish to support congressional candidates who believe in Israel.

But you don't.

All you have to do is believe in America.

You see, if U.S. interests in the Middle East were threatened, it would take months to mount a significant presence there. With Israel as an ally, it would take only days.[54]

The same month another NatPAC ad appeared in the *New York Times*. Under a photograph of Yasir Arafat were the words, "Next year in Jerusalem?" followed by the text:

Yasir Arafat has publicly stated that he would like the people of Israel wiped off the face of the earth.

This is not only a threat to the people of Israel, but also to America.

Israel is our strongest military ally in that part of the world. But the ties between our two countries go much deeper than that. Israel is the *only* democratic nation in the Middle East.

Its people share the same values and the same goals as we do.[55]

NatPAC raised approximately one million dollars in its first year. In the 1982 elections, it gave $547,000 to 109 candidates, with no donation of less than $5,000.[56] In October, 1982 Josephson announced that NatPAC was expanding and hoped to be involved in every Senate and House race in 1984.

Other Pro-Israel PACs

These figures on political contributions were reported for the 1983-84 election cycle:[57]

Americans for Better Citizenship: $4,500 to 4 candidates.
Americans for Better Congress (ABC): $11,850 to 7 candidates.
Americans for Good Government: $102,250 to 56 candidates.
Arizona Politically Interested Citizens: $55,800 to 36 candidates.
BALPAC Political Action Committee: $24,600 to 23 candidates.
Bay Area Citizens PAC (BACPAC): $15,500 to 25 candidates.
BAYPAC: $31,350 to 35 candidates.
Chicagoans for a Better Congress: $15,000 to 8 candidates.
Citizens Concerned for the National Interest: $56,000 to 21 candidates. (Chicago)
Citizens Organized PAC: $174,000 to 37 candidates. (Los Angeles)
Committee for "18": $30,000 to 25 candidates. (Denver)
Congressional Action Committee of Texas: $40,500 to 32 candidates.
Connecticut Good Government PAC: $6,750 to 10 candidates.
Delaware Valley PAC: $187,300 to 132 candidates.
Desert Caucus: $142,000 to 56 candidates.
Florida Congressional Committee: $114,500 to 59 candidates.
Friends of Democracy PAC: No contributions to any candidate.
Government Action Committee: $12,000 to 21 candidates.
Hudson Valley PAC: $111,941 to 105 candidates.
Joint Action Committee for Political Affairs: $260,550 to 118 candidates.
Massachusetts Congressional Campaign Committee: $66,000 to 27 candidates.
Mississippians for Responsive Government PAC: $1,710 to 9 candidates.
National Action Committee: $84,799 to 35 candidates.
National Bipartisan PAC: $40,700 to 36 candidates.
National PAC (see above): $749,500 to 148 candidates.
Roundtable PAC: $106,750 to 91 candidates.
San Franciscans for Good Government: $111,000 to 39 candidates.
St. Louisans for Better Government: $132,000 to 51 candidates.
South Carolinians for Representative Government: $1,250 to 2 candidates.
To Protect Our Heritage: $35,498 to 17 candidates.
Washington PAC: $196,800 to 178 candidates.
Youngstown PAC: No contributions during this cycle.
Capital PAC (CAPPAC) $16,030 to 32 candidates.*

* CAPPAC was formed in late 1983 in Washington D.C. Chaired by Philip Friedman, it—like many other PACs—seeks to attract young professionals between the ages of twenty and forty. CAPPAC describes itself as "dedicated to strengthening American support for the State of Israel" and contributes to candidates who "support economic and military aid to Israel; recognize Israel's strategic value to the United States; demonstrate a moral commitment to the survival of Israel; and are committed to ensuring the security of Israel."[58]

Conference of Presidents
of Major American Jewish Organizations

Date established: 1959
Chairman: Kenneth J. Bialkin
Executive Vice-President: Yehuda Hellman
Address: 515 Park Avenue, New York, NY 10022
Publications: *Annual Report, Middle East Memo*

General Background and Structure
Efforts leading to the establishment of the Conference of Presidents of Major American Jewish Organizations, usually referred to as the Presidents Conference or simply the Conference, began in 1955. The now-accepted story, whether apocryphal or not, is that it arose as a direct result of the complaint of Undersecretary of State Henry Byroade that too many Jewish organizations were competing to get an audience with President Eisenhower to discuss the issue of Israel and U.S. policy toward the Middle East. Nahum Goldmann, who became the first chair of the conference, took the initiative in bringing together an *ad hoc* group of sixteen organizations, each represented by its president or director. The original organizations involved were: American Jewish Congress, American Trade Union Council for Labor Israel, American Israel Committee for Public Affairs (later AIPAC), American Zionist Council (later disbanded), B'nai B'rith, Hadassah, Jewish Agency-American Section, Jewish Labor Committee, Jewish War Veterans, Labor Zionist Organization of America, Mizrachi Organization of America, National Community Relations Advisory Committee, Union of American Hebrew Congregations, Union of Orthodox Jewish Congregations, United Synagogue of America, and the Zionist Organization of America.

Originally known as the Presidents Club, the Presidents Conference was formally established in 1959 with a headquarters, budget and staff. In 1966 the members voted to become a representative body of organizations rather than one of organization presidents. Today the Presidents Conference lists thirty-seven affiliated organizations; those who joined after the original sixteen are: American Mizrachi Women, American Zionist Federation (replacing the AZ Council), Anti-Defamation League, B'nai B'rith Women, B'nai Zion, Central Conference of American Rabbis, Emunah Women of America, Herut Zionists, Jewish National Fund, Jewish Reconstructionist Foundation, Labor Zionist Alliance, National Committee for Labor Israel (incorporating the American Trade Union Council for Labor Israel), National Council of Jewish Women, National Council of Young Israel, National Federation of Temple Sisterhoods, National Jewish Welfare Board, North American Jewish Youth Council, Pioneer Women, The Rabbinical Assembly, Rabbinical Council of America,

Women's American ORT, Women's League for Conservative Judaism, Workmen's Circle, and the World Zionist Organization-American Section. The AJC and CJF are both observers. The criteria for membership are that an organization be national in scope, have an independent budget, at least one staff member dealing with national affairs, and make its own policy independent of others.

The prestigious position of chairperson is filled approximately every two years, usually by the president of a constituent group who is nominated by an eight-member board and then elected by the rest. The current chair, elected in June 1984, is lawyer Kenneth J. Bialkin, who has been in the leadership of ADL for many years. Julius Berman, head of the Union of Orthodox Jewish Congregations, chaired the Conference from June 1982 until 1984. Berman, an Orthodox-ordained rabbi, was the first Orthodox leader ever to hold the position of Conference chair. The chairman for the preceding two years (June 1980–June 1982) was Howard Squadron of the AJCongress. Yehuda Hellman, a close friend of Nahum Goldmann, has held the paid position of executive vice-president since 1959. Richard Cohen is the public relations consultant for the Conference.

The Presidents Conference is supported mainly by dues and contributions from its member groups. The budget in the late 1970s was approximately $150,000 a year and reached $350,000 in 1982.

Role

While AIPAC is the lobby of the pro-Israel community and is known for its clout and political maneuvering, the Presidents Conference could be termed the diplomatic branch. Its power is based on the claim to represent the consensus of its constituent organizations on questions relating to Israel and other international issues. This claim is unparalleled, as Conference head Julius Berman noted in an interview:

I believe that the Presidents Conference is an unbelievable phenomenon in the history of the American Jewish community. We all realize that American Jews are the most over-organized entity in the world. Over-organized usually means disorganized, with everyone speaking for himself or herself. The ability of the various national organizations, now totalling 36, to come together and work out a consensus on a specific subject and to continue to work together on that issue, without in any way homogenizing the rest of the organizational world and covering up the numerous areas in which there might be disagreement, can be called a miracle of modern times. Over the years, slowly but surely, both within the American Jewish community and within the public at large, including the powers in Washington, a consensus has grown that the Presidents Conference reflects the position of the total American Jewish community.[59]

The original role of the Presidents Conference was to provide an internal forum for addressing issues related to Israel, and also act as an external voice, reflecting the consensus of American Jewish leaders. From this basic orientation there have developed several major interrelated functions: first, to interpret and convey the position of American Jewry to the U.S. government, policy makers, and media, to the Israeli government, and to other countries and international bodies; second, to interpret and convey the U.S. government and public's position to the Israeli government and the American Jewish community; and third, to present the Israeli position to the U.S. government, the American Jewish community, and the general public.

Thus it is in a very real sense that the Presidents Conference is often termed the foreign policy association of the American Jewish establishment. It is not a lobby, either legally or in practice, but it is more than simply an articulator of a consensus. It is simultaneously a concerned participant and an occasional mediator, a role that depends on maintaining a consensus and having close relations, and thus legitimacy, with those in power in the United States and Israel.

That the Presidents Conference has been granted this legitimacy is demonstrated by the numerous private meetings with and special access to high-ranking officials of both countries.[60] Julius Berman was elected president of the Conference on 9 June 1982; though his term officially began on July 1, within twenty-four hours he was in the White House with a Conference delegation to meet with Vice President George Bush (President Reagan was in Europe at the Versailles Conference). According to its annual report for the year ending 31 March 1982, members of the Presidents Conference had meetings with Reagan, Bush, Secretary of State Haig, Secretary of Defense Weinberger, UN Representative Kirkpatrick, and National Security Advisor Richard Allen throughout the year. The contacts on the Israeli side are even closer. In addition to frequent visits to Israel, the Presidents Conference is routinely briefed by high-level Israeli diplomats in the United States and by visiting officials. When Menachem Begin came to the United States in 1981, one of his first acts was to meet privately in his hotel suite with members of the Conference. He then left for Washington for meetings with Reagan and other officials; on his return to New York he met again with the Presidents Conference to share the results of his talks. The Israelis also use the Conference as a conduit to the administration. In November 1981, a special Knesset delegation led by Moshe Arens and Chaim Herzog briefed the Presidents Conference on the Israeli position toward the Fahd peace plan; the very next day a Conference delegation met with Reagan and Bush to discuss the same Fahd plan. On 26 August 1982, Israeli defense minister Ariel Sharon met with the Conference and presented his assessment of the Lebanon war and the coming period. (He was introduced by Julius Berman as "the chief architect of Israel's great victory.") In the late afternoon of the same day, a thirteen-member Presidents Conference delegation met with Secretary of State Shultz for two hours—to discuss U.S. Middle East policy following the war. Just one week later, representatives of the Conference held

193

another long private meeting with Shultz, this time to discuss the Reagan plan. The Conference is also used as a public forum for messages; on 14 February 1984, Deputy Prime Minister David Levy used his speech to the Conference to criticize the United States strongly for not consulting sufficiently with Israel regarding the withdrawal of the Marines and the meetings with Egypt's President Mubarak and Jordan's King Hussein. (The Conference was holding an annual meeting in Jerusalem.)

Other examples of the Presidents Conference role as the arbiter and/or diplomat of the American Jewish communities abound:

According to its annual report, the "1980 Presidential campaign catapulted the Presidents Conference onto the front pages of the nation's newspapers as each major candidate appeared before it to present his views and answer questions on critical foreign policy issues that American Jews would take into account as they cast their ballots." After each such meeting, Conference president Howard Squadron held a well-attended press conference. While not officially endorsing a candidate, after the meeting with the incumbent, Jimmy Carter, Squadron said, "I think that on some issues people left the room still concerned"; following the meeting with Reagan, Squadron noted that he had "said the right things."

After the July 1981 Israeli bombing of Beirut, U.S.–Israeli relations were strained, and the Conference was used to mend fences:

As the U.S.-Israeli relationship grew tense, Mr. Begin invited Howard Squadron and Yehuda Hellman to visit Jerusalem for a wide-ranging discussion of the situation. On their arrival in Jerusalem, Squadron and Hellman met with Prime Minister Begin for a thorough review of the state of American public opinion, with particular reference to Israel and the Middle East. In the stormy aftermath of the Beirut raid, Prime Minister Begin had come to recognize the extent and depth of negative U.S. public opinion. "A key figure in this process," said the *New York Times* in a review of events, "was Howard Squadron."[61]

Squadron worked on mediating the American side as well. He brought with him on the trip House Foreign Affairs Committee members Tom Lantos (D-Ca.) and Millicent Fenwick (R-N.J.), who also met with Begin. Outlining the Conference's task in the U.S., he said, "We'll have to work hard to persuade senators and congressmen that something very serious was going on in the north [Galilee] and the civilian casualties [in Beirut] are not only regretted, but not likely to happen again. . . ."[62]

In early July 1981, Squadron and Hellman visited West Germany and met with Chancellor Helmut Schmidt, whom they criticized for his position on the Middle East. They also held meetings with opposition leader Helmut Kohl, who used the meeting as a forum for pledging "to pursue a pro-Israel policy on assuming political leadership. . . . " After his election as chancellor, Kohl met again with the Presidents Conference during a 1982 visit to the United States and once more asserted his pro-Israel position and laid the groundwork for a state visit to Israel which took place in early 1984.[63]

In September 1983, a delegation from the Presidents Conference met one hour with Secretary of State Shultz and another hour with Richard Murphy, the newly appointed assistant secretary of state for Near Eastern Affairs. The major reason for the latter appointment was to allow the Conference to meet and approve Murphy, who had been ambassador to Saudi Arabia for the previous two years.

The Conference met with Secretary–General Waldheim at the UN and threatened to "pursue a campaign for cuts in American financial aid to the United Nations if that body continued on its present course." The Conference was also the first outside group that Jeane Kirkpatrick addressed following her appointment as permanent representative. In her speech she assured them that: "As long as I am at the UN, Israel will never have to face her enemies alone."

Political Position, Consensus and Dissent

The Presidents Conference role as official spokesman and statesman for the American Jewish community is based on its claim to speak for the unified position or consensus of its diverse constituency, which includes groups that differ politically and ideologically (Zionist or non-Zionist, religious or secular, liberal or conservative) and organizationally (fraternal, rabbinical, community relations). The success of the Conference in reaching consensus is helped by the fact that it need only address issues relating to Israel and international affairs, and that consensus is needed only for issues on which the Conference takes a position; theoretically, at least, if no consensus is reached, no position is taken.

There are now five points that have been put forward as the "bottom-line" consensus of the Presidents Conference and thus of the American Jewish community as a whole. These were developed in June 1979, when Prime Minister Begin invited a Presidents Conference delegation to Israel to study the issue of the autonomy negotiations. The delegation met with Begin and other leaders, toured "Judea and Samaria" by helicopter, and met with West Bank settlers. On the basis of the delegation's report, the Presidents Conference policy meeting reached the following statement of consensus, which continues to be cited to this day:

1. Israel's settlements on the West Bank are legal.
2. There must be no "Palestine state" on the West Bank. Such a state would be a dagger pointed at the heart of Israel.
3. There must be no dealings with the PLO by the United States.
4. Jerusalem is indivisible. As the spiritual capital of the Jewish people, it must remain the political capital of Israel, a united city under Israeli sovereignty.
5. It is our conviction that Israel is committed to carrying out both the letter and spirit of the Camp David accords.

This consensus has long been the unstated understanding of American Jewish friends of Israel. But it is well to publish it lest there be any miscalculation of the unity of American Jews and the strength of their commitment to the security and dignity of Israel and its people.[64]

Other positions taken by the Presidents Conference tend to mirror those of the Israeli government; there has been no deviation on any major issue. During the 1982 invasion of Lebanon, Howard Squadron held a press conference and called on President Reagan and the United States to support the invasion and its goals, and to reject any sanctions against Israel. In a statement issued on the first anniversary of the invasion, the Conference assessed it as "worth the cost." The Israeli position regarding the Reagan plan was also adopted by the Conference, albeit in milder tones. Julius Berman wrote a letter to Reagan stating that the plan " ... does violence to the spirit of Camp David in that it substitutes a specific American plan for the free give-and-take essential if the parties to the dispute are to solve their differences."[65] In a Jerusalem press conference, held after a meeting with Begin, Berman went even further, accusing Reagan of reneging on his campaign promise to support a united Jerusalem.[66]

During the Israeli invasion of Lebanon and the ensuing massacres in Palestinian camps, a generally more hidden aspect of the Presidents Conference role became apparent by the sheer weight of its diplomatic credentials, establishment leaders, and broadly-based membership: the Conference effectively maintains the important illusion of consensus rather than acting as a genuine vehicle for debate. The perception of a monolithic Jewish community, solidly united behind Zionist policy and the Jewish establishment, is essential to the legitimacy of both the Presidents Conference and the Israeli government.

In this instance, the Conference acted to defuse criticism of the Israeli role through articles, speakers, and press conferences. It also attempted to deny the existence of division in the Jewish community's ranks and to prevent open expression of dissent. Within days of the invasion, Chairman Berman met with Vice President Bush to express "the American Jewish community's understanding and support of Israel's incursion into Lebanon." When Begin visited the United States, the Conference organized a demonstration in support of the war. On 22 June, a small group from the Conference met with Defense Secretary Weinberger, where they again stressed that the community was "totally united" in support of the war.[67] The Conference also helped coordinate an 11 July *New York Times* ad entitled "An End of Terror—A Start Toward Peace," which was signed by 131 leaders of Jewish organizations, public officials, academics, and others, including present and past leaders of the Conference. (The ad was probably a response to statements and ads from Jews and others protesting the invasions.)

A similar scenario unfolded in reaction to the Sabra and Shatila massacre. In a *Middle East Memo* entitled "Tragedy and Truth—The

Beirut Massacre," the Conference deplored the killings, but went on to assert that only a Moslem-Christian "blood feud" was responsible, to praise Israeli democracy, criticize the PLO, denounce the international double standard and hypocrisy against Israel, and attack the Arab regimes for intransigence. Regarding the position of American Jews, the memo stated:

Until there is peace, Israel must act to defend itself. American Jews understand this reality. We accept what Israel must do in order to survive. Therefore there will be no "split," no "rift," no "erosion" of the love and support we give to Israel.

To ensure that the broader public was reached, Berman held a press conference in Jerusalem on 6 October, following a private meeting with Begin, where he again denied that there was any split in the American Jewish community over Israel's policies.[68]

The Presidents Conference also adheres to the position adopted by virtually all Jewish establishment organizations: any dissenting view or criticism must be expressed privately; it is unacceptable, even treacherous, to disturb or challenge publicly the image of unity. The Conference's structure facilitates this practice. For one thing, its membership is the entrenched leadership of established organizations, who generally share the same interests, and thus the consensus. (They also decide which other groups are eligible to join.) In addition, because of the Conference's dual role as internal forum and public representative, any expression of dissent is limited, by mandate, to the internal forum and thus has no possible public outlet or expression, since official (public) statements must represent consensus. Rabbi Balfour Brickner wrote to Julius Berman:

Much publicity has been given to the Jan. 26, 1983 conference which the Presidents Conference is convening to discuss relations between the United States Jewish community and Israel. Some have even suggested that this meeting would also explore the matter of "dissent" within the American Jewish community. That must be an erroneous report since none of the better-known "dissenting types" seem to have been invited.

At least none are publicized as being panelists at the advertised discussion. Certainly, no one would accuse Rabbi Glazer or Dr. Sidorsky of being "dissenters" from the "establishment view." They both have distinguished reputations as being strong supporters of the present Israel government's policies. Dr. Thurz may have reservations about those policies. If so, his views are not as yet well known.

I would hope that the Presidents Conference would, indeed, consider convening A Consultation on Dissent, one that would be open, not closed, one to which the Jewish press would be invited, one at which spokespeople from the various positions in the ever-broadening spectrum of American Jewish public opinion would be invited, one where, for at least a first time, we could honestly, as Arthur Hertzberg likes to say, "break a lance or two."

I am certain that the Presidents Conference is not afraid openly to debate with Jews not in the Presidents Conference some of the issues which now tear at the

197

seam of American Jewry's cloak. Such dialogue would not only be interesting, it might also prove to be important and as informative as I am sure your closed session with Glazer, Sidorsky and Thurz will be. I notice that Ken Bialkin will be summarizing the findings. Will, at least, that summary be shared with members of the organizations whose "leaders" will be attending the closed session, or will they have to rely on a report from their presidents?[69]

Brickner has also publicly criticized the Presidents Conference role in stifling dissent. In March 1983, he led a contingent of eighteen rabbis to Washington. They met with twenty senators and representatives to assert that there are Jews who do not share establishment views and who, in particular, "do not support the Israel Government on policies in the West Bank; call for a freeze on new Israeli settlements in the West Bank; call for all avenues to be explored to involve Palestinians in negotiations." Brickner said it was the "closed door" policy of the Conference that led to the delegation's actions and noted that they had no alternative within the Jewish establishment: " . . . none of these views are aired publicly by prestigious establishment groups such as the Presidents Conference, AIPAC and organizations with massive memberships like Hadassah for one. Groups that make periodic pilgrimages to Washington to make their views known at no point give those holding alternative views a chance to be heard and quoted."[70]

The White House, the Presidents Conference, and Republican Jews

The system that makes access to the White House and, to a lesser degree, the State Department the prerogative of the Presidents Conference has generally been accepted because it is clear to all concerned that unity is strength and that one voice is more likely to achieve sustained access to the White House than scores of individual pro-Israel groups. But at the same time, the Jewish community (or communities), with its proliferation of organizations and duplication of tasks, has long rejected any overall control or hierarchy. It seems likely that the traditional Jewish establishment maintains the Presidents Conference as official representative for several reasons. First, there is more consensus regarding Israel than any other issue, and it is in the interest of all to protect this—including the U.S. and Israeli governments. Second, the Conference is not threatening: its power is not inherent, but stems from the complicity of and legitimacy granted by the other groups involved. It exerts no control over the constituent organizations, who continue their own work, programs, and meetings with politicians (including the U.S. president). Finally, the position of chairman—which brings with it the most perks, publicity, and meetings with heads of state—is carefully allocated among the various members.

While the Conference is not and never has been the White House's sole access to American Jews, it is expedient to be able to emerge from a meeting and announce "The Jewish community thinks this about Israel."

If by some chance there are disagreements, other organizations and avenues can always be approached.

This convenient scenario received its most serious challenge with the coming of Ronald Reagan and his administration. As Wolf Blitzer wrote in the *Jerusalem Post*, "Since President Reagan took office, relations between the White House and the Presidents Conference have been strained. Administration officials regard the group as fundamentally Democratic in its orientation and, therefore, automatically hostile to the president. . . . "[71]

In the opinion of some Jewish groups, including the Presidents Conference, Reagan is guilty of overlooking, and thus undermining, the Conference and turning instead to a group of wealthy Republican Jews, most of whom were active in the Jewish Coalition for Reagan-Bush during the 1980 campaign. First among them is Albert Spiegel of Los Angeles, a personal friend of Reagan and chair of the Coalition. According to the *Jerusalem Post*, "More than anyone else in the Republican Jewish leadership, Spiegel has access, clout and credibility in the White House."[72] (Spiegel is a businessman who has long been active in the Los Angeles B'nai B'rith Hillel Foundation and the Joint Distribution Committee.) Another close Jewish friend of Reagan is Ted Cummings, also a Los Angeles businessman and Republican; he was an honorary co-chair of the Coalition and became ambassador to Austria after the election. The other most well-known and active Jewish Republican is Detroit businessman Max Fisher, who was close to the Nixon and Ford administrations. He, too, was an honorary co-chair of the Republican National Jewish Coalition, and a member of the board of governors of the Jewish Agency. Other prominent and active Jewish Republicans include Gordon Zacks of Columbus, Ohio, Richard Fox of Philadelphia, and George Klein of New York. Virtually all of them are large contributors to AIPAC and pro-Israel PACs as well. The institutional framework within which these men operate is the National Republican Jewish Coalition, of which Richard Fox was elected chair in June 1983 and Max Fisher is honorary chair. According to Fox, a role of the Coalition is to act as a "sounding board" between the Reagan administration and the Jewish community.[73]

Since the degree of access to high officials, especially the President, constitutes the basis of an organization's or individual's power and credibility, the Presidents Conference quickly responded to the threat posed by Spiegel and others. The Presidents Conference annual report for the year ending 31 March 1981 contains the statement that:

The question of the role of the Coalition's members in representations to the White House had been resolved by a unanimous vote of the Presidents Conference declaring that Jewish community discipline demanded that only the democratically-constituted voice of the Jewish community be entrusted with the task of dealing with the incoming administration—not any self-appointed group of political supporters of the President, no matter how distinguished its individual members might be.

While this statement sounds definitive, in fact it appears in brackets after reference to Squadron and Hellman's first meeting with Alexander Haig, which was also attended by Max Fisher. Since most of the Presidents Conference's meetings with high administration officials since the Reagan election have been attended by Spiegel, Fisher, or other Republican Jews, it seems that there was a quiet compromise to share access. The Presidents Conference, which maintains its role as public representative, tolerates Reagan's private meetings with the Republican Jewish group as partisan necessities.

This compromise temporarily exploded in 1982. The spark was an April 1982 meeting with Reagan attended by Spiegel, Fisher, Zacks, Fox, Klein, and Larry Weinberg, a Democrat and former AIPAC president. It was the participation of Weinberg to which the Presidents Conference most objected: first, he was a staunch Democrat, so there could be no excuse that this was a private, partisan meeting; and second, his attendance fueled the existing competition between AIPAC and the Conference. This was due to AIPAC's ever-growing clout and prestige, exacerbated in this instance by what was seen as a violation of AIPAC's mandate to focus on Congress and leave the executive branch to the Conference. The fact that Spiegel, who organized the meeting, chose to invite Weinberg but not Squadron (then head of the Conference) was a blow. Squadron responded with a public statement criticizing the visit, which read in part:

The American Jewish community is past the point where we need or want "court Jews" to speak for us to our government. The members of this self-appointed group—all but one of them active Republicans—were not authorized by the Jewish community to address the President. Such meetings do not help Israel and do not advance the cause of Jewish dignity and self-respect. . . . From the beginning of this Administration, an effort has been made to bypass the Presidents Conference so that the White House could designate its own "Jewish leaders." The effort was vigorously rejected by the organized Jewish community on the grounds that it is not up to the President to select the Jews who represent the Jewish community. It is up to the Jewish community itself.[74]

The statement was widely covered in the American Jewish and Israeli press—all of whom deplored the fact that it was made public. Compromise once again became the order of the day, as all concerned recognized the importance of preserving at least the appearance of unity. When Julius Berman became head of the Presidents Conference, one of his pledges was to improve relations with AIPAC and Republican Jews. In turn, the Coalition has stated publicly that it does not have exclusive representation of Jewish community interests. However, the individual Republican Jews whom Reagan favors still seem to be in ascendancy. Spiegel has proposed that he coordinate White House access; subsequent meetings with Reagan, though often publicly announced as headed by the Presidents Conference, invariably include Spiegel or members of the Republican Coalition.

The importance and impact of this conflict within the American Jewish establishment is difficult to assess. It is certainly connected to the shift in Israel support work away from the more old-fashioned, behind-the-scenes methods of the Presidents Conference toward the more modern and aggressive policies of AIPAC and the PACs, which do not hesitate to intervene directly and openly in political affairs. More generally, this conflict also reflects the deeper chasm evidenced by the neoconservative direction of certain sectors of American Jewry, and the inevitable clash with the traditional support of the Democratic party and the at least symbolic liberalism such allegiance still represents.

Other Activities

While the main role of the Presidents Conference is that of public spokesman, it also engages in more pragmatic work, along the same lines as other pro-Israel organizations.

The Conference occasionally initiates national campaigns on specific themes or issues. In 1979, in the middle of the Andrew Young-PLO affair, the following announcement was sent to "every Jewish communal leader and publication throughout the country":

The Conference of Presidents of Major American Jewish Organizations has undertaken a national campaign urging the United States Jewish community to make known to the White House our deepening concern about the current trend of American Middle East policy. The themes of this campaign are: No appeasement of PLO terror. No surrender to Arab blackmail.[75]

In its annual report, the Conference described its own activities in the campaign: on 9 September, Conference president Theodore Mann published a letter entitled "America's Case Against the PLO" in the *New York Times*; the letter was reprinted by the Conference as a *Middle East Memo* and "disseminated widely." Mann was interviewed in *US News and World Report;* on 12 September, Mann held a press conference where he made public a 30 August letter from Secretary of State Cyrus Vance, reasserting the U.S. commitment to Israel; the next day the *Daily News* interviewed Mann. On 25 September, a *Middle East Memo* about the PLO was released. In March 1982, the Conference launched another nationwide information campaign, this time "to deepen American appreciation of the significance of Israel's withdrawal from Sinai and to protest Administration policies that could damage the Middle East peace process and imperil U.S. strategic interests in the region."[76] This campaign culminated in a National Leadership Conference of Solidarity with Israel, held in a Washington, D.C. synagogue. The conference was addressed by Senators Robert Byrd, Henry Jackson, and David Durenberger.

The Presidents Conference also sponsors demonstrations. The best known one was the Rally Against Arab Terror, held to protest Yasir Arafat's speech at the United Nations in 1974. Julius Berman has claimed, "When necessary, we can get out a major demonstration in 48 hours."[77] During the June 1982 invasion of Lebanon, the Conference called for a pro-Israel demonstration when Menachem Begin addressed the UN General Assembly. The demonstration was coordinated with NJCRAC and the local New York Jewish Community Relations Council; according to their figures, three thousand people attended.

Like other pro-Israel groups, the Conference places newspaper advertisements. On the occasion of a Begin visit to the United States in early September 1981, the Conference (together with the UJA, Israel Bonds, and others) placed an ad that read:

Deeply committed to the well-being and dignity of Israel's people, we extend a heart-felt welcome to Prime Minister Begin. We join in fervent prayer for the cause of peace that brings you to our shores.[78]

On 25 April 1982, to salute the Israeli withdrawal from the Sinai, the Conference placed a *New York Times* ad entitled "Betting Their Lives on Peace." In a more unusual action, the Conference placed a full-page *New York Times* ad—at a cost of $23,362—after an Israeli airline El Al strike ended in 1982. It read, "El Al—We Missed You!"

Press conferences are a frequent activity of the Presidents Conference and generally receive wide coverage. In addition to the annual National Leadership Conference, the Conference also holds the smaller banquets and conferences at which leading U.S. and Israeli figures are speakers or honored guests.

Its publications are *Annual Report*, which summarizes the activities and political developments of each year (from April to March), and the one or two-page *Middle East Memo*, which provides statements or essays on topical events. Typical brochures include "America's National Interest in the Middle East," "PLO—The Nazis of Our Day," "The Arab Claim to Palestine—An Analysis," and "The Jewish People's Historic Rights in the Land of Israel." Press relations kits with feature stories and photographs on Israel are distributed to newspapers and other media around the country.

Jewish Institute for National Security Affairs

Year established: 1977
President: Saul I. Stern
Executive Director: Shoshana Bryen
Address: 1411 K Street, N.W., Washington, DC 20005
Publication: *Newsletter* (monthly)

General Background

During the latter part of the 1970s, a Washington-based pro-Israel cluster of military analysts emerged to constitute a "Pentagon watch" on strategic issues related to the Middle East. The appearance of this "Pentagon watch" was inspired in part by the characterization of Israel as a military "burden" to the United States by General George Brown, chairman of the Joint Chiefs of Staff, in 1976.

The major themes that these analysts emphasize in regard to U.S. relations with Israel are the following: (1) Israel is a strategic asset to the United States in the Middle East, whereas the Arab states are unreliable allies; (2) U.S. support for Israel must be strategic, not merely moral and political; (3) since the security interests of the United States and Israel are so closely intertwined, exposure of Israel to pressure from the Soviets or their surrogates endangers U.S. interests in the region; (4) the Soviet Union has designs to control the Middle East, and its responsibility for most of the problems posed to Israel by Arab forces should be exposed.[79]

JINSA was established in 1977 to serve as a center for the "Pentagon watch" and to affect national security policy. Stephen Bryen, former aide to the Senate Foreign Relations Subcommittee on Near Eastern and South Asian Affairs, was instrumental in founding JINSA.*

Announcing its formation in June 1977, JINSA circulated a printed "Dear Friend" letter signed by David Bar Elan (active in the Jerusalem-based Jonathan Institute, which sponsors invitation-only seminars on international terrorism), Rita Hauser (of the AJC), Max Kampelman (U.S. ambassador to the Madrid Conference on Security and Cooperation in Europe and currently head of the U.S. delegation for negotiations on nuclear and space arms), Walter Laqueur, Norman Podhoretz, Eugene V. Rostow, and Rabbi Stanley Rabinowitz (former ZOA president and chair of the Rabbinical Cabinet of the UJA). After wondering rhetorically "Why our national stocks of military equipment were so low that we lacked adequate reserves from which to resupply Israel in her hour of need during the Yom Kippur War," and what led General Brown to characterize Israel as a "burden," they argued that the answers required "a great deal of specialized information which is of crucial importance for all of us." There

---

*See note on p. 167.

is a need, they reasoned, for a Jewish organization to provide the proper perspective on these issues: "In our judgment, we Jews have a similarly vital stake in, and special perspective on, America's overall national security policy." JINSA promised to provide that perspective.

JINSA's first *Newsletter* projected a classical Cold War approach to the Soviet Union. "A serious problem faces the Free World . . . as a consequence of the continuing Soviet arms buildup," the *Newsletter* starts. The Jewish community (presumably the liberal segments of it) was admonished for not appreciating sufficiently the dangers of Soviet military buildup and for not acquainting itself with the appropriate technical data in this area. JINSA then vowed "to do our share to inform the American public, and in particular the Jewish community, about the dangers posed by the increasing Soviet military capability and the prudent actions we can take to respond to this danger."

It appears that JINSA's establishment was in part a reaction to the liberal support for detente that was prominent within the Jewish community. Most of those associated with JINSA's establishment, and who are currently on its board of directors, represent the conservative segments of American Jewry.

Funding

Based on its IRS Form 990 for November 1980 to October 1981, JINSA's declared total revenues for that year were $99,000, of which 75 percent came from "direct public support," 11 percent from "indirect public support," and the rest from membership dues and interest. Its total expenditures for the year were slightly over $97,000. The largest expense category (28 percent) was "consulting fees" (the bulk of it went to management); 15 percent was spent on the *Newsletter,* 13 percent on fundraising; and 13 percent on conferences, dinners, and meetings.

Activities

Since its establishment, JINSA has been primarily a liaison between the Jewish community and the defense establishment in Washington, and a point of the triangle connecting selected defense analysts in Washington with the Israeli defense establishment. In a 1983 progress report, JINSA claimed that it has succeeded in "fostering a dialogue with the U.S. military services," in part by facilitating the process through which about two hundred Jewish community leaders were invited to the Pentagon since 1977. Furthermore, it helped to arrange smaller meetings for "many times that number" with Pentagon officials in Washington and around the country.[80]

JINSA hosts dinners honoring staunch supporters of Israel and critics of the Soviet Union, such as the late Senator Henry Jackson, and arranges for delegations to Israel. According to a report by JINSA's president Saul I. Stern, for example, a JINSA-sponsored delegation to Israel in October

1982, with the assistance of the Israeli Defense Forces, held high-level meetings aimed at strengthening Israel as a U.S. strategic ally.

JINSA's activities help to build a network of military-minded people who share the same ideological premises and who are willing to introduce them into the public discourse. JINSA-facilitated activities help to create an atmosphere of familiarity and constant contact among American defense officials, American Jewish leadership, and Israeli defense officials. As an American officer noted in JINSA's *Newsletter:* "If push comes to shove the Israelis are in our pocket, and we are in theirs."[81]

The *Newsletter* is a monthly publication, ranging in length from six to eight pages. Its board of advisors has included Senator Rudy Boschwitz, Lieutenant General Devol Brett (Ret.), Representative Jack Kemp, AIPAC founder Si Kenen, Walter Laqueur and Max Kampelman (both on the advisory board of the Georgetown Center for Strategic and International Studies), Ivan Novick (former president of ZOA), Jacques Torczyner (former president of ZOA and an officer of the WZO-American Section), Eugene Rostow, Edward Sanders (former adviser to President Carter), Lieutenant General Eugene Tighe (Ret.), General John Vogt (Ret.), and Admiral Elmo Zumwalt (Ret.).

Articles in the *Newsletter* stress the dangers posed by the USSR: how the Soviet arms buildup is outpacing NATO's, the growth of Russian facilities in the Horn of Africa, "rethinking the unthinkable" about a Soviet attack on the United States, and "Why Did We Underestimate Soviet Military Spending for 10 Years?"

Prominent analysts, government officials, and retired military personnel write for JINSA's *Newsletter.* The lead article in the December 1982/January 1983 issue, for example, "The Bulgarian Connection" (about the attack on the Pope) was contributed by Michael Ledeen, a JINSA board member, a senior fellow in international affairs at the Georgetown Center for Strategic and International Affairs, and a former special advisor to Alexander Haig. Another article, on "The MX and U.S. Defense Doctrine," was written by Ronald Lehman, deputy assistant secretary of defense for nuclear policy. The main article in the February 1983 issue, "Electronic Combat: Warfare of the Future," was written by Lieutenant General Kelly H. Burke (Ret.), former Air Force deputy chief of staff.

The Context of JINSA's Work

While JINSA is the only Jewish organization specifically directed toward security matters, it carries out its work in the context of a heightened interest in military affairs among the organizations of the Jewish establishment. The ADL, for example, has begun to arrange "military missions." The first delegation consisted of six former military commanders, including retired Major General George S. Patton, and was accompanied by Lewis M. Perlstein, of the Association of the U.S. Army. They went to Lebanon at the time of the Israeli invasion, " . . . under ADL auspices to assess the situation for themselves. Their conclusion: Israel acted 'extremely cautiously' to avoid civilian casualties in Southern Lebanon."[82] Thirteen retired U.S. generals and admirals participated in its second military mission to Israel and Lebanon. The retired officers included Major General Gerald J. Carey, USAF; Lieutenant General Richard E. Carey, USMC; Major General Robert Cocklin, USA; Admiral Donald Davis, USN; Lieutenant General Harry Kinnard, USA; Major General Doyle Larson, USAF; Lieutenant General Thomas H. Miller, USMC; Lieutenant General William R. Nelson, USAF; Lieutenant General Adolph G. Schwenk, USMC; Vice Admiral William St. George, USN; General Volney F. Warner, USA; and Admiral Maurice P. Weisner, USN. The delegation met with the Israeli chief of staff and other high-ranking officers and toured military installations, including an armored division headquarters in Lebanon's Bekaa Valley.[83]

Similarly, AIPAC's literature now includes military analysis. Its monograph, *The Strategic Value of Israel*, for example, makes a detailed argument about the strategic benefits Israel offers to its U.S. ally, including an explicit discussion of the logistical advantages that use of bases in Israel could confer upon U.S. military units engaged in battle in the Gulf.

JINSA's basic perspective on the U.S.-Israeli alliance is also shared by other centers devoted to international security analyses. A number of experts associated with Georgetown University's Center for Strategic and International Studies, for example, hold opinions similar to those advocated by JINSA and participate in its work, including Walter Laqueur, Michael Ledeen, and Max Kampelman.

The Center for International Security (CIS), although not specifically a Jewish organization and not limited in scope to concerns about Israel and the Middle East, has played a major role in publicizing the priorities about Israeli security that it shares with JINSA. The director and founder of the CIS is Dr. Joseph Churba. He was a childhood friend of Rabbi Meir Kahane, the founder of the Jewish Defense League. In 1965, the two men cooperated in setting up Consultant Research Associates, whose first task was to mobilize campus support for the war in Vietnam. In 1971, Churba taught Middle Eastern studies at the U.S. Air Force University on Maxwell Air Force Base in Alabama; a year later, he was appointed as a special advisor on the Middle East to General George F. Keegan (Ret.). In 1976, he assailed General George Brown's pronouncements on Israel as "dangerously irresponsible"; he then lost his special security clearance and resigned. It was at this point that he founded the Center as an organization of former military officers. The Center's Advisory Board includes: Professor Gil Carl Alroy; Frank Gervasi; Lieutenant General Daniel O. Graham, USA (Ret.); Major General George F. Keegan, Jr., USAF (Ret.); Dr. J.B. Kelly; Honorable William R. Kintner; Robert Morris; Professor William V. O'Brien; Merrill Simon; Rear Admiral Phillip W. Smith, USNR (Ret.); William R. Van Cleave; and Bernard Yoh.

As the Center explains, in its geostrategic world view, "peace requires strength, both moral and military.... For better or worse, America's future is tied to an international community in which Western Europe, Japan, Israel, Canada, Australia and New Zealand strive to remain democratic, secure and friendly, while Africa, Asia and Latin America remain independent of the Soviet Union and Communist China."[84]

CIS' position on Israel emanates from that of its director. In 1977, following his disagreement with the Pentagon, Churba published *The Politics of Defeat.* He specified that he wanted the book "to highlight the dangers inherent in the defeatist idea that Israel constitutes a 'burden'." The book was given further credibility by an introduction by Admiral Elmo Zumwalt, chief of naval operations, USN (Ret.). "The purpose of this book is simple," Churba wrote in the preface. "It is to demonstrate that the vitality of Israel is crucial to the United States and that the United States must therefore categorically commit itself to the defense and preservation of that nation." This is so "primarily because she is—and will remain—of paramount strategic value to the security of the U.S."

In a 1980 interview with *Forbes* magazine, Churba chastised President Carter for "lying" about America's strike capability in the Arabian Gulf and accused American Middle East diplomacy of failure for not knowing "where the real ball game was." The real ball game, in Churba's analysis, is not the Palestine question, but the Arabian Gulf and how "to prevent ... the epicenter of world politics from disintegrating." [85]

His second book, *Retreat From Freedom*, carried an introduction by Richard V. Allen, who later became the chief of President Reagan's National Security Council. In it, Churba argued that "Israel is without question the only reliable and effective ally the U.S. has in the Middle East.... It is essential, therefore, that American policy-makers force the leaders of the feeble regimes bordering the Persian Gulf to accept the overwhelming fact of this epoch—that their existence is bound up with American arms, and that those arms can be used effectively only in an alliance with Israel.... The inherently unstable Arab states can be auxiliaries to Israel-American might—they can never substitute for it."[86]

Notes

Introduction

1. Quoted from AIPAC promotional material.
2. *Jerusalem Post*, 29 October 1982.
3. Stephen S. Rosenfeld, "AIPAC," *Present Tense*, Spring 1983: 16.
4. Sources for voter and financial information are Edward Bernard Glick, *The Triangular Connection: America, Israel, and American Jews*. London: George Allen and Unwin, 1982; and Stephen D. Isaacs, *Jews and American Politics*. Garden City, N.Y.: Doubleday, 1974.
5. *Jerusalem Post*, 16 November 1983.
6. *New York Times*, 10 August 1982.

AIPAC

7. Isaiah L. Kenen, *Israel's Defense Line: Her Friends and Foes in Washington*. Buffalo, N.Y.: Prometheus Books, 1981: 66.
8. *Ibid:* 69.
9. *Ibid:* 111.
10. *Ibid:* 113.
11. *Congressional Quarterly Weekly Report*, "Middle East Lobbying," 39/34 (22 August 1981): 1525; Kenen: 113.
12. Wolf Blitzer, "The AIPAC Formula," *Moment* 6/10 (November 1981).
13. Sue Hoechstetter, "Michael Gale, Jewish Liaison for the White House," *The American Jewish Congress Monthly*, 50/4 (June 1983): 14.
14. Quarterly Financial Reports, 1980-1984; and IRS Form 990 for 1980, 1981 and 1984.
15. AIPAC, "Why U.S. Aid to Israel?" February 1983.
16. AIPAC, "The Strategic Value of Israel," 6 June 1983.
17. Kenen: 71.
18. *Washington Post*, 9 February 1983.
19. *Washington Post*, 13 February 1983.
20. Blitzer.
21. *Jerusalem Post*, 5 November 1982.
22. William J. Lanouette, "The Many Faces of the Jewish Lobby in America," *National Journal*, 13 May 1978: 751.
23. Both quotes from AIPAC promotional letter dated February 1982.
24. *Congressional Quarterly Weekly Report*, "Middle East Lobbying": 1524.
25. Roberta Strauss Feuerlicht, *The Fate of the Jews*. New York: Times Books, 1983: 271.
26. Rosenfeld: 15.
27. Lanouette: 751.
28. Rosenfeld: 15.
29. AIPAC, "AIPAC Workshop on Politics," 16 October 1983.
30. Lanouette: 752.
31. Charles McC. Mathias, Jr., "Ethnic Groups and Foreign Policy," *Foreign Affairs*, 59/5 (Summer 1981): 993.
32. Lanouette: 752.
33. *Ibid:* 751.
34. *Wall Street Journal*, 3 August 1983.
35. *U.S. News and World Report*, 27 March 1978: 25.
36. Rosenfeld: 15.
37. Lanouette: 752.
38. Both incidents are described in Russell Warren Howe and Sarah Hays Trott, *The Power Peddlers*. New York: Doubleday, 1977: 271-273, 294-297.
39. AIPAC, "The Jordan Arms Sale," 7 June 1983.

10. *Jerusalem Post*, 29 October 1982.

Political Action Committees

41. See *The Mideast Observer*, 1 November 1983; *Political Focus* 6/15 (1 August 1983); *Wall Street Journal*, 3 August 1983.
42. *Wall Street Journal*, 3 August 1983.
43. Morris J. Amitay, "A Field Day for Jewish PACs," *The American Jewish Congress Monthly*, 50/4 (June 1983): 11.
44. *Ha'aretz*, 29 May 1983.
45. Amitay: 11.
46. *Wall Street Journal*, 3 August 1983.
47. *The Mideast Observer*, 6/19 (1 November 1983).
48. *Wall Street Journal*, 3 August 1983.
49. *Decatur Herald Review*, 30 March 1982.
50. *Wall Street Journal*, 26 February 1985.
51. *Wall Street Journal*, 22 August 1983 (letter).
52. *Jewish Telegraphic Agency*, 13 October 1982.
53. *Wall Street Journal*, 3 August 1983.
54. *National Review*, 1 October 1982 (advertisement).
55. *New York Times*, 13 October 1982 (advertisement).
56. *Wall Street Journal*, 3 August 1983.
57. Federal Election Reports, 1983-1984 election cycle.
58. *Washington Report on Middle East Affairs*, 14 November 1983.

Presidents Conference

59. *Jewish Telegraphic Agency*, 30 June 1982.
60. Sources for meetings, activities and statements are *Report(s) of the Conference of Presidents of Major American Jewish Organizations, For the Year(s) Ending March 31, 1980; March 31, 1981; March 31, 1982; and March 31, 1983* (hereinafter referred to as "Report," with date).
61. "Report," for year ending 31 March 1982.
62. *Ibid.*
63. Jewish Week, 19 November 1982.
64. "Report," for year ending 31 March 1980.
65. *Jerusalem Post*, 8 September 1982.
66. *Jewish Telegraphic Agency*, 6 October 1982.
67. "Report," for year ending 31 March 1983.
68. *Jewish Telegraphic Agency*, 6 October 1982.
69. Letter published in *The Jewish Post and Opinion*, 9 February 1983.
70. *The Jewish Post and Opinion*, 23 March 1983.
71. *Jerusalem Post*, 7 June 1982.
72. *Jerusalem Post*, 21 January 1982.
73. *Jewish Telegraphic Agency*, 21 June 1983.
74. *Jewish Telegraphic Agency*, 14 April 1982.
75. "Report," for year ending 31 March 1980.
76. "Report," for year ending 31 March 1982.
77. *Jewish Week*, 11 July 1982.
78. "Report," for year ending 31 March 1982.

JINSA

79. These themes are elaborated in the JINSA *Newsletter*(s); AIPAC's "The Strategic Value of Israel"; and in Joseph Churba's *The Politics of Defeat: America's Decline in the Middle East.* New York: Cyrco Press, 1977.

80. *JINSA Newsletter,* March 1983.
81. *Ibid.*
82. *ADL Bulletin,* October 1982.
83. *ADL Bulletin,* February 1984.
84. CIS, "Statement of Purpose," *Spotlight on the Americas* (undated).
85. *Forbes,* 27 October 1980.
86. Joseph Churba, *Retreat From Freedom.* Washington D.C.: Center for International Security, 1980. Introduction by Richard V. Allen: 2.

Target Areas and
Special Focus Organizations

Target Areas and
Special Focus Organizations

CAMPUS

Jewish establishment organizations have long focused special attention and resources on the academic sector of American society and on the campus environment. Until about fifteen years ago, the B'nai B'rith Hillel was the primary organization working to create a pro-Israeli context on U.S. campuses. Established in 1923, the Hillel Foundation provided religious, educational, social and counseling programs for Jewish students, including Hebrew courses and lectures on Zionism and Israel.

The Student Zionist Organization, the now-defunct precursor of the Zionist Student Organization and the American Zionist Youth Council, was particularly active in presenting an array of Israel-related programs, often through the Hillel Foundation. The SZO's 1963 publication, *A Program Manual for Zionism on the Campus,* offered a detailed guide on how to "create a Zionist climate" on campus, with discussions on "how to organize a new chapter," "public relations," "relations with other organizations on and off campus," "leadership training," "Israel trips," and other topics.

Since the 1967 war, and particularly since the 1973 war, there has been a marked intensification of pro-Israel work on campuses, largely in response to the perceived challenge arising from a new degree of public criticism of Israeli policies.

Although attempts by Jewish establishment organizations to influence campus opinion have not been confined to work with Jewish faculty and students, they have taken advantage of the strong Jewish presence on campuses. A 1964 estimate by Dr. Alfred Jospe, national director of the Hillel Foundation, suggested that approximately 80 percent of Jewish college-age youth attend colleges or universities, in comparison with a rate of about 40 percent for the general college-age population.[1] A 1973 publication of the Synagogue Council of America called attention to "the first in-depth study of the rapid rise of Jews in academia since World War II," which was prepared by Seymour M. Lipset and Everett C. Ladd, Jr., and based on the Carnegie Commission Study on Higher Education:

The Carnegie Commission data gathered in 1969 indicate that Jews comprise almost 15 percent of the social science faculties in American colleges and universities, 25 percent of the law faculties, 16 percent of the social work faculties, and 22 percent of the medicine faculties. Moreover, Jewish faculty members tend to be concentrated in the Northeastern and prestige schools, where high-percentage-Jewish student bodies are also found. In addition, the Lipset and Ladd study notes that Jewish academics are higher than average achievers, being among those scholars most inclined toward research and publishing.[2]

There are two general concerns behind efforts targeting the campus: (1) to influence present and future intellectual discourse among students and faculty in favor of Israel and against sympathy for the Palestinian position; and (2) to affect student political opinion, since students are voters or potential voters with a much higher rate of participation in the electoral process than their counterparts off campus. To these ends, and in addition to ongoing campus activities, various programs are organized to bring students directly to Israel. In its September 1983 report filed with the U.S. Department of Justice, for example, the WZO-American Section indicates that during the previous six-month period:

A. Recruitment, screening, and registration for the 1983-84 American class at Kibbutz Kfar Blum were completed.... At the end of August, 26 high school students departed for a year in Israel, representing the fifteenth class in this program.

B. Recruitment and planning continued for adult, student and youth travel-study programs to Israel. The first group departed in May, and the final group at the end of July. The groups were as follows:

1. Brandeis University—20 graduate students studied problems of Jewish communal work and Israel.

2. Providence Group—15 afternoon school teachers were selected by the Providence Bureau of Jewish Education to spend three weeks in Israel studying at the Hebrew University. Their course in pedagogical methods was specifically designed by the Melton Center of H. U. [Hebrew University] and the Department in N.Y. to meet the needs of the community in Providence.

3. Reform Teachers—An intensive study-tour for 25 educators (and spouses) who had never been to Israel, or only visited briefly. Lectures and visits to educational institutions were integrated into a travel program.

4. Early Childhood Seminar—15 Early Childhood professionals from Florida participated in workshops and field trips.

5. High school students from Dallas, Baltimore, Indianapolis and Cleveland toured the country, studied Hebrew Language, and worked on special projects. They numbered about 160 participants.

6. T.O.V.S. Group—Approximately 30 schoolteachers spent the summer in Israel on volunteer teaching, tutoring, etc. in cities and towns throughout the country.

7. NY-BJE Group—Programs financed by a grant from the Joint Education Program in Israel. 22 educators were selected by NY-BJE. Program included

months of lectures and readings in N.Y. in preparation for course of study in Israel.

    8. Ulpan Akiva—Students spent 8 weeks in extremely intensive Hebrew study at one of the oldest, best known Ulpan programs in Israel.

    9. Queens College Group—40 graduate students from the Department of Education in Queens College studied the Israeli educational system in a full credit course led by their professor.

    10. SUNY—A full credit course and travel program offered in conjunction with the State University of New York, Hebrew University and WZO. There were about 30 participants.

C. All groups returned by the end of August. Planning, promotion, and recruitment activities are underway for winter program:

    1. Early Childhood Seminar—December
    2. Philadelphia Jewish Campus Activities Program—December-January Planning and promotion has also begun for Summer 1984, as well as active recruitment for the 1984-85 American class at Kfar Blum.

    In addition to efforts to project a positive image of Israel, a strategy has been developed to counter individuals, organizations, and academic institutions that voice negative views of Israel, or that are perceived to voice such views or to slight Israeli concerns, since the campus provides one of the few arenas for pro-Palestinian groups and speakers. This strategy is threefold and involves (1) presenting the Jewish students on campus with methods of counteracting "anti-Israel propaganda"; (2) challenging faculty members who are critical of Zionism and/or Israel; (3) monitoring and criticizing Middle East studies centers in American universities.

AIPAC's "Battle for the Campus"

    One organization that has increasingly targeted the campus is AIPAC, whose Political Leadership Development Program, initiated in 1980, provides on-campus political workshops intended to train, organize and provide coordination for pro-Israel student activists.* Program director Jonathan Kessler claims the campus political action workshops are used to familiarize students with both pro- and anti-Israel arguments. They provide specific techniques for neutralizing or disrupting pro-Palestinian events and speakers, influencing the campus media, and building coalitions. Students are also urged to get involved in local off-campus political campaigns. Once a workshop is held, that campus is hooked into the

---

*At the 1983 AIPAC policy conference, two evenings were devoted to the subject of campus activity. In addition to talks led by four staff members of the Leadership Development Program, there was a session called "Building Coalitions on Campus," illustrating AIPAC's goal of broadening the forces involved in pro-Israel student work. Guest speakers in this session were leading representatives from the College Republican National Committee, College Democrats of America, NAACP, Christian Ministry Among Jewish People (sic), Frontlash, and Young America's Foundation.

AIPAC Leadership Development Program's ongoing network. Local campus contacts are asked to monitor all pro-Palestinian or Middle East-related speakers, and send tapes or notes to AIPAC. Kessler then prepares "dossiers" to arm participants in the network against future appearances of targeted speakers. Ammunition includes damaging quotes from past speeches and advice on suggestions for the most effective style of questioning or criticism. Suggested questions are carefully varied for different campuses so the target does not become familiar with them, and students are asked to distribute the questions as widely as possible. According to a participant in the 1983 AIPAC policy conference, the suggested strategy for the coming year was to attack Arab countries and society in order to deflect criticism from Israel. The AIPAC center also helps develop strategies for preventing or obstructing the appearance of pro-Palestinian speakers altogether. If the student union approves guest speakers, pro-Israel groups are encouraged to join it; if the school administration makes the decision, Kessler recommends raising the complaint that such speakers advocate violence or support the PLO. He notes that even if these techniques do not result in cancellations, the controversy alone will discourage colleges from inviting pro-Palestinian speakers.

One of Kessler's political action workshops was held in Madison, Wisconsin on 12 September 1982.* The first part identified and suggested responses to major issues raised by critics of Israel: Zionism and racism, civilian casualties in Lebanon, the media, Begin as a terrorist, Israeli arms sales to repressive regimes, and the Israeli settlements policy.

The second part addressed strategy and tactics for pro-Israel campus work. The objectives presented were: building coalitions, fortifying Jewish students and giving them information to respond to anti-Zionists, winning over those with open minds, providing information to the curious, letting the Arabs know they cannot get away with what they are doing, destroying the credibility of speakers and undercutting their arguments, and "disequilibrating" Arab students. An effective response, Kessler noted, must be an appropriate response, and an appropriate response is one that works—it is not a moral question. The vehicles for response that he provided include:

(1) No response at all.

(2) Monitor: go to events and photograph speakers and audience; tape speakers and send cassettes to other campuses so that leaflets can be prepared in advance. Noting that it is not illegal to take photographs, he said that "if anyone lays a hand on you it can be legal assault; people can be thrown off the campus and out of the country," and he added that it was

---

* The following summary of the workshop was provided by a participant who has requested to remain anonymous.

necessary to "show the Arabs they can't get away with that stuff in this country."

(3) Newspaper campaigns: respond to critical articles, letters, ads, and so forth. Develop relationships with media people and with "people who count."

(4) Leaflet before, after, and during an event. Here Kessler suggested that students "play to the racist tendencies of the American people" by telling police "you are afraid for your safety; say something like 'Arabs don't like us because of their different perspective' or that Arabs might get violent because of their 'different perspective'."

(5) Use what he called counter or preemptive programming. Debates, he suggested, should be turned down if there is a possibility of losing. How? By announcing that "We don't want confrontation; we want communication, we want dialogue." If they turn you down: "All they want is confrontation."

(6) Raise questions from the audience; use plants. Have the questions prepared, spread out in the audience, take off yarmulkas ("God will forgive").

(7) Plant hecklers: they should be succinct, loud enough for everyone to hear, devastatingly clever or funny; pitch to the audience accordingly.

(8) Prevent pro-Arab events from taking place: appeal to the administration either to cancel the event or to forbid posters. (He also suggested taking posters down on the grounds that the Arabs incite violence and racial hatred.) Alternately, ask whether money would be used to bring a white supremacist to campus; argue that these people don't deserve free speech. Unless the administration feels that free speech is sacrosanct, Kessler told his audience, they will win, although he noted that this approach is sometimes counterproductive.

(9) Spread disinformation, or accurate information in a form that misleads. Kessler's example was an AIPAC pamphlet made to look like those of the Palestine Human Rights Campaign, but labeled Human Rights Campaign and presenting pro-Zionist views. This was given out at events in order to confuse the audience.

AIPAC has also administered a questionnaire entitled "The AIPAC College Guide: A Survey of Political Activism (Campus Survey)." This extremely detailed survey covers the political climate on campus, the Arab-Israeli battle on campus, the campus press, pro-Israel groups, anti-Israel groups, and the relationship between pro- and anti-Israel groups. The results of the survey would obviously be extremely useful in planning an even more systematic campaign for campus-oriented work or publishing a study on the general subject. The questions are so detailed that responses could also be used to target a particular campus, a student group or publication, or even a certain program or individual. One sequence of questions reads: "Please name any individual faculty who assists anti-Israel groups. How is this assistance offered? If there is a

Middle East Study Center, please elaborate on its impact on campus."

It is important to note here that AIPAC's recent stress on academia points to the likelihood of more aggressively and carefully targeted involvement on campuses in the future by all pro-Israel groups.

Challenging Israel's Critics on Campus

The challenge to faculty members critical of Israel sometimes even precedes—and obstructs—their appointment. In 1982, for example, a well-known and highly respected Third World scholar was invited to occupy a professorship in political science at the Newark campus of Rutgers University. The members of the political science department supported the appointment, but after the scholar was assured of the position, the university provost told him "it didn't work out" because of budgetary constraints. Privately, however, he was told that the American Professors for Peace in the Middle East, a pro-Israeli group, had organized a delegation to visit the president of the university, Edward J. Blaustein, and convinced him not to approve the appointment because of the candidate's pro-Palestinian views. In order to avoid the appearance of discrimination, because the candidate was amply qualified for the position, the president simply abolished the position and cited financial considerations.

In another case, the Israeli consulate became directly involved in the matter of a faculty member who is an outspoken critic of Israel. A number of Jewish faculty members from a respected university were invited to a meeting at the Israeli consulate in the area; one of the items on the agenda was "how to curb the influence" of a Palestinian professor.

One of the most highly publicized instances of pressure on a faculty member because of his approach to Zionism and Israel was that of Dr. Ernest Dube, then assistant professor of Africana studies at the State University of New York at Stony Brook. On 15 July 1983, Selwyn Troen, a visiting professor from Israel, wrote a letter of complaint to Egon Neuberger, dean of social and behavioral sciences at Stony Brook. Troen told the dean that "The information that I received indicated that the bounds of usual academic objectivity in inquiry and evaluation were transgressed as the instructor, Dr. Dube, employed his position for the propagation of personal ideology and biases." Troen had not observed Dube's classes, nor had he communicated with him personally: he based his charges on the account of a single student and a review of a syllabus and term paper topic list that Dube had distributed for his course on "The Politics of Race." One of the suggested term paper topics was the proposition "Zionism is as much racism as Nazism was racism." Dube lectured on the thesis that Zionism is a form of racism for part of one class. Dube, a South African exile, also lectured on Nazism and apartheid as forms of racism.

After writing the letter, Troen left the country, his two-year residence at Stony Brook completed, and resumed his position as a dean at Ben-Gurion University of the Negev. The dean at Stony Brook who received the complaint passed it along to a faculty committee; as the dean wrote to Dube, "I am afraid the matter has escalated beyond our expectations or desires. I was interviewed by a *Newsday* reporter and visited by the local representative of the Anti-Defamation League, neither at my invitation." The faculty committee, which was the University Senate's Executive Committee, reported on 17 August that in its "considered judgment . . . the bounds of academic freedom have not been crossed in this case." The head of the committee, Joel Rosenthal, a professor of history, later told the *New York Times*, "Frankly, I thought what Professor Troen said was bull."[3]

Rabbi Arthur Seltzer, ADL regional director on Long Island, reacted strongly against the faculty committee's conclusion, however, and pressed for action against Dube. He told a Long Island newspaper, "Here we have a university, operating under its standard procedures, which reaches what we see as baseline anti-Semitism."[4] He asked for a meeting with an aide to New York governor Mario Cuomo; the aide, Rabbi Israel Moshowitz, has responsibility for "human affairs," and in particular for liaison with the Jewish community. The governor shortly thereafter made a public statement attacking the Stony Brook faculty for their "thunderous silence" and questioning the faculty committee's report. "If the report of the faculty committee is posited in such a way as to construe . . . it as an endorsement of the [Zionism is racism] doctrine or the soundness of its reasoning, then I reject that report," Cuomo declared. The governor also expressed his abhorrence of the equation of Zionism with a form of racism: "It is a teaching which is, in my opinion, intellectually dishonest."[5]

A statement from Dean Neuberger then asserted that "academic freedom requires the exercise of academic responsibility," and called for "extreme sensitivity" on the part of instructors in discussing "controversial topics."[6]

The Stony Brook campus became polarized over the issue. Dube's colleagues in the Africana studies department criticized the manner in which the administration had handled the controversy, and especially what they perceived as insufficient support for Dube. A group of professors who described themselves as "senior faculty" circulated a memo in response to the critique by the Africana studies faculty, declaring their willingness to defend Dube's academic freedom but calling "the statement linking Zionism to racism and Nazism abhorrent." Dean Neuberger announced that he associated himself with the "senior faculty" memo.

A newspaper account described a considerable amount of resentment on campus toward the external interference:

University President John Marburger said he resented the influence of "outside forces which contributed to the polarization of the campus." Student government president David Gamberg said Cuomo "stirred things up." The student newspaper editorialized against Cuomo's comments, labeling them "convenient political sloganeering." An outspoken sociology professor, Bruce Hare, said Stony Brook "neared hysteria" as the media, outside groups "and the governor fanned the flames."[7]

By the conclusion of the uproar, President Marburger had met with thirty-five local and national Jewish groups and issued a statement in which he declared, "The Stony Brook Administration, for which I speak officially here, absolutely divorces itself from the views expressed in this course and from any view that links Zionism with racism or Nazism. Furthermore I personally find such linkages abhorrent."

Professor Dube subsequently dropped the unit of his course dealing with the connection between Zionism and racism.*

Monitoring Middle East Centers

The third component in the strategy to counter any influences on campus that oppose or are construed to slight Israel is a special effort to scrutinize the activities of Middle East studies centers.

The 1981 report on Middle East centers prepared for the AJC (and discussed in that section, *supra*) particularly questioned "the expanding pattern of funding by Arab governments or pro-Arab corporations" for Middle East studies, asserting that "guidelines notwithstanding, it exercises at least a subliminal influence on the participants, whether student or faculty, as well as on the nature, content and outcome of the programs."

The Middle East studies centers' outreach programs were a matter of special concern to the AJC study. These programs had been established to comply with federal guidelines specifying that 15 percent of federal support be allocated to outreach. The more recent federal guidelines do not specify a percentage of funds to be earmarked for outreach, but the programs are still mandated. The study found that the outreach programs "do in many curriculum development and evaluation projects, evince a determination to improve the image of the Arab world, or, as in the case of business-oriented outreach programs, project a decidely entrepreneurial orientation, geared almost exclusively toward the Arab Middle East." Its conclusion urged that universities "should exercise close oversight" over the outreach programs in view of the "extreme" importance and sensitivity of the issues aroused by any consideration of the Middle East.[8]

In 1981, the Tucson Jewish Community Council (TJCC) complained to University of Arizona officials that the outreach program of the Near Eastern Studies Center was using "propagandistic materials" and that the instructors in the program displayed an "anti-Israel" bias. The particular

---

*According to information provided by the Africana studies department at Stony Brook (7 October 1985), Professor Dube was denied tenure.

target was Dr. Sheila Scoville, who had become head of the outreach program four years earlier. The initial reaction of the University president was that the U.S. Department of Education (DED) was responsible for oversight of federally-funded outreach programs. DED, in turn, placed the responsibility for oversight on the university itself. The TJCC, in the meantime, launched a campaign of letters to Representative Jim McNulty and Senator Dennis DeConcini of Arizona, university officials, the Arizona Department of Education, and DED.

University officials subsequently met with members of a TJCC delegation and invited them to document their charges. On 19 March 1982, the TJCC submitted its report, which remained completely under wraps. The director of the Oriental studies department then formed an *ad hoc* committee to discuss the findings of the TJCC report and closed the departmental library pending settlement of the case.

During this time, the university gained a new president, Henry Koffler, himself a member of the TJCC. For some yet-unexplained reason, a second university panel was appointed to study the TJCC accusations. This panel produced another report that became known as the "extended response to the TJCC." It, too, was kept under wraps. However, unsatisfied by this report, the university president decided to appoint a third review committee of Middle East experts from outside the university to stand as an arbitration committee. The TJCC was given a veto power over the nominees.

As a result of the campaign, the school board had by May 1983 agreed to rescind credit retroactively for high school teachers who had participated in Dr. Scoville's workshops. As for the arbitration panel, though all parties had agreed that its recommendations would be binding, the TJCC announced during the summer of 1983, just before the panel was to meet, that it had never entered into such an agreement. It insisted, further, on broadening the scope of the "investigation" to include other materials of the outreach program and sources of funding, and the university president concurred. In early August 1983, the panel submitted its findings, which appear to have exonerated the outreach program. The president refused to circulate the report, however, indicating that it would constitute only a part of the final report that he intended to write himself.[9]

Recently, as a result of the work of the AJCongress, the state of Illinois passed a disclosure act (Act 83-0641), which "requires the disclosure of monies in excess of $100,000 made to state institutions of higher education by foreign governments or individuals." According to Sylvia Neil, the Midwest legal director of the AJCongress, the target of the act is Arab money. Required in the disclosure statement are the source and purpose of the donation and the conditions on its use. The state of Maryland is considering a similar act.[10]

A number of organizations, or specified programs and departments within existing Jewish community organizations, have been set up since

221

1967 specifically to target campuses and academia. American Professors for Peace in the Middle East (APPME), with a predominantly Jewish membership, was established in 1967. In 1973, the AJCongress set up the National Academic Committee of Jewish Professors. As noted above (Chapter 3), in 1970 UJA established its University Programs Department, and in 1975, its Faculty Advisory Cabinet, both of which promote faculty and student support for UJA campaigns.

American Professors for Peace in the Middle East

Year established: 1967
National President: Marver Bernstein
Executive Director: George Cohen
Address: 330 Seventh Avenue, Suite 606, New York, NY 10001
Publications: *Middle East Review* (quarterly), *APPME Bulletin,*
Special Reports

General Background

APPME grew out of an *ad hoc* committee set up during the 1967 war "to gather signatures for a statement indicating support within the academic community for a resolution of the crisis which would achieve and maintain a just and lasting peace in the Middle East including the preservation of the State of Israel." The statement appeared as a two-page advertisement in the *New York Times* on 8 June 1967, published under the name of "Americans for Democracy in the Middle East—Ad Hoc Committee of American Professors." It characterized the Arab blockade of the Straits of Tiran and the Gulf of Aqaba as "an attack on the very life of the state of Israel and its people." Citing "massive [Arab] mobilization to destroy Israel," it called on the U.S. Congress to maintain its commitment to Israel and "restore freedom of passage through the Gulf of Aqaba." Hundreds of American professors, the majority of whom were Jewish, signed the ad.

After the war was over, the "Ad Hoc Committee of American Professors" placed another advertisement in the *New York Times* on 13 July 1967: the statement, an open letter to President Johnson, UN secretary general U Thant, and others, called for "recognition of Israel's right to exist as a sovereign state on equal terms with other sovereign states in the region." Moreover, it criticized the UN for inactivity, and the U.S.S.R. for its "biased attack on Israel," its equation of Israel with the Nazis, and its encouragement of "Arab extremism and intransigence." Finally the statement appealed for more signatures, volunteers, and help in financing the cost of such advertisements.

By the time the group published its third advertisement on the war *(New York Times,* 24 October 1967), it was no longer an "Ad Hoc Committee," but APPME. The theme of this ad was "The road to peace: direct negotiations." The text criticized "Arab intransigence," and advocated negotiations between "Israel and her neighbors." It called on the UN to honor its principle that "negotiation is essential," and on President Johnson to uphold "his statements that '... the parties to the conflict must be the parties to the peace....'" Boasting the support of ten thousand professors on about 170 U.S. campuses, APPME stated that its aim was "to help achieve a just and lasting peace in the Middle East that will guarantee the security of the State of Israel."

Structure

APPME is a membership organization open to all faculty members and administrators in academia; the American Academic Association for Peace in the Middle East (AAAPME) is its non-profit branch, which receives tax-deductible contributions and also sponsors publications, such as *Middle East Review.* In 1980, an APPME brochure declared that "about 15,000 individuals . . . , in one way or another, are formally or informally connected with our organization and . . . subscribe to its overall objectives." These individuals were distributed over six hundred U.S. campuses.

APPME shows the same New York City address as the American Zionist Federation's Zionist Academic Council (discussed above in Chapter 1). APPME is structured on a regional basis; as of March 1983, there were fifteen regions, each under a regional chairman.*

Each regional chairman has a regional council that consists of the campus representatives in the region. All regional chairmen, in turn, serve on the national executive committee, which meets regularly. APPME's deliberative body, the national council, meets in the spring of each year and includes campus representatives, APPME's officers, and executive committee members. APPME has also an active liaison office in Jerusalem.

Role and Israel Support Work

To the American academic community, APPME advertises itself as "the oldest and largest organization of academics devoted to bringing the scholarly resources of the academic community to bear on the basic conflict areas in the Middle East." Although it declares that it is "dedicated to a just and lasting peace between Israel and her Arab neighbors," it insists that it "does not engage in direct political action, nor does it espouse specific policy positions."[11] It acknowledges, however, that its position "implies advocacy of certain objectives that we regard as fundamental, of which the continued existence of Israel, not only in security but also in a context of normal relations with its Arab neighbors, is the most significant."[12]

---

* The regions and their regional chairmen are: New York Metropolitan, Joseph Rothschild (Columbia); New York Upstate, Jeffrey Ross; Eastern Pennsylvania, Bernard Stern (Villanova); Western Pennsylvania, Myron Taub (University of Pittsburgh); Central Pennsylvania, Elmer Lear (Penn State); District of Columbia, Harvey Lieber (American University); Midwest, Stephen Feinstein, (University of Wisconsin, River Falls); Chicago, Milton Shulman (De Paul); Southeast, Ted Lansman (University of Florida, Gainesville); Southwest, Leo Cefkin (Colorado State, Fort Collins); Texas, Sidney Weintraub (University of Texas, Austin); Southern California, Norman Abrams (UCLA, Law School); Northern California, Ralph Kramer (Berkeley); Northwest, Morton Jacobs (Lewis and Clark); New England, Norman Lichtin (Boston University).

APPME conducts regional and national meetings on campuses, academic conferences, special panels at meetings of professional associations, briefing sessions, and study missions to the Middle East and distributes books, reports and its journal, *Middle East Review*. APPME organizes missions to the Middle East, campus meetings, regional conferences, and annual national conferences. The AAAPME conducts Middle East panels at professional meetings.

In 1979/1980, AAAPME's Committee on Campus Journalism monitored over three hundred college newspapers, with the help of a grant from the Newton Becker CPA Review Course Philanthropic Fund, to examine the presentation of the Middle East debate in the campus press. The conclusion, as reported in *Middle East Review*, showed that Arab students express "radical views," while American commentators keep referring to PLO moderation.

Recently APPME has been gathering information on critics of Israeli policy who speak on campuses; a memorandum sent to all regional chairmen and campus representatives in March 1983 reported:

We have received a list of speakers who are being toured through the university circuit by other groups to present the Arab point of view. The problem with many of these presentations is that they smack more of propaganda than of education. In order of frequency and virulence the speakers are: Hatem Hussaini, Edward Said, Noam Chomsky, Fawaz Turki, Stokely Carmichael, James Zogby, Hassan Rahman, Chris Giannou, M.D., Israel Shahak, and Gail Pressberg. It would be helpful if you would let us know whether any of these speakers appeared on your campus or on a neighboring university, what they said and what the question and answer period was like. We would be equally interested to know whether any speakers presenting the Israeli point of view visited in your area and what transpired. While there are doubtless many speakers who espouse the Israeli position, it seems to us that there is no organized, centrally controlled, information plan like the one we are seeing on the Arab side.[13]

Such a characterization is ironic, in light of APPME's 1982 expenditure of $425,000, as well as the fact that APPME is only one of many pro-Israel organizations that target the American campus.[14]

In 1982, AAAPME formed a new "Middle East Media and Information Service" to respond quickly to media requests for experts on the Middle East and to encourage media to submit such requests. In 1983, AAAPME received a research grant from the Bruner Foundation "to measure informational and attitudinal changes among faculty and students resulting from having Middle East scholars in residences for 3-day periods on selected campuses in the far West." The call was for professors who are willing "to serve as our paid contacts for the project." The selected universities were in Arizona, Idaho, Montana, Nevada, New Mexico, Oklahoma, and Utah. AAAPME has a campus radio program, called "Middle East Dialogue," which is distributed free to over 200 campuses.[15]

Publications

The major activity of the APPME/AAAPME is the publication and dissemination of background papers, special reports, conference proceedings, journals and books.

Among the background papers that APPME has produced and made available to the academic public are: "Saudi Oil Pricing and Production: Good Will or Self-Interest," by Alan Dowty; "AWACS and the Next Arab-Israeli War," by Martin Greenberg; "The Immoderation of Saudi Arabia," by Michael Curtis; "The Arab Lobby," by Fredelle Z. Spiegel; "The Israel Lobby and the National Interest," by Seymour Martin Lipset; and "Western Europe and the Middle East: Venice or Munich," by Michael Curtis.

The quarterly *Middle East Review* (*MER*) published by AAAPME was known as the *Middle East Information Series* until 1974. In 1981, it claimed a circulation of 10,000 copies. Its self-description states that "its contents focus on the varied and complex problems involved in the Arab-Israel conflict;" that it is prepared by "international authorities;" and that it is read by reaching academics and scholars and is used as class, text and source material.

In the wake of the Israeli invasion of Lebanon, AAAPME initiated a series of monthly *MER Special Reports,* distributed free of charge upon request. Three of these reports, written by Michael Curtis, AAAPME's chairman of the board and a professor of political science at Rutgers University, deal with "Lebanon: Past, Present, Future" (August 1982), "Options for Peace in the Middle East" (February 1983), and "Academic Freedom and the West Bank" (April 1983).

In the Lebanon report, produced at the height of the Israeli seige of Beirut, Curtis maintained that, "As a result of PLO activity, Lebanon as a viable political structure has disappeared," and that "Israel intervened in Lebanon in order to eliminate the PLO bases and thus end their use as springboards for attacks on Israeli soil."

In the report on "Options for Peace in the Middle East," Curtis wrote: "The essence of the Arab-Israeli conflict remains what it has always been: the refusal of Arab states or political forces, except Egypt, to accept the existence and legitimacy of the state of Israel."

Curtis' report on "Academic Freedom and the West Bank" is the clearest example of his, and APPME's, role as apologists for official Israeli policy. Curtis' thrust in this report is to refute the charge that Israel suppresses academic freedom in Palestinian educational institutions on the West Bank; Curtis minimizes those abuses that are too blatant to dismiss as instances of "overzealous censorship" or "occasional brutalities."

In 1983, controversy arose over a Middle East textbook that AAAPME commissioned. The book, *The United States and the Middle East,* was written by Philip L. Groisser, a former high school superintendent, and published by the State University of New York Press in 1981. The American Arab

Anti-Discrimination Committee charged that the book contained anti-Arab bias; in the wake of the allegations, SUNY Press discontinued publishing the book, though it claimed its decision was due to financial considerations only.[16]

CHURCH

Historically, Jewish community relations organizations have targeted the church as an area for generating positive sentiments and engaging in opinion-molding on behalf of Israel. Churches exert influence through study programs, radio and television broadcasts, newsletters, and newspapers reaching millions of persons. Churches operate hundreds of universities and seminaries and a huge number of elementary and secondary schools. Despite the growing secularization of American life, the churches remain a significant source of moral and cultural influence. The enormous diversity among the churches in organization, outlook, and policy, however, makes precise measurement of their influence difficult.

Since the 1940s, American Jewish organizations engaged in Israel support work have worked to identify sympathetic theological trends, sought to neutralize "pro-Arab" elements within the churches, and organized sympathetic clergy and laity. For example, in 1946, after the Christian Council on Palestine and the American Palestine Committee merged to form the American Christian Palestine Committee, the American Zionist Emergency Council subsidized the new organization's activities with grants ranging from $75,000 to $150,000 a year. Distinguished Protestant theologians Reinhold Niebuhr and Paul Tillich were among the organization's most enthusiastic spokesmen.

Over time, the Jewish community relations organizations have been able to adapt their strategy toward the churches to changing conditions in American church life. Thus, during the last few years, with the ascendancy of New Right fundamentalists among U.S. Protestants and the increasingly significant support of the Christian right for Israel, many Jewish groups have shifted their attention away from the "mainline" Protestant churches and toward these conservative Protestants.

"Mainline" Protestants

The "mainline" churches are generally regarded as those with membership in the National Council of Churches of Christ in the United States (NCC). At present there are thirty-one member "communions" in the NCC. Their influence is disproportionate to their relatively small numbers—presently around 30 million members. As Peter Johnson argues, they "have shaped the public ethos not because their members are a majority of the U.S. population but because they are the churches of the upper class . . . the churches of the WASP, the White Anglo-Saxon Protestant. . . . "[1]

During the post-World War II era, the growth of liberation movements, successful political decolonization of many Third World nations, and concurrent demands for control over their societies' institutions posed new demands on the mainline denominations. They were challenged to transform their "paternalistic" styles of missionary behavior. International ecumenical bodies, most notably the World Council of Churches, increasingly articulated theological and socioeconomic points of view antagonistic to the "principalities and powers." The development of liberation theology brought an emphasis on class analysis to Biblical understanding. Minority groups within the mainline churches demanded more meaningful participation and often tended to be more sympathetic in their outlook toward Third World movements.

As the mainline churches sought to accommodate these new trends, they designed new programs and offered support to organizations outside the traditional definition of church activity. They tended to espouse a liberal social agenda: they were active supporters of the civil rights movement during the 1950s and 1960s, and many mainline church leaders publicly opposed the Vietnam war. They supported the organizing efforts of the United Farmworkers and the J.P. Stevens textile workers and were a major component in the Nestlé boycott and other campaigns for greater corporate responsibility.

These activities, however, alienated large segments of their membership. Mainline church membership dropped, and denominational and ecumenical leaders found themselves under increasing attack for being "out of touch with the man in the pew." By mid-1980, it was apparent that a major political offensive was being waged against them.

One of the most vociferous critics of the NCC and related mainline denominations has been Rael Jean Isaac, the founding member of Americans for a Safe Israel, whose attack on Breira appeared in *Commentary* in 1977. A spate of hostile articles have also appeared in the nation's business press with titles such as "Unholy Alliance" (*Barron's*), and "When Capitalism and Christianity Clash" (*Forbes*).[2] At the same time, the "neoconservatives" were often able to effect alliances with conservative caucuses and individuals in the mainline churches to attack their liberal social positions from within. Isaac, for example, has drawn heavily upon the resources of the Institute for Religion and Democracy, a think-tank with close relations to the neoconservative Social Democrats, USA, and with the Movement for a Democratic Majority.

Attacks on the NCC

The entire social and political agenda of the NCC and mainline churches, not merely these bodies' policies and practices relating to the Middle East, came under attack. However, the NCC's "Middle East Policy

228

Statement" became the *cause célèbre* that catalyzed the convergence of attacks from the political right and the Jewish establishment.

The NCC's "Middle East Policy Statement" was adopted by a 162-0 vote of their governing board in November 1980. In the section on "Israel and the Palestinians" the statement stops just short of advocating recognition of the PLO, referring to it as "the only organized voice of the Palestinian people [which] appears to be the only body able to negotiate on their behalf." At the same time, NCC called for "either an amendment of the Palestine National Covenant of 1968 or an unambiguous statement recognizing Israel as a sovereign state and its right to continue to exist as a Jewish state." The Policy Statement then called for the following "affirmations":

a) Cessation of acts of violence in all its forms by all parties;

b) Recognition by the Arab states and by the Palestinian Arabs of the state of Israel with secure, defined and recognized borders; and recognition by Israel of the right of national self-determination for the Palestinian Arabs and of their right to select their own representatives and to establish a Palestinian entity, including a sovereign state. In the meantime, unilateral actions in respect to such issues as settlement policy and land and water use in the occupied areas can only inflame attitudes, and reduce the prospects of achieving peace;

c) Agreement on and creation of a mode of enforcement of international guarantees for the sovereign and secure borders of Israel and of any Palestinian entity established as part of the peace process. This would mean the implementation of the principles enunciated in United Nations Security Council Resolution 242 (1967);

d) Provision for solution to problems of refugees and displaced persons, Palestinian Arab, Jewish, and other, affected by the Israel-Palestinian and related conflicts dating from 1948, including questions of compensation and return;

e) Agreement on the future status of Jerusalem, a focus of the deepest religious inspiration and attachment of three faiths, Judaism, Christianity and Islam. Existing international treaties (Paris, 1856 and Berlin, 1878), and League of Nations actions regulating the rights and claims of the three modern monotheistic religions to Holy Places should remain unaltered. At the same time, the destiny of Jerusalem should be viewed in terms of people and not only in terms of shrines. Therefore, the future status of Jerusalem should be included in the agenda of the official negotiations including Israel and the Palestinian people for a comprehensive solution of the Middle East conflict. Unilateral actions by any one group in relation to Jerusalem will only perpetuate antagonisms that will threaten the peace of the city and possibly of the region.

The statement had been in formulation for more than a year. In October 1979, the NCC appointed a high-level panel, chaired by Rev. Tracey Jones, general secretary of the United Methodist Board of Global Ministries, and including the heads of six denominations. The panel visited the Middle East, conducted hearings, and sought the input of a wide variety of persons.

However, the panel found itself under attack from the American Jewish establishment well before its process was completed. By early February 1980, the *New York Times* carried stories noting the intention of major American Jewish organizations, including the ADL, to boycott the panel's discussions. The ADL characterized the NCC as having a "disturbing and troubling record of pro-Arab and pro-PLO leanings."[3]

The ADL conveyed its critique of the draft of the proposed statement to Rev. Jones in a stinging letter dated 18 August 1980, and signed by the chair of ADL's National Program Committee and the co-chairs and co-directors of the Interfaith Affairs Committee.[4] The letter spoke of ADL's "very deep concern" with the draft, because "this document is so philosophically incompatible with the quest for a just and lasting peace." The ADL warned Rev. Jones that "unless you and your Committee reexamine the foundations of your proposed Policy Statement, you will have produced a document which will fail to withstand the test of reality and credibility." The draft, the ADL's letter declared, "does NOT serve the best interests of peace" (emphasis in original). To assist the NCC in "rethinking the recommendations of the Policy Statement," the ADL appended a twenty-page document entitled "The Middle East Today: Questions and Answers for Church Leaders," which generally reflected official Israeli positions.

Dissatisfaction with the NCC and suspicion that it was "pro-PLO" had been brewing among the Jewish community relations organizations for several years. In May 1979, Judith Banki, writing for the Interreligious Affairs Department of the American Jewish Committee, produced *Anti-Israel Influence in American Churches: A Background Report*. In the introduction, Rabbi Marc Tannenbaum, then AJC's national interreligious affairs director, described the document as the "first to survey systematically the sources of anti-Israel influence within American Christian Churches." Banki argued: "A pro-Arab disposition is strongly in evidence among Protestant denominations with long-standing involvement in missions to the Arab Middle East; in churches and church-related groups engaged in aiding Arab refugees; among certain left-wing 'liberationist' ideologues; and in communions with predominantly Arab constituencies, whether Catholic or Eastern Orthodox." Banki's criterion for determining "pro-Arab disposition" was "the use of double standards—harsher judgments and stricter demands made on Israel than on her Arab antagonists—biased or loaded renderings of history; and sometimes, resort to theological arguments hostile to Judaism."

The American Jewish committee was particularly active during the spring of 1979 in response to resource materials that were being produced for an interdenominational study on the Middle East undertaken by the NCC and its member communions. "Middle East Mosaic" was selected as the theme of the 1979-1980 annual mission study; the process of assembling resource materials for the study had been initiated in 1977 under the

230

guidance of the NCC-related Friendship Press. Eventually, the materials were to include a novel intended to generate interest, a more factual book to complement the novel, a leader's guide, a supplemental packet, along with a film and film guide.

The AJC was permitted an opportunity for critical review of the written materials at every stage of their production, which amounted to considerably greater access than that accorded to the NCC's counterpart, the Middle East Council of Churches. The AJC did not have similar access to the film, "Hope for Life," and to the film guide during their production, and these became the subjects of the AJC's harshest criticisms.[5] The guide was produced, withdrawn, and rewritten twice before the third and final version passed scrutiny by the AJC; even then the guide was not wholly to AJC's liking.

Rabbi James Rudin, in coordination with Rabbi Marc Tannenbaum, Judith Banki, and Inge Gibel, produced a point-by-point critique and analysis of the guide. Linda Burnett, an associate professor of English and film at the Community College of Philadelphia, prepared what amounted to nearly a frame-by-frame analysis of the film itself. In a letter to United Methodist pastor Bob White, she wrote:

Whether intended or not, the overall effect encourages the Christian viewer to liken those interviewed with Christ, thus magnifying their words, actions, political positions, and making these acceptable without question. . . . The arrangement of sequence, starting with ecumenical visuals (fishermen at Galilee, Moslems and Jews at prayer, garbage collectors in Egypt) relaxes the viewer and lulls critical faculties until well along in the film before the first political accusation is made; after which the pace quickens, the political content thickens to an almost militaristic call to action. . . .

Various commentators on the film objected to the self-identification of a Gaza social service representative as "a refugee from Haifa, Palestine," and the remark of a kindergarten teacher on the West Bank that "this is the generation which we hope will grow up to live in freedom." Jules Whitman, president of AJC's Philadelphia chapter, wrote to United Methodist Bishop James Ault to seek "immediate withdrawal of this film from distribution." Whitman argued that the film contained "subtle and at times overt political judgments that are clearly hostile to Israel," and concluded that, "The film is a distinct setback to building positive interreligious relations between Methodists and Jews. . . . "

Church spokespersons defended the film against its detractors in the Jewish community relations organizations. Edwin Maynard, acting general secretary of the United Methodist Communications Office at the time, said " . . . the film intends to show ministries of Christian churches to persons in the Middle East who are refugees." The One Great Hour of Sharing Committee, which was using the film to rally support for the projects depicted, concluded that "within the context of documenting ministry by the Christian community in this area of the Middle East . . . the film and its companion guide fulfill their purposes adequately."

"Hope for Life" won an award for excellence in the motion picture category from the Religious Public Relations Council and was considered in the finals of the twenty-first Annual American Film Festival.

Yet another NCC effort at public information on the Middle East drew the particular ire of the ADL. A month after Warren Day, executive director of the NCC's Office of News and Information, distributed a kit on "American Churches and the Arab-Israeli Conflict" to editors and reporters in December 1979, a strong letter of criticism was sent to NCC president Rev. M. William Howard with the signatures of five rabbis, all ADL officials. They complained that the "unmistakable thrust" of an attempt was "to undermine and reverse Christian support of Israel."[6]

While the critical supervision that the Jewish community organizations have attempted to exercise over the developing positions of mainline Protestant churches toward the Middle East has concentrated on the NCC, it has not been limited to that level. Offices of individual denominations and local church activities have come under scrutiny as well.

For example, the director of the ADL's Department of Interreligious Cooperation criticized a report on the thirtieth session of the UN General Assembly, which was prepared by the United Nations Office of the United Methodist Church (UNOUM), and which appeared in the February 1976 issue of *Engage-Social Action*. The ADL official wrote to Robert McClean, associate director of UNOUM: "I find it difficult to square some of your observations with an empathetic approach to the Jewish community and to its concerns about Israel," and expressed concern about the report's "evident tone of indifference toward the State of Israel and the disinterest in the flood of anti-Semitism which has been let loose in the 30th Session of the General Assembly." The United Methodists responded in a letter to the ADL that defended the report on the General Assembly and commented: "We have been happy to join with your organization on issues such as Racial Discrimination, Civil Rights and the Anti-War Movement. However, quite frankly, the present pressure has attempted to build on the Christian's latent anti-Semitism, coupled with their fear of that prejudice and desire to escape it. This campaign is almost wholly political and indicates that those who are concerned with the human and civil rights of all persons in the Middle East are somehow anti-Semitic."

The local affiliates of the Jewish community relations organizations play an analogous role in regard to the Middle East activities of local clergy and congregations. The AJC's Community Service Department, for example, reported among its chapter activities during the fall of 1982 that, "The Seattle Chapter took the leadership in challenging the virulent anti-Israel statements of Protestant clergymen following their Middle East tour which was underwritten by the PLO. The chapter also mobilized pro-Israel Christian leaders to speak out in support of Israel."[7]

The Jewish community relations organizations have advanced pro-Israel positions within the mainline churches through the Christian-Jewish dialogue. Sensitive to charges of anti-Semitism, and searching for means to root inherited anti-Semitic tendencies out of Christian theology, mainline church leaders have established active programs of interfaith dialogue with the American Jewish community and especially with the cooperation of the AJC. However, reporting on one such dialogue held in August 1982, the *New York Times* noted that relations have become more strained since the 1982 Israeli invasion of Lebanon.[8]

The AJC's Inge Gibel spearheaded another recent effort, this one particularly aimed at church women. The "Women of Faith in the 80s" organization held their second conference during early January 1984. Advance material for the conference indicated that one of the presentations was to be from Thelma Adair, president of Church Women United, and who was "in Copenhagen," a reference to the First International Women's Conference. The material, under Gibel's name, continued, "her paper will deal with what happens to Third World women who are caught in the middle of Palestinian women as the chief order of business and the type of anti-apartheid, anti-racism platform whose real focus is to hit at Israel and Zionism (sic) . . . "

U.S. Catholics

In a recent study of *American Christianity, the Jewish State, and the Arab-Israeli Conflict*, Thomas Wiley quotes a 1946 editorial from *Commonweal* magazine to summarize the attitudes of U.S. Catholics: "We have never been able to make up our minds on the subject of Jewish immigration into Palestine. We fully recognize the desperate need of Europe's remaining Jews for a homeland in which they can be reasonably confident of living unmolested . . . but we are . . . suspicious of Zionist nationalism and we cannot withhold our sympathy from the natives of Palestine."[9]

Despite such ambivalence, by 1949 U.S. Catholics tended to follow the tone established by the Vatican, which declared recognition contigent upon repatriation of the refugees, protection of the holy sites, and settlement of all territorial questions. The Vatican still has not recognized Israel and maintains a "Pontifical Mission to Palestine" in Jerusalem. The Catholic church continues to assist the Palestinian refugees through the Catholic Near East Welfare Association, established in September 1948.

It was not until 1973 that an Israeli leader was granted papal audience. Pope Paul VI informed Israeli prime minister Golda Meir that the Vatican would not recognize Israel "as long as the Middle East conflict remains unresolved." Relations were further strained by the Vatican's stand at the UN Habitat Conference in 1976, when it supported a resolution denouncing racism as "defined in UN resolutions," a reference that included the UN resolution calling Zionism a form of racism. The Vatican position on Israel softened somewhat following Israel's release of

Archbishop Hilarion Capucci in 1977 (he had been accused of smuggling arms to the Palestinian resistance and imprisoned), but tensions were again heightened after Pope Paul II granted an audience to PLO chairman Yasir Arafat.

U.S. Catholics, particularly since the 1967 war, have tended to be more pro-Israeli in their outlook than the Vatican. According to Wiley, this is "reflected not only in Catholic journals and periodicals, but also in clergy and lay activity." He continues: "This shift in attitude is due not only to the ecumenicalism of the period but also, of course, to the changing climate of public opinion in the United States since the Six-Day War."[10]

Rev. Joseph Ryan likewise notes public statements from Catholic organizations that reject the UN resolution on Zionism as racism and oppose efforts to expel Israel from the United Nations. Analyzing three major U.S. Catholic policy statements from the 1970s, Ryan details "several central elements":

1) The rights of Israel: to existence as a sovereign state within secure and recognized boundaries;
2) The rights of the Palestinian Arabs: to participate in negotiations affecting their destiny, and to a homeland of their own;
3) Compensation: just compensation should be provided for all parties concerned, of whatever national origin, deprived of home and property by the three decades of conflict;
4) The status of Jerusalem: recognition of its unique religious significance which should be preserved through an international guarantee of access to the holy places, and through the preservation of a religiously pluralistic citizenry;
5) UN Resolution 242: its continuing utility as a basis for a just settlement in the region.[11]

These pronouncements closely parallel the position of the NCC, the major body speaking for mainline Protestants.

Evangelicals

Estimates of the number of evangelicals in the United States vary from thirty million to more than fifty million. The term "evangelical" is itself quite ambiguous and encompasses persons with widely divergent political views. Pollster George Gallup characterizes evangelicals as persons who have had a "born again conversion, accept Jesus as personal saviour, believe the Scriptures are the authority for all doctrine, and feel an urgent duty to spread the faith." His survey, "Religion in America 1977-1978," determined the number of adult evangelicals in the United States to be about forty million. Fundamentalist evangelicals, who take the word of the Bible literally, are generally thought to number around ten million persons. While evangelicals may constitute one-third of the membership of the mainline churches, most are clustered within the conservative wing of the Protestant church, which includes the nation's largest single denomination, the Southern Baptists, as well as the Assemblies of God, the Missouri Synod Lutheran, the Church of Christ, and many others. Their national umbrella organization, the National Association of Evangelicals, has thirty-four member denominations.

By all measurements, however, while the mainline denominations have been experiencing a period of declining membership, the conservative evangelicals have celebrated major growth. Their books are a major component of religious book sales, which constitute more than one-third of the total gross sales of the commercial book market; approximately thirteen hundred radio stations, one in seven in the United States, is evangelical-owned and operated; in the late 1970s, evangelical broadcasters were adding a new television station to their ranks every thirty days.[12] Evangelical schools have attracted the largest growth of private school enrollment. In 1983, the *New York Times* reported: "In the decade from 1970 to 1980, enrollment in non-Catholic church-related schools increased 47 percent in the Northeast and 49 percent in the North-Central region. . . . But in the West enrollment in such schools doubled in the same period and in the South it quadrupled."[13]

The fundamentalist churches have become a significant target for the Jewish community relations organizations for three major reasons. First, the growth of the fundamentalists, particularly relative to the decline of the mainline Protestant churches, gives them a special importance. Second, evangelical theology, with its exaltation of Israel, predisposes many fundamentalists to support the state of Israel. Third, the fundamentalist churches are closely associated politically with the New Right, and their base is highly mobilized to participate in political activity that favors Israel. These latter two factors will be discussed next.

Evangelicals and Israel

"PRAY AGAINST THE SPIRIT OF ISLAM," exhorted a newsletter of the Pittsburgh "consulate" of the International Christian Embassy in Jerusalem. It then asserted:

The evil spirits of Islam are responsible for:
   a. The spiritual bondage of the Arab world.
   b. Much anti-Semitism around the world.
   c. Bitter anti-Israel attitude in all Middle Eastern nations, and other nations of the world that are predominantly Muslim.
   d. The idea of "oil blackmail" against the nations of the world who are supportive of Israel.
   e. A great mockery of God . . . a Moslem mosque sits on the most holy site, Mt. Moriah. This is a reproach on the sacred temple site.
   f. In Lebanon, it is Islam that has sought to destroy Lebanon's Christians for a decade now. Hundreds of thousands of Christians have been killed.[14]

The International Christian Embassy in Jerusalem (ICEJ) was established during the last week of September 1980 after thirteen governments withdrew their embassies from the city. A 1980 *Jerusalem Post* feature concluded: "The embassy promotes every kind of propaganda for the cause it cherishes, through press, radio, films, tapes, meetings, 'love-Israel' nights."[15] The ICEJ carries out its programs both in Jerusalem and internationally. In Jerusalem, in addition to providing lectures to tour groups, it has organized "Christian" contingents to march in Israeli national celebrations. Upon concluding a tour of the Holocaust Memorial, Yad Vashem, one recent visitor to Jerusalem was asked whether he was Jewish or Christian. When he replied Christian, the receptionist handed him a tract prepared by the ICEJ.

Most of the ICEJ's activities outside Jerusalem are organized through its "consulates," which are mobilized to carry out wide-ranging programs of support for Israel. They conduct seminars, organize efforts aimed at promoting the sale of Israeli goods, provide speakers from the Jewish National Fund and other Zionist organizations, organize tours, suggest guidelines for letters to congressional representatives, publish newsletters and articles, and sponsor prayer groups for Israel, among other activities. Fifteen "consulates" currently operate in the United States.

The ICEJ, moreover, is only one of a plethora of evangelical Christian groups operating in the United States in support of Israel; others include Mike Evans Ministries, Evangelicals United for Zion, TAV (named for the last letter of the Hebrew alphabet), Bridges for Peace, and the Temple Mount Fund Society. Many of the country's best known "televangelists," including Jack Van Impe, Pat Robertson, James Robison, and Jerry Falwell, regularly advocate support for Israel.

Shaping the perceptions of many of the most active individuals and organizations among the evangelicals is an understanding of history and theology known as dispensational premillennialism. The central belief of premillennialists is that the second coming of Christ will be accompanied by his rule on earth for one thousand years before the "final judgment." Many dispensationalist beliefs relate directly to Israel. They are convinced a series of specific events will occur as history unfolds to its climax, including the return of the Jews to the land of Palestine, the establishment of a Jewish state, the preaching of the Gospel to all nations, including Israel, and the Battle of Armageddon, taking place literally at Armageddon by the Mediterranean, in what is now northern Israel, where the armies of the Antichrist will be finally defeated by Christ.

In the United States, the view of theology is often wedded to a particularly chauvinistic understanding of history. The United States is seen as particularly singled out and blessed by God, a repeating undercurrent of American thought. Thus, Jerry Falwell commonly explains, "God has blessed America because we have blessed the Jews." Mike Evans, appearing on Pat Robertson's television program, "The 700

Club," asserted a miraculous improvement in Alabama's economic welfare after its state legislature sent a letter of support to Israel. On his own hour-long television program, "Israel, America's Key to Survival," which airs on dozens of stations, Evans has characterized the PLO as "small bands of ruthless outlaws," and "just a bunch of nuts."[16] Guests such as General George Keegan, columnist Jack Anderson, and the former head of Israeli intelligence, Isser Har'el, have linked the PLO with the Soviet Union, while Israel's positive ties with the United States and God's will are stressed.

Fundamentalist Theology and Rightist Strategy

The impetus behind the emergence of the New Right is commonly traced to a handful of conservative political activists, including Richard Viguerie, Howard Phillips, Ed McAteer, Robert Billings, and Paul Weyrich. Dismayed at President Gerald Ford's 1974 selection of the "liberal" Nelson Rockefeller as his vice president, Viguerie called together a group of friends to begin strategizing on how to develop a new conservative movement.

Viguerie was a pioneer in the use of direct mail as a political organizing tool. By the early 1980s, his clients included opponents of the Panama Canal Treaty, gun control, busing, abortion, and labor law reform. Among the organizations using his services were the Conservative Caucus, Gun Owners of America, the Committee for the Survival of a Free Congress, and the National Conservative Political Action Committee. A distinctive feature of Viguerie's operation is that when engaged by an organization to raise funds, Viguerie retains control of the names of any contributors his efforts generate. Thus, by 1980, he had lists numbering some 4.5 million conservative contributors.

In an informative and insightful article written for the *New York Review of Books* in 1981, Frances Fitzgerald described how organizers of the New Right

... found their way into the fundamentalist church movement through Edward McAteer, a former sales manager for Colgate-Palmolive and the national director for the Christian and Freedom Foundation, and Robert Billings, a former high school principal, who had become an organizer of the Christian school movement. McAteer and Billings introduced them to Jerry Falwell, James Robison, and a number of other television preachers. From their combined efforts came the three political organizations of the fundamentalist right: the Moral Majority (directed initially by Billings), the Religious Roundtable (run by McAteer) and the Christian Voice (a California organization founded independently but affiliated with this group).[17]

From their inception, the Religious Roundtable and the Moral Majority paid particular attention to combining theology and political developments. They projected a picture of a United States threatened

237

from within and without. Domestically, moral decay, the dissolution of the nuclear family, homosexuality, drugs, and all manner of social ills were the hallmarks of Satan's work, with the assistance (perhaps unwitting, perhaps willing) of "liberal" church leaders and "secular humanists." Abroad, the U.S. defeat in Indochina and its waning ability to control Third World nations were surely the work of Satanic forces, namely the Communists.

The Religious Roundtable is the body established to coordinate the Christian right's agenda. Formed in 1979, it includes many of the largest and most financially successful operators of the religious right: Viguerie, Falwell, Robertson, McAteer, Billings, Phyllis Schlafly, Paul Weyrich, and Bill Bright. Organizations include the Wycliffe Bible Translators and the Church League of America (an extremely secretive research organization that keeps files on thousands of "known communists," and monitors "communist infiltration" of the National Council of Churches, the United Methodist Church and other churches).[18]

While support for Israel on both strategic and theological grounds is a central tenet of the Christian right, it is important to note that the activities of the Religious Roundtable's constituent members are not limited to Israel and the Middle East. The Campus Crusade for Christ, headed by Bill Bright, a frequent participant at "National Prayer Breakfasts for Israel," for example, presently spends some $90 million a year around the globe and has an active program for Central America. Deborah Huntington wrote of this facet of its work that:

... Campus Crusade, Assemblies of God and other U.S. based organizations active in Central America reinforce black-and-white Reagan Administration perceptions among their U.S. constituency, thereby mobilizing constituency support for U.S. government policy. In its "country profile" designed to explain the organization's field work, Campus Crusade introduces El Salvador: "In the final analysis there is a struggle for the people's freedom with democracy installed versus the tyrannical rule of communism as in Cuba, the Soviet Union, or in Eastern Europe."[19]

One of the most active campaigners for Israel from the religious right has been the Moral Majority's Jerry Falwell. Falwell is pastor of the Thomas Road Baptist Church in Lynchburg, Virginia, which claims more than seventeen thousand members. He has been broadcasting for years, and his "Old Time Gospel Hour" radio and television broadcasts are carried by more than six hundred stations. However, it was not really until he assumed leadership of the Moral Majority that he received national prominence. Falwell's pronouncements on the Middle East illustrate the combination of theological and strategic thoughts on supporting Israel. In his book, *Listen, America*, Falwell tells us that: "Israel is a bastion of democracy in a part of the world characterized by near lunacy." Later, he states: "This tiny nation will once again be attacked by her enemies, led by the great Russian armies and her Arab allies, but as

238

the prophet Ezekiel prophesied in Ezekiel 38 and 39, Russia will be defeated, and Israel will once again be spared by the hand of God." According to Falwell, the United States has no choice: "If this nation wants her fields to remain white with grain, her scientific achievements to remain notable, and her freedom to remain intact, America must continue to stand with Israel."[20]

In addition to his public pronouncements, Falwell is one of many who utilize Holy Land tours as a vehicle for strengthening ties between Israel and American Christian participants. Highlights include visits to the Valley of Armageddon and other Biblical sites, and an American-Israel Friendship Banquet, usually featuring a prominent Israeli as a keynote speaker.

Falwell has been particularly sensitive to charges of anti-Semitism and has taken steps to repudiate this charge. The March 1984 issue of *Moral Majority Reports* carried both a review and a major advertisement for the newly published book, *Jerry Falwell and the Jews*. It was written by Merill Simon, a research associate at Tel Aviv University's Center for Strategic Studies.

In fact, Falwell's labors were directly encouraged by Israeli Prime Minister Begin, who presented Falwell with the Jabotinsky Award for outstanding service to the state for Israel. When Israel bombed the Iraqi nuclear reactor in 1981, Falwell was one of the first persons Begin called, soliciting his help to "explain" the action to the U.S. public.

Another figure who illustrates the connection between Israel support groups and the New Right is Douglas Krieger, reportedly the Middle East advisor to Ed McAteer of the Religious Roundtable. Krieger, who has served as the chairman of the National Prayer Breakfast for Israel, is the executive director of the Jerusalem Temple Foundation, and vice-chair of the American Forum for Jewish-Christian Understanding, as well as executive director of the Alaska Land Leasing, Inc. company.

An American businessman and Christian fundamentalist, Terry Reisenhuver, established the Temple Mount Foundation to fulfill the Biblical prophecy of rebuilding a Third Temple. A 1983 article in the Israeli newspaper *Davar* reported that the foundation had already raised $10 million, which it was going to use to donate to settlements, purchase land from Muslim religious endowments, and help re-establish the Temple of Solomon on the Temple Mount, where the Dome of the Rock (a major shrine of Islam) presently stands. According to the same article, which indicates that the foundation has close ties with Israeli Knesset members Yehuda Perach and Geula Cohen, Krieger characterized the possibility of the destruction of the Dome of the Rock as "incidental." Krieger was the co-organizer with Reisenhuver of an ad protesting the arrest of Israeli settlers in conjunction with a March 1983 plot to take over the Temple Mount area. Reisenhuver and Krieger reportedly paid the legal expenses of the arrested settlers.[21]

Evangelicals in South Lebanon

A new page in missionary history was opened when George Otis and his High Adventure Ministries began broadcasts on the "Voice of Hope" radio station in southern Lebanon.

Otis, former general manager of the Lear Jet Corporation, launched his effort in the spring of 1979, following a conversation with Major Saad Haddad, commander of the Israeli-supported Christian militia in southern Lebanon. Otis saw Haddad as "the leader of that last fragment of Lebanon that was still free and controlled by Lebanese and not by the Palestine Liberation Organization or the Syrians," and characterized "Haddadland" and its population as "a small group of some 100,000 people with the courage to provide a buffer, to reduce the infiltration of the terrorists killing and harming Israelis." With help from American entertainer Pat Boone, he raised the necessary $600,000 to $700,000 in about six months; in September 1979, the station commenced its broadcasts, which Otis called a "Gospel radio station in the very heart of the Middle East." It served up a daily fare of American gospel music, country and western and pop music, Bible lessons, and Haddad propaganda. One of Haddad's lieutenants served as the station's news director.

Otis described High Adventure's goals in an interview: "The bottom line is to ignite a hunger for the Word of God and the things of God, to remind an insane region that turning their back on God and beginning to depend on power and violence has produced the kind of trouble, heartache and bloodshed they've experienced." "A revival," he declared, "is the only answer to the problems of the Middle East."

To demonstrate that his activities have secured divine blessings, Otis tells "miracle" stories. In an account titled "Miracle at Beaufort Castle" in *Christian Life* magazine, Otis described how the station was under bombardment from guns positioned at Beaufort Castle. Angered, Otis shouted defiantly at the guns, then gathered his workers for prayer. Suddenly, he related, "there appeared before us a sight which none of us would ever, ever forget. The entire top gun floor of Beaufort was 'atomized' before our eyes. Fire, cannons, turrets, rockets and smoke shot hundreds of feet in the air. But not a shot was being fired against it from Israel or by Haddad's cannons. . . . We leaped from the vans and gave a mighty cheer. . . . To this day, no one seems sure about what actually happened. However, we attribute it to a supernatural work of God."

During the 1982 Lebanon War, Otis and High Adventure stepped up their operations, complementing their message with desperately needed relief supplies for the besieged population of the south. In a fundraising letter, Otis was positively ecstatic: *"He (God) has in fact delivered a nation into our hands."* The letter then goes on, "Your Voice of Hope stations have been used during these past years to pry open this once tightly closed door, and *today it stands wide open.* And together we must seize the unparalleled opportunities before the rich harvest is lost" (all emphases in original), High Adventure with its "Lebanon Aid" program was one of a handful of relief organizations allowed to operate in southern Lebanon by Israel and the Haddad militia during the summer of 1982.*

Targeting the Evangelicals: Goals and Contradictions

The shift in focus of Jewish community relations groups from the mainline churches toward the evangelicals began shortly after the 1967 war. It was pursued quietly in the 1970s but assumed greater importance with the political ascendancy of the Israeli Likud party in 1977. Mainline Protestants were increasingly suspected of being at best unreliable supporters of Israel, susceptible to pressure from their mission interests in the Middle East, vulnerable to influence from the Eastern Christian churches, and given to sympathy for the Palestinians as Third World people struggling for their rights. The coming to power of Prime Minister Begin coincided with the politicization of the leadership of the fundamentalists; these U.S. conservatives were, moreover, more comfortable with the Bible-quoting Begin and the generally conservative outlook of the Likud than they had been with the more secular manner and politics of the Labor party leadership.

By the latter part of the 1970s, persons and organizations among the Jewish community relations groups, which had formerly concentrated on the mainline Protestants, were pointing out the advantages of activity among the evangelicals. Jerry Stober, formerly on the staff of the AJC, commented in 1977: "The real source of strength that Jews have in this country is from the evangelicals." He coordinated a series of ads in more than forty newspapers proclaiming: "The time has come for Evangelical Christians to affirm their belief in Biblical prophecy and Israel's Divine Right to the Land."[22]

Participants in the annual AIPAC strategy conference in June 1983 declared that AIPAC expected the liberal churches to take an increasingly "pro-Arab" position, and that AIPAC consequently would focus more on the support of fundamentalist Christians. AIPAC had assigned a full-time staff person to its "Christian Outreach Program." The Rabbinical Council of America held a meeting for Orthodox Jews and evangelicals in February 1983 to "reharness White House support for Israel" and appointed Rabbi Abner Weiss as its liaison to the evangelical community.[23]

The NJCRAC's Joint Program Plan for Jewish Community Relations for 1982-83 posited:

While opposing those among the fundamentalists who eschew pluralism and demand alliance to only one set of responses to social issues, we should seek out

* The station in South Lebanon has since disbanded due to a series of bombings. According to an 11 January 1986 National Public Radio program, George Otis has moved his operation to Central America. In an interview he stated his concern was to preach Biblical truths to counter work done in the name of liberation theology.

241

those among the mainstream moderate evangelicals whose support of Israel's survival is well demonstrated and whose positions on social issues closely correspond to those of the Jewish community. This may provide an opportunity to ameliorate the tensions triggered by the strong current of pro-Arab, anti-Israel sentiment among some members of the Governing Board of the National Council of Churches.[24]

As the NJCRAC statement hints, this shift toward the evangelicals has not been without strain. Many of the nation's major Jewish organizations had been active supporters of the liberal social agenda: the search for political allies in support of Israel presented significant contradictions in the domestic political realm. A current of opinion, apparently a minority one, has expressed concern about relations with the fundamentalists. Rabbi Alexander Schindler of the Union of American Hebrew Congregations, Edgar Bronfman of the World Jewish Congress, and other Jewish community leaders have criticized the new alignment. The Commission on Social Action of Reform Judaism, under the chairmanship of Alexander I. Ross, published a lengthy critical study on the subject, *The Challenge of the Religious Right: A Jewish Response*. Rabbi Ira Youdovin, executive director of ARZA, circulated a memorandum, "Moral Majority: A Danger."

Another paradox in the work of Jewish community organizations with the evangelicals revolves around the tension between the evangelicals' desire to proselytize and the suspicion about the resistance to missionary activity on the part of American Jews. The theological doctrines of many of the conservative Protestants, while identifying the creation of the state of Israel as fulfillment of Biblical prophecy, also hold that the "ingathering" of the Jews merely presages their mass conversion prior to the second coming of Christ. Some activists on both sides are striving to lessen this tension; supporters of the International Christian Embassy, for example, are encouraged to seek converts from any religious group except Jews, among whom they are forbidden to conduct missionary activity.

The American Jewish Yearbook lists hundreds of organizations that engage in one form or another of Israeli support work but do not fit neatly under the categories of Zionist, community, funding, or lobby. While time and space limitations do not allow an examination of all such organizations, some stand out because of their particular target or focus, or because of their political extremism, and the consequent organizational priority given to pro-Israel work.

In the first category are the America-Israel Friendship League (which targets non-Jewish Americans), the Youth Institute for Peace in the Middle East (youth), and the National Committee for Labor Israel and the American Trade Union Council for Histadrut (labor). In the second category are Americans for a Safe Israel and the National Council for Young Israel, which are very different organizationally but share a hawkish political view that is reflected in their programs. Each is representative of a certain trend or focus among American Jewry.

America-Israel Friendship League

Year established: 1971
President: Herbert Tenzer
Executive Director: Ilana Artman
Address: 134 East 39th Street, New York, NY 10016
Publications: *News Bulletins*

Role and Structure

Like other friendship organizations, the aim of the America-Israel Friendship League (AIFL) is to enhance relations between the United States and Israel, especially on a person-to-person basis. It describes itself as "representatives of a community of Americans with differing interests and beliefs who share in their recognition of the common interests and values of the peoples of the United States and the peoples of the State of Israel."[1]

The AIFL is unique among special interest pro-Israel groups in that most of its outreach and programs are sponsored by and aimed at the non-Jewish community. It has developed a roster of sponsoring politicians and prominent personalities of various races and creeds whose names read like a political "Who's Who" list.*

---

*AILF's 1983 National Council consisted of: Hon. Abraham Muller (Chairman), Rep. Joseph P. Addabbo, Gov. George R. Ariyoshi, Sen. William L. Armstrong, Rep. Les Aspin, Rep. Mario Biaggi, Dr. Mary Rose Black, Sen. Dennis De Concini, Rep. William R. Cotter, Sen. John C. Danforth, Rep. Thomas J. Downey, Rep. Geraldine Ferraro, Ambassador Seymour

In September 1983, a fundraising letter went out under the names of Senators Daniel Moynihan and Robert Packwood. Stressing the threat posed by anti-Israel forces in the U.S. and reiterating the moral and strategic links between the United States and Israel, the letter urged readers to support AIFL financially. In Minnesota, the same text went out with a cover letter endorsing the appeal by State Attorney General Hubert H. Humphrey, III, written on stationery with the state seal. The Humphrey letter noted that "we ourselves are not Israeli, but our self-interest is compatible with Israeli interests. ... "[2] (Humphrey's father was a founding member of AIFL; the son has also published a guest column in AIFL's newsletter.)

Such fundraising letters appear to be quite successful for AIFL, which is a tax-exempt organization. According to its IRS 990 report, in 1982 the AIFL received a total of $580,000 in direct public support. Of this, approximately $40,000 went for management, $120,000 for fundraising, and $397,000 (or 68 percent) for programs. Also included in its report were donations to AIPAC (which is not tax-exempt) and to the *Jerusalem Quarterly* (a Jerusalem-based publication).

Israel Support Work

Project Interchange. This national program, established in 1982, is based in Washington, D.C. Its major role is to arrange American delegations to Israel for "the new generation of U.S. opinion leaders and policy makers. ... " The visits involve a ten-day seminar in Israel and meetings

M. Finger, Rep. Hamilton Fish, Jr., Dr. Eugene Fisher, Rep. Harold E. Ford, Rep. William D. Ford, Rep. Robert Garcia, Rep. Sam M. Gibbons, Rep. Benjamin Gilman, Rep. Barry Goldwater Jr., Rep. William Green, Rev. William Harter, Sen. Paula Hawkins, Hon. Margaret M. Heckler, Sen. H. John Heinz, Rep. Frank Horton, Gov. James B. Hunt, Sen. J. Bennett Johnson, Jr., Rep. James R. Jones, Rev. Elmer Josephson, Rep. Jack F. Kemp, Gov. Richard F. Kneip, Rep. William Lehman, Rep. Norman F. Lent, Dr. Franklin Littel, Rep. Stanley Lundine, Sen. Charles Mathias, Jr., Sen. Spark Matsunaga, Rep. Raymond McGrath, Rep. Matthew McHugh, Gov. William Milliken, Rep. Joseph Minish, Rep. Richard Ottinger, Sen. Claiborne Pell, Rep. Claude Pepper, Rep. Melvin Price, Rep. James Quillen, Rep. Charles Rangel, Rep. Charles Schumer, Rep. Paul Simon, Gov. Richard Snelling, Rep. Stephen Solarz, Rep. Fernand St. Germain, Rep. Samuel S. Stratton, Gov. Robert Straub, Rabbi Marc Tannenbaum, Rep. Morris Udall, Rep. Henry Waxman, Rep. Ted Weiss, Rep. Charles Wilson, Rep. Timothy Wirth, Dr. James Wood, Rep. Jim Wright, and Rep. Gus Yatron.

Honorary Sponsors include: Hon. Robert Abrams, Hon. Birch Bayh, Hon. Abraham Beame, Sen. Lloyd Bentsen, Sen. Rudy Boschwitz, Hon. Hugh Carey, the late Sen. Frank Church, Sen. Alfonse D'Amato, Hon. Robert F. Drinan, Max M. Fisher, Hon. Gerald Ford, Hon. Arthur J. Goldberg, Sen. Gary Hart, Sen. Ernest Hollings, Sen. Henry Jackson, Mrs. Charlotte Jacobson, Hon. Jacob Javits, I.L. Kenen, Sen. Edward Kennedy, Lane Kirkland, Sen. Frank Lautenberg, Hon. Phillip Klutznick, Sen. Howard Metzenbaum, Hon. Arthur Markewich, Rabbi Israel Miller, Sen. Daniel Moynihan, Hon. Thomas P. O'Neill Jr., Sen. Robert Packwood, Hon. Ogden Reid, Rep. Peter Rodino, Samuel Rothberg, Bayard Rustin, Jacob Stein, Rabbi Alexander Schindler, Mrs. Bernice Tannenbaum, Sen Lowell Weicker, Jr., Jack D. Weiler, and Elie Wiesel.

with top specialists. The national advisory board for Project Interchange includes Theodore Bikel, Senator Rudy Boschwitz, Senator Alan Cranston, Stuart Eizenstat, former president Gerald Ford, I.L. (Si) Kenen, Lane Kirkland, Dan Rather, and George Will, among others.

In 1983 delegations were organized for congressional aides and for Hispanic American leaders. The Hispanic delegation included the legislative director of the Congressional Hispanic Caucus (Susan Herrera) and the special assistant to the chairman of the Democratic National Committee (Len Rose-Avila). Pointing out that Hispanics are expected to be the largest minority within the United States, an AIFL director noted the value of the program:

It is very important that the leaders of the community have a first-hand experience of Israel as they move into public policy-making positions. Furthermore, we all have a great deal in common. Israel is grappling with many of the same social problems facing the Hispanic community in the U.S. Secondly, American Jews have faced similar dilemmas now facing Hispanics. Increased dialogue and cooperation between the two communities can only benefit both.[3]

National Christian Leadership Conference for Israel (NCLCI). AIFL participated in establishing the NCLCI and still contributes to its financial support. AIFL writes of the NCLCI: "This coalition of 25,000 clergy and laity in 20 states and regional groups is a network which responds quickly to the needs of the moment. During the Lebanese War, the NCLCI took a group of 55 Christian leaders to Israel on a fact finding tour and placed an ad of Christian solidarity with Israel in the *New York Times* and other major U.S. papers."[4] In addition, AIFL arranges clergy study tours of Israel for diocese educators, clergy, and senior divinity students. (These have been cosponsored by institutions such as Seton Hall University in New Jersey.)

Ambassadors-for-Peace. This is the AIFL's U.S.-Israel high school student exchange program. It was begun in 1978 with the cooperation of the U.S. Office of Education, the Council of the Great City Schools, and the Israeli Ministry of Education and Culture. Since its inception, over seven hundred Israeli and American students have participated in exchange visits. In addition, the program sponsors education forums on Israel in schools throughout the United States, again with government cooperation. The Council of the Great City Schools, representing thirty-two major urban school districts, has also endorsed an AIFL publication entitled "Israel and the USA: A Comparison of Two Allies," which is distributed free of charge to schools and elsewhere.

People-to-People. This is another exchange program, involving writers, community leaders, performing arts groups, athletes, and young scientists. It is coordinated with the international Cultural Center for Youth in Jerusalem, the AIFL's international affiliate, and with government ministries, municipalities, kibbutzim, and cultural programs in Israel. Music groups have included the Horace Mann High School Glee Club, the Fredonia (NY) College Chamber Singers, and the Concord Choral of New Hampshire. (Costs to the AIFL for the last two were $31,740 and $55,366, respectively.) The program now travels the other direction as well, with AIFL sponsoring U.S. tours for Israeli arts groups.

The AIFL sponsors Israeli speakers for church, community, and civic groups, and publishes pamphlets such as "The Birth of Two Nations: An Historical Account of a Nation Born and a People Reborn" (which compares the history of the United States and Israel). It also reprints and distributes other material, including several thousand copies of Martin Peretz's *New Republic* article, "Misreporting Lebanon."

Youth Institute for Peace in the Middle East

(formerly Youth Committee for Peace and Democracy in the Middle East)

Year established: 1968
Chairman: Carl Gershman
Executive Director: Kristeen A. Bruum
Address: 275 Seventh Avenue, New York, NY 10011
Publication: *Crossroads*

Background, Role and Structure

The Youth Institute for Peace in the Middle East (YIPME) was formed in 1974 as the successor to the Youth Committee for Peace and Democracy in the Middle East. In a 1974 letter announcing YIPME's formation, its chairman, Carl Gershman, stated that "in our view Israel is in the midst of a long-term struggle for survival, and the continued understanding of her problems, especially by those who will be the future leaders of America, is essential." He announced that YIPME would be continuing the educational programs on Israel that had been conducted by the Youth Committee but pointed out "one big difference"—that YIPME's tax-exempt status as an educational organization, along with its tax-deductible contributions, should secure its financial situation.[5]

In a mass-mailing membership recruitment letter sent out in 1978, YIPME's executive director, Kristeen Bruum, urged young people to join YIPME because, in the face of threats to Israel such as "this administration's decision to sell more death-dealing jets to the Arabs," the "horrible violence of the PLO," and "declining American support," "the institute's work among students and young workers is the single most effective effort on Israel's behalf today."

Unlike many pro-Israel organizations in the United States, YIPME targets primarily non-Jewish youth among students and workers. YIPME's declared goals involve the development of educational programs that will sensitize young Americans "to the importance of democratic Israel's survival and the need to bring about true peace in the Middle East," and specifically, to

—give young people an accurate understanding of the history of the Arab-Israeli conflict;
—emphasize the vital importance of preserving and extending democratic institutions in the Middle East;
—explain the nature of American interests in the Middle East and explore the kinds of policies that will further the cause of peace and democracy;
—arouse young people's awareness of the need to defend Israel's existence and work for genuine Arab-Israeli reconciliation;
—encourage understanding of the need to build coalitions to further support for democracy.[6]

247

Among the organizations that YIPME suggests it can work closely with are the Social Democrats, U.S.A., Black Americans to Support Israel Committee (whose director is Bayard Rustin), Frontlash, the League for Industrial Democracy, and "other liberal groups." This choice of coalition partners, along with the circumstances of its establishment and its sponsors, places it within the neoconservative cluster that is anti-Communist, anti-Soviet, and labor-dominated.*

Israel Support Work

YIPME's activities are intended to provide young people with what it considers to be an accurate presentation of the conflict in the Middle East. These include: seminars and briefings for "youth leadership education" across the country; "action programs," such as rallies, demonstrations, and petition drives; delegations to Israel aimed specifically at "promising American youth leaders," and leadership training workshops designed to educate about Israel, "the long and close friendship between Israel and American labor, and about the nuts and bolts of organizing."[7] In practice, YIPME's programs transmit the official Israeli point of view. During the invasion of Lebanon, for example, the Institute circulated materials prepared by the Israeli consulate in New York and simply blocked out the source identification on the front page.[8]

---

* Among the sponsors are: Sol C. Chaikin (ILGWU), Lane Kirkland (AFL-CIO), Emanuel Muravchik (JLC), Matthew Schoenwald (ATUC), Marie Syrkin, Allen Pollack, Joseph Neyer (APPME), Midge Decter, Paul Seabury, Penn Kemble (all Committee for the Free World), Norman Podhoretz, Ben Wattenberg (American Enterprise Institute and founder of the Committee for Democratic Majority), A. Philip Randolph, John Roche, and Bayard Rustin (all Social Democrats, U.S.A), Walter Laqueur, and Martin Peretz.

National Committee for Labor Israel
(formerly National Labor Committee for the Jewish Workers in Palestine, National Committee for Labor Palestine)

Year established: 1923
President: Aaron L. Solomon
Executive Vice President: Eliezer Rafaeli
Address: 333 East 67th Street, New York, N.Y 10021
Publication: *Shalom* (quarterly)

General Background

Following the establishment of the Israeli labor federation, Histadrut, in 1920, efforts began in the United States to mobilize labor support systematically for the Histadrut's programs and for the broader goals of Zionism. The NCLI was formed to provide the organizational link between the Histadrut and American labor groups.

The organized labor movement is an integral component of support for Israel in the United States. This support goes back as far as 1917, when the American Federation of Labor (AFL)* passed a resolution recognizing "the legitimate claims of the Jewish people for the establishment of a national homeland in Palestine on a basis of self-government."[9] The current leadership of the AFL-CIO points to that resolution when they state the relationship between Israel and the U.S. labor movement is "far older than the state of Israel itself . . . the leaders of organized labor were far ahead of most other Americans in supporting the Zionists' dream."[10]

While the initial impetus for labor support of Zionism came largely from unions with substantial Jewish membership, such as those in the needle and garment trades, support of Zionism became virtually unanimous among the leadership of the U.S labor movement. This unanimity of support transcends strong differences within the AFL-CIO on other foreign policy issues. The more conservative unions, such as the building and construction trades, which favor a strong defense policy and supported U.S. involvement in Vietnam, and the more progressive unions, such as the United Auto Workers, the American Federation of State, County, and Municipal Employees (AFSCME), and the International Association of Machinists (IAM), which favor reduced military spending and oppose U.S. intervention in Central America, have all been strong supporters of Israel.

Jewish workers and union leaders constitute an important component of labor pro-Israelism. The Jewish Labor Committee (JLC) is a pre-

---

*The Congress of Industrial Organizations split off from the AFL in 1935 and rejoined in 1954 to form the AFL-CIO, thus the alternate references to the AFL, the CIO and the AFL-CIO in this section.

dominantly liberal organization that claims to "speak for the totality of Jewish workmen" in the United States.[11] In 1982, Emanuel Muravchik, the JLC's executive director, summed up the goals of his organization:

Mobilizing and facilitating trade union support for a secure Israel, for human rights and for assistance to Soviet Jews continues to be at the top of JLC's agenda. Alongside this now stands, as an equal partner, the mobilization of Jewish community support for liberal economic and social policies. On these twin bases the alliance between organized labor and the organized Jewish community can now be established.[12]

In the summer of 1981, the JLC launched a "Labor for a Secure Israel" program. This is a national effort to develop support for Israel within government and the general community by mobilizing labor in areas where the Jewish community is weak, but where the influence of labor is strong. The program is based in the AFL-CIO's headquarters in Washington.

Structure and Role

The NCLI is an umbrella organization for American Jewish labor groups. It is a member of the Presidents Conference and claims a membership of 500,000. It has sixteen regional groups and 5,000 local affiliates. Its most active constituent member is the American Trade Union Council for Histadrut. A second NCLI affiliate is the American Histadrut Cultural Exchange Institute. The NCLI has two fundraising branches, the Israel Histadrut Campaign and the Israel Histadrut Foundation.

The NCLI "provides funds for the social, welfare, vocational, health, and cultural institutions and other services of Histadrut to benefit workers and immigrants and to assist in the integration of newcomers as productive citizens in Israel." It further identifies its role as educating the people in the United States about "the ideals and accomplishments of the Israel labor movement."[13]

Funding

The NCLI fundraises through the Israel Histadrut Campaign, which in turn raises money primarily through fundraising dinners and other events sponsored by its local committees and councils. In 1981, the NCLI reported a total revenue of $2,881,355 and a total expenditure of $2,847,771. Nearly $2 million was spent on program services in the form of grants and allocations to the following: Histadrut Assistance Fund ($1,024,668), Israel Histadrut Foundation ($370,019), and American Histadrut Cultural Exchange Institute ($9,500).

American Trade Union Council for Histadrut

Year established: 1947
Chairman: Morton Bahr
Address: 33 East 67th Street, New York, NY 10021
Publication: *Shalom* (with NCLI)
Slogan: "Worker to Worker in the Free Democratic Trade Union Movement"

General Background, Role and Structure

The American Trade Union Council for Histadrut (ATUCH or ATUC) is an affiliate of the NCLI; it was founded at a Labor Zionist emergency conference in 1947 and has since played a major role in mobilizing U.S. labor support for Israel. Both the AFL and CIO urged their affiliated unions "to take an active part in the promotion of the American Trade Union Council in the aid of the Histadrut and the establishment of a national homeland for the Jewish people."[14] The ATUC has a dual purpose: educating people in the United States about the Histadrut and Israel, and fundraising. It describes itself as "the ideological and pragmatic link between the two free trade union movements of Israel and the United States."[15]

As a network of local councils, the ATUC works closely with the Canadian Trade Union Council for Histadrut; in 1981, it put the number of active Trade Union Councils in the United States at forty-seven, with two more in Canada. Although the ATUC is technically an affiliate of the NCLI, it is an independent member of the Presidents Conference.

Since the establishment of the ATUC, leaders of major American and Canadian labor unions (including the United Auto Workers, International Brotherhood of Teamsters, and major AFL-CIO affiliated unions) have served as honorary chairs. The combination of Jewish and non-Jewish labor provides the ATUC with a much wider legitimacy than if it were only representing Jewish labor. ATUC and other NCLI events are often co-sponsored by the AFL-CIO and its member unions. AFL-CIO leaders also present awards and serve as masters of ceremonies at NCLI and ATUC events.

The ATUC periodically releases statements aimed at influencing U.S. public opinion and foreign policy. A "Resolution of Policy" adopted at its annual conference in November 1970 stated in part:

We petition the U.S. Government ... to bring to Israel without delay the added strength and support it now needs. This manifestly includes such planes and other armaments as have been requested, or may need to be requested, by the Government of Israel. It may well include vastly increased economic and financial assistance.[16]

251

In addition to their regular fundraising efforts, the ATUC has been able to raise large sums of money in emergency funds. In January 1969, ATUC's executive board raised $1 million in emergency funds from trade unions, their officers, and members, citing "the explosive situation" in the Middle East.[17] The New York chapter (Greater NY/TUCH) held a drive in August 1970 to raise $100,000 for emergency medical services for wounded soldiers and civilians in "response to the news of increased fighting along Israel's borders during the past summer."[18]

Americans for a Safe Israel

Year established: 1971
Chairman of the Board: Herbert Zweibon
Director: Peter Goldman
Address: 147 East 76th Street, New York, NY 10021
Publication: *Outpost* (newsletter)

General Background, Role and Structure

Americans for a Safe Israel (AFSI) stands out among pro-Israel organizations for its hard-line positions. Unlike the Jewish Defense League and its offshoots, which tend to be shunned by the Jewish establishment, AFSI is accepted as a legitimate force representing a political trend that exists in the U.S. and in Israel. This acceptance is crucial to AFSI's basic role: not only to articulate an extremist line, but to provide constant pressure on others, especially within the Jewish community, to move to the right. In the words of AFSI, "We encourage other organizations and movements to take stronger stands in support of Israel, and we have had substantial success in this area."[19]

Politically, AFSI advocates virulent anti-Communism and militant Zionism in the tradition of Jabotinsky. AFSI is against any withdrawal from the occupied territories and supports the building of further settlements; it considers U.S. policy "appeasing" and anti-Israel; it opposed the Camp David Accords and the Sinai withdrawal and still considers Egypt an enemy; it strongly supported the invasion of Lebanon, and it believes that "the existence of a strong Israel is an absolute condition for the security of the United States and Western interests in the Middle East, providing a brake to Soviet expansion and Arab imperialism."[20]

When established in 1971, AFSI described itself as a "think-tank of professors and other experts in international affairs."[21] It has an executive committee, a national council, and an academic advisory committee composed of professors from around the country. Among its most active members are chairman Herbert Zweibon, director Peter Goldman (former director of Joseph Churba's Center for International Security in Washington and of the Denmark-Israel Association of Copenhagen), Herut supporter Rael Jean Isaac, and Rabbi Avraham Weiss (of the Hebrew Institute of Riverdale and Yeshiva University).

Israel Support Work

In its early years, AFSI focused on publishing attacks against its "enemies." One of these was a scathing diatribe against the American Friends Service Committee for its alleged anti-Israel and pro-PLO position, entitled "The Friendly Perversion, Quakers as Reconcilers: Good People and Dirty Work." Another was the attack against Breira by Rael Jean Isaac.

253

Today AFSI no longer bills itself as a think tank, but as a membership organization whose activities include publications, press conferences, press releases, demonstrations, radio and television appearances, and media monitoring. In 1982, AFSI coordinated the coalition to protest "America's increasing abandonment of Israel," which culminated in an April 1982 demonstration in Washington.[22] In February 1983, it sponsored an Israel delegation that came to the United States to campaign against the Reagan plan; among the delegation members were the right-wing settlers Rabbi Eliezer Waldman of the Kiryat Arba city council and Yigal Kutail, executive director of the "renewed Jewish community in Hebron," who also used their visit to solicit for more settlers from America.[23] AFSI itself has actively participated in Israel's settlement drive as the agent for the sale of Palestinian land on the West Bank exclusively to American Jews. Following the invasion of Lebanon, they demonstrated against NBC News and produced the widely distributed video file called "NBC in Lebanon: A Study of Media Representation." Likewise, they sponsored a five-month campaign against the *Boston Globe* for alleged anti-Israel bias; the campaign culminated with a "Ban the *Globe* Day," which resulted in a meeting between AFSI and the *Globe*'s publishers and editors. AFSI has also used its newsletter, *Outpost*, to solicit American volunteers for the Israel Recruitment Drive, aimed at offsetting the workforce shortage caused by the continued Israeli occupation of Lebanon.

Relations with the Jewish Establishment

The special role of AFSI, however, is found in its targeting of American Jewish organizations and leaders. A 1982 *Jerusalem Post* article noted that ASFI was established "in reaction to what its founders perceived to be the dominance of liberal and dovish attitudes towards Israel among American Jewish intellectuals." In the same article, AFSI director Peter Goldman accounted for Jewish criticism of the Lebanon war by saying that "the American liberal media overplay the importance of noisy and unrepresentative Jewish intellectuals" and accused American Jewish leaders of having "lost touch with American Jews who by and large support the Israeli operation." AFSI chairman Herbert Zweibon exhorted such leaders to realize that Israel is facing "big business corporations and the left-dominated media, both of which want to encourage the U.S. to abandon Israel. Without a more forceful reaction to their efforts, the American Jewish community is in danger of committing the same sin of silence it committed during the Holocaust."[24]

AFSI engages in many attacks against the "liberal trend," not simply in alternative groups such as Breira, but in mainstream organizations as well. A favorite target is Seagrams' owner Edgar Bronfman, head of the World Jewish Congress, whom AFSI dubs the "Whiskey King" and accuses of siding with the PLO against Israel when he calls for negotiations over the West Bank and Gaza Strip. An especially virulent attack by

Rael Jean Isaac appeared in AFSI's November 1982 *Outpost* under the title, "The American-Jewish Congress and the Union of American Hebrew Congregations: Self-Destructiveness in the Organized Jewish Community." The article expressed outrage and horror that these two groups had joined a coalition for nuclear freeze with such "anti-Israel organizations" as the American Friends Service Committee, the Mobilization for Survival, the Fellowship of Reconciliation, and Clergy and Laity Concerned. According to Isaac, the nuclear freeze movement constitutes a double threat because its members are "bitterly hostile to Israel" and because it "would weaken the ability of the United States to withstand global Soviet designs, including its designs on the Middle East." Isaac asserts that the AJCongress and UAHC are not ignorant of this but act from baser motives:

These Jewish organizations support the freeze because, lamentably, there are Jewish leaders whose primary goal is maintaining the purity of their "liberal credentials," whatever the cost to Jewish interests. Currently fashionable in trendy liberal circles, the freeze above all offers Jewish organizations the chance to cooperate once more with mainline Protestant bureaucracies whose stream of hostile pronouncements against Israel have soured relations in the last decade. Jewish leaders can now hope to relive former days when they could march together with Protestant clerics in good cause.[25]

Another AFSI criticism is leveled against what it considers the Jewish establishment's appeasement of the American administration. AFSI's responses here have included the coalition to stop the American "abandonment" of Israel and an attack on AIPAC and other groups that spoke at all favorably of the Reagan peace initiative. Indeed, AFSI went so far as to demonstrate against the Reagan plan at a UJA dinner that featured Secretary of State Shultz as the keynote speaker.

Funding

AFSI enjoys a tax-exempt status under the Internal Revenue Code. According to its 1981 IRS return (Form 990), AFSI's total revenue for that year was $84,219 (compared to $7,000 in 1977; AFSI's total revenues have been doubling annually since 1977). Total expenditures were $78,563, of which 56 percent went for program services, including about two-thirds for advertising; 29 percent was attributed to professional fundraising fees. In July 1982, at the height of the war in Lebanon, WZO-American Section granted AFSI $5,000 "to assist in the cost of publication of this organization."[26]

National Council of Young Israel

Year established: 1912
President: Harold Jacobs
Executive Vice-President: Ephraim Sturm
Address: 3 West 16th Street, New York, NY 10011
Publication: *Young Israel Viewpoint* (monthly newspaper)

General Background, Structure and Role

The Young Israel movement was initiated in 1912 with the aim of strengthening Orthodox Judaism in America by making it more modern and relevant. To this end, certain changes were introduced in religious practices, such as communal singing and sermons in English; however, the movement was and remains strictly Orthodox, with a constitutional mandate committing all member branches to the standards of Halachic law.

The base of the movement is the Young Israel synagogue, which is comprised of hundreds of branch congregations, mainly in the United States but also in Canada, Mexico, and Israel. Each synagogue is seen as "the vital first step in building or rebuilding any successful Orthodox community." Community is the key word, since Young Israel is not a rabbinical body or mere grouping of synagogues, but a movement to create and maintain an Orthodox way of life in America, especially in the face of the "threat" posed by Conservative and Reform movements.[27]

The National Council of Young Israel (NCYI or National Council) is the national body and coordinator of the movement. Branch members participate in the NCYI through their delegates, who elect officers at the national convention. Branches also help support the NCYI—a religious tax-exempt organization—with fundraising drives. In return, the NCYI provides leadership and a wide range of services covering much more than religious issues. A partial listing includes an endowment fund for interest-free loans to branches; health insurance programs; a travel department; youth and athletic clubs; a Senior League that provides kosher meals and trips to Israel for the elderly; a Torah tape library and Torah retreats; a Women's League; and a campus program whose main aim is to combat cults and missionaries recruiting Jewish students and to provide kosher meals on campus.

Political Positions: Israel and the Torah

The NCYI is characterized by its "strong consensus in favor of vigorous support of the State of Israel and encouraging Aliyah," to a degree that stands out even within the extremely pro-Israel stance of American Jewish religious organizations. In relation to current events in general, the NCYI seeks "to champion the Torah point of view on the critical public policy issues of our time."[28]

256

The person who does most of the "championing" at NCYI is Harold Jacobs, president of the National Council, member of the U.S. Naval War College, and former member of the Jewish Agency's Executive, now on its Actions Committee. In February 1982, for example, Jacobs demanded that President Reagan ask for the resignation of Secretary of Defense Caspar Weinberger. He claimed that Weinberger had a conflict of interest because of his past connection with Bechtel Corporation and "has consistently demonstrated a bias against Israel even in issues far beyond his direct responsibilities. . . . "[29] Following the Sabra and Shatila massacre, at a time when many American Jewish leaders deplored the killings and supported the call for an Israeli inquiry, Jacobs declared that:

Israel had nothing to do with the massacre. It was hot blood on the part of Phalangists who took revenge after seven years of the killing of Christians. It was people out of control. It is not in the Jewish nature to kill people. I don't believe there was any conspiracy on the part of the Israelis to let the Phalangists into the camps to kill.[30]

In November 1983, Weinberger invited the NCYI to meet with him and other Defense Department officials at the Pentagon. The fifty-member NCYI delegation was led by Jacobs, who also brought with him the heads of Emunah Women of America, AMIT (Mizrachi women), the national commander of the Jewish War Veterans (who is also president of Young Israel of Canton, Ohio), as well as New York City controller Harrison Goldin. The discussion focused on U.S. military policy and the security of Israel, with special stress on why the United States declined Israeli help following the September 1983 attack on the Marines in Beirut.[31]

In a December 1982 message, Jacobs warned American Jewish organizations and individuals not to endorse the nuclear freeze and "not to allow themselves to become unwitting tools of communist propaganda. . . . " He also urged the Jewish community to endorse, on a bipartisan basis, the Reagan administration's efforts to rebuild U.S. military power "to protect the freedom of our people and our allies throughout the world, including Israel."[32]

In a rare positive statement issued in January 1984, Jacobs praised Reagan's warm reception of Israeli prime minister Shamir as "a refreshing and long overdue change."[33] (Their talks had focused on formation of a joint study committee for increased U.S.-Israeli cooperation.)

According to a February 1984 article in NCYI's monthly newspaper, *Young Israel Viewpoint*, Jacobs strongly and publicly "condemned the rejection by Americans on the Jewish Agency Board of Governors of the nomination by Israeli government leaders of Ariel Sharon to the chairmanship of the World Zionist-Jewish Agency Aliyah Department. He decried the 'continuing persecution and character assassination directed

257

against a great Israeli leader.' " He went on to say that Sharon's policies have been proven correct, and that even U.S. officials regret that Israel is not following the same course. However, according to Jacobs, the most important aspect is that:

... the prestige of Ariel Sharon among those Jews who are seriously considering Aliyah is higher than ever. He represents a vision of Israel which is both proud and idealistic. In the post of chairman of the Jewish Agency's Aliyah Department, Sharon would rally many idealistic Jews to the cause of Aliyah, and inspire them to devote their lives to building and living in Israel. By sabotaging the appointment in an effort to scapegoat one of Israel's modern heroes, those who voted against Sharon have done a disservice to the cause of Zionism, Aliyah, and the future of the State of Israel.[34]

Israel Support Work

An important aspect of NCYI's pro-Israel work that permeates the entire organization is the inevitable use of its member synagogues (which claim to reach half a million people in the United States and Canada) as a forum for propagating NCYI's position on current events. Congregations are also a ready-made vehicle for mobilizing members to carry out concrete tasks or hook into national campaigns. The NCYI plays an active role in the Presidents Conference and supports the work of AIPAC; when telegrams need to be written or delegations sent to members of congress, Young Israel congregations are active. Judging by reports in the *Young Israel Viewpoint*, branches fully share the positions of the national body; for example, when the Young Israel of East Brunswick, New Jersey organized a series of lectures for its Adult Education Program, the first speaker they invited was JDL's Meir Kahane (described as a candidate for the Knesset and the only Jewish leader coming out against the candidacy of Jesse Jackson).[35]

Most of NCYI's pro-Israel work in the United States is carried out by the Public Affairs Committee of the National Council, whose chairman is Matthew J. Maryles. A NCYI summary of its 1983 activities includes this item:

Young Israel Mobilized Support For Israel—In the aftermath of deepening American involvement in Lebanon, the National Council has redoubled its efforts to reinforce support for Israel both within and outside the Jewish community. Its Public Affairs Committee, comprised of representatives from branches throughout the movement, is organizing an instant response network and has opened a telephone mobilization hotline to help individuals respond more effectively in support of Israel and other Jewish issues.[36]

In January 1984, Maryles and Fred Ehrmans, chair of the Israel Committee of the Union of Orthodox Jewish Congregations of America, issued a joint statement calling for the formation of an international tribunal to bring Yasir Arafat and "PLO terrorists" to justice. The statement also castigated the United Nations for supervising the PLO evacuation from Tripoli in December 1983, criticized the United States for assessing the subsequent meeting between Arafat and Egyptian president Mubarak as positive, and said that the PLO should be treated like the Nazis at Nuremberg.[37]

The Public Affairs Committee also sought to mobilize members to register to vote in the 1984 primaries and general elections:

At one time, 90% of the Jewish community was registered and voted in every election, making it a potent political force which has been of vital importance to Israel, politically and economically. With the increased reliance of Israel on U.S. government economic aid, it is doubly important for the Jewish community to maintain its political credibility and clout. Mr. Maryles also noted that every single Jewish vote can take on national importance. For instance, in the last election, an arch enemy of Israel, Congressman Paul Findley, was ousted from his seat by a margin of only 1,400 votes. Maryles also noted that registering to vote does not entail any increased risk of being called for jury duty, or any other penalty.*[38]

The Young Israel Movement in Israel

Primarily as a result of its policy of strongly encouraging *aliyah*, the Young Israel movement has become increasingly active in Israel itself, where it now has approximately thirty-five congregations. The NCYI supports its Israeli branches with its Eretz Israel Commission, whose work includes national membership, the annual dinner (fundraising), and encouraging American Young Israel branches to adopt Israel branches. Also involved is the Israel Activities for the National Council, whose director is Isaac Hagler.

---

*A footnote to NCYI's pro-Israel work in the United States can be illustrated in a series of ads that appeared in the *New York Times* during and after the war in Lebanon. One ad showed the picture of a young Palestinian girl over the headline: "Thanks to Israel, she won't grow up to be mutilated, flogged or beheaded," followed by text stressing how democratic and pro-Arab Israel is, in contrast to the repressiveness of the Arab states. The ad was placed by Americans for Peace and Democracy in the Middle East, Faye Katz and Joel Kessler, co-chairpersons, but the address for this group was given as 3 West 16th Street, New York, NY, the head-quarters of the NCYI. The same group placed a series of full-page ads (see *New York Times*, 12 August 1982) that simply listed hundreds and hundreds of names under the headline: "We Americans wholeheartedly endorse the Israel Government's Peace for Galilee campaign; express our appreciation to President Reagan for his efforts to remove all foreign armies and terror groups from Lebanon; hail the extraordinary measures taken by the Israel Defense Forces to limit and avoid civilian casualties." Following the massacre in Beirut, another ad appeared in the *New York Times* (9 November 1982) under the heading: "Mr. President." The text stated: "It is in the highest national interest of our country to provide maximum support for Israel. Strategic considerations require it. The moral values our two countries share demand it." This time, however, the ad was placed by American Friends for Israel, Faye Katz, coordinator, but the address again was 3 West 16th Street, New York, NY.

Young Israel clearly enjoys support and recognition from the Israeli state on both the political and religious levels. In February 1982, President Yitzhak Navon received the Young Israel Shofar Award at a banquet in Jerusalem, an event that was also a fundraiser for the growth of Young Israel in Israel. As NCYI leader Harold Jacobs noted in his speech, "The participation of President Navon is an indication of the rapid growth of the Young Israel movement in Israel, and its rapidly expanding influence in Israeli society."[39] The event also marked the opening of a Young Israel branch on the campus of Haifa University.

The next year Young Israel opened an international center in Jerusalem in the Yeshurun synagogue. The center's programs include the Young Israel Institute for Jewish Studies, which offers daily lectures on the Torah and cultural topics; a young adult congregation; a youth center for students and young singles; and the Resource Center for Americans in Israel, "providing referrals and arranging Young Israel visitations for Americans visiting or studying in Israel."[40]

From the United States, the NCYI promotes travel to Israel with programs such as its *Achva* Summer Mission for youth and special tours for senior citizens, and it encourages members to make *aliyah*, now facilitated by the Young Israel branches in Israel. Also advertised in NCYI's *Young Israel Viewpoint* is Mishab Housing Construction and Development Co., which offers to "build your home in Israel"; Mishab's offices, according to the ads, are located in Jerusalem, Tel Aviv, Haifa, and at 3 West 16th Street in New York, the headquarters of the NCYI.[41]

Notes

Campus

1. "Jewish Academics: New Signs of Life in a 'Disaster Area,'" *Analysis*, Institute for Jewish Policy Planning and Research of the Synagogue Council of America, 15 September 1973.

2. *Ibid.*

3. *New York Times*, 11 October 1983.

4. *Newsday*, 20 September 1983.

5. *New York Times*, 11 October 1983.

6. This and other quotes are from internal Stony Brook memoranda and correspondence, including: letter from Professor Selwyn Troen to Dean Egon Neuberger, 15 July 1983; memorandum from Professor Joel Rosenthan, president *pro tem* of the University Senate, to Dean Neuberger; "Dean's Statement," 22 August 1983; memorandum from the Africana Studies Department, 22 August 1983; and memorandum from Dean Neuberger, 26 September 1983.

7. *Newsday*, 20 September 1983.

8. Gary S. Schiff, "Middle East Centers at Selected American Universities," *Report to AJC*, 1981.

9. Sources for the Tucson incident are confidential memoranda and interviews.

10. *Jewish Telegraphic Agency*, 27 November 1983.

11. APPME, "An Invitation to Join APPME" (brochure).

12. *MESA Bulletin*, December 1980.

13. *APPME Newsletter*, March 1983.

14. AAAPME 1982 Annual Report, Charitable Organization, for year ending 31 August 1982, filed with the New York State Department of State.

15. *APPME Bulletin*, 1982, 1983.

16. *New York Times*, 21 September 1983.

Church

1. Peter Johnson, "Mainline Churches and United States Middle East Policy," in *American Church Politics and the Middle East*, edited by Basheer K. Nijim. Belmont, Massachusetts: Association of Arab American University Graduates, 1982: 64.

2. *Barron's*, 2 June 1980; *Forbes*, 1 September 1980.

3. *New York Times*, 10 February 1980.

4. Copies of this and other correspondence are on file with the author.

5. During the period these study materials were being produced, the author of this section, Larry Ekin, was working with the Middle East Council of Churches, on assignment from the United Methodist Board of Global Ministries. He assisted the Middle East Council of Churches and the "Hope for Life" film crew in the West Bank, Gaza Strip, and Beirut. In addition, he obtained interviews with the film's producer, Don Meyers, now deceased. The AJC saw the proposal, working draft, all revisions and the galleys, and critiqued the materials at every stage of production.

6. *Jewish Week*, 27 January 1980.

7. AJC, "In the Communities," Fall 1982.

8. *New York Times*, 15 August 1982.

9. Thomas Wiley, "American Christianity, The Jewish State and the Arab-Israeli Conflict." Washington, D.C.: Georgetown University, Center for Contemporary Arab Studies, Occasional Paper Series, 1983: 7.

10. *Ibid:* 10.

11. Joseph S. Ryan, "Religion and United States Foreign Policy Toward the Middle East: A Catholic Perspective," in Nijim, *American Church Politics and the Middle East:* 100-101.

12. Jeremy Rifkin and Ted Howard, *The Emerging Order: God in the Age of Scarcity.* New York: G.P. Putnam and Sons, 1979: 105.

13. *New York Times,* 13 April 1983.

14. International Christian Embassy in Jerusalem, "Pittsburgh Consulate Newsletter", (undated).

15. *Jerusalem Post* (International Edition), 5-11 October 1980.

16. "700 Club" broadcast, 26 April 1982.

17. Frances Fitzgerald, "The New Right and Phyllis Schlafly," *New York Review of Books,* 19 November 1981.

18. Deborah Huntington and Ruth Kaplan, "Corporate Ties to the Evangelical Christian Groups," *Report to the World Student Federation,* 28 August 1980.

19. Deborah Huntington, "The Salvation Brokers: Conservative Evangelicals in Central America," *NACLA* 8/1 (January/February 1984).

20. Jerry Falwell, *Listen, America!* Garden City, N.Y.: Doubleday, 1980: 107, 112-113.

21. Jerusalem Temple Foundation brochure; Grace Halsell, "Americans Waging Zionists' Al-Aqsa War," *Arab News,* 27 April 1983; Ingram Kelly, "Where the Money to Blow-Up Al-Aqsa Comes From," *The Middle East* 119 (September 1984).

22. *Washington Post,* 1 November 1977.

23. *Washington Post,* 26 February 1983.

24. NJCRAC, *Joint Program Plan, 1982-83:* 53.

Special Focus Organizations

AIFL

1. Promotional letter, September 1983.
2. *ADC Reports,* January-February 1984.
3. AIFL, *News* 3/1 (Summer 1983): 3.
4. September 1983 letter, *supra.*

YIPME

5. *Pennsylvania Jewish Life,* July 1974 (letter to the editor): 17.
6. YIPME, "Democracy Challenged: Israel and the Struggle for Peace in the Middle East."
7. *Ibid.*
8. "Lebanese Call for International Inquiry," 21 July 1982.

NCLI

9. *AFL-CIO American Federationist,* 10 September 1983.
10. *Ibid.*
11. *Jewish Labor Committee News,* Spring 1982.
12. *Ibid.*
13. NCLI promotional brochure (undated).

ATUCH

14. ATUCH and NCLI, *Shalom,* Fall/Winter 1982.
15. *Ibid.*
16. ATUCH and NCLI, *Shalom,* December 1970.
17. *Free Trade Union News,* July 1970.
18. ATUCH and NCLI, *Shalom,* October 1970.

AFSI

19. AFSI, "Why AFSI."
20. *Ibid.*
21. *Ibid.*
22. *Jewish Week,* 21 March 1982.
23. AFSI, *Outpost,* no. 21, March 1983.
24. *Jerusalem Post,* 16 July 1982.
25. AFSI, *Outpost,* no. 19, November 1982.
26. WZO-American Section, 1982 Report filed with U.S. Department of Justice.

NCYI

27. NCYI, "The National Council of Young Israel: Experience, Leadership and Accomplishments in the American Jewish Community Since 1912," ca. 1982-1983.
28. *Ibid.*
29. *The Jewish Press,* 26 February 1982.
30. *New York Times,* 21 September 1982.
31. *The Jewish Press,* 11 November 1983.
32. *Jewish Week*, 3 December 1982.
33. NCYI, *Young Israel Viewpoint,* January 1984.
34. NCYI, *Young Israel Viewpoint,* February 1984.
35. NCYI, *Young Israel Viewpoint,* January 1984.
36. NCYI, "National Council Highlights for 5744."
37. NCYI, *Young Israel Viewpoint,* January 1984.
38. *Ibid.*
39. *The Jewish Press,* 26 February 1982.
40. NCYI, "National Council Highlights for 5744."
41. NCYI, *Young Israel Viewpont,* January 1984.

The Pro-Israel Paradigm

The Pro-Israel Paradigm

The 1983 National Survey of American Jews, which focused on attitudes of American Jews toward Israel, was commissioned by the American Jewish Committee (AJC) because "many recent developments have fostered speculation that American Jews are becoming alienated from Israel. The hard-line posture of the Begin government, the rise to public prominence of Sephardic Israelis, recurrent Jewish and Arab violence on the West Bank, the 1982 war in Lebanon, and highly publicized disagreements between American and Israeli officials all have prompted some to suggest that the once-strong cultural, spiritual and political connections between American Jews and Israel are weakening."[1] This is of particular concern to the American Jewish establishment, as the AJC notes:

If true, such a development would have far-reaching consequences, particularly in two areas. First, the commitment of American Jews to Israel has undoubtedly helped generate a strong pro-Israel American foreign policy stand, and a perceived dampening of American Jewish enthusiasm could eventually translate into reduced U.S. economic, military and diplomatic support for the Jewish state. Second, for more than three decades, and especially since 1967, Israel has been a major element of American Jewish group identity. Support for Israel has been central to many philanthropic and other communal endeavors, and Israel has figured prominently in the spiritual life of American Jewry. Any changes in these attitudes and actions are likely to have profound consequences for contemporary Jewish identity and institutional life.[2]

In fact, however, the 1983 National Survey found " ... little or no erosion in the most fervent and passionate support for Israel. Caring for Israel still ranks with attending a Passover Seder and lighting Hanukkah candles as among the most popular and widespread contemporary expressions of American Jewish commitment."[3] While there is definite conflict over specific Israeli policy issues such as building Jewish settlements in the West Bank and Gaza Strip or holding negotiations with the PLO,*

*In his accompanying analysis to the 1983 National Survey, Steven Cohen found that American Jews fell into three groups: "About 45% may be seen as doves; that is, roughly, the proportion that support territorial compromise, favor suspending settlement activity, and are willing to consider a Palestinian homeland on the West Bank and Gaza that does not threaten Israel. About 30% may be seen as hawks ... Between the doves and the hawks were the roughly 25% who were ambivalent or inconsistent...."[4]

the lack of a complete consensus has not weakened the dominance of pro-Israelism on American Jewry's programmatic and political agenda in any meaningful way. The underlying support and identity with Israel the "symbol" remains substantially stronger than any doubts generated by a particular Israeli government, and it is highly unlikely that the pro-Israel ideology which unifies and motivates organized American Jewry will be radically weakened in the near future.

The core of this phenomenon is the inherent relationship between pro-Israelism and what is termed "Jewish survivalism" or group interest. In the opinion of Jonathan Woocher, a Brandeis University professor of Jewish Communal Service, the American Jewish community and its institutions now constitute a political system or polity in which " 'Jewish survivalism' ... defines the purposes of the polity as the insurance of Jewish physical and cultural continuity and (insofar as possible) of the well-being of every Jew."[5] Especially in twentieth-century America, with the weakening of religious identification and the symbiotic threat of assimilation and anti-Semitism, he argues, " 'Jewish survivalism' has, in effect, swallowed up alternative ideologies by integrating them into a grand synthesis. Old distinctions—between Zionist and non-Zionist, religious and secular, separatists and integrationists ... have either disappeared or been papered over by the overarching framework of the 'survivalist' vision of communal Jewish destiny and purposes."[6] Inevitably, the essence of survivalism for modern Jewry is the passage from the Holocaust to the state of Israel.*

The survivalist component of American Jewry's pro-Israelism creates a paradox which protects and perpetuates the pro-Israel status quo, diminishing or even negating the impact of apparently divisive developments. For example, while respondents to the 1983 National Survey evidenced greater willingness to criticize Israel, survivalism led them to express certain important qualifications: " ... criticism is acceptable only if it is internal to the group, and the more internal the better ... Criticism by non-Jews—whose views and motives are always suspect—of the Jewish State, her leaders, policies, and society is not acceptable."[7] The paradoxical effect is clearest when Israel commits a controversial act: though some Jewish organizations may feel critical, their reaction to the expression of non-Jewish criticism is to view Israel as vulnerable and thus in need of support, despite misgivings.**

---

* Other contemporary survivalist agenda items are Soviet Jewry, education on the Holocaust, anti-Semitism, intermarriage and Jewish family life, and Jewish education and culture.

** During the 1982 Israeli invasion of Lebanon, surveys found that the percentage of American Jews rejecting territorial compromise actually *increased;* Cohen posits that critical media coverage at the time caused American Jews to perceive Israel as threatened and vulnerable, and thus in need of less qualified support.[8]

The advent of the Likud government in Israel, with its aggressive and hawkish policies, highlighted actual and potential conflicts between the traditionally liberal/Democratic American Jewish establishment and Israel; however, virtually all the organizations discussed in this book provided at least tacit support to such Israeli actions as increased settlements, the invasion and occupation of Lebanon, and arms trade with authoritarian regimes in Latin America and elsewhere. Even those groups most rooted in the liberal establishment, while sincerely deploring many Israeli policies, voiced their disquiet through private channels or simply remained silent because, within the survivalist paradigm, joining their voices to those of non-Jewish critics constitutes self-hatred or betrayal of group interests.

The linkage of support for Israel and survivalism is the basis of Cohen's premise that pro-Israelism emerged as "the politics of ethnic survival . . . a mass-based movement supplanting liberalism as the center-piece of activity for most major Jewish organizations."[9] (Liberalism was defined as "the politics of group integration.") The ascendancy of pro-Israelism and survivalism are major factors in the decline of Jewish liberalism, as evidenced not only by Jewish positions and alliances on Middle East issues, but by such domestic survivalist issues as quotas, affirmative action, and community control over public education. The likelihood that this trend to the right will continue is supported by a 1984 AJCongress report which found that while American Jews are still disproportionately Democrats and nonconservative, whether or not this continues to be true "may depend on whether the liberal establishment becomes identified with the anti-Israel camp."[10]

The impact of pro-Israelism reaches all areas of Jewish organizational life. Its emotional, political and financial centrality has granted Israel and her supporters great authority in the community. Daniel Elazar writes:

The authoritative role of Israel functions in two ways. First, Israel is itself authoritative. Those who wish to dissent from any particular Israeli policy or demand must be very circumspect when they do so. Those Jews who reject Israel's claims upon them are more or less written off by the Jewish community. They are certainly excluded from any significant decision-making role in the community. Second, leaders who can claim to speak in the name of Israel or on behalf of Israel gain a degree of authority that places them in very advantageous positions when it comes to other areas of communal decision-making.[11]

Pro-Israelism has become the financial cornerstone of the American Jewish communal network. Contributions to the annual UJA-Federation campaign are solicited primarily by appeals to support Israel, though the funds generated are allocated to both domestic and overseas needs. The American Jewish establishment supports Israel and is in turn supported and empowered by its allegiance to the Jewish state. To quote Woocher again:

269

The State of Israel has served as a unifying focus for polity activity and as a central symbol in the polity's "civil religious" faith. Its existence and needs have catalyzed structural changes and shifts in the balance of power within the polity. Israel serves as the primary basis for generating resources, and behavior with respect to it constitutes virtually the only area where communal norms can be even minimally enforced.[12]

Indeed, according to the AJCongress report cited above, Israel is so central to American Jews that "in some significant ways the future of the American Jewish community in the 21st century will be shaped by the future of American Jewish-Israeli relations."[13]

Any discussion of the dynamics between American Jews and Israel is incomplete without accounting for the role and impact of the third major party, the United States. Economic, military and diplomatic support for Israel has been an inherent component of U.S. strategy for successive administrations. The obvious effect of this political reality is to dramatically increase the effectiveness of American Jewry's Israel support work. A more complex result, however, is that U.S. policy reinforces the identification of American Jews with Israel because it removes the potential conflict of dual loyalty by legitimizing the construct that 'what is good for Israel is good for America.' The 1983 National Survey notes:

As a result of deep commitments to both Israel and the United States, American Jews firmly reject the notion that a commitment to one in any way contradicts a commitment to the other. Over 9 in 10 affirmed that "U.S. support of Israel is in America's interest," while fewer than 1 in 4 agreed that "There are times when my devotion to Israel comes into conflict with my devotion to America."[14]

Whether or not this construct will continue unchallenged (and essentially unchallengeable) rests primarily with the United States. No U.S. administration or substantial sector of U.S. society has consistently advocated a policy that seriously clashes with any potentially or actually controversial Israeli policy, such as demanding and attempting to enforce a halt to Israeli settlements in the West Bank and Gaza Strip. Barring cataclysmic upheaval within Israel itself, so long as U.S. and Israeli strategic interests are perceived as compatible by the ruling elites of each country, there is no objective basis for serious conflict to arise over such issues as dual loyalty or dissent, and no reason to anticipate a shift in American Jewry's support for Israel in the foreseeable future.

1. Steven M. Cohen, *Attitudes of American Jews Toward Israel and Israelis: The 1983 National Survey of American Jews and Jewish Communal Leaders.* Institute on American Jewish-Israel Relations, AJC: 1.

2. *Ibid.*

3. *Ibid: 3.*

4. *Ibid: 26.*

5. Jonathan S. Woocher, "The American Jewish Polity in Transition," *Forum* 46/47 (Fall/Winter 1982): 63.

6. *Ibid.*

7. *Attitudes of American Jews,* 24.

8. *Ibid: 17.*

9. Steven M. Cohen, *American Modernity & Jewish Identity,* New York and London: Tavistock Publications, 1983: 154.

10. *Washington Post,* 25 March 1984.

11. Daniel J. Elazar, "Decision Making in the American Jewish Community," in Marshall Sklare (ed.), *American Jews/A Reader.* New York: Behrman House, Inc., 1983: 209-210.

12. Woocher: 68.

13. *Washington Post,* 25 March 1984.

14. *Attitudes of American Jews,* 12.

Appendix

Attitudes of American Jews Toward Israel and Israelis
The 1983 National Survey of
American Jews and Jewish Communal Leaders

Steven M. Cohen

Institute on American Jewish-Israel Relations
The American Jewish Committee

(Excerpt)

The Surveys

As noted, this study consists of two surveys, one of a representative nationwide sample of American Jews, the other of board members of five prominent Jewish communal organizations.

The public sample survey data collection was conducted by A.B. Data Corporation of Milwaukee, a firm that conducts direct marketing campaigns of Jewish communities. In the last year, A.B. Data compiled approximately 80,000 Distinctive Jewish Names (DJN) which it applied against lists of the country's 70 million telephone subscribers to yield well over a million households with a high probability of containing a Jewish member. Using this list, the survey was initially sent (in June, 1983) to a sample of 1600 households. About a quarter of these, in turn, were ineligible or unreachable (non-Jewish, deceased, moved with no forwarding address, etc.). Of the remaining 1200 or so, about half (N=640) eventually returned the questionnaire. Many had received as many as five mailings: an introductory letter, the first questionnaire, a postcard reminder, a second and a third questionnaire, as well as a follow up reminder phone call. The survey's last respondents replied in late July 1983.

The leadership sample consists of board members from five national organizations: the American Jewish Committee, the American Jewish Congress, the Anti-Defamation League of B'nai B'rith, the International B'nai B'rith, and the United Jewish Appeal. Again, about half of the eligible respondents returned the questionnaire (N=272). Results below are reported collectively for the five organizations.

275

TABLE 1

Indicators of Psychic Attachment to Israel

	Public	Leaders
Caring about Israel is a very important part of my being a Jew	78%	90%
If Israel were destroyed, I would feel as if I had suffered one of the greatest personal tragedies in my life	77	83
I am sometimes uncomfortable about identifying myself as a supporter of Israel	10	4
Feelings about Israel		
Very Pro-Israel	43	63
Pro-Israel	43	35
Neutral	6	0
Anti-Israel	2	2
Very Anti-Israel	1	0

TABLE 2

Indicators of Personal Involvement with Israel

	Public	Leaders
Pay special attention to newspapers and magazine articles about Israel	93%	99%
Often talk about Israel with friends and relatives	75	97
Consider myself very well-informed about Israel	56	93

TABLE 3

Indicators of Contact and Communication with Israel

	Public	Leaders
Visited Israel		
Once or more	40%	94%
Twice or more	17	78
Have any family in Israel	34	35
Have any personal friends in Israel	35	69
Ever seriously considered living in Israel	17	17

TABLE 4

To What Extent Do You Think Each of the Following Descriptions Applies to Most Israelis?

	To A Great Extent	
	Public	Leaders
Industrious	81%	69%
Aggressive	68	71
Heroic	66	66
Peaceloving	53	75
Progressive	50	44
Idealistic	30	14
Arrogant	29	29
Materialistic	21	19
Secular	20	41
Intolerant	13	14
Religious	12	4
Conservative	8	6
Generally, I feel closer kinship with Israeli Ashkenazim than Israeli Sephardim	59	55

TABLE 5

Reported Acts of Support for Israel

	Public	Leaders
Contribute directly to Israeli educational or charitable institutions	46%	94%
Have given the UJA/Federation $100 or more in the last 12 months	34	97
Contributed money to a political candidate in the last 12 months because "he/she would support Israel"	30	76
Written a newspaper or elected official in support of Israel in the last 12 months	20	70

TABLE 6

Israel, American Jews, and the Larger Society

	Public	Leaders
U.S. Support for Israel is in America's interest.	91%	96%
There are times when my devotion to Israel comes into conflict with my devotion to America.	24	17
Consider self a Zionist	39	50
Most Americans think that U.S. support for Israel is in America's interest.	47	60
When it comes to the crunch few non-Jews will come to Israel's side in its struggle to survive.	54	41
I am worried the U.S. may stop being a firm ally of Israel.	55	48
Jews should not vote for candidates unfriendly to Israel.	73	66
Anti-Semitism in America may, in the future, become a serious problem for American Jews.	69	55
Anti-Semitism in America is currently not a serious problem for American Jews.	37	64
Virtually all positions of influence in America are open to Jews.	27	44

TABLE 7

Are Each of these American Groups Generally Friendly, Mixed or Neutral, or Generally Unfriendly to Israel?

	Friendly Index[a]	
	Public	Leaders
Democrats	60%	76%
Liberals	46	44
Congress	38	76
Labor Unions	33	58
President Reagan	16	55
Republicans	14	42
The Military	12	24
Conservatives	10	27
"Mainstream" Protestants	8	10
Evangelical Protestants	3	63
News Media	-3	-20
Catholics	-5	9
State Department	-11	-53
Corporations	-15	-29
Blacks	-41	-58

[a] Friendly Index = (the difference between the % who answered "generally friendly" and the % who answered "generally unfriendly")

TABLE 8

Opinions About Israeli Security Policies

	Public			Leaders		
	Yes	No	Not Sure	Yes	No	Not Sure
Israel should maintain permanent control over . . . the West Bank.	42	29	30	21	59	20
Israel should offer the Arabs territorial compromise in . . . the West Bank and Gaza in return for credible guarantees of peace.	42	34	23	74	16	10
Israel should suspend the expansion of settlements in . . . the West Bank . . . to encourage peace negotiations.	51	28	21	55	25	20
Israel should talk with the PLO if the PLO recognizes Israel and renounces terrorism.	70	17	13	73	17	11
Palestinians have a right to a homeland on the West Bank and Gaza, so long as it does not threaten Israel.	48	26	27	51	28	22

TABLE 9

Favorability Ratings of Six Israeli Political Leaders

	Public		Leaders	
	Favorability Rating [a]	% No Impression	Favorability Rating [a]	% No Impression
Abba Eban	72	8	72	0
Yitzhak Rabin	41	28	45	4
Yitzhak Navon	36	45	57	14
Shimon Peres	31	23	32	6
Menachem Begin	31	3	6	0
Ariel Sharon	5	7	-39	0

[a] Favorability Rating $= 1$ X (% "Very Favorable" $-$ % "Very Unfavorable")
$+0.5$ x (% "Somewhat Favorable" $-$ % "Somewhat Unfavorable")

TABLE 10

Expressions of Overt Criticism of Israeli Policies and Leaders

	Public			Leaders		
	Yes	No	Not Sure	Yes	No	Not Sure
I am often troubled by the policies of the current Israeli government.[a]	48	29	23	70	21	9
The policies of Prime Minister Begin and his government have hurt Israel in the U.S.	50	22	28	68	15	18
Israeli leaders have sometimes been unnecessarily tactless in their dealing with American officials.	50	24	26	81	10	9
The policies of Menachem Begin and his government have damaged Israel.	35	38	27	43	32	25
Israel's commitment to democratic values has eroded in recent years.	24	52	24	22	64	14
Continued Israeli occupation of the West Bank will erode Israel's democratic and humanitarian character.	28	42	31	47	33	20
Continued Israeli occupation of the West Bank will erode Israel's Jewish character.	22	50	27	43	36	21

[a] Answers to the first question only are "Agree," "Disagree," "Not Sure."

TABLE 11

Attitude Toward Criticism of Israeli Policies

	Public			Leaders		
	Agree	Dis-agree	Not Sure	Agree	Dis-agree	Not Sure
Israelis who strongly criticize some of the government's policies are bad for Israel.	17	70	13	7	85	7
American Jewish organizations should feel free to publicly criticize the Israel government and its policies.	60	27	13	42	37	21
American Jews should not criticize the government of Israel's policy publicly.	31	57	11	31	57	12
Jews should hold Israel to higher standards of conduct than other countries.	52	37	11	50	39	10
Non-Jews should hold Israel to higher standards of conduct than other countries.	15	67	19	12	79	9
Those who stop giving to the UJA because they oppose Israeli government policies are right to do so.	20	61	19	10	78	13

Bibliography

Sources for the study are listed here chapter by chapter, with subgroups of books, documents, newspapers, magazines and journals, and organizational publications. For the convenience of the reader, references that were used in more than one chapter are cited accordingly. Many of the organizational publications are flyers or promotional materials which lack dates, sometimes page numbers, and occasionally titles.

General Sources

Books

Who's Who in American Jewry. Los Angeles: Standard Who's Who, 1980.

Barwell, Beatrice (ed.). *Zionist Yearbook 1981-82.* London: The Zionist Federation Educational Trust, 1982.

Chomsky, Noam. *The Fateful Triangle: The United States, Israel & the Palestinians.* Boston: South End Press, 1983.

Cohen, Steven M. *American Modernity & Jewish Identity.* New York and London: Tavistock Publications, 1983.

Elazar, Daniel. "Decision Making in the American Jewish Community," in *American Jews/A Reader,* edited by Marshall Sklare. New York: Library of Jewish Studies, Behrman House, Inc., 1983.

Feuerlicht, Roberta Strauss. *The Fate of the Jews.* New York: Times Books, 1983.

Goren, Arthur A. *The American Jews.* Cambridge and London: The Belknap Press of Harvard University, 1982.

Grose, Peter. *Israel in the Mind of America.* New York: Alfred A. Knopf, 1983.

Himmelfarb, Milton and David Singer (eds.). *American Jewish Yearbook,* vols. 82, 83. New York: American Jewish Committee, 1982, 1983.

Liebman, Arthur. *Jews and the Left.* New York: Wiley, 1979.

Maslow, Will. *The Structure and Functioning of the American Jewish Community.* Published jointly by the American Jewish Congress and the American Section of the World Jewish Congress, 1974.

Schiff, Gary S. "American Jews and Israel: A Study in Political and Organizational Priorities," in *Understanding American Jewish Philanthropy,* edited by M.L. Raphael. New York: KTAV Publishers, 1979.

Sklare, Marshall (ed.). *The Jewish Community in America.* New York: Behrman House, 1974.

Wallach, Michael (ed.). *The Jewish Yearbook 1982.* London: Jewish Chronicle Publications, 1982.

Journals and Periodicals

Friedman, Murray. "A New Direction for American Jews." *Commentary* 72/6 (December 1981).

Hertzberg, Arthur. "Israel and American Jewry." *Commentary* 44/2 (August 1967).

Himmelfarb, Milton. "Are Jews Becoming Republican?" *Commentary* 72/2 (August 1981).

Podhoretz, Norman. "The New American Majority." *Commentary* 71/1 (January 1981).

Urofsky, Melvin I. "American Jewish Leadership." *American Jewish History* 70/4 (June 1981).

————. "A Cause in Search of Itself: American Zionism after the State." *American Jewish History* 69/1 (September 1979).

Woocher, Jonathan. "The American Jewish Polity in Transition." *Forum* 46/47 (Fall/Winter 1982).

Newspapers

Jerusalem Post:

Hoffman, Charles. "Researcher Says U.S. Jews Not Disappearing." 4 April 1984.

Siegel, Judy. "AJC Report Predicts Sharp Division of U.S. Jewry by 2000." 3 April 1984.

Jerusalem Post International Edition:

Hadar, Leon. "New Voices in U.S. Jewry." 7-13 June 1981.

Jewish Press:

Rodan, Yaacov. "Reagan Returning to Orthodox Voters." 13 January 1984.

Jewish Telegraphic Agency:

Polakoff, Joseph. "Jewish Republicans, Jewish Democrats Assess Meaning of Election Sweep by Reagan." 6 November 1980.

Jewish Week:

"Metropolitan N.Y. Now Numbers 1,668,000 Jews—15% of Total." 9 May 1982.

Yaffe, Richard. "Carter's Jewish Vote Hits Bottom in Reagan Sweep." 9 November 1980.

New York Times:

Smith, Terence. "Carter Post-Mortem . . . " 9 November 1980.

Wall Street Journal:

Inman, Virginia. "One of 95 Jews in U.S. Adopted the Religion . . ."
16 April 1984.

Putka, Gary. "As Jewish Population Falls in U.S., Leaders Seek to
Reverse Trend." 13 April 1984.

Washington Post:

Hyer, Marjorie. "Convention to Study Projected Decline in U.S.
Jewish Population." 25 March 1984.

Organizational Publications

Cohen, Steven M. *Attitudes of American Jews Toward Israel and Israelis:
The 1983 National Survey of American Jews and Jewish Communal Leaders.*
Institute on American Jewish-Israel Relations, AJC, 1983.

287

Chapter I

Books

Cohen, Steven M. *American Modernity & Jewish Identity.* New York and London: Tavistock Publications, 1983.

Grose, Peter. *Israel in the Mind of America.* New York: Alfred A. Knopf, 1983.

Halperin, Samuel. *The Political World of American Zionism.* Detroit: Wayne State University Press, 1961.

Lilienthal, Alfred M. *The Zionist Connection II: What Price Peace?* New Brunswick, New Jersey: North American, 1982.

Maslow, Will. *The Structure and Functioning of the American Jewish Community.* New York: Published jointly by the American Jewish Congress and the American Section of the World Jewish Congress, 1974.

Sachar, Howard M. *A History of Israel From the Rise of Zionism to Our Time.* New York: Alfred A. Knopf, 1982.

Shapiro, Yonathan. *Leadership of the American Zionist Organization 1897-1930.* Urbana: University of Illinois Press, 1971.

Sochen, June. *Consecrate Every Day: The Public Lives of Jewish American Women.* Albany: SUNY Press, 1981.

Documents

Covenant Between the Government of Israel and the Zionist Executive Also Called the Executive of the Jewish Agency. Jerusalem, 26 July 1954. For the Government: Moshe Sharitt (*sic*), Prime Minister, For the Zionist Executive: Berl Locker and Dr. Nahum Goldmann, Chairman. (Copy of document on file with the U.S. Department of Justice.)

IRS Form 990:
Hadassah, for fiscal year 1 July 1951 to 30 June 1982.
JA-American Section, for 1 April 1982 to 31 March 1983.
WZO-American Section, for fiscal year 1 April 1982 to 31 March 1983.

U.S. Department of Justice. WZO-American Section Registration Statements, 1982-83 (filed every six months).

U.S. Senate. *Activities of Nondiplomatic Representatives of Foreign Principals in the United States.* Hearing before the Committee on Foreign Relations, 88th Congress, First Session, 23 May 1963 (Fulbright Hearings).

Newspapers

Boston Globe:
"U.S. Misplaces Its Enthusiasm" (letter). 23 January 1984.

Ha'aretz:
Jaffe, Eliezer. "Philanthropic Politics." 22 June 1983.

Jerusalem Post:
   "Exposing Youth to Israel." 20 July 1983.
   Hadar, Leon. "Zionist Election 'Witch-Hunt.' " 22 April 1982.

Jewish Newsletter:
   9 January 1961.

Jewish Press:
   "Herut Forum on Dec. 7th." 2 December 1982.

Jewish Telegraphic Agency:
   "ZOA Leader Urges Reagan to 'Grasp the Moment' in Lebanon." 14 June 1982.
   "UAHC Distributes Videocassettes Depicting PLO Terrorist Tactics." 1 September 1982.
   "Jabotinsky Prizes Announced." 15 November 1983.
   "UAHC Demands End of 'Discrimination Against Non-Orthodox Judaism' in Allocation of Diaspora Funds in Israel." 17 November 1983.
   Rabi, Yitzhak. "Effort Being Made to Improve Zionist Activities in the U.S." 3 March 1982.
   Zuckoff, Murray. "Dulzin Calls for a New 'Challenging Partnership' Between Israel and the Diaspora." 18 November 1982.

Jewish Week:
   "Record of PLO Terror Now on TV Cassettes." 3 September 1982.
   "Labor Zionists Back Plan." 10 September 1982.

National Observer:
   Mosher, Lawrence. "Zionist Role in U.S. Raises New Concern." 18 May 1970.

New York Times:
   "U.S. Jewish Spokesmen Assert that Israelis Are Not to Blame for Massacre." 21 September 1982.
   Teltsch, Kathleen. "A $100,000 Award is created . . . " 24 August 1983.

Washington Post:
   Hyer, Marjorie. "Jewish Council Excluded New Group over Views on Rights of Palestinians." 4 June 1983.

Magazines and Journals

   "Caesarea: The Jerusalem Program." *Forum,* no. 41 (Spring/Summer 1981). Special Issue.
   "Mitzpeh Har Chalutz." UAHC.
   "For Israel." *Washington Report on Middle East Affairs,* 13 June 1983.

American Council for Judaism. *Special Interest Report*, June-July 1983.

Gold, Mark. "The Condition of the Patient is Deteriorating: A Report from the 30th Zionist Congress." *Israel Horizons*, March/April 1983.

Jaffe, Eliezer. "Wanted: A New Agency." *Moment*, April 1983.

Nelson, Nancy Jo. "The Zionist Organizational Structure." *Journal of Palestine Studies* 10/1 (Autumn 1980).

Schenker, Avraham. "Zionism in Distress." *Forum* 46/47 (Fall/Winter 1982).

Tabory, Ephraim. "The Conservative and Reform Movements in Israel." *Midstream*, May 1983.

Urofsky, Melvin J. "A Cause in Search of Itself: American Zionism After the State." *American Jewish History* 69/1 (September 1979).

Likhowsky, Eliyahu. "The Zionist Legal and Constitutional Context: An Insider Account." Speech delivered at the Post-Elementary Teachers Seminar, Jerusalem, 3-4 February 1981. Translated by Uri Davis (unpublished).

Organizational Publications

ARZA

"Almost Everything You Wanted To Know About ARZA: History, Goals, Israel," September 1980.

ARZA *Newsletter*, March-April 1983; Fall 1983.

"The Law of Return: 1. Action Suggestions for Reform Congregations, 2. Background materials on the Law of Return and religious pluralism in Israel, 3. Appendix with addresses, resolutions, and sample letters and telegrams." Compiled by Rabbi Eric H. Yoffie, ARZA pamphlet, 1983.

AZF

"Report to the American Zionist Federation Sixth Biennial Convention," 9-11 November 1980. New York: Grossingers, 1980.

"A Manual for a Zionist Information and Education Program in the United States," November 1975.

"The Palestinians—Some Facts," 28 November 1975 (flyer).

David Szonyi, "The Jerusalem Program: Its Meaning and Implications for American Jewry." *AZF Issue Analysis*, no. 19 (June 1982).

"The American Zionist Federation" (background, with structure, goals, and program), June 1983.

Spectrum 1/4 (Summer 1983).

Hadassah

"Facts About Hadassah," May 1983 (pamphlet).

"Hadassah Goes International," 69th Annual Convention Report, 1983.

Jewish Agency
Founding Assembly of the Reconstituted Jewish Agency. Jerusalem: Israel Communications, 1971.
"The Jewish Agency for Israel: A Brief Description." UJA flyer, ca. 1981.

World Confederation of United Zionists
"Non-Party Zionism Means Jewish Unity: Join the World Confederation of United Zionists" (undated pamphlet).
Zionist Information Views, August-September 1983.

WZO
"The World Zionist Organization." Organization and Information Department, 1972.
"Anti-Zionism, a Threat to: Israel/the Jewish People/Democracy" (undated pamphlet).
"A Guide to Israel Programs," 1983.

ZOA
The American Zionist, May-June 1976; April-May 1983.
Ayin L'tzion, The Masada Magazine, Fall 1982.
"The World of Masada of the ZOA" (undated).
"ZOA Projects in Israel" (undated).
"ZOA Impact: In the U.S., In Israel, On Jewish American Youth" (undated brochure, ca. 1982).

Chapter II

Books

Cohen, Naomi. *Not Free to Desist: The American Jewish Committee, 1906-1966.* Philadelphia: The Jewish Publication Society of America, 1972.

Cohen, Steven M. *American Modernity & Jewish Identity*. New York and London: Tavistock Publications, 1983.

Feuerlicht, Roberta Strauss. *The Fate of the Jews*. New York: Times Books, 1983.

Forster, Arnold and Benjamin Epstein. *The New Anti-Semitism*. New York: McGraw-Hill, 1974.

Glick, Edward Bernard. *The Triangular Connection: America, Israel, and American Jews*. London: George Allen and Unwin, 1982.

Goren, Arthur A. *The American Jews*. Cambridge, Mass. and London: The Belknap Press, 1982.

Grusd, Edward E. *B'nai B'rith: The Story of a Covenant*. New York: Appleton-Century, 1966.

Halperin, Samuel. *The Political World of American Zionism*. Detroit: Wayne State University Press, 1961.

Liebman, Arthur. *Jews and the Left.* New York: Wiley, 1979.

Maslow, Will. *The Structure and Functioning of the American Jewish Community.* New York: Published jointly by the American Jewish Congress and the American Section of the World Jewish Congress, 1974.

Perlmutter, Nathan and Ruth Ann. *The Real Anti-Semitism in America.* New York: Arbor House, 1982.

Raphael, M.L. (ed.). *Understanding American Jewish Philanthropy.* New York: KTAV Publishers, 1979.

Sklare, Marshall (ed.). *American Jews/A Reader.* New York: Behrman House Inc., 1983.

Sloan, Irving J. (ed.). *The Jews in America 1621-1970.* Dobbs Ferry, N.Y.: Oceana Publications, 1971.

Documents

IRS Form 990:

American Jewish Committee, for year ending 31 December 1982.

American Jewish Congress, for year ending 31 December 1982.

Anti-Defamation League, for fiscal year 1 July 1981 to 30 June 1982.

Council of Jewish Federations Annual Report—Charitable Organization, for year ending December 1982, filed with the New York State Department of State.

O.S.S. Document no. B-165. "American Zionists and the Palestine Resolution." 9 March 1944.

Newspapers

Baltimore Jewish Times:

Rosenblatt, Gary. "The Life and Death of a Dream." 7 November 1980.

Boston Globe:

Berman, John. "Corporations to Reveal Funds Spent on AWACS Lobbying." 24 February 1983.

Chicago Tribune:

O'Shea, James. "Jewish Group Wants AWACS Lobbying Revealed." 26 December 1982.

Christian Science Monitor:

"Jewish Bid to Bar PLO from U.S. Fails." 1 April 1974.

Richey, Warren. "AWACS: American Jewish Congress Takes on Corporate America." 17 March 1983.

Zakim, Leonard. "The Arab-Arab Drama." 27 January 1983.

Detroit Free Press:

"Pentagon Seeks U.S. Jewish Support." 18 April 1974.

Detroit News:
 Gilbert, Armand. "Arabs Charge Defamation." 13 January 1982.

Jerusalem Post:
 "B'nai B'rith Seeks Closure of 'Racist' U.S. Radio Station." 29 May 1983.
 Hadar, Leon. "Enquiry Into Corporate Lobbying on Mid-East Issues." 9 December 1982.
 _____. "Rightward Ho!" *International Edition,* 7-13 December 1980.
 Blitzer, Wolf. "Reagan Says U.S. to be Israel's 'Rock of Support.' " 12 June 1983.

Jewish Exponent:
 18 February 1977.

Jewish News:
 "ADL Sees Climate for Jewish Security as Worsening." 21 November 1974.

The Jewish Press:
 "Leaders of 120 Jewish Agencies Assail U.S. Arms-Sales to Arabs." 5 March 1982.
 "ADL Releases Guides for Students." 18 June 1982.
 "Supporters of PLO as Guilty as Terrorists." 17 September 1982.

Jewish Telegraphic Agency:
 "Schindler Says There is a Link Between Rightwing Christians and Increase of Anti-Semitic Attacks." 24 November 1980.
 "Moral Majority Official Under Fire for Anti-Jewish Remarks." 9 February 1981.
 "ADL Official Warns Arms Sales Endangers Israel." 8 June 1982.
 "NJCRAC Urges Action that Will End Use of Lebanon by Terrorists." 9 June 1982.
 "Begin Scheduled to Address CJF 50th General Assembly in L.A." 13 October 1982.
 "ADL Study Shows Hate Groups Are Turning to Violence." 29 October 1982.
 "ADL Urges Probe of Reported Use of UNRWA Facility by PLO." 3 November 1982.
 "ADL Reports that Anti-Semitic Vandalism in U.S. Declined in 1982." 11 January 1983.
 "21 U.S. Jewish Community Leaders Return from Mexico Reassured About Situation of Jews There." 23 January 1983.
 "ADL Official Raps UN-Sponsored Conclave on Israel and South Africa." 27 July 1983.

"High Court Asked to Review Treasury Department Refusal to Reveal Dollar Holdings of Arab States in the U.S." 7 October 1983.

"CJF Announces 1983 Smolar Award Winners: JTA Gets Special Citation." 11 October 1983.

Freeman, Kevin. "AJCongress to Launch Program to Determine Extent of Mideast Lobbying Activities by U.S. Firms." 7 December 1980.

_____."Jewish Leaders Back Israel." 8 June 1982.

Friedman, David. "U.S. Proclaims Nov. 12 'ADL Day.'" 18 November 1983.

Silver, Helen. "Jackson Urged 'Unwavering' Support." 10 June 1983.

Zuckoff, Murray. "At the GA of the CJF: Resolution on the Mideast Emphasized Importance of U.S.-Israel Being in Accord on Peace Goals and Strategies." 23 November 1983.

Jewish Times:

Perlmutter, Phillip. "Bluntly Speaking." 14 June 1973.

Jewish Week:

"Massacre Used by PLO to Spur Anti-Israel Acts, Forster Says." 15 October 1982.

"Court Asked to Show Arab Holdings." 7 October 1983.

Feldstein, Donald. "Why AJCommittee Won't March on Washington." 29 July 1983.

Greenberg, Eric. "Anti-Jewish Incidents Here Down 40%." 8 July 1983.

Schloss, Steve. "U.S. Jews Must Flood Congress, President with Pro-Israel Mail . . . " 23 July 1982.

Yaffe, Richard. "At Federations General Assembly: Israel Central to U.S. Jewish Life, Delegates Told." 19 November 1982.

Los Angeles Times:

Meisler, Stanley. "B'nai B'rith Backs Israel Again After 'Anguish' and 'Pain.'" 23 October 1982.

Mideast Observer:

"Weinberger Speaks to AJC." June 1983.

New York Times:

"Rights Panel Choices Defended by Leader of B'nai B'rith Wing." 5 June 1983.

Bialkin, Kenneth J. "A Palestinian Professor Unqualified to Be Called a 'Moderate'" (letter). 12 January 1984.

Bookbinder, Hyman H. "Israel's Lebanon Gains" (Op-Ed). 10 June 1983.

Forster, Arnold. "American Opinion Makers' Mideast Errors" (letter). 25 November 1983.

Foxman, Abraham H. "Mideast Radicals Furthering Soviet Aims" (letter). 1 January 1984.

Gruen, George E. "Lessons For Arabs" (Op-Ed). 26 April 1983.

Shenker, Israel. "Anti-Semitism is called Evasion of Self-Criticism." 10 January 1971.

Spiegel, Irving. "Study Finds Rise in 'Radical Jews.' " 10 January 1971.

_____. "Anti-Semitism Found on Far Right and New Left." 26 January 1971.

San Francisco Examiner:
"Rabbi Scores Arab Propaganda." 19 February 1969.

Village Voice:
Hentoff, Nat. "Defamation League." 18 February 1971.

_____. "Vanessa, the Professor, the PLO, and Free Speech." 1 June 1982.

_____. "Is This Any Way To Treat a Blacklisted Lady?" 8 June 1982.

Washington Post:
Kiernan, Laura A. "Suits on Terrorist Raid in Israel Filed Here Against Libya, PLO." 12 March 1981.

Medsger, Betty. "Stolen FBI Documents Analyzed." 9 May 1971.

Muscatine, Alison. "Drop Reported in Anti-Semitic Violence in U.S." 11 January 1983.

Valentine, Paul W. "A Challenge to the 'Zionism' of B'nai B'rith." 7 February 1971.

Magazines and Journals

"Blind Loyalty and Palestinian-Baiting: Jewish Groups on the Offensive." *ADC Reports,* no. 19 (Summer 1983).

"Middle East Lobbying." *Congressional Quarterly Weekly Report* 39/34 (22 August 1981).

Avishai, Bernard. "Breaking Faith: Commentary and the American Jews." *Dissent,* Spring 1981.

Ben Cohen, Truman (pseud). "How Non-Governmental is B'nai B'rith?" *Arab World,* May-June 1970.

Dawidowicz, Lucy S. "America & the Jews," review of *The Real Anti-Semitism in America,* by Nathan and Ruth Ann Perlmutter. *Commentary,* 74/4 (October 1982).

Elinsen, Elaine. "Special Report: Anti-Defamation League Defames the Sandinistas." *Palestine Focus,* November 1983.

Fein, Leonard. "The Domestic Element: American Jewry and U.S.-Israel Relations." Institute for Jewish Policy Planning and Research of the Synagogue Council of America. *Analysis,* no. 49 (1 December 1974).

295

Fischel, Jack R. "Rabbis and Leaders: Silver and Wise." *The American Zionist*, April-May 1983.

Friedman, Murray. "A New Direction for American Jews." *Commentary* 72/6 (December 1981).

Goodman, Walter. "Fair Game/Forster & Epstein." *The New Leader*, 27 May 1974.

Hertzberg, Arthur, "Israel and American Jewry," *Commentary* 44/2 (August 1967).

Lanouette, William J. "The Many Faces of the Jewish Lobby in America." *National Journal*, 13 May 1978.

Peretz, Don. "Israel: Land and People or State and Nation." *Petahim* (undated).

Rose, Sharon and Joe Stork. "Zionism and American Jews," *MERIP Reports*, no. 29 (June 1974).

Samuelson, Norbert. "How the American Jewish Community Could Be Democratic: A Political Model." *interChange* 1/8 (April 1976).

Urofsky, Melvin. "American Jewish Leadership." *American Jewish History* 70/4 (June 1981).

————. "Do American Jews Want Democracy in Jewish Life?" *interChange* 1/7 (March 1976).

Woocher, Jonathan. "The American Jewish Polity in Transition." *Forum* 46/47 (Fall/Winter, 1982).

Organizational Publications

NJCRAC

1982-83 Joint Program Plan for Jewish Community Relations, 1983.
1983-84 Joint Program Plan for Jewish Community Relations, 1984.

American Jewish Committee

Periodicals, Pamphlets, Flyers
Commentary, 1965-1983.
Present Tense, 1978-1983.

"Decades of Decision: A Brief History of the American Jewish Committee," May 1983.

"The Energy Crisis: Questions and Answers," February 1974.

"15 Questions and Answers on U.S. Arms for Saudi Arabia," May 1981.

"Milestones of the American Jewish Committee," May 1983.

"Planning Guide for the Christian Visitor to Israel," (undated).

"Questions and Answers on Middle East Problems," (undated).

"Questions People Ask About Israel and America's National Interests," July 1975.

"Teaching About the Holocaust," May 1978.

Feingold, Henry L. "A Jewish Survival Enigma: The Strange Case of the American Jewish Committee," May 1981.

Karlikow, Abraham S. "Jews in Arab Countries," September 1968.

Background Reports, Studies, and Surveys

Banki, Judith Hershcopf. *Christian Reactions to the Middle East Crisis.* November 1967.

———. *The UN's Anti-Semitism Resolution: Christian Responses.* October 1976.

———. *Anti-Israel Influence in American Churches.* May 1979.

Cohen, Steven M. *Attitudes of American Jews Toward Israel and Israelis: The 1983 National Survey of American Jews and Jewish Communal Leaders.* Institute on American Jewish-Israel Relations, AJC, 1983.

Ellerin, Milton. "The AWACS Debate: Is There Anti-Semitic Fallout?" *Trends Analyses Report,* 17 February 1982.

Gottesman, Lois. *Islam in America.* 1979.

Mittelman, Sheila. "Ad Hoc Groups: New Pleaders for the Arab Cause." *Trends Analyses Report,* 11 October 1982.

Schiff, Gary S. "Middle East Centers at Selected American Universities." A Report Presented to the American Jewish Committee. AJC: 1981.

Yankelovich, Skelly, and White. *Anti-Semitism in the United States,* Vol. 1, The Summary Report. July 1981.

Background Memoranda

"The Arab War Against Israel: The UN Battleground," July 1975.

"Some of Our Best Friends . . . . The Claim of Arab Tolerance," December 1975.

"Israeli, U.S. and Egyptian Positions on Jerusalem," 21 January 1980.

"Jerusalem: Renewed Focus of Controversy," 29 September 1980.

"The Golan Heights Controversy: Symptom of a Deeper Crisis in U.S.-Israel Relations," 23 December 1981.

"The Golan Heights Controversy as Seen in Israel," 20 January 1982.

"President Reagan's Mideast Peace Initiative," 15 September 1982.

"United States-Saudi Relations: Time for a Reevaluation," March 1983.

"Moscow's Moves in the Mideast," 16 May 1983.

Press Releases

"News from the American Jewish Committee," 23 June 1967; 12 February 1976; 11 May 1979; 16 May 1982.

"News from *Commentary,*" 27 October 1975.

Miscellaneous

"10 Questions and Answers on Lebanon," 6 July 1982.

"Statement on the Middle East." Adopted at the 73rd Annual Meeting, Waldorf Astoria, New York, 13 May 1979.

"Statement on Arab-Israel Peace and the Middle East." Adopted at the 74th Annual Meeting, Waldorf Astoria, New York, 18 May 1980.

Proceedings, 70th Anniversary Meeting, Washington Hilton, Washington, D.C., 13-16 May 1976.

Peters, Joan. "An Exchange of Populations." Reprinted from *Commentary*, August 1976.

American Jewish Congress

Issues of *Congress Monthly*, 1948-1983.

Brochures

"A Program for the American Jewish Congress in 1983."

"America Must Not Quit on Social Justice" (undated).

"Not Charity But Justice: The Story of the American Jewish Congress," (undated).

"Where We Stand: Anti-Semitism." Adopted by the National Governing Council, 1 February 1981.

"Where We Stand: The Evangelical Right." Adopted by the National Governing Council, 6 March 1983.

"Where We Stand: The Mass Media." Adopted by the National Governing Council, 6 March 1983.

"Why Join the American Jewish Congress?" (undated).

Anti-Defamation League

ADL Bulletin, 1948-1983.

Not the Work of a Day: The Story of the Anti-Defamation League of B'nai B'rith, 1965.

"ADL: Purpose and Program," 1966.

"ADL: Campaign '80."

"The Middle East Today: Questions and Answers for Church Leaders," (undated).

"Extremist Groups in the United States: A Curriculum Guide," 1982.

"Television Network Coverage of the War in Lebanon," October 1982.

Campus *Hashara* Network: Letter to "Campus Jewish Leaders," November 1983; letter to "Zionist Activist/Student," 7 November 1983; booklet on anti-Israel organizations and individuals.

"The Arab Propaganda Offensive," November 1975.

"Pro-Arab Propaganda in America: Vehicles and Voices," January 1983.

Memoranda

To: ADL Regional Offices
From: Abraham H. Foxman
Date: 18 September 1970
Subject: Uri Avnery

To: Regional Offices
From: Ken Jacobson
Date: 16 June 1982
Subject: Israel's military action against the PLO

To: Rabbis
From: Interfaith Affairs Committee
Date: 28 June 1982
Subject: Same as 16 June 1982

To: Regional Offices
From: Allen Cohen
Date: 23 July 1982
Subject: Media Distortion—the "Big Lie," and PLO reign of terror in
        Lebanon

To: Regional Directors
From: Theodore Freedman
Date: 5 October 1982
Subject: Unpublished paper critiquing any comparison of Israelis
        with Nazis

To: National Executive Committee
From: Abraham H. Foxman
Date: 12 October 1982
Subject: The Black press and Lebanon

To: Regional Offices
From: Abraham H. Foxman
Date: 10 December 1982
Subject: Israel and the Middle East after Lebanon

To: ADL National Commission
From: Abraham H. Foxman
Date: 20 June 1983
Subject: Big 50 press survey

To: Regional Offices
From: Ken Jacobson
Date: 1 September 1983
Subject: *New York Times* editorial and response

To: Regional Directors
From: Lynn Ianniello
Date: 16 September 1983
Subject: Menahem Begin profile (to be used as Op-Ed piece)

To: Regional Directors
From: Abraham H. Foxman
Date: 5 October 1983
Subject: U.S. Marines in Lebanon

To: Regional Offices
From: Ken Jacobson
Date: 10 October 1983
Subject: *Hanna K.*

Council of Jewish Federations
45th General Assembly Program. Philadelphia, 10-14 November 1976.
48th General Assembly Program. Montreal, 14-18 November 1979.
General Assembly Program 1980.
50th General Assembly Program and 1981 CJF Annual Report.
51st General Assembly Program and 1982 Annual Report.
CJF News Release, 9 September 1980; 10 October 1980; 25 March 1981;
19 September 1983.
What's New in the Federations? July 1983; February 1983.
"Program Ideas/Shroder Award Submissions 1982." Community
Planning Department.
Citrin, Martin E. "Community and Campaign," 8 January 1982.
_____. "Caesarea Process—A Diaspora View," 22 June 1983.

National Jewish Community Relations Advisory Council
*Joint Program Plan for Jewish Community Relations, Guide to Program,
1982-83; 1983-84.*
Planning of the Constituent Organizations (Annual, 1953-1983).

Chapter III

Books

American Jewish Committee, *American Jewish Yearbook.* New York:
1983.
Glick, Edward Bernard. *The Triangular Connection: America, Israel and
American Jews.* London: George Allen and Unwin, 1982.
Jaffe, Eliezer D. *Giving Wisely: The Israel Guide to Non-Profit and
Volunteer Services.* Jerusalem: Koren Publishers, 1982.
Jewish Chronicle Publications. *The Jewish Yearbook.* London: 1982.
Karp, Abraham J. *To Give Life: The UJA in the Shaping of the American
Jewish Community.* New York: Schocken Books, 1981.
Maslow, Will, *The Structure and Functioning of the American Jewish
Community.* New York: Published jointly by the American Jewish Congress
and the American Section of the World Jewish Congress, 1974.

Halperin, Samuel. *The Political World of American Zionism*. Detroit: Wayne State University Press, 1961.

Meir, Golda, *My Life*. New York: G.P. Putnam and Sons, 1975.

Raphael, M.L. (ed.) *Understanding American Jewish Philanthropy*. New York: KTAV Publishers, 1979.

Sachar, Howard M. *A History of Israel From the Rise of Zionism to Our Time*. New York: Alfred A. Knopf, 1982.

Silverberg, Robert. *If I Forget Thee O Jerusalem: American Jews and the State of Israel*. New York: Morrow, 1970.

Weizmann, Chaim. *Trial and Error*. New York: Harper, 1949.

Documents

Annual Reports Filed with the New York State Department of State:
American ORT Federation Inc., Annual Report—Charitable Organization for Year Ended 31 December 1982.

Jewish National Fund, Annual Report—Charitable Organization for Year Ended 30 September 1982.
IRS Form 990:
UJA for years 1978, 1979, 1980 and 1981.

Jewish Agency-American Section for fiscal year 1 April 1982 to 31 March 1983.

Government of Israel. *Laws of the State of Israel*, vol. 14 (5720-1960): Jerusalem.

U.S. Senate. *Activities of Nondiplomatic Representatives of Foreign Principals in the United States*. Hearing before the Committee on Foreign Relations, 88th Congress, First Session, 23 May 1963 (Fulbright hearings).

U.S. Government. Departments of State and Justice. *"U.S. Assistance Provided for Resettling Soviet Refugees."* Report to the Congress by the Comptroller General of the U.S., 20 June 1977.

U.S. International Development Cooperation Agency. "Voluntary Foreign Aid Programs, 1980, 1981." Washington, D.C.: AID, Bureau for Food for Peace and Voluntary Cooperation.

World Zionist Organization-Jewish Agency (Status) Law. *Laws of the State of Israel*, vol. 7 (1952-1953).

Newspapers

Boston Globe:
Walsh, Edward. " 'Levinson Affair' Shakes Labor Party in Israel." 26 February 1984.

Financial Times:
Lennon, David. "Arabs Stage Protests at Israeli Land Grab." 31 March 1983.

Ha'aretz:

Jaffe, Eliezer D. "Philanthropic Politics." 22 June 1983.

Jerusalem Post:

"UJA Donors to Dine at Home with Israelis." 1 February 1982.

"Henry Montor Dies in Jerusalem, Chief Architect of Bond Organization." 16 April 1982.

"UJA Gears Operation for Lebanon Campaign." 15 June 1982.

"$35 m. in Bonds Sold at Begin Luncheon." 20 June 1982.

"JDC Pledges Money for Lebanon Relief." 22 June 1982.

"Jewish Leaders Here on War Mission." 29 June 1982.

"Galilee Settlement Campaign Begins." 24 November 1982.

Friedler, Ya'akov. "High Place in Galilee." 8 April 1983.

Krivine, David. "Ampal is $736m. Foreign Investment Giant." 18 October 1982.

Rubinstein, Aryeh. "Fact-finding Grand Tour." 9 May 1982.

_____. "Unfair to Galilee." 21 November 1982.

_____. "Galilee Settlers Offered Cheap Land for Homes." 24 November 1982.

Siegel, Judy. "Hunting the Big Givers." 6 May 1982.

Jewish Digest:

Bloom, Melvin. "The Good and the Bad About UJA Fundraising." November 1981.

Jewish Telegraphic Agency:

"United Synagogue of America Launches National Park in Galilee." 5 January 1982.

"First UJA Winter President's Mission Raises Almost $3.3 Million for 1982 Campaign." 23 February 1982.

"UJA 'Super Sunday' Raised Over $25.2 Million, Updated Figures Show." 24 Feburary 1982.

"Bush Says Charge of Dual Loyalty is 'Scurrilous'." 6 April 1982.

"Funds Raised for Israel." 21 June 1982.

"JDC Relief Aid for Lebanon." 22 June 1982.

"U.S. Jewish Community Leaders Endorse a 1983 UJA Special Fund." 28 July 1982.

"Report U.S. Jews Responding to Israel's Humanitarian Needs." 19 August 1982.

"JDC Relief Commitment to Lebanon Reached $1 Million." 8 October 1982.

"UJA Gathering in Israel Generates $24 Million in 1983 Pledges." 15 October 1982.

"UJA National 'Yachad' Mission Will Bring 1,500 Young Americans to Israel in April." 15 December 1982.

"UJA Joint Mission to Israel Raises More than $3 Million." 1 July 1983.

Freeman, Kevin. "Modai, Rothberg Promise Bond Leaders Cross-Israel Canal Will Be Completed Within Decade." 14 June 1983.

Friedman, David. "Lautenberg: 'What's Good for Israel is Good for the U.S.' " 25 May 1983.

Kohn, Judith. "Visitors to Lebanon Say Their Experience Contradicted Reports in the American Media." 23 July 1982.

Landau, David. "Special Interview with Robert Loup." 4 May 1982.

_____ . "Jewish Agency Governors Kick Off Campaign with $10 Million." 25 June 1982.

_____ . "Bond Leaders Renew Pledge." 2 July 1982.

_____ . "Begin: War in Lebanon Has Ensured Peace for the Foreseeable Future." 18 October 1982.

_____ . "Focus on Issues: Aid from U.S. Jews to Lebanon After the War Topped $1 Million." 10 November 1982.

Rabi, Yitzhak. "750 U.S. Jewish Leaders Pay Tribute to Israel and Its President." 22 November 1983.

Jewish Week:

Sedan, Gil. "Bond Leaders in Israel." 29 June 1982.

"Hatikvah, Tel Aviv's 'Twinned' Area, in Project Renewal, Needs More Aid." 7 February 1982.

"Campaign Mission to Israel Set for April 22-May 2nd." 14 February 1982.

"Bond Leaders Back from Israel Trip, Pledge All-out Economic Aid in 1982." 14 February 1982.

"Lord & Taylor to Get Israel Peace Medal." 21 February 1982.

"Volunteer Thousands Ring Up More than $2m for 1982 Drive." 21 February 1982.

"First National UJA Palm Beach Dinner Nets $11½ Million for '82." 14 March 1982.

"Prime Minister Begin Urges Israel Bond 'Demonstration of Solidarity' Effort." 4 April 1982.

"April 25 Designated as 'Unity with Israel Day'." 11 April 1982.

"Finally, Hatikvah Slum Turns Around, Real Progress Seen." 11 April 1982.

"New Israel Envoy Tells UJA-Fed Leaders Need for Aid is Unending." 2 May 1982.

"Unique Group Set Up by UJA-Fed Helped Success of Rally." 16 May 1982.

"Project Renewal Seen as One of Greatest Challenges Ever Faced by Israel, World Jewry." 13 June 1982.

"Unprecedented Response Reported for June 18 Israel Bond Luncheon Welcoming Begin after UN Speech." 13 June 1982.

"After 37 Years of Publicizing UJA-Fed Campaign, Smith Retires." 20 June 1982.

"$10 Million Sent by UJA-Fed Drive for 'Urgent Needs'." 20 June 1982.

"Full U.S. Jewry Support for Israel Urged by National UJA: $10 Million UJA-Fed Gift Cited as Example to All." 27 June 1982.

"Bonds Welcome Begin with $35 Million in Cash." 27 June 1982.

"Bond Leaders Pledge in Israel: Will Raise Additional $100 Million in Ten Weeks." 11 July 1982.

"Leaders from All Parts of World to Meet in Israel in October to Show 'Unshaken Unity' of All Jews." 11 July 1982.

"Mobilization '82 Breaks All Records." 16 July 1982.

"Back from Lebanon, Mission Leaders Offer War Background." 20 July 1982.

"Special $50 Million Campaign Launched for Israel." 6 August 1982.

"How to Help, What to Do." 13 August 1982.

"Peres Lauds U.S. Support for Israel; Launches U.S. $200 Million Campaign." 13 August 1982.

"Local Bond Leaders Return from Israel Study Visit." 13 August 1982.

"Justice of Israel's Actions Will Soon Be Apparent, says Elaine Winik." 20 August 1982.

"Controversial Letter Forgotten, Watt Meets UJA Young Leaders." 27 August 1982.

"Secretary Shultz to Open UJA's 1983 Campaign." 3 September 1982.

" 'Terrorism Can Be Defeated,' Sharon Says; Begin Call for Bond Leaders' Economic Aid." 3 September 1982.

"New UJA-Fed Campaign General Chairman. . . . " 10 September 1982.

"U.S. Moral Support Critical, Shamir Tells UJA-Fed Leaders." 15 October 1982.

"Haig Urged Non-Confrontational Stance Between Israel and U.S." 12 November 1982.

"Eight Leaders Get Israel 35th Anniversary Awards." 19 November 1982.

"Surprising Things Ensue—After First Visit to Israel." 10 December 1982.

"Delaware Senator: U.S. Does Not Want Israeli Pullout." 7 October 1983.

Smolar, Boris. " 'Hidden Millionaires' to Be Sought as National UJA Aims for 40% Increase over '82 Results." 16 May 1982.

New York Post:
"Begin Hails Koch's Courage." 19 June 1982.

New York Times:
"Losing a Fare But Coming Out Ahead." 29 December 1983.

Briggs, Kenneth A. "Jewish Groups in U.S. Supporting the Invasion." 23 June 1982.

Feren, James. "Sharon Calls on U.S. Jews for Support." 13 October 1982.

Montgomery, Paul. "'We Need the Cash,' Begin Says at Bonds Lunch." 19 June 1982.

Shipler, David. "A New Focus for U.S. Jews: Israeli Slums." 26 June 1983.

Wall Street Journal:
Levin, Doren P. "Jewish Charities Raise Huge Sums in U.S. but Resistance Grows." 1 April 1983.

Washington Post:
Klaidman, Stephen. "Jewish Appeal: The Power of Charity." 20 February 1972.

Lardner, George, Jr. "Jewish Charity Sets up Tours to Counter 'Distortion' over War." 1 August 1982.

Murphy, Caryle. "U.S. Jewish Leaders Pledge Aid for Israel." 29 August 1982.

Magazines and Journals

American Council for Judaism. *Special Interest Report,* August 1983.

Blitzer, Wolf. "Who Gives, Who Doesn't—and Why?" *Present Tense,* Summer 1983.

Bradlee, Ben, Jr. "Israel's Lobby." *Boston Globe Magazine,* 29 April 1984.

Davis, Uri and Walter Lehn. "And the Fund Still Lives." *Journal of Palestine Studies* 7/4 (Summer 1978).

Elazar, Daniel. "The Jewish Agency and the Jewish People—After Caesarea." *Forum* 42/43 (Winter 1981).

Elliman, Wendy. "Your Dollars and Your Sons." *Forum* 44 (Spring 1982).

Lehn, Walter. "The Jewish National Fund." *Journal of Palestine Studies* 3/4 (Summer 1974).

Nelson, Nancy Jo. "The Zionist Organizational Structure." *Journal of Palestine Studies* 10/1 (Fall 1980).

Rosen, Michael. "The UJA as a Detriment to Jewish Survival." *Israel Horizons* 28/5-6 (May/June 1980).

Urofsky, Melvin I. "American Jewish Leadership," *American Jewish History* 70/4 (June 1981).

Woocher, Jonathan. "The 1980 United Jewish Appeal Young Leadership Cabinet: A Profile." *Forum* 42/43 (Winter 1981).

UJA

"Do's & Don'ts of Personal Solicitation" (undated brochure).
"We Give To Life" pamphlets for the 1983 Regular campaign and Israel Special Fund.
"How your contribution helps" (undated brochure).
UJA Annual Report, May 1981

JDC

"The American Jewish Joint Distribution Committee, Inc."
1982 Annual Report of the American Jewish Joint Distribution Committee, Inc.
"Reports from the Field," 1 August 1983.

JNF

JNF Focus 1/1 (Spring 1979).
Land & Life, Summer 1981.
JNF Illustrated, Winter 1982/1983.
"JNF Fact Sheet."
"The Role of the JNF in the Context of a Middle East Peace Agreement."
H. Freeden. "Jewish National Fund—70 Years of Growth." New York.
"Gift Partnerships for the '80s."
Adler, Esther. "The Little Blue Box."

PEF Israel Endowment Fund

60th Annual Report, 1982.

IBO

Israel Bond *Forum*, March 1983.
"The Corporate Share in Building Israel."
"Israel Bond $1 Billion Economic Development for Peace Loan Issue."
"How You Can Help Yourself and Israel Through a Tax-Sheltered Retirement Plan."
"Your Bond with Israel."
Prospectus brochures: $50,000,000—10 June 1983; $200,000,000—28 February 1983; $1,000,000,000—30 April 1982.

AMPAL

"Share in Israel's Progress, Share in the Earnings."
AMPAL 1982 Annual Report.

PEC Israel Economic Corporation

1982 Annual Report.

NIF
Annual Report 1982.
The New Israel Fund *Bulletin*, August 1983.

Promotional brochures from: American Red Magen David for Israel. American Friends of the Hebrew University, American Friends of Beit Halochem, American ORT Federation, Federated Council of Israel Institutions, American Friends of Haifa University.

Chapter IV

Books

Chomsky, Noam. *The Fateful Triangle: The United States, Israel and the Palestinians.* Boston: South End Press, 1983.

Churba, Joseph. *The Politics of Defeat: America's Decline in the Middle East.* New York: Cyrce Press, 1977.

_____. *Retreat from Freedom.* Introduction by Richard V. Allen. Washington, D.C.: Center for International Security, 1980.

Feuerlicht, Roberta Strauss. *The Fate of the Jews.* New York: Times Books, 1983.

Glick, Edward Bernard. *The Triangular Connection: America, Israel and American Jews.* London: George Allen and Unwin, 1982.

Grose, Peter. *Israel In The Mind of America.* New York: Alfred A. Knopf, 1983.

Howe, Russell Warren and Sarah Hays Trott. *The Power Peddlers.* New York: Doubleday, 1977.

Isaacs, Stephen D. *Jews and American Politics.* Garden City, N.Y.: Doubleday, 1974.

Kenen, Isaiah L. *Israel's Defense Line: Her Friends and Foes in Washington.* Buffalo, N.Y.: Prometheus Books, 1981.

Klutznick, Philip M. *No Easy Answers.* New York: Farrar, Straus, and Giroux, 1961.

Raphael, M. E. (ed.). *Understanding American Jewish Philanthropy.* New York: KTAV Publishers, 1979.

Documents

IRS Form 990:
AIPAC, for fiscal year 1 March 1980 to 28 February 1981 and 1 March 1981 to 28 February 1982.

Conference of Presidents of Major American Jewish Organizations, for fiscal year 1 April 1982 to 31 March 1983.

Jewish Institute for National Security Affairs, for fiscal year 1 November 1980 to 31 October 1982.

AIPAC Quarterly Financial Report, 1980 through 1983 (filed with the Secretary of State and the Clerk of the House of Representatives).

Federal Election Reports, 1983-1984 election cycle. Washington, D.C.

Newspapers

Decatur Herald & Review:
    "U.S. Jews Try to Unseat Paul Findley." 30 March 1982.

Ha'aretz:
    Marcus, Yoel. "United States: The Pro-Israel Lobby on the Offensive."
29 May 1983.

Jerusalem Post:
    "Presidents Conference: Outlaw PLO." 10 June 1982.
    "U.S. Israel Lobbyist on Visit to Israel." 24 November 1982.
    Blitzer, Wolf. "Who Speaks for American Jews?" 2 May 1981.
    _____ . "AWACs Battle Draws Near." 7 June 1981.
    _____ . "Reagan's Link to U.S. Jews." 21 January 1982.
    _____ . "Lawyer/Rabbi May Lead U.S. Jews." 7 June 1982.
    _____ . "U.S. Jewish Leaders Question Reagan Plan." 8 September
1982.
    _____ . "Lessons for a Lobby." 29 October 1982.
    _____ . "U.S. Jews Make Their Mark." 5 November 1982.
    _____ . "Reagan Felt Worried Before Beirut Bomb." 28 October
1983.
    Davis, Leonard J. "Changing Role for U.S. Jews." 16 November 1983.

Jewish Monthly:
    Silverberg, David. "The Quest For Access To the White House."
February 1984.

The Jewish Post and Opinion:
    Letter from Balfour Brickner, 9 February 1983.
    Herschaft, Jean. "18 Rabbis Tell Senators of Opposition to Israel
Policies." 23 March 1983.

Jewish Press:
    Amitay, Morris J. "Report from Washington" column, 18 June 1982
and 3 September 1982.

Jewish Telegraphic Agency:
    Friedman, David. "Squadron: U.S. Jews Have the Obligation to Fight
for Israel." 15 March 1982.
    _____ . "Squadron: Meeting Between Reagan and Six Jewish
Leaders..." 14 April 1982.
    _____ . "Packwood: Term 'Jewish Lobby' Should be Considered a
'Statement of Honor.'" 13 May 1982.
    _____ . "Jewish Leaders Meet State Department Officials..." 14
September 1983.

_____ . "Behind the Headlines Organizing for Political Action." 11 October 1982.

Freeman, Kevin. "Presidents Conference Urges Administration to Understand Need for Israel's Action." 9 June 1982.

_____ . "GOP Group is 'Sounding Board.' " 21 June 1983.

Rabi, Yitzhak. "Special Interview: Berman Sees Presidents Conference as Reflecting Views of American Jewry." 30 June 1982.

Sedan, Gil. "Presidents Conference Leader Denies Split in U.S. Jewish Community Over Israel's Policies." 6 October 1982.

Jewish Week:

"10,000 People Donate to NatPAC to Aid Israel." 29 October 1982.

"New German Chancellor Vows to Strengthen Israel Ties." 19 November 1982.

Kestenbaum, Ray. "Conference of Organizations Urges Reagan to Join Israel in Major Mideast Peace Try." 13 June 1982.

_____ . "Presidents Conference May Be More More Activist, New Chairman Indicates." 11 July 1982.

Long Island Jewish Week:

Ain, Stewart. "Conference Is Place to Debate & Form Consensus." 24 December 1982.

New York Times:

"Jews and Jackson Meet." 18 November 1983.

"Israeli Official Assails U.S. for Not Consulting." 15 February 1984.

"Study Finds Pro-Israeli PACS Active in '84 Races." 16 August 1984.

Churba, Joseph. "Israel's Left vs. American Security Interests" (Letter to the editor). 21 November 1982.

Dine, Thomas A. "America, Be Warm to Israel" (Op-Ed). 23 May 1983.

Gwertzman, Bernard. "Leading Pro-Israel Lobbyist Sees 'A Lot of Value' in Reagan Plan." 7 September 1982.

Phelps, Robert H. "Mideast Lobbies Active in U.S." 6 April 1970.

Weisman, Steven R. "Reagan Aides and Jewish Groups See Less Strain." 10 August 1982.

Village Voice:

Cockburn, Alexander. "Press Clips." 26 October 1982.

Wall Street Journal:

Bialkin, Kenneth J. "PAC Backing for Israel in the U.S." (letter). 22 August 1983.

Fialka, John J. "Pro-Israel Politics . . . " 3 August 1983.

Fialka, John J. and Brooks Jackson. "Jewish PACs Emerge as a

Powerful Force in U.S. Election Races: They Gave $3.6 Million in 1984 and Helped Beat Percy." 26 February 1985.

Washington Post:
    Dine, Thomas A. "Pressuring Israel is Dumb." 13 February 1983.
    Evans, Rowland and Robert Novak. "Israel Lobby's New Offensive." 9 February 1983.

Magazines and Journals

    "Israel's Potent Lobby Faces Biggest Test." *U.S. News and World Report,* 27 March 1978.
        "What Lies Behind the AIPAC Spread?" *The Middle East,* June 1980.
        "Middle East Lobbying." *Congressional Quarterly Weekly Report* 39/34 (22 August 1981).
        "Political Action Committee to Support Israel Formed." *Political Focus* (NAAA) 6/15 (1 August 1983).
        "Will Community Doubts Shake Lobby?" *The Middle East,* September 1983.
        "Pro-Israel PACs Predominate." *The Mideast Observer* 6/19 (1 November 1983).
        "Lobby Activities." *Washington Report on Middle East Affairs,* February 1983; June 1983; November 1983.
        "Political Action Committee to Support Israel Formed." *Political Focus* (NAAA) 6/23 (1 December 1983).
        "ADL Military Mission." *ADL Bulletin,* February 1984.
        American Council for Judaism. *Special Interest Report,* May 1983.
        Amitay, Morris J. "A Field Day for Jewish PACs." *Congress Monthly* 50/4 (June 1983).
        Blitzer, Wolf. "The AIPAC Formula." *Moment* 6/10 (November 1981).
        Brohy, Beth. "Defense Expert Joseph Churba: Carter is Lying." *Forbes,* 27 October 1980.
        Hoechstetter, Sue. "Michael Gale, Jewish Liaison for the White House." *Congress Monthly,* June 1983.
        Lanouette, William J. "The Many Faces of the Jewish Lobby in America." *National Journal,* 13 May 1978.
        Marcus, Yoel, "America's Israel Lobby." *Atlas World Press Review,* June 1978.
        Mathias, Charles McC., Jr. "Ethnic Groups and Foreign Policy." *Foreign Affairs* 59/5 (Summer 1981).
        MEPARC (Middle East Policy and Research Center). *Status Reports,* January 1984.
        Reisman, Roberta Fahn. "Lebanon: A Different View." *ADL Bulletin,* October 1982.
        Rosenfeld, Stephen S. "AIPAC." *Present Tense,* Spring 1983.

Organizational Publications

AIPAC
"Effective Community Action," May 1978.
"Dear Fellow American," February 1982.
"Legislative Update Year End Report 1982."
"Why U.S. Aid To Israel," February 1983.
"Is America For Sale?" March 1983.
"The Campaign to Discredit Israel." *AIPAC Papers on U.S.-Israel Relations,* no. 3, June 1983.
"The Strategic Value of Israel" (memorandum), 6 June 1983.
"Jordan Arms Sale" (memorandum), 7 June 1983.
"Legislative Talking Points for June 14 Lobbying on Hill" (memorandum), 8 June 1983.
"Workshop on Politics." Chicago, 16 October 1983.
"The AIPAC College Guide: A Survey of Political Activism (Campus Survey)" (undated).
"Making More Effective Use of the Student Newspaper." Prepared by The Youth Institute for Peace in the Middle East, distributed by AIPAC.
Unofficial transcripts: September 1982 AIPAC campus workshop in Madison, Wisconsin; June 1983 24th Annual Policy Conference in Washington, D.C.
Rosen, Steven J. "The Strategic Value of Israel." *AIPAC Papers on U.S.-Israel Relations,* no. 1, 1982.
Near East Report, 1970-1983.

Center for International Security
Spotlight on the Americas (undated newsletter). Washington, D.C.

Conference of Presidents of Major American Jewish Organizations
Middle East Memo, 10/1-7 (28 September 1982—28 November 1983).
Report of the Conference of Presidents of Major American Jewish Organizations, for the years ending 31 March 1980, 1981, 1982, 1983.

Jewish Institute for National Security Affairs
Newsletter. June 1977; November 1982; December 1982/January 1983; February 1983; March 1983; April 1983.

Chapter V:

CAMPUS

Books

Chertoff, Mordecai (ed.). *The New Left and the Jews.* New York: Pitman, 1971.

Chomsky, Noam. *Peace in the Middle East?* New York: Vintage Books, 1974.

Howe, Irving and Carl Gershman. *Israel, the Arabs and the Middle East.* New York: Bantam Books, 1972.

Documents

AAAPME Annual Report—Charitable Organization, for year ending 31 August 1982, filed with the New York State Department of State.

Newspapers

Jerusalem Post:

Siegel, Judy. "U.S. Professors Helping Israel's Cause Abroad." 2 January 1974.

Jewish Telegraphic Agency:

"Illinois Mandates Public Disclosure of Gifts to State Universities by Foreign Governments or Persons." 22 November 1983.

New York Times:

Maeroff, Gene I. "Book on Israel Discontinued After Dispute." 21 September 1983.

Winerip, Michael. "The Stony Brook Rift: Racism and Zionism." 2 October 1983.

_____ . "Academic Freedom Tenet Is Tested." 11 October 1983.

Newsday:

D'Antonio, Michael. "Curse on Prejudice Stirs Clash." 5 August 1983.

_____ . "State U Upholds Teacher Linking Zionism, Nazism." 18 August 1983.

_____ "Of Politics and Teachers' Rights." 20 September 1983.

Magazines and Journals

"Fall Propaganda Offensive." *Near East Reports,* 10 September 1982.

"Jewish Academics: New Signs of Life in a 'Disaster Area.' " *Analysis* (Institute for Jewish Policy Planning and Research of the Synagogue Council of America), 15 September 1973.

Washington Report on Middle East Affairs, 8 August 1983.

Baum, Bernard H. "Zionist Influence on American Higher Education." *Issues* (American Council for Judaism), Autumn 1965.

Borosage, Robert, and Peter Weiss. "The Fight Around the Institute for Policy Studies." *Midstream*, February 1981.

Forrest, A.C. "What Happened When I Criticized Israel." *The Observer* (United Church of Canada), 1 April 1968.

Menuhin, Moshe. "The Stifling and Smearing of a Dissenter." *Issues*, Summer 1966.

MESA Bulletin 14/2 (December 1980).

Organizational Publications

AAAPME

Bulletin, September 1975; 1982; 1983.

Special Reports:

Curtis, Michael. "Lebanon: Past, Present, Future." August 1982.

———. "Options for Peace in the Middle East." February 1983.

———. "Academic Freedom and the West Bank." April 1983.

Martin, Lenore C. "Inter-Arab Disputes in the Middle East." March 1983.

Newsletter, March 1983.

Middle East Review (formerly Middle East Information Series).

"An Invitation to Join APPME" (undated promotional brochure).

AJC

Schiff, Gary S. "Middle East Centers at Selected American Universities." Report presented to the American Jewish Committee. AJC, 1981.

Student Zionist Organization

A Program Manual for Zionism on the Campus, 1963.

Other sources include interviews and correspondence with individuals who requested anonymity.

CHURCH

Books

Ahlstrom, Sydney E. *A Religious History of the American People.* New Haven and London: Yale University Press, 1972.

Falwell, Jerry. *Listen, America!* Garden City, N.Y.: Doubleday, 1980.

Handy, Robert T. *A Christian America: Protestant Hopes and Historical Realities.* London, Oxford, New York: Oxford University Press, 1971.

Nijim, Basheer, K. (ed.). *American Church Politics and the Middle East.* Belmont, Mass.: Arab-American University Graduates, 1982.

Rifkin, Jeremy with Ted Howard. *The Emerging Order: God in the Age of Scarcity.* New York: G.P. Putnam Sons, 1979.

Van Impe, Jack. *Israel's Final Holocaust.* Nashville: Thomas Nelson Publishers, 1979.

Wells, David F. and John D. Woodbridge. *The Evangelicals: What They Believe, Who They Are, Where They Are Changing.* Nashville & New York: Abingdon Press, 1975.

Documents

NJCRAC. *Joint Program Plan, 1982-83.*

Newspapers

Bay Area Jewish Newsletter:

Mouly, Ruth. "The Religious Right and the Israel Connection." February 1984.

Jerusalem Post (International Edition):

"Christian 'Embassy' in Capital." 5-11 October 1980.

McWhirter, Joan. "Ambassadors of Friendship." 12-18 October 1980.

Morris, Benny. "Huge Turnout for Jerusalem March." 5-11 October 1980.

New York Times:

Austin, Charles. "U.S. Jews Received by Church Council." 15 August 1982.

Briggs, Kenneth A. "Evangelicals Hear Plea: Politics Now." 24 August 1980.

Cleninden, Dudley. "'Christian New Right's' Rush to Power." 18 August 1980.

Cummings, Judith. "Non-Catholic Christian Schools Growing Fast." 13 April 1983.

Herbers, John. "Ultraconservative Evangelicals a Surging New Force in Politics." 17 August 1980.

Shipler, David K. "Odd Friends: Israel and the Evangelical Protestants." 1 December 1981.

Vecsey, George. "Jewish Groups Shun Churches' Mideast Hearing." 10 February 1980.

Newscope:

"Anti-Israel Charges Contested; Film Guide Revised." 18 May 1979.

Pacific News Service:

Viviano, Frank. "U.S. Fundamentalists Battle Liberation Theology for El Salvador's Refugees." July 1981.

Washington Post:
　　"Evangelicals' Concern for Israel." 1 November 1977.
　　Herbert, Paula. "Evangelicals, Rabbis Join to Back Israel." 26 February 1983.
　　Hyer, Marjorie. "Fundamentalists Join Jews in Strong Support for Israel." 13 November 1982.

Magazines and Journals

　　Beegle, Dewey. "The Promise and the Promised Land." *Sojourners,* March 1977.
　　Boland, John C. "The Unholy Alliance." *Barron's,* 2 June 1980.
　　Davis, James D. "J.W. van der Hoeven Answers Questions About the Embassy." *Charisma,* 8 June 1983.
　　Earl, Howard. "What Your Church Can Do." *Charisma,* 8 June 1983.
　　Feinberg, John S. "Why Christians Should Support Israel." *Fundamentalist Journal,* September 1982.
　　Fitzgerald, Frances. "The New Right & Phyllis Schlafly." *New York Review of Books,* 19 November 1981.
　　Gall, Norman. "When Capitalism and Christianity Clash." *Forbes,* 1 September 1980.
　　Gorfain, Louis. "Pray TV." *New York Magazine,* 6 October 1980.
　　Halsell, Grace. "Americans Waging Zionists' Al-Aqsa War." *Arab News,* 27 April 1983.
　　Hopkins, Joyce. "UMs Disagree on Affairs Briefing." *United Methodist Reporter,* 29 August 1980.
　　Huntington, Deborah. "The Salvation Brokers: Conservative Evangelicals in Central America." *NACLA* 8/1 (January/February 1984).
　　In the Communities. Fall 1982 (AJC publication).
　　Ingram, Kelly. "Christian Zionism." *The Link,* November 1983.
　　_____. "Where the money to blow up Al-Aqsa comes from." *The Middle East* 119 (September 1984).
　　Jackson, Jim. "The Others Left in Protest." *Charisma,* 8 June 1983.
　　Michaelson, Wes. "The Evangelical Right and Israel: What Place for the Arabs?" *ADC Issue Paper,* no. 8 (undated, ca. 1982).
　　_____. "Biblically Buttressed Land Grab." *Sojourners,* July 1979.
　　Mouly, Ruth. "The Religious Right and Zionism." *The Humanist,* May/June 1982.
　　_____. "Zionism in American Premillenarian Fundamentalism." *American Journal of Theology and Philosophy,* September 1983.
　　Verdase, Danae. "Israel, You Are Not Alone." *Charisma,* 8 June 1983.
　　Wigodor, Geoffrey. "Stressing the Fundamentals." *Jerusalem Post Magazine,* 16 April 1982.
　　Williams, Russ. "Heavenly Message, Earthly Designs." *Sojourners,* September 1979.

Zunes, Stephen. "Strange Bedfellows." *The Progressive* 28 (November 1981).

Zweir, Robert and Richard Smith, "Christian Politics and the New Right." *Christian Century,* 8 October 1980.

Organizational Publications

Huntington, Deborah and Ruth Kaplan. "Corporate Ties to the Evangelical Christian Groups." Report to the World Student Federation, 28 August 1980.

Wiley, Thomas. "American Christianity, the Jewish State, and the Arab-Israel Conflict." Occasional Paper Series. Washington, D.C.: Center for Contemporary Arab Studies, Georgetown University, 1983.

International Christian Embassy in Jerusalem
 Shalom—Selah! 1/1 (November 1983); 2/1 (January 1984).
 Director's Letter, October/November 1983.
 Prayer Letter, November/December 1983.
 Prayer Letter, January 1984.
 "International Christian Embassy in Jerusalem," informational brochure.
 Jerusalem Temple Foundation brochures.

Mike Evans Ministries
 Middle East News Alert 1/1 (August 1983).
 Fundraising letter, November 1980.
 Several undated fundraising letters.

George Otis/High Adventure Ministries
 Letter from Saad Haddad, dated 12 June 1983.
 Several undated fundraising letters.
 Other undated publications from High Adventure Ministries.

International Christian Aid
 ICA News, 1982-1983.

NJCRAC
 Joint Program Plan, 1982-1983.

World Vision
 1982 Annual Report.

World Relief (service arm of the National Association of Evangelicals)
 Touching, 1982-1983.

Moral Majority
 Moral Majority Reports, 1979-1984.

America-Israel Friendship League

America-Israel Friendship League, Inc. Annual Report—Charitable Organization, for year ending 31 December 1982, filed with the New York State Department of State.

"New Perspectives." *New York Times,* 22 November 1983.

"Minnesota's Foreign Policy" *ADC Reports*, January-February 1984.

Organizational Publications

America-Israel Friendship League *News* 3/1 (Summer 1983).

AIFL promotional letter, September 1983.

Cohen, Jack S. "Israel and the USA: A Comparison of Two Allies" 1980 (pamphlet).

"The Birth of Two Nations," 1980 (pamphlet).

YIPME

Gershman, Carl. "Letter to the Editor." *Pennsylvania Jewish Life,* July 1974.

Organizational Publications

Flyers: "Genocide: The Arab Goal"; "The Russian Menace to Israel"; "Israeli MIAs, POWs in Syria."

Promotional letter, 25 May 1978.

"Democracy Challenged: Israel and The Struggle for Peace in the Middle East."

"Lebanese Call for International Inquiry," 21 July 1982.

"No to the PLO."

Crossroads (YIPME Bulletin) 13/3 (Fall 1982).

NCLI and ATUCH

Glick, Edward Bernard. *The Triangular Connection: America, Israel and American Jews.* London: George Allen and Unwin, 1982.

Halperin, Samuel. *The Political World of American Zionism.* Detroit: Wayne State University Press, 1961.

AFL-CIO American Federationist, 10 September 1983.

Free Trade Union News (AFL-CIO Department of International Affairs), 1947-1984.

Labor in Palestine (General Federation of Jewish Labour in Eretz Israel), 1947-1948.

Service Employee, May 1983.

"Arthur Moore's visit to Israel highlights ongoing involvement with Bonds." *Jewish Week,* 2 May 1982.

Organizational Publications

Histadrut Bulletin (National Committee for Labor Palestine), June/July 1944.

Histadrut News (National Committee for Labor Palestine, ATUC), 1945-1948.

Histadrut Foto News, 1948-1970.

NCLI organizational brochures.

Shalom, March 1968—Fall 1983.

JLC

Jewish Labor Committee News, Summer 1981; Spring 1982.

Jewish Labor Committee 1982 Biennial Convention Resolutions.

AFSI

IRS Form 990, for fiscal year 1 September to 31 August 1982.

WZO-American Section. Report filed with U.S. Department of Justice, 1982.

"March to Precede Protest Rally in Capital." *Jewish Week*, 21 March 1982.

Goldman, Peter. "Letter to the Editor." *Christian Science Monitor*, 10 January 1983.

Hadar, Leon. "The Sounds of Silence." *Jerusalem Post*, 16 July 1982.

"Statement by Zweibon and Goldman of AFSI." *Jewish Press*, 19 November 1982.

Maurer, Marvin and Peter Goldman, "Lessons of the Lebanese Campaign." *Midstream* (April 1983).

Organizational Publications

"Why AFSI" (undated statement).

Outpost (AFSI newsletter) no. 19 (November 1982); no. 20 (March 1983).

National Council of Young Israel

"Senator Moynihan Guest Speaker at Y.I. Dinner." *Jewish Press*, 29 January 1982.

"Y.I. President to Honor Navan in Jerusalem." *Jewish Press*, 26 February 1982.

"Young Israel Leader Demands Ouster of Weinberger for Conflict of Interest." *Jewish Press*, 26 February 1982.

"Young Israel Leaders Quiz Weinberger at Pentagon Meeting." *Jewish Press*, 11 November 1983.

"Applying Torah Standards Urged." *Jewish Telegraphic Agency*, 21 June 1982.

"Jacobs Cautions on U.S. Nuclear Freeze Plank." *Jewish Week*, 3 December 1982.

"U.S. Jewish Spokesmen Assert that Israelis Are Not to Blame for Massacre." *New York Times* 21 September 1982.

Organizational Publications

"The National Council of Young Israel: Experience, Leadership and Accomplishment in the American Jewish Community Since 1912" (undated brochure, ca. 1982-1983).

"National Council Highlights for 5744" (statement), 1983.

Young Israel Viewpoint, January 1984; February 1984.

Index

Italicized numbers indicate the main discussion of an organization.

Abourezk, James, 70
Abram, Morris B., 73, 74
Abrams, Elliott, 39, 168
Adelman, Lynn, 185
AFL-CIO, 249, 250
Allen, Richard, 193, 207
Allen, Woody, 188
Allied Jewish Campaign, 110-111
Allied Jewish Federation of Denver, 60
Alroy, Gil Carl, 206
Altman, Richard, 160, 161, 183, 188
Ambassadors-for-Peace program, 245
America-Israel Friendship League, (AIFL), *243-246*
American Academic Association for Peace in the Middle East (AAAPME), 224-226
American Associates of Ben-Gurion University, 146
American Christian Palestine Committee, 227
American Committee for Shaare Tzedek Hospital, Jerusalem, 146
American Committee for the Weizmann Institute for Science, 146
American Council for Judaism, 53
American Federation of State, County, and Municipal Employees (AFSCME), 249
American Financial and Development Corporation. *See* State of Israel Bonds Organization
American Friends of Haifa University, 146
American Friends of Peace, 81
American Friends of the Hebrew University, 146
American Friends of the Israel Museum, 146
American Friends of the Jerusalem Academy, 146
American Friends of the Jerusalem Mental Health Center, 146
American Friends of the Midrashia, 146
American Friends of the Rambam Society, 146
American Friends of the Tel Aviv Museum, 146
American Friends of the Tel Aviv University, 146
American Friends Service Committee (AFSC), 53, 70, 90, 99, 253
American Histadrut Cultural Exchange Institute, 250
American-Israel Cultural Foundation, 146

American-Israel Dialogue Symposium, 89
American Israel Public Affairs Committee (AIPAC), 15, 54, 60, 153, 154, *158-182*, 191, 200, 206, 215-218, 241, 255
American-Israeli Lighthouse, 146
American Jewish Alternatives to Zionism, 53
American Jewish Committee (AJC), 49, 50, 59, 60, 63, 64, 69-70, *72-83*, 84, 85, 90-92, 110, 159, 171, 191, 192, 230-233, 267
American Jewish Congress (AJCongress), 49, 59, 63, 64, 69-70, 72, *84-92*, 159, 221, 222, 255, 269, 270
American Jewish Joint Distribution Committee, 110-112, 114, 115, 119, *128-129*
American Jewish Relief Committee, 110, 128
American Jewish Yearbook, 82
American Mizrachi Women, 191
American ORT Federation, 129, 146
American Physicians Fellowship for Medicine in Israel, 146
American Professors for Peace in the Middle East, (APPME), 218, 221-222, *223-227*
American Red Magen David for Israel, 146
American Sephardi Federation, 30
American Technicon Society, 146
American Trade Union Council for Histadrut (ATUC), 250, *251-252*
American Trade Union Council for Labor Israel, 191
American Zionist Council (AZC), 20, 158, 191
American Zionist Emergency Council, 227
American Zionist Federation (AZF), 15, 18, 26, *29-33*, 43, 191, 224
American Zionist Fund, 39
American Zionist Youth Council, 213
American Zionist Youth Foundation, 30, 32
Americans for a Safe Israel (AFSI), 228, *253-255*
Americans for Better Citizenship, 190
Americans for Better Congress (ABC), 190
Americans for Good Government, 190
AMIT, 257
Amitay, Morris, 159-160, 167, 168, 178, 183, 184
AMPAL-American Israel Corporation, *142*
Anti-Defamation League of B'nai B'rith (ADL), 49, 50, 59, 60, 63, 69-70, 75, 85, 90-91, *93-103*, 171, 187, 191, 205-206, 219, 230, 232
Anti-Semitism, 53, 67, 69, 78-79, 93-94, 97
Appeal for Human Relations, 75
Arab American Anti-Discrimination Committee, 227
Arafat, Yasir, 186, 234, 259
Arens, Moshe, 61, 124, 193
Arizona Politically Interested Citizens, 190
Asher, Robert, 162, 183
Association for the Welfare of Soldiers, 136
Association of Americans and Canadians in

Israel, 136
Association of Parents of American Israelis, 30
Association of Reform Zionists of America
    (ARZA), *42-44,* 242
AuCoin, Les, 185
Ault, James, 231
Avishai, Bernard, 80
Avner, Gershon, 83
Avnery, Uri, 99-100

Balaban, Barney, 166
BALPAC Political Action Committee, 190
Bank Hapoalim, 142
Banki, Judith, 230, 231
Bar Elan, David, 203
Bar Ilan University in Israel, 146
Barrett, William, 167
Bay Area Citizens PAC (BACPAC), 190
Bayh, Birch, 178
BAYPAC, 190
Beame, Abe, 124
Becker, Newton, CPA Review Course
    Philanthropic Fund, 225
Begin, Menachem, 61, 102, 109, 125, 133, 139,
    169, 193-196, 202, 239
Ben-Gurion, David, 17, 74, 137
Bentsen, Lloyd, 178
Berger, Elmer, 53
Berkowitz, William, 131
Berman, Howard, 169, 173
Berman, Jay, 168, 178
Berman, Julius, 192, 193, 196, 197, 200, 202
Bernstein, Irving, 118
Bernstein, Philip, 160
Bialkin, Kenneth, 187, 192
Biden, Hecht, 168
Biden, Joseph, 36
Billings, Robert, 237, 238
Bingaman, Jeff, 186
Bingham, Jonathan, 168
Blaustein, Edward J., 218
Blitzer, Wolf, 181, 199
Bloomfield, Douglas, 160
B'nai B'rith, 93, 159, 191, 213. *See also* Anti-
    Defamation League of B'nai B'rith
B'nai B'rith Women, 93, 191
B'nai Zion, 191
Bond, James D., 168
Bookbinder, Hyman, 55, 76, 77
Boone, Pat, 240
Boschwitz, Rudy, 156, 168, 205
Brandeis, Louis, 38, 72, 84, 126, 135
Breger, Marshall, 161
Breira, 53, 81, 228, 253
Brett, Devol, 205
Brickner, Balfour, 197-198
Bridges for Peace, 236

Bright, Bill, 238
Bronfman, Edgar, 242, 254
Brown, George, 203
Bruner Foundation, 225
Bruum, Kristeen, 247
Bryen, Stephen, 167, 203
Bund, 99
Burdick, Quentin, 186
Burke, Kelly H., 205
Burton, Phillip, 185
Bush, George, 120, 193, 196
Business Roundtable, 91
Byrd, Robert, 186, 201

Caesarea Conference, 21-22
Camp Tel Yehuda, 37
Campus activities, 213-227
Campus Crusade for Christ, 238
Capital PAC (CAPPAC), 190
Capucci, Hilarion, 234
Carey, Gerald J., 206
Carey, Richard E., 206
Carnegie Commission Study on Higher
    Education, 213-214
Carter, Jimmy, 194
Catholic Near East Welfare Association, 233
Catholics, 233-234
Celler, Emmanuel, 167
Center Conference of American Rabbis, 191
Center for International Security (CIS), 206
Chicagoans for a Better Congress, 190
Chomsky, Noam, 53, 90
Churba, Joseph, 206, 207
Church League of America, 238
Church-related activities,
    Catholics, 233-234
    evangelicals, 179, 234-242
    mainline Protestants, 227-233
Citizens Concerned for the National
    Interest, 186, 190
Citizens Organized PAC, 187, 190
Citrin, Martin, 57
Cleveland Federation Israel Task Force, 59
Cocklin, Robert, 206
Cohen, Abba, 101
Cohen, Geula, 239
Cohen, Richard, 192
Commentary, 79-81
Commission on Law and Social Action, 85
Commission on Social Action of Reform
    Judaism, 242
Committee for "18," 190
Community organizations, 49-55
    American Jewish Committee, 49, 50, 59, 60,
        63, 64, 69-70, *72-83,* 84, 85, 90-92, 110,
        159, 171, 191, 192, 230-233, 267
    American Jewish Congress, 49, 59, 63, 64,

69-70, 72, 73, *84-92*, 159, 221, 222, 255, 269, 270
Anti-Defamation League of B'nai B'rith, 49, 50, 59, 60, 63, 69-70, 75, 85, 90-91, *93-103*, 171, 187, 191, 205-206, 219, 230, 232
Council of Jewish Federations, 49, 50, *56-62*, 69-70, 75, 95, 111, 114, 119, 192
National Jewish Community Relations Advisory Council, 49, 51, 52, 60, *63-71*, 202, 241-242
Community Relations Committees (CRCs), 63-65
Conference of Presidents of Major American Jewish Organizations, 15, 43, 54, 76, 90, 153, 171, *191-202*
Congressional Action Committee of Texas, 190
Connecticut Good Government PAC, 190
Council of Jewish Federations (CJF), 49, 50, *56-62*, 69-70, 75, 95, 111, 114, 119, 192
Council of the Great City Schools, 245
Covenant of 1954, 19-20
Cultural Center for Youth, Jerusalem, 245
Cummings, Ted, 199
Cuomo, Mario, 219
Curtis, Michael, 226
Cutler, Lynn, 176

Daniels, Mitchell, 172, 176
Daughters of Zion Study Circle, 34
Davis, Donald, 206
Davis, Ken, 168
Davis, Leonard, 160, 161, 162, 181
Day, Warren, 232
DeConcini, Dennis, 186, 221
Decter, Moshe, 181
Defense organizations, 49. *See also* Community organizations
Delaware Valley PAC, 190
Department of Agriculture, U.S., 129
Department of Commerce, U.S., 91
Department of Education, U.S., 221
Department of Health and Human Services, U.S., 58
Department of Justice, U.S., 20, 26
Desert Caucus, 190
Dick, Bess, 167
Dillar, Barry, 188
Dine, Thomas A., 154, 163, 164, 167, 168, 171 172, 182
Dinitz, Simcha, 77
Dixon, Julian, 179
Dodd, Christopher, 168
Douglas, Paul H., 166
Downey, Thomas J., 177
Dowty, Alan, 226
Dube, Ernest, 218-220
Dulzin, Leon Arieh, 21

Durbin, Dick, 185, 186
Durenberger, David, 168, 186, 201
Dworkin, Susan, 181
Dymally, Mervyn, 176

Eban, Abba, 124, 128
Edelstein, Leo, 116
Ehrmans, Fred, 258
Eisenhower, Dwight, 94
Elazar, Daniel, 269
Elon, Amos, 80
Emergency Advisory Committee on Community Relations in the Middle East, 59
Emergency Committee for Zionist Affairs, 29
Emunah Women of America, 191, 257
Energy Information Service, 82
Enlarged Jewish Agency. *See* Jewish Agency
Epstein, Benjamin, 97
Evangelical Right, 86
Evangelicals, 234-242
Evangelicals United for Zion, 236
Evans, Mike, 236-237

Falwell, Jerry, 236, 238
Fascell, Dante, 184, 185
Federated Council of Israel Institutions, 146
Federation of American Zionists, 38
Federations, 49, 50. *See also* Community organizations
Fellowship of Reconciliation, 99
Fenwick, Millicent, 194
Fenyvesi, Charles, 181
Fernea, Elizabeth, 101
Findley, Paul, 185-187
Fine, Sidney, 167
Fisher, Max M., 20, 74, 162, 199, 200
Flacks, Paul, 39-40
Florida Congressional Committee, 190
Ford, Carl, 168
Ford, Gerald, 77
Foreign Affairs Department Background Memoranda, 82
Foreign Agents Registration Act of 1938, 20, 26
Forster, Arnold, 97
Fox, Richard, 199, 200
Foxman, Abraham, 97, 99, 102
Frank, Barney, 168
Frankfurter, Felix, 84
Freedom of Information Act, 91
Friedman, Bernard, 168
Friedman, Howard I., 74
Friends of Democracy PAC, 190
Friends of the Rothschild University Hospital, 146
Frost, Martin, 185
Fugate, Tom, 167

Fund for Higher Education, 146
Fundamentalist Christians. *See* Evangelicals
Funding organizations, 109-113
  American Jewish Joint Distribution
    Committee, 110-112, 114, 115, 119,
    128-129
  AMPAL-American Israel Corporation, *142*
  Jewish National Fund, 30, 36, 112, 121,
    130-134, 191
  New Israel Fund, *144-145*
  PEC-Israel Economic Corporation, 112, *143*
  PEF Israel Endowment Fund, 112, *135-136*
  State of Israel Bonds Organization, 109, 112,
    137-141
  United Israel Appeal, 20, 21, 23-25, 57, 112,
    114, 119, *126-127*
  United Jewish Appeal, 20-21, 24, 25, 57, 111,
    112, *114-125,* 126, 128, 129, 137, 222

Gale, Michael, 160, 161
Gavras, Costa, 101
Gejdenson, Sam, 184, 185
Georgetown University Center for Strategic
  and International Studies, 206
Gershman, Carl, 81, 247
Gervasi, Frank, 206
Gibel, Inge, 231, 233
Gilman, Benjamin, 168
Glazer, Nathan, 80
Goldberg, Arthur J., 74
Goldin, Harrison, 257
Goldman, Peter, 253, 254
Goldmann, Nahum, 191, 192
Goldmuntz, Lawrence, 82
Goott, Amy, 180, 182
Gottesman, Lois, 83
Gould, Don, 121
Gouletas-Carey, Evangeline, 134
Government Action Committee, 190
Graham, Daniel O., 206
Greenberg, Martin, 226
Gronich, Fred, 160
Groisser, Philip L., 226
Gruen, George E., 82, 83

Hadassah (Women's Zionist Organization of
  America), 16, 29, *34-37,* 49, 63, 159, 191
Hadassah Medical Relief Association, 35
Hadassah University Hospital, 35
Haddad, Saad, 240, 241
Hagler, Isaac, 259
Haig, Alexander, 125, 193
Hailes, Edward, 179
Hamlisch, Marvin M., 124
Hanna K., 101
Hauser, Rita, 188, 203
Hebrew Immigrant Aid Society (HIAS), 58,
  115

Hebrew University, Jerusalem, 135
Hebrew University-Hadassah Medical Schoo
  Jerusalem, 35
Hebrew University-Technion Joint
  Maintenance Appeal, 146
Hecht, Chic, 168, 184, 186
Heinz, John, 186
Hellman, Yehuda, 192, 194
Herrera, Susan, 244
Hertzberg, Arthur, 80, 87
Herut Zionists, 191
Herzl, Theodor, Foundation, 27
Herzl, Theodor, Institute, 27, 80
Herzl Press, 27
Herzog, Chaim, 61, 77, 193
High Adventure Ministries, 240-241
Hillel Foundation, 58, 213
Himmelfarb, Milton, 80, 82
Histadrut, 249
Histadrut Assistance Fund, 250
Hoffman, Philip E., 74
"Hope for Life" film, 231-232
Howard, M. William, 232
Hudson Valley PAC, 190
Humphrey, Hubert, 77
Humphrey, Hubert H., III, 244
Hurwitz, Harry, 39

In the Communities, 81-82
Institute for Israel Studies, 41
Institute for Religion and Democracy, 228
Institute of Human Relations, 74, 75
Institute on American Jewish-Israeli
  Relations, 79
Institutionally-specific funding
  organizations, *146*
International Association of Machinists
  (IAM), 249
International Association of Reform Zionist
  Organizations (ARZENU), 43
International Christian Embassy in Jerusalem
  (ICEJ), 235-236, 242
International Conference of Mayors, 88-89
Isaac, Rael Jean, 228, 253-255
Israel Activities for the National Council, 259
Israel Aliyah Center, 32
Israel Bonds Organization. *See* State of Israel
  Bonds Organization
Israel Histadrut Campaign, 250
Israel Histadrut Foundation, 250
Israel Land Administration, 132
Israel Music Foundation, 146
Israel Seminar Foundation, 32
Israel support work
  America-Israel Friendship League, 244-246
  American Israel Public Affairs
    Committee, 163-166

American Jewish Committee, 75-79
American Jewish Congress, 86-90
American Professors for Peace in the
   Middle East, 224-225
American Zionist Federation, 31-33
Americans for a Safe Israel, 253-254
Anti-Defamation League, 95-99, 102-103
Association of Reform Zionists of
   America, 44
Community organizations, 50-55
Council of Jewish Federations, 59-62
Hadassah, 35-37
National Council of Young Israel, 258-259
National Jewish Community Relations
   Advisory Council, 64-71
United Jewish Appeal, 116-122
World Zionist Organization-American
   Section, 27
Youth Institute for Peace in the Middle
   East, 247-248
Zionist Organization of America, 39-41

Jackson, Henry, 168, 178, 186, 201, 204
Jackson, Jesse, 179
Jacobs, Harold, 257-258, 260
Jacobson, Ken, 103
Jaffe, Eliezer D., 144
Javits, Jacob, 167, 178
Jerusalem Program, 15, 17-18, 22
Jewish Agency (JA), 19-23, 36, 56-57, 110, 114
Jewish Agency-American Section, 20, 21, 24,
   25, 191
Jewish Agency for Israel, 20, 24-25, 126, 127, 132
Jewish Community Council of Greater
   Washington, 40
Jewish Education Service of North America, 58
Jewish Institute for National Security Affairs
   (JINSA), 153, 203-207
Jewish Labor Committee (JLC), 49, 63, 191,
   249-250
Jewish National Fund (JNF) (Keren Kayemeth
   LeIsrael), 30, 36, 112, 121, 130-134, 191
Jewish Reconstructionist Foundation, 191
Jewish War Veterans, 49, 63, 159, 191, 257
Johnson, Lyndon, 94
Joint Action Committee for Political
   Affairs, 190
Joint CJF/UJA/Jewish Welfare Board Task
   Force on Television, 58
Joint Defense Appeal, 95
Joint Program for Jewish Community
   Relations, 64-69
Jones, Tracey, 229, 230
Josephson, Marvin, 162, 183, 188-189

Kagedon, Allen L., 83
Kahane, Meir, 258

Kallen, Horace Meyer, 84
Kampelman, Max, 167, 203, 205, 206
Kane, Irving, 160
Kanovsky, Eliyahu, 82
Kasten, Robert, 168, 174
Keating, Kenneth, 167
Keegan, George F., Jr., 206
Kelly, J.B., 206
Kemp, Jack, 184, 205
Kenen, Isaiah (Si), 158-161, 166, 167, 171, 176,
   181, 205
Kenen, Peter B., 82
Kennedy, Edward, 168, 186
Kennedy, John F., 94
Keren Hayesod (Foundation Fund), 20, 21, 24,
   25, 114, 126, 127
Keren-Or, 146
Kessler, Jonathan, 215-217
Keyserling, Billy, 172-173
Kfar Silver Campus, Ashkelon, 41
Kibbutz Yahel, 44
Kinnard, Harry, 206
Kintner, William R., 206
Kirkpatrick, Jeane J., 36, 81, 193
Klein, George, 188, 199, 200
Koffler, Henry, 221
Kohl, Helmut, 194
Kollek, Teddy, 158
Kotlowitz, Rafael, 25
Kraft, Michael, 167
Kraus, Adolf, 72
Krieger, Douglas, 239
Kutail, Yigal, 254

Labor Zionist Alliance, 191
Labor Zionist Organization of America, 191
Ladd, Everett C., Jr., 213
Lakeland, Albert, 167
Lantos, Tom, 169, 184, 185, 194
Laqueur, Walter, 203, 205, 206
Large City Budgeting Conference
   (LCBC), 58, 64, 75, 95
Larson, Doyle, 206
Lautenberg, Frank, 168, 186
League for Conservative Judaism, 192
Ledeen, Michael, 205, 206
Lehman, John, 168
Lehman, Ronald, 205
Lesser, Allen, 181
Levine, Mel, 169, 173
Levy, David, 194
Lewis, Ann Frank, 172
Lipset, Martin, 226
Lipset, Seymour M., 213
Livingston, Sigmund, 93
Long, Clarence, 185
Loup, Robert, 118, 124

Luttwak, Edward, 81

Maass, Richard, 74
McArthur, F. Stephan, 160, 161, 179
McAteer, Edward, 237, 238
McCall, Richard, 168
McClean, Robert, 232
McHugh, Matthew, 185
MacIver, Robert, 63-64
Mack, Julian W., 84
McNulty, Jim, 221
Mainline Protestant churches, 227-233
Mann, Theodore, 201
Marburger, John, 219, 220
Marshall, Louis, 110
Maryles, Matthew J., 258
Masada, 41
Maslow, Will, 91
Massachusetts Congressional Campaign
    Committee, 190
Mathias, Charles, 175
Matsunaga, Spark, 186
Maynard, Edwin, 231
Meir, Golda, 111-112, 233
MER Special Reports, 226
Metzenbaum, Howard, 168, 186
Middle East centers, 220-221
"Middle East Policy Statement," NCC, 229-230
Middle East Review, 224-226
Mike Evans Ministries, 236
Millenson, Roy, 167
Miller, Thomas H., 206
Milson, Menachem, 81
Ministry of Education and Culture, Israeli, 245
Ministry of Labor, Israeli, 36
Mishab Housing Construction and
    Development Co., 260
Mississippians for Responsive Government
    PAC, 190
Mitchell, George, 184, 186
Mittleman, Sheba, 83
Mitzpeh Har Chalutz, 44
Mizrachi, 16, 29, 191
Mondale, Walter, 139, 178
Monthly Dinner Club, 41
Montor, Henry, 137
Moral Majority, 237
Morgenthau, Henry, Jr., 137
Morris, Robert, 206
Morse, Wayne, 166
Moshowitz, Israel, 219
Moynihan, Daniel, 168, 186
Muravchik, Emanuel, 250
Murphy, Richard, 195

NAACP, 179
National Academic Committee of Jewish
    Professors, 222

National Action Committee, 190
National Association of Arab Americans, 91
National Bipartisan PAC, 183, 190
National Christian Leadershp Conference for
    Israel (NCLCI), 245
National Committee for Labor Israel
    (NCLI), 191, *249-250*, 251
National Community Relations Advisory
    Committee, 191
National Coordinating Committee Fund, 111
National Council of Churches of Christ in the
    United States (NCC), 53, 90, 98, 227-233
National Council of Jewish Women, 49, 63,
    159, 191
National Council of Young Israel (NCYI), 191,
    256-260
National Endowment for the Humanities
    (NEH), 101-102
National Federation of Temple
    Sisterhoods, 191
National Inter-Religious Task Force on Soviet
    Jewry, 40
National Jewish Community Relations
    Advisory Council (NJCRAC), 49, 51, 52,
    59, 60, *63-71*, 202, 241-242
National Jewish Welfare Board, 191
National PAC, 190
National Political Action Committee
    (NatPAC), 183, 184, 188-189
National Survey of American Jews, 1983,
    267-268, 270
National Women's League for Conservative
    Judaism, 49, 63
Navon, Yitzhak, 260
Near East Report (NER), 181
Neil, Sylvia, 221
Nelson, William R., 206
Nesher, Aryeh, 124
Neuberger, Egon, 218, 219
New Israel Fund (NIF), 144-145
New Jewish Agenda (NJA), 40, 101
New York Association for New Americans
    (NYANA), 115
New York Jewish Community Relations
    Council, 202
New York Office of Charities Registration, 26
News and Views, 81-82
News from the Committee, 83
Newsletter, 204, 205
Niebuhr, Reinhold, 227
NJCRAC Israel Task Force, 68-70, 78
North American Aliyah Movement, 32
North American Jewish Youth Council, 191
Novick, Ivan, 40, 205

O'Brien, William V., 206
Ochs, Adolph, 93

326

Ockenden, Stephen, 168
Office of Education, U.S., 245
Organization for Rehabilitation through
    Training (ORT), 129
Orthodox Central Committee for the Relief of
    Jews, 128
Otis, George, 240
O'Toole, Donald, 167

Packwood, Robert, 156, 168, 244
Palestine Congress of North America, 91
Palestine Information Office, 91
Patt, Gideon, 39
Patt, Raymond, 31-32
Patton, George S., 205
PEC-Israel Economic Corporation, 112, *143*
PEF Israel Endowment Fund, 112, *135-136*
Peled, Matityahu, 70
People-to-People program, 245
People's Relief Committee, 128
Perach, Yehuda, 239
Peretz, Martin, 188
Perle, Richard, 167
Perlmutter, Nathan, 97
Perlstein, Lewis M., 205
Picon, Molly, 124
Pincus, Louis, 20
Pioneer Women, 191
Pipes, Richard, 81
Poale Zion, 16, 29
Podhoretz, Norman, 79, 81, 203
Political action committees (PACs), 153, 169,
    183-190
Pope John Paul II, 234
Pope Paul VI, 233
Present Tense, 81
Presidents Conference. *See* Conference of
    Presidents of Major American Jewish
    Organizations
Pro-Israel lobby, 153-157
  American Israel Public Affairs Committee,
    15, 54, 60, 153, 154, *158-182*, 191, 200,
    206, 215-218, 241, 255
  Conference of Presidents of Major American
    Jewish Organizations, 15, 43, 54, 76, 90,
    153, 171, *191-202*
  internationally-specific funding
    organizations, *145-146*
  Jewish Institute for National Security
    Affairs, 153, *203-207*
  National Political Action Committee, 183,
    184, *188-189*
  political action committees, 153, 169, *183-190*
Project Energy Independence, 40
Project Interchange, 244-245
Project Renewal, 118
Protestants

evangelical, 234-242
  mainline, 227-233
Publications
  America-Israel Friendship League, 245, 246
  America-Israel Public Affairs
    Committee, 180-182
  American Jewish Committee, 79-83
  American Jewish Congress, 86, 91
  American Professors for Peace in the
    Middle East, 226-227
  American Zionist Federation, 33
  Anti-Defamation League, 103
  Conference of Presidents of Major American
    Jewish Organizations, 202
  Jewish Institute for National Security
    Affairs, 205
  World Zionist Organization-American
    Section, 27
  Zionist Organization of America, 41

Rabbinical Assembly, 191
Rabbinical Council of America, 191
Rabin, Yitzhak, 60
Rabinowitz, Stanley, 203
Rashish, Myer, 168
Reagan, Ronald, 94, 123, 193, 194, 199
Reconstitution Agreement of 1971, 20-21
Redgrave, Vanessa, 90
Reisenhuver, Terry, 239
Religious Roundtable, 237-238
Ribicoff, Abraham, 167, 177, 178
Robertson, Pat, 236, 238
Robinson, David, 187
Robison, James, 236
Rose-Avila, Len, 244
Rosen, Steven, 160
Rosenbaum, Aaron, 160, 181
Rosenberg, M.J., 181
Rosenne, Meir, 36
Rosenthal, Benjamin, 168
Rosenthal, Joel, 219
Ross, Alexander I., 242
Rostow, Eugene V., 203, 205
Roth, William, 186
Rothberg, Sam, 139
Roundtable PAC, 190
Rudin, James, 231
Rutgers University, 218

St. George, William, 206
St. Louisans for Better Government, 190
Samuels, Shimon, 101
San Franciscans for Good Government, 190
Sanders, Edward, 160, 205
Sarbanes, Paul, 186
Sartawi, Issam, 70
Sasser, James, 184, 186

Schiff, Gary S., 78
Schindler, Alexander M., 22, 43, 98-99, 242
Schmidt, Helmut, 194
Schwenk, Adolph, 206
Scoville, Sheila, 220-221
Seltzer, Arthur, 219
Shapira, Hermann, 130
Sharon, Ariel, 25, 125, 139, 193, 257-258
Sharon, Natan, 71
Sharrett, Moshe, 158
Shultz, George, 61, 124, 193-195
Siegel, Mark, 183
Siegman, Henry, 87
Silber, Tina, 181
Silberman, Morton, 162
Siljander, Mark, 173
Silver, Abba Hillel, 29, 41, 128
Simon, Merrill, 206, 239
Sisco, Joseph, 59, 77
Skelton, Ike, 185
Smith, Larry, 168, 169, 173, 174
Smith, Philip W., 206
Solarz, Stephen, 168
South Carolinians for Representative
    Government, 190
Soviet Jewish Resettlement Project, 58
Sparkman, John, 166
Special focus organizations, 243
    America-Israel Friendship League, 243-246
    American Trade Union Council for
        Histadrut, 250, 251-252
    Americans for a Safe Israel, 228, 253-255
    National Committee for Labor Israel, 191,
        249-250, 251
    National Council of Young Israel, 191,
        256-260
    Youth Institute for Peace in the Middle
        East, 247-248
Specter, Arlen, 39
Spiegel, Albert, 199-201
Spiegel, Fredelle Z., 226
Squadron, Howard, 90, 192, 194, 196, 200
State of Israel Bonds Organization (IBO), 109,
    112, 137-141
State University of New York at Stony Brook,
    218-220
State University of New York Press, 226
Stern, Saul I., 204
Sternstein, Joseph, 31
Stevenson, Adlai, 177
Stoker, Jerry, 241
Stone, Richard, 178
Straus, Richard, 160, 161
Student Zionist Organization (SZO), 213
Survivalism, 267-269
Swig, Melvin M., 187
Synagogue Council of America, 51, 58

Szold, Henrietta, 34

Talmadge, Herman, 178
Tannenbaum, Bernice S., 20
Tannenbaum, Marc, 230, 231
Target area organizations. See Campus
    activities; Church-related activities;
    Special focus organizations
Task Force on Federation-Synagogue
    Relations, CJF, 58
TAV, 236
Temple Mount Foundation, 239
Temple Mount Fund Society, 236
Tigay, Alan, 181
Tighe, Eugene, 205
Tillich, Paul, 227
Timerman, Jacobo, 90
To Protect Our Heritage, 190
Torczyner, Jacques, 205
Torricelli, Robert, 173
Treasury Department, U.S., 91
Trends Analysis Report, 83
Troen, Selwyn, 218
Truman, Harry, 94
Tucker, Robert W., 81
Tucson Jewish Community Council (TJCC),
    220-221

UJA-Federation campaign, 59, 70, 109, 114-116,
    122-125. See also United Jewish Appeal
Union of American Hebrew Congregations
    (UAHC), 42, 44, 49, 58, 63, 94, 191, 255
Union of Orthodox Jewish Congregations, 49,
    63, 191, 255
United Auto Workers, 249
United Charity Institutions of Jerusalem, 146
United Israel Appeal (UIA), 20, 21, 23-25, 57,
    112, 114, 119, 126-127
United Jewish Appeal (UJA), 20-21, 24, 25, 57,
    111, 112, 114-125, 126, 128, 129, 137, 222
United Jewish Fund, 50, 95
United Nations, 233-234, 259
United Nations Office of the United Methodist
    Church (UNOUM), 232
United Palestine Appeal (UPA), 110, 111, 126,
    128, 129
U.S. Catholics, 233-234
United States Committee Sports for Israel, 146
United Synagogue of America, 63, 134, 191
University of Arizona, 220-221
Urbina, Jorge, 36

Van Cleave, Michelle, 168
Van Cleave, William R., 206
Van Impe, Jack, 236
Vatican, 233-234
Viguerie, Richard, 137, 138

Vogt, John, 205

Waldeman, Eliezer, 254
Wall, Harry, 102
Warburg, Felix M., 110
Warner, Volney F., 206
Washington PAC, 190
Watt, James, 77
Wattenberg, Ben, 168
Waxman, Henry, 168
Weicker, Lowell, 156, 184, 186
Weinberg, Barbara, 186-187
Weinberg, Lawrence, 160, 162, 183, 186-187, 200
Weinberger, Caspar, 77, 193, 196, 257
Weisner, Maurice P., 206
Weiss, Avraham, 253
Weizmann, Chaim, 29, 110, 126
Welfare funds. See Community organizations;
    Federations
Wheeler, Winslow, 178
Whitman, Jules, 231
Wilson, Charles, 169
Winter, Elmer L., 74
Wise, Isaac, 42
Wise, Louise Waterman, Youth Hostel, 88
Wise, Stephen S., 72, 84, 85
Wishner, Maynard, 74
Wolfensohn, James, 188
Wollack, Ken, 160, 161
Women Under Siege, 101
Women's American Organization for
    Rehabilitation through Training, 49, 63,
    192
Women's League for Israel, 30, 146
Women's Social Service for Israel, 146
Women's Zionist Organization of America. *See*
    Hadassah
Woocher, Jonathan, 268, 270
Workmen's Circle, 192
World Confederation of United Zionists
    (WCUZ), 15, 22, 26, 35
World Council of Churches, 228
World Jewish Congress-North American
    Section, 43
World Union for Progressive Judaism, 43
World Zionist Organization (WZO), 15, 16,
    19-25, 43, 60, 126, 130
World Zionist Organization-American
    Section, *26-28,* 40, 192
Wouk, Herman, 163
Wycliffe Bible Translators, 238

Ya'acobi, Gad, 132
Yankelovich, Skelly and White, Inc., 78, 122
Yanowitz, Bennett, 51, 52, 68, 69, 71
Yates, Sidney, 168, 184, 185
Yoh, Bernard, 206

Youdovin, Ira, 242
Young Israel. *See* National Council of Young
    Israel
Young Judea Camps, 36, 37
Youngstown PAC, 190
Youth Aliyah, 36
Youth Committee for Peace and Democracy
    in the Middle East. *See* Youth Institute for
    Peace in the Middle East (YIPME), *247-248*

Zablocki, Clement, 185
Zacks, Gordon, 199, 200
Zionism, 8, 15-18, 85
Zionist Academic Council, 33
Zionist Information News Service, 40
Zionist Organization of America (ZOA), 16,
    17, 29, *38-41,* 191
Zionist organizations, 15-18
    American Zionist Federation, 15, 18, 26,
        29-33, 43, 191, 224
    Association of Reform Zionists of America,
        42-44, 242
    Hadassah, 16, 29, *34-37,* 49, 63, 159, 191
    Jewish Agency, *19-23,* 36, 56-57, 110, 114
    Jewish Agency for Israel, 20, *24-25,* 126,
        127, 132
    World Zionist Organization, 15, 16, *19-25,*
        43, 60, 126, 130
    World Zionist Organization-American
        Section, *26-28,* 40, 192
Zionist Student Organization, 213
ZOA House, Tel Aviv, 41
Zumwalt, Elmo, 76, 205, 207
Zweibon, Herbert, 253, 254

329

About the author

Lee O'Brien was born and raised in New York City. She was educated at the University of California, Berkeley, and Georgetown University. At present she is a writer and lives in Washington, D.C.

American Jewish Organizations and Israel
was typeset in Baskerline.